AF605802

TROPES OF ENGAGEMENT: CHAUCER'S ITALIAN POETICS OF INTERTEXTUALITY

LEAH SCHWEBEL

Tropes of Engagement: Chaucer's Italian Poetics of Intertextuality

UNIVERSITY OF TORONTO PRESS
Toronto Buffalo London

Toronto Buffalo London
utorontopress.com
Printed in the USA

ISBN 978-1-4875-5260-2 (cloth)
ISBN 978-1-4875-5261-9 (EPUB)
ISBN 978-1-4875-5262-6 (PDF)

Library and Archives Canada Cataloguing in Publication

Title: Tropes of engagement: Chaucer's Italian poetics of intertextuality / Leah Schwebel.
Other titles: Chaucer's Italian poetics of intertextuality
Names: Schwebel, Leah, author.
Description: Includes bibliographical references and index.
Identifiers: Canadiana (print) 20240282574 | Canadiana (ebook) 20240282582 | ISBN 9781487552602 (cloth) | ISBN 9781487552626 (PDF) | ISBN 9781487552619 (EPUB)
Subjects: LCSH: Chaucer, Geoffrey, –1400 – Criticism and interpretation. | LCSH: Boccaccio, Giovanni, 1313–1375 – Influence. | LCSH: English poetry – Middle English, 1100–1500 – History and criticism. | LCSH: Influence (Literary, artistic, etc.) – History – To 1500.
Classification: LCC PR1924 .S39 2024 | DDC 821/.1–dc23

Cover design: Rebecca Lown
Cover illustration: Andrea Mantegna, *The Triumphs of Caesar. The Picture Bearers*. Alamy Stock Photo

We wish to acknowledge the land on which the University of Toronto Press operates. This land is the traditional territory of the Wendat, the Anishnaabeg, the Haudenosaunee, the Métis, and the Mississaugas of the Credit First Nation.

University of Toronto Press acknowledges the financial support of the Government of Canada, the Canada Council for the Arts, and the Ontario Arts Council, an agency of the Government of Ontario, for its publishing activities.

Canada Council for the Arts
Conseil des Arts du Canada

Funded by the Government of Canada
Financé par le gouvernement du Canada
Canada

For my parents

Contents

Abbreviations

Inf	*Inferno*
Pg	*Purgatorio*
Pd	*Paradiso*
Vn	*Vita nuova*
Cv	*Convivio*
Ve	*De vulgari eloquentia*
Fam	*Epistolae Familiares*
Sen	*Epistolae Seniles*
SA	*Sources and Analogues of the "Canterbury Tales"* (1941 and 2002/5 editions)

Citations of Dante's *Commedia* are taken from Giorgio Petrocchi, *La Commedia secondo l'antica vulgata*, 4 vols (Milan: Mondadori, 1966–7; corr. repr. edn Florence: Le Lettere, 1994); translations are from Robert M. Durling and Ronald L. Martinez's edition, *The Divine Comedy of Dante Alighieri* (Oxford: Oxford University Press, 1996–2011). References to Boccaccio's works are from Branca's *Tutte le opere di Giovanni Boccaccio* (Milan: Mondadori, 1964–98), unless otherwise indicated. Abbreviations of titles of Chaucer's works are taken from the *Riverside Chaucer*, p. 779.

Acknowledgments

Writing this book has been a fifteen-year process, throughout which I have followed in the footsteps of many brilliant scholars. I first studied Chaucer at McGill University, where Jamie Fumo taught me to read the *Canterbury Tales* through the writings of Ovid, Boethius, and Dante. At the same time, I was taking classes with Elena Lombardi, who opened my mind to the world of *Trecento* and *Quattrocento* Italian poetry. I took such pleasure in learning about, and discovering, intertextual resonances in medieval literature with these two professors, and it is a pleasure to recognize them here.

Perhaps the greatest debt I owe is to C. David Benson, who is charisma personified. I have the most wonderful memories of David's seminars on Chaucer, Piers Plowman, and the medieval city. The most important lessons I learned from him were, however, those he set by example. David showed me how to navigate the often thorny woods of academia with grace, humility, and dignity, and it was in watching him teach that I discovered the kind of professor I wanted to be. To paraphrase Statius's words to Virgil, through you I am a scholar; through you I am a teacher. My endless thanks also go to Fiona Somerset. As a professor, I often think back to Fiona's seemingly limitless generosity toward her students. The door to her office was always open, and I spent many hours therein discussing my work. With Fiona, I experienced what it was like to be taken seriously as a scholar while still a student. I hope every budding medievalist has a Fiona.

Fortune has given me the best of friends, especially in Andrew Kraebel, Steven Rozenski, and Juliette Vuille. Andrew has read drafts of and provided invaluable feedback on this book at every stage. He and Steve are my twin pillars; they have stood by me through the darkest hours and times of happiness alike. Incidentally, some of the happiest times involve Steve and our annual hundred-mile hikes. I hope he knows how much I cherish these trips. Juliette and I spoke nearly every day during the COVID lockdown. Through her, I rediscovered a love of my work and found joy in the revision process. Richard Firth Green has been a longtime friend, and I have benefited greatly from his support and guidance. I gave my first Chaucer paper on one of David Raybin and Susanna Fein's *Chaucer Review* panels. This paper developed into my first article, published, appropriately, in the *Chaucer Review*. It is not an overstatement to say that my development as a Chaucerian has been shaped by this journal and its two editors. To my Texas coterie, Barbara Zimbalist, Liz Scala, and Nancy Warren, y'all make this massive state feel small. Thank you for reading my work and supporting my development as a scholar. Many thanks also go to Taylor Cowdery, Hal Cushman, Lynn Shutters, Michael Calabrese, Mary Flannery, Kara Gaston, Laura Saetveit Miles, Franco Masciandaro, K.P. Clarke, Robert Meyer-Lee, Frank Grady, R.D. Perry, Jeremy DeAngelo, Jeanette Zissell, Robert Hasenfratz, and Jean Marsden, all of whom have been helpful readers and worthy interlocutors. I am likewise grateful to Patricia Ingham, Holly Crocker, Wendy Hoofnagle, Alessandra Petrina, Marilyn Desmond, Derek Pearsall (whose absence is felt by many of us), Pam Benson, Ruth Evans, Catherine Sanok, Julia Boffey, Betsy McCormick, Mark Pearsall, Esther Frank, David Hensley, and Ivana Djordjevic, for their mentorship and generosity of expertise. To Bri Winder, Avi Greene, Igor Gurevich, Lisa de Repentigny, Dianne Goodale, Teresa Reed, Andy Snider, and Venetia Bridges, thank you for your friendship. I started this project as a PhD student at the University of Connecticut, where I had the unbelievable luck and good judgment to befriend Beata Moskal, Vanessa Petroj, and Miller Oberman, my UConn *mishpocha*. I'm equally fortunate in my colleagues at Texas State, many of whom I count among my dearest friends, especially Julie McCormick Weng, Eric Leake, and Cecily Parks. Thanks, too, to Elizabeth Skerpan-Wheeler, Sara Ramírez, Geneva Gano, Rob Tally, Tom Grimes, Cyrus Cassells, Debra Monroe, Susan Morrison, Dan Lochman, Deb Balzhiser, Natasha Mikels, and Ruben Zecena. My students, especially Aricelda Flores Calderon, Alex Harlan, and Amrin Madhani, are a constant source of inspiration. I am lucky to have grown with them over the years.

I am grateful to the University of Connecticut for providing essential funding in my final year as a graduate student, which enabled me to focus on my dissertation. I am also grateful to Texas State University for giving me a Research Enhancement Grant, which funded summer archival work. This book would not exist without the financial support of Texas State's English Department and College of Liberal Arts. I am so thankful to my chair, Victoria Smith, and dean, Mary Brennan, for their support and generosity. The three anonymous readers of my manuscript vastly improved my book with their discerning and valuable suggestions. My thanks go to them. I also want to extend my gratitude to the University of Toronto Press and to my editor, Suzanne Rancourt. As a young scholar, I read through UTP's medieval catalogue with great admiration. It is a dream to publish my book with this press.

I've saved my family for last because I cannot begin to express what I owe to them. When I was growing up, my parents made it clear that I had a choice of three professions. Fortunately, a professor was one of them. To my father, my first mentor: thank you for reading to me as a child and for taking me to Italy as a young adult. Because of you, I was never scared of failing. My mother gifted me my first copy of the *Canterbury Tales*, which was an illustrated children's book, and instilled in me the value of a good education. I get my strength and perseverance from her. I am infinitely proud of my siblings, who are models of dedication and devotion to one's craft. My brother Aaron is not only the best violinist in the world but also the best human. My sister Paula is a paragon of grace and wisdom; I've benefited greatly from her always being one step ahead of me, in academia and in life. Chava is a born leader: despite my being older, it is I who follow her example and not the other way around. Shoshana is as uncompromising in her values as she is in the way she lives her life. Josh is a brilliant artist and a man of great integrity. I admire him for habitually skirting the easy path in favour of the ethical one. Heela, my sister in everything but name, I have always wanted to be just like you, and I'm a better person for it. To the Chans, Wees, and especially Josephine and Randy Dela Cruz, you've been an unflagging source of love and support over the last few years; I'm so honoured to call you family. Carina, Jordan, Bar, Kaia, and Leo, I cannot wait to watch you grow up.

I am constantly in awe of my wife, Jo Chan, for whom I'm grateful every day. If everything else was stripped away, and it was just we two alone, I'd still be ecstatically happy, and we'd laugh at gilded butterflies and hear poor rogues talk of court news. With Luna and Blue, you are my everything.

TROPES OF ENGAGEMENT

Introduction

Every allusive text makes also some broader reflexive statement: "I am poetry," or "fiction," or "I belong in a tradition."

– Alessandro Barchiesi, *Speaking Volumes*[1]

Immature poets imitate; mature poets steal.

– T.S. Eliot, *Philip Massinger*[2]

Good artists copy; great artists steal.

– Pablo Picasso[3]

A good composer does not imitate: he steals.

– Igor Stravinsky[4]

The bad artists imitate, the great artists steal.

– ~~Pablo Picasso~~ Banksy[5]

In the third book of Geoffrey Chaucer's *House of Fame*, the narrator sees illustrious authors from antiquity holding up the fame of their literary creations. Josephus the Hebrew carries the fame of "Jewerye" (III.1436), Statius hoists the glory of Thebes and Achilles (III.1460–3), while Virgil lifts the fame of Aeneas (III.1483).[6] Standing on a pillar of iron, and supporting the heavy fame of Troy, is a much larger party: Homer, Dares Phrygius, Dictys Cretensis, Lollius, Guido delle Colonne, and "Englyssh Gaufride" all bear the weight of the fallen city (III.1466–70).

The scene is one of pomp and spectacle, yet it is not without resentment. Dramatizing the common medieval characterization of Homer as a liar, a perspective popularized by later translations of the pseudo-historical works of Dares and Dictys, Chaucer imagines an encounter coloured by quiet acrimony. He admits that "betwex" these authors "was a litil envye" (III.1476), because

> Oon seyde that Omer made lyes,
> Fenynynge in hys poetries.
> And was to Grekes favorable;
> Therefor held he hyt but fable. (III.1477–80)

Chaucer's emphasis on Homer as the target of his fellow authors' ire seems oddly deflective, for huddled unobtrusively among these famous chroniclers of Troy is none other than the spurious Lollius, Chaucer's invented Latin source for *Troilus and Criseyde*, a work that translates the Italian poem, *Il Filostrato*.[7] Absent from this company is the actual author of the *Filostrato*, Giovanni Boccaccio, whom Chaucer never names, despite relying on his works for not only the *Troilus* but also *Anelida and Arcite*, the "Knight's Tale," the "Franklin's Tale," and the "Monk's Tale." While the absence of an identified source in medieval literature is not itself extraordinary, Chaucer's treatment of Boccaccio is far more vexed than a simple failure of acknowledgment. Indeed, rather than acknowledge his debt to his Italian author, Chaucer variously attributes Boccaccio's writings to "Corynne" (*Anel.* 21), "Stace of Thebes" (*Anel.* 21; *KnT* I.2294), "olde stories" (*KnT* I.859), an anonymous Breton lay (*FranT* IV.709–13), "Trophee" (*MkT* VII.2117–18), "Petrak" (*ClT* VII.2325), and, of course, his "auctor Lollius" (*Tr.* I.3995, V.1653). If Homer is a liar, Chaucer seems to be suggesting, then so too is he.

The question of Boccaccio's startling anonymity in Chaucer's poetry stands perennially at the margins of studies on Chaucer and his Italian sources. Scholars have long explored connections between Chaucer and Boccaccio's poetry, yet relatively few have hazarded an explanation as to why Chaucer relies on, yet never names, his vernacular source.[8] Those scholars who have offered a justification of this treatment fall generally, if not exclusively, into two categories, attributing it to either Chaucer's ignorance or his anxiety.[9] Scholars in the first group tend to look at Chaucer's Boccaccian works individually, arguing, in each case, that Chaucer was simply unaware that he was translating Boccaccio's poetry. William E. Coleman, for example, speculates that perhaps the version of the *Teseida* Chaucer consulted did not include Boccaccio's name.[10] Piero Boitani wonders if Chaucer's manuscript of the *De casibus virorum illustrium* was "anonymous and mutilated."[11] For critics including Robin Kirkpatrick, since Chaucer names Petrarch yet not Boccaccio as his source for the "Clerk's Tale," "it is unlikely that Chaucer was acquainted with Boccaccio's version."[12] Although this number has dwindled over the last fifty years, certain scholars suspect that Chaucer did not know the *Decameron* at all.[13]

A variation of this first theory suggests that when Chaucer names an invented source, he believes this source to be historically real, if not necessarily the original author of the work he is translating. Douglas Bush and Lee Patterson, for example, claim that Chaucer's Corynne was perhaps an "obscure Theban poetess," while Walter William Skeat suggests that Chaucer intended a reference to Corinnus, an epic poet who supposedly lived during the Trojan war.[14] George Livingstone Hamilton, Frederick Tupper, Robert A. Pratt, and Oliver Farrar Emerson propose that when Chaucer names Trophee as a source for his portrait of Hercules in the "Monk's Tale," he is referring to Guido delle Colonne, who, in the *Historia destructionis Troiae*, described Hercules establishing pillars at the edges of the world.[15] Other critics, including George L. Kittredge and Pratt, maintain that Lollius owes his existence to Chaucer's misunderstanding of a vocative in Horace's epistles.[16] For scholars in this first group, when Chaucer neglects to acknowledge Boccaccio in favour of naming another source, he intends no deception but simply lacks crucial information, like his author's name.

Perhaps because it relies on the supposition of Chaucer's sustained credulity or error, the theory of Chaucer's ignorance has fallen somewhat out of fashion in recent years.[17] More popular, and, to my mind, more convincing, is the explanation that Boccaccio's vernacularity presented a challenge for Chaucer. Adopted most stridently by Kittredge, but articulated more recently by Alastair Minnis and David Wallace, the argument of these scholars is that Chaucer chose to identify authors who sounded Latinate and ancient (e.g., Lollius, Statius, Corynne) while minimizing his reliance on contemporary, vernacular models, whose names perhaps lack the authority and antiquity of their classical counterparts.[18] Minnis, for example, suggests that Chaucer does not name Boccaccio "for the same reason that Guido did not mention Benoît's Roman de Troie: these writers were casting themselves in the role of historian ... and therefore 'modern' works in whatever vernacular would not serve their purpose. Instead, auctores had to be cited, 'ancient' writers who had written in Latin."[19] Wallace offers a similar explanation of Chaucer's erasure of Boccaccio under the cover of translating a fictional Latin source. Noting that Boccaccio himself claimed to follow the testimony of a fictional priest named Ilario in the *Filocolo*, he proposes that these imaginary authors allowed each poet to "take up a particular authorial posture."[20] By "affirming that his work incorporates the historical witness of an *auctour*," Chaucer "suggests that his modern vernacular narrative is supported by a backbone of ancient authority."[21] Boccaccio, by contrast, "remained an outsider to the courtly world," and, were Chaucer to acknowledge him by name, he would risk "prompt[ing] comparisons that he was willing to avoid."[22]

According to these scholars, Chaucer was anxious about Boccaccio's status as a modern poet, and he fabricated Latin authorities while camouflaging his heavy debt to Boccaccio to give his poetry the illusion of textual longevity. This explanation is extremely valuable in that it rightly considers Chaucer's erasure of Boccaccio throughout his works, rather than on a case-by-case basis, and is grounded in historical conversations surrounding Latin versus vernacular authority in the Middle Ages.[23] Nevertheless, this theory brings with it a new set of questions and contingencies. In the first place, Chaucer frequently relies on his Latin sources in a way that undermines, rather than exploits, their authority, a tendency that at the very least complicates the assumption that he feigns reliance on these *auctores* to "'cash in' on their antiquity and *auctoritas*."[24] Under the pretext of following Virgil's lantern in the *Legend of Dido*,[25] to recall one of the more conspicuous examples of this manoeuvre, Chaucer instead tells a thoroughly Ovidian version of the romance of Dido and Aeneas, a decision so provocative that it led fifteenth-century poet Gavin Douglas to declare that his "mastir Chauser gretly Virgill offendit."[26] Of course, Minnis would be the first to remind us that Chaucer can gain prestige from naming his Latin *auctoritates* while simultaneously giving their beards a good yank (or their "waxen noses" a good "wrench").[27] Yet Chaucer does not reserve this sort of treatment for his classical sources, and assessing Chaucer's engagement with his authors according to a binary – one that sees his invention and manipulation of his ancient sources as a "shield and defense" (or a tweaking of antiquity's collective nose), yet his erasure and mistranslation of his vernacular sources as evidence of his anxiety – is not wholly satisfying.[28]

It remains unclear why we should read Chaucer's erasure of Boccaccio as proof of his concern with his source's perceived authority, yet his mishandling of his ancient sources as a ludic wrench of antiquity's nose. Might not these manoeuvres stem from a similar impulse?[29]

A second challenge with the argument that Chaucer erases Boccaccio to imbue his works with ancient as opposed to vernacular authority is that he names Petrarch and Dante frequently, both of whom wrote in Italian as well as Latin, and whose reputations were for Chaucer tied as much to their vernacular as to their Latin poetry. Although it is likely that Petrarch himself would be mortified by this revelation, Chaucer mines Petrarch's vernacular writings for material, famously translating one of his sonnets in the *Troilus* (I.400–20) and alluding to the *Trionfo della fama* in the Monk's portrait of Zenobia (VII.2321–6).[30] Of course, in the "Clerk's Tale," he emphasizes Petrarch's Latin translation of the Griselda story over Boccaccio's original novella in the *Decameron*, which was written in the vernacular. Even here, however, Chaucer eulogizes "Petrak" as, first and foremost, an Italian poet, commemorating him (I think rather facetiously) as bard to "al Ytaille" (IV.33).[31]

Dante is likewise petitioned as a vernacular authority, and to an extent even greater than Petrarch.[32] Eager to prove to a vicious summoner that he will soon rank among these authors, due to his own hellishly informative "experience" (III.1517), the fiend in the "Friar's Tale" names Dante alongside Virgil as one of the great chroniclers of the underworld (III.1519–20). It is specifically Dante as the author of the *Inferno* who is invoked here, his Italian work set on par with Virgil's Latin epic. In the "Wife of Bath's Tale," the ugly old woman cites Dante's *Convivio* as her main authority on virtue, pointing the rapist-knight to the "wise poete of Florence, / That highte Dant" (III.1125–6) for the lesson that nobility cannot be passed down to us by our ancestors. There is no sense that Dante's vernacularity, or, for that matter, the female vessel through which his words are conveyed, is of issue here. On the contrary, this scene hinges on overturning entrenched systems of authority, with the low-born hag presented as the "intellectual and moral superior" of the churlish aristocrat.[33] But what is especially interesting is the context of the Dantean citation. Not only does the old woman "preach" – in English, no less – the wisdom of a contemporary vernacular poet, but she also appeals to Dante *in defence of the vernacular*. As Minnis observes, "implicit" in Dante's discussion of nobility is the glorification of the *volgare* "at Latin's expense."[34] Just as a person does not require an illustrious pedigree to behave virtuously, so "a language does not have to be ancient (like Latin) to be noble."[35] Truly, "vulgarization rarely gets more prestigious than this."[36]

To suggest that it is Boccaccio's modernity and Italianism that prompt Chaucer to erase him is thus not entirely convincing, because Chaucer regularly and unproblematically invokes Dante and Petrarch as vernacular *auctoritates*.[37] What is more, Boccaccio himself was a polyglot, known in the Middle Ages for both his vernacular and Latin poetry. Indeed, as James Kriesel has recently argued, Boccaccio repeatedly emphasized his own versatility – his fluid movement between the vernacular and Latin, and his production of both scholarship and erotic writings – as a way of distinguishing himself from his two near contemporaries, Dante and Petrarch.[38] Chaucer for his part drew on and translated a full range of Boccaccio's works, from the encyclopedic Latin *De casibus virorum illustrium* and *De mulieribus claris* to the Italian *Filocolo*, *Teseida*, and *Filostrato*.[39] What obstacle did Chaucer face in naming Boccaccio that citing Petrarch and Dante did not pose?

Scholars such as Leonard Michael Koff and Peter Beidler have answered this question by suggesting that it was *what* Boccaccio wrote rather than in which language he composed that presented a problem for Chaucer.

Boccaccio's *Decameron* had a reputation as an "immoral" text in medieval Europe, and Chaucer did not acknowledge its author because he did not want to tarnish his own good name, they claim.[40] Certainly, Boccaccio painstakingly considered the reception of his *Decameron*. Depending on how we interpret his letter to Mainardo Cavalcanti (1372), in which he asks his friend to prevent the women in his household from reading his *libellos*, he may even have regretted its dissemination.[41] But that Chaucer would have numbered among those put off by the *Decameron*'s tone and content – so much so that he would have avoided acknowledging the poet while consistently translating his works – seems unlikely. For one thing, Chaucer gleefully stocks the *Canterbury Tales* with fart jokes and fabliaux, many of which have analogues (if not origins) in the *Decameron*, and which he claims to transcribe from figures far more proximate, albeit invented – e.g., his Miller, Reeve, and Shipman – than Boccaccio. These tales may not clarify the extent of his familiarity with the *Decameron*, but they do make it difficult to imagine that it was Boccaccio's reputed salaciousness with which Chaucer took issue.

Another impediment to this line of reasoning is that other near-contemporary French and English authors exhibit no similar disinclination to name the Italian poet, at the very least raising the question of the extent, range, and duration of Boccaccio's perceived immorality.[42] As I discuss in my fifth chapter, the devout Monk of Bury, John Lydgate, enthusiastically cites Boccaccio as his source throughout his poetry, at times even crediting "Bochas" for another author's work.[43] In the *Fall of Princes*, for example, he designates Boccaccio's Latin treatise, the *De casibus*, as his textual model, despite relying predominantly on Laurent de Premierfait's Old French prose translation of Boccaccio's work. To be sure, Lydgate's acknowledgment of "Bochas" could speak to a change in the status of both Boccaccio and the Italian vernacular since the time that Chaucer was writing. As critics including David Rundle have shown, Italian humanism took root in fifteenth-century England, which corresponded to a critical increase in the study, reproduction, and dissemination of Italian-authored works.[44] And here, too, there is the distinction between Boccaccio's Latin and Italian works to consider, with the latter occasionally disparaged by fourteenth- and fifteenth-century humanists.[45] Filippo Villani's *De origine civitatis florentinae et eiusdem famosis civibus* (1375–1404), edited by Coluccio Salutati, for example, elevates Boccaccio's Latin writings over his vernacular efforts, which include "pleraque continuatione prosaica, in quibus lasciventis iuventitis ingenio paula libera evagatur" ("many in prose, in which he strays a bit too freely according to the inclination of lustful youth").[46] Still, as Timothy Kircher notes, there is increasing evidence that *Quattrocento* humanists also "recognized the value of [Boccaccio's] vernacular composition," with some even adapting the *Decameron* "for the ends of moral virtue."[47] It is possible, in this regard, that Lydgate's exaggeration of Boccaccio's influence at the expense of crediting other authors has little to do with how Boccaccio and his works are perceived in fifteenth-century England, and is instead an example of the author camouflaging his source. Perhaps, in other words, in his treatment of Boccaccio, Lydgate is emulating Chaucer's poetics of authorial erasure.

The question of what motivated Chaucer to efface his extensive debt to Boccaccio is at the heart of this book, the aim of which is twofold. First, I will argue that when Chaucer camouflages his debt to Boccaccio under the cover of translating another source, he is mimicking strategies of translation practised by his classical and continental predecessors. Rather than evidence of Chaucer's ignorance or anxiety, authorial erasure, invention, and manipulation are, as this study suggests, recognizable literary topoi, used by poets to suggest their connection to, and place within, a broader authorial tradition.[48] Nor does Chaucer's imitation of his sources' intertextual practices indicate his hostile response to his literary ancestors, motivated by fear of similarity or inferiority, as Harold Bloom might argue.[49] On the contrary, from antiquity forward, authors would seem to initiate their predecessors into the fellowship of literary history by obscuring or distorting one another's influence. Manoeuvres such as these are not only intentional but also playful, a characteristic of *translatio studii* that has heretofore remained underappreciated. Chaucer develops his sources' poetics to align his writings with theirs, in anticipation of similar treatment at the hands of later authors, and with the aim of ensuring his own artistic longevity.[50] Even as they appear antagonistic, these strategies are thus *affiliating* devices: used to forge textual associations, they reveal fame as something that is conferred upon poets by posterity.[51]

Should we look beyond the "Knight's Tale" to previous and subsequent works on Thebes, for example, we detect a pattern of authorial obfuscation. Like Oedipus himself, Theban poets including Statius, Boccaccio, Chaucer, and Lydgate erase the influence of their authorial fathers, converting their theme of patricide into a poetics of intertextual commentary. It is likewise not only *Troilus and Criseyde* that contains a conspicuously fraudulent historicizing device. As I discuss in my fourth chapter, nearly every poem on Troy, including the pseudo-eyewitness accounts of Dares and Dictys and their medieval historiographic translations, contains a fabricated source or origin story, a pretence to textual authority that deconstructs itself, and, in the process, the very illusion of historical accuracy. With his creation of Lollius, Chaucer thus joins the ranks of a long line of fictionalizers intent on showcasing their own art. Obscuring their actual sources while performing what Sarah Spence calls a

"Rosencrantz-and-Guildenstern-type adaptation" of the Troy legend, these poets align themselves with Homer and an epic tradition of confabulation even as they decry the writings within this tradition as inauthentic.[52] These gestures are not unique to Chaucer, or even to an English tradition. On the contrary, they are modes of authorial engagement – literary tropes originating in antiquity, which are employed throughout the Italian Middle Ages before being adopted by Chaucer to suggest his place in an epic genealogy. In the words of T.S. Eliot, Picasso, Stravinsky, and Banksy, who, together, have provided me with my introduction's second epigraph, "Good poets imitate, great poets steal." It is as much the open act of theft as it is the borrowed refrain, appearing again and again in slightly different permutations, that creates an artistic tradition through playful allusion.[53]

The second aim of this book is methodological, and concerns how we as a field recognize and discuss literary influence. Where previous scholars have thought about intertextuality in terms of verbal and plot echoes, I explore the transmission and development of the very *strategies* of authorial engagement from antiquity to the Middle Ages. While still attentive to verbal correspondences, each chapter looks beyond Chaucer's immediate literary models to how his authors themselves translate one another's writings. Thereby combining an attention to the cultural, historical, and material circumstances surrounding literary production (an attention that critics like Minnis and Wallace so rightly encourage) with a mode of source study that looks both at and beyond Chaucer's most discernible influences, I recognize authors self-consciously erasing and misreading each other as part of a process of mutual and self-promotion. My argument is not so much that Chaucer has or has not read one or another author, in this regard, as that we can only appreciate how he engages with his literary models by first seeing how these authors themselves engaged with their sources.[54]

Tropes of Engagement thus seeks to broaden the ways we think and talk about literary influence to encompass borrowings that lack overt textual markers. At the same time, by investigating patterns of authorial erasure, invention, and dissimulation across literary traditions – i.e., narratives of Thebes, Troy, Griselda, and Fortune's Wheel – I situate Chaucer within a network of poets adapting the intertextual methodologies of their predecessors for the sake of inscribing themselves in literary history.

Source Study and Its Critics

Traditionally, the study of Chaucer's sources has been overwhelmingly positivistic. Despite efforts to distinguish between various kinds of textual influence, including by the contributors to both the original and more recent *Sources and Analogues* (1941, 2002 [vol. 1] and 2005 [vol. 2]), our process for discovering literary borrowings involves investigating allusions that appear primarily in the form of verbal echoes and plot parallels, at times at the expense of analysing broader strategies of translation between languages.[55] To be sure, this work is extremely valuable, and it has enabled many important developments in our understanding of Chaucer's works. Nevertheless, we lack the vocabulary to describe Chaucer's intertextual engagement when it presents itself in more indirect ways.[56]

Our difficulty in identifying Chaucer's sources stems from more than a mere terminological deficiency. Because archival research makes it possible to establish a paper (or parchment) trail, to identify, potentially, which manuscript Chaucer was reading and on what date, when we are unable do so we take it as evidence of its absence.[57] Suggesting that in the late Middle Ages "ideas did not travel in the air, in the water supply, or in the wine," for example, Minnis insists that our methodology for establishing Chaucer's influences must document the process of transmission.[58] "If one wishes to argue that Chaucer was influenced by a certain idea," he suggests, "the criterion of historical plausibility must be satisfied with reference to its two facets, namely, dissemination and provenance."[59] If a scholar cannot lay claim to a text or idea being "in the right place at the right time," they "should recognize the danger of solipsism and bow out gracefully."[60] Minnis justifiably sets a very high bar for identifying Chaucer's influences. At the same time, it is unclear that this bar could ever be cleared by some sources, which cultivate manoeuvres of authorial erasure and manipulation as part of their intertextual aesthetic. (This is to say nothing of Chaucer's more informal models, of which we really have no sense. We can only speculate on the kinds of encounters or conversations Chaucer had while in Italy, and to what extent he was influenced by them.) The peril of a system like Minnis's is, therefore, that it might dispense with, before even considering, many texts and authors with which Chaucer plausibly engages, simply because we cannot place a copy of these works in his hands.

A further obstacle in retracing Chaucer's literary models is the sheer paucity of evidence of this sort. Whereas we have a great deal of information on the manuscript traditions of some of Chaucer's Italian sources, we have no autograph manuscripts of Chaucer's writings, nor do we have any manuscripts of his works that were created during the poet's lifetime.[61] This makes retracing the poet's reading and writing practices considerably more difficult than such a process would be for Boccaccio or Petrarch, to name two examples, both of whom rigorously controlled the production and reception of their various works.[62] Our speculations on Chaucer's familiarity with specific codices of *Trecento* writings stem invariably, by contrast, from his two diplomatic trips to Italy, in 1373 and 1378. Yet, recent estimates of the percentage of medieval manuscripts lost over the years have been staggeringly high, particularly in cases of private ownership.[63] We should hardly assume that for Chaucer to have had access to a manuscript, so too must we. Nor, I think, does our lack of substantive evidence with regard to which works Chaucer read mean we cannot usefully interpret these texts together, as part of a larger literary tradition.

Compounding these challenges already present in our approach to uncovering Chaucer's sources is the poet's repeated refusal to either acknowledge his literary models or engage with his predecessors in an obvious or emulative manner. Rather than identify his sources consistently (or in Boccaccio's case, at all), or translate texts with the aim of preserving their original *sentence*, Chaucer at times appears more invested in combusting narrative authority than in capitalizing on it, and in exposing the fault lines along which his authors collide. I have already mentioned his claim to follow Virgil in the *Legend of Dido*, "Glory and honour, Virgil Mantuan, / Be to thy name! and I shal, as I can, / Folow thy lantern, as thou gost biforn" (1–3), a statement he undercuts immediately by mourning "How Eneas to Dido was forsworn" (4). Despite his seeming awareness that their two versions of the romance between Dido and Aeneas "simply cannot be reconciled," Chaucer turns from Virgil to Ovid as his source.[64] But this is hardly an isolated incident. Chaucer repeatedly petitions patristic and classical authorities only to use their teachings erroneously or out of context, reminding us, for instance, that woman is not man's ruin but rather his "joie and al his blisse" (VII.3166),[65] that "all that is written" – including his works that "sownen into sin" (X.1085) – "is written for our doctrine" (VII.3441–2, X.1083),[66] and that Midas owes his humiliation not to his barber but to his wife.[67] Should we protest against this anarchy of misprision – should we read his "tale of a cock" (VII.3252) as either an allegory or a simple beast fable,[68] that is, or resist his Christological justification of Griselda's trials in the provocatively unsettling "Clerk's Tale" – the fault lies in our exegetical abilities alone. We must "blameth nat" him but ourselves.[69]

What we have, then, is a confluence of incongruities: our system for identifying Chaucer's sources is keyed to investigating positive presences, yet Chaucer himself trafficks in erasure and manipulation. Rather than develop a more flexible model for identifying Chaucer's less obvious sources, we have, moreover, doubled down on our demand for substantive evidence, crediting Chaucer's anomalous attributions to manuscript or scribal corruption, and calling for proof of provenance and dissemination before considering Chaucer's knowledge of a work. Certainly, this call for philological and historical rigour is necessary, and the labour put into establishing Chaucer's immediate sources has been foundational to our understanding of the poet's literary milieu. In some cases, however, our tendency to seek only presences and parallels, verbal or otherwise, in Chaucer's poetry and in the poetry of his sources hampers our recognition of the very tropes of authorial engagement that underlie textual transmission. Studies that investigate only direct or obvious borrowings are thus limited in their capacity to convey the full complexity of Chaucer's engagement with his authors and their works.

I am hardly the first person to recognize that applying a positivistic lens to Chaucer's complex and unruly intertextual practices yields an incomplete picture of these engagements. Over thirty years ago, Wallace declared a moratorium on the method of "quantifying Chaucer's indebtedness to Boccaccio by matching details of plot, imagery and characterization."[70] Acknowledging that Boccaccio's influence on the English poet was far more intricate than a record of semantic borrowings could ever demonstrate, he encouraged scholars to take a historically informed, pan-European approach to Chaucer's Italian works, fundamentally changing how we read the relationship between Chaucer and his sources. More recently, in her work on Chaucer's French influences, many of whom Chaucer also obscures, Ardis Butterfield has emphasized that there are "further, and perhaps other, ways of thinking about translation" than traditional source study.[71] Indeed, such an approach is "as distorting as it has been illuminating. We are left puzzling over the simultaneously thick stuff of reference and the minute detail of its cross-hatched character," while Chaucer himself veers "from text to text, at one moment through word-by-word translation and at another through large-scale structural amplification or compressions."[72] We have found ourselves accordingly caught between theory and practice: "it seems we can only be really sure a writer has read another writer if we home in on closer and closer correspondences, but the difficulty is that this presupposes a very limited model of both writing and reading."[73]

Instead of disappearing altogether, however, traditional source study simply became more niche. Certain scholars remain dedicated to uncovering the specific authors and texts on which Chaucer relied, and to honing the language required for classifying these borrowings.[74] Others, following the example of Wallace and Butterfield, have gone in a different direction. Modern research on Chaucer and his Italian sources has developed new modes of theorizing Chaucer's relationship to Boccaccio that go beyond documenting linguistic and narrative echoes. Warren Ginsberg has conceived of Chaucer's Italian tradition "not as the accumulation of localized borrowings" but as the product of Chaucer reading Dante, Petrarch, and Boccaccio "in the light one could throw on the other."[75] He directs our attention to Chaucer's use of Boccaccio as a mediating figure in his reading of Dante, and vice versa, as well as to the ways in which Chaucer rejected his Italian models. Robert R. Edwards argues that Chaucer took from Boccaccio his very concepts of antiquity and modernity.[76] George Edmondson encourages readers to view Chaucer's relationship to his sources horizontally instead of vertically. Rather than adopt a traditional "genealogical" model of literary influence, Edmondson very helpfully positions Chaucer and Boccaccio as neighbours.[77] In recent years, our field has further enjoyed what K.P. Clarke (drawing on Stephen G. Nichols) describes as a "turn to the manuscript matrix" in both Chaucer and Italian studies, and in his own fascinating study, Clarke focuses on both text and paratext, manuscript and glosses.[78] Philology has returned as praxis, but accompanied now by attention to both history and the material text.[79] Most recently, Kara Gaston has suggested that it is through the writings of his Italian sources that Chaucer grapples with questions of form, formation, and reception in relation to time.[80]

To recognize the limitations of traditional source study in our analyses of Chaucer and Boccaccio is thus in part retreading the intellectual fieldwork of these other scholars. But I suspect that the backlash created by earlier positivistic approaches to Chaucer and Boccaccio – and our subsequent resistance to source studies as a theoretical framework – has also hamstrung our ability to assess the richness of Chaucer's intertextual engagement. Without a suitable model for identifying less proximate models – without the language to talk about allusions that take forms other than positive presences – we have, as it were (to borrow Minnis's phrase), "bowed out gracefully" from a more fruitful, perhaps more versatile, discussion of Chaucer's literary influences. While we will not always find evidence of Chaucer's artful intertextuality only in verbal echoes or plot parallels, however, nor will we find it by stepping away from source studies entirely. On the contrary, as I will show, by investigating patterns of authorial erasure, manipulation, and dissimulation, we develop a richer understanding of not only how Chaucer saw and used his literary predecessors, but also how he was read in turn by his contemporaries and later poets.

Classical Studies of Intertextuality

What I am proposing is a return to the question of what constitutes a source in Chaucer's poetry, but informed by new methodologies and in anticipation of outcomes beyond cataloguing Chaucer's library.[81] In this age of considering why medieval studies matters, and the ways in which it is and can be appropriated, it is in our interest to read Chaucer's poetry alongside other critical and national traditions. In addition to examining his works in light of their lengthy Latin and continental textual histories, I have thus turned to classical poetry, and to studies of intertextuality and allusion in classical poetry, as a model for how we might interpret and codify influence. In contrast to the trend toward positivism in Chaucer scholarship, several studies of Roman poetry have developed far more flexible models for analysing sources, and for theorizing modes of allusion that extend beyond imitation.[82] Stephen Hinds, for example, reminds us that "openness in borrowing" is not always a prerequisite of allusion among ancient poets.[83] Hinds cites Macrobius on Virgil's obfuscation of a Homeric narrative vignette. Eustathius and Evangelus are discussing Virgil's knowledge of the Greek orators. Eustathius points out that Virgil's mirroring of Homer's epic is common knowledge, even if Virgil himself does not always showcase this debt: "interdum sic auctorem suum dissimulanter imitator, ut loci inde descripti solam dispositionem mutet et faciat velut aliud videri" ("Sometimes Virgil disguises an imitation of his model author, by just changing the format of a passage copied from him, and making it look like something else" [*Saturnalia* 5.16.12]).[84] Dissimulation (*dissimulanter*) is not merely negative here. Rather, as Hinds notes, drawing on Horace's edict from the *Ars Poetica*,

> from another ancient point of view this Virgilian manoeuvre might be cited as a wholly positive example of a principle which will often (though not inevitably) run athwart the principle of openness: namely, that the imitator should appropriate the imitation by avoiding too-faithful literalness in his rendering.[85]

Indeed, allusion – as much for Chaucer as for Virgil – can involve "indirection as much as direction, concealment as much as revelation," an idea that serves as the basis for my chapter on the "Knight's Tale," and for much of this book.[86]

Virgil's practice of intertextual dissimulation has been scrutinized by several scholars of Roman poetry, some of whom link this approach to a tradition of misreading.[87] In his study on Trojan narratives, for example, Ralph Hexter notes that Virgil's treatment of Homer appears to emulate Homer's previous engagement with his own sources (such as they were). By the time Virgil wrote the *Aeneid*, Hexter notes, there had emerged an "'aporetic' Homer," whose "inconsistencies and divergences from other mythological traditions were carefully noted, whose every character, in deed and word, was measured against the canon of 'the proper' … or the likely or credible."[88] Rather than attempt to harmonize these inconsistencies, Virgil lays them bare for his reader's consideration. Reading a Homer "already rendered problematic by the disputatious discussions that swirled around" his texts, he creates a new version of the Troy story that is "aporetic from the ground up."[89]

For Joseph Pucci, Virgil's unacknowledged yet significant borrowing from Homer is an act of artistic *mirroring*, rather than mere imitation.[90] It is, moreover, contingent on a powerful reader, who recognizes the Latin poet's allusions to his predecessor and brings this hidden process to light. Like Hinds, Pucci turns to the discussion between Eustathius and Evangelus in Macrobius's *Saturnalia* to illustrate this process of allusion:

> While acknowledging that Virgil is, indeed, a literary borrower, Eustathius is careful to use a verb suggestive of creation in describing Virgil's engagement of Homer. Virgilian borrowing in the *Aeneid* is cast in this response, therefore, not in the context of slavish copying – as the verb *mutuari* can imply. It is, rather, a function of *formare*, of a creative and artistic response on the part of Virgil to Homer's poetry.[91]

Pucci portrays Virgilian borrowing as an interactive process – one that demands the presence of a "full-knowing reader, whose competencies are required in order for the Homeric context of Virgil's poetry ... to be recognized and interpreted."[92] Pucci's reader has as much control over the activation of an allusion as does the author: the *Aeneid* "hinges on the ability of Virgil's readers to work their way through his translations," and spy "for themselves the reflections of Homer that form the backdrop of Virgil's poetry and that lead ultimately to a more authoritative interpretive perspective, grounded as much in readerly as in authorial power."[93]

Among Virgil's "full-knowing" readers are Roman poets Ovid and Statius, both of whom make a practice of obfuscating and erasing their literary debts.[94] Again, we find these examples of unaccredited borrowing noted by the authors' near contemporaries and readers, which suggests a frankness with regard to their intertextual methods on their part. In a passage that recalls Eustathius's conversation with Evangelus about Homer's influence on Virgil, for example, Seneca the Elder documents Ovid's conspicuous use of the Virgilian phrase "plena deo" ("full of a god") in a now-lost work. As he reports, his friend Gallio observed that Ovid "very much liked this phrase: and that as a result the poet did something he had done with many other lines of Vergil – with no thought of stealing it, but meaning that his piece of open borrowing should be noticed."[95] Indeed, Ovid borrows brazenly from Virgil, staging what Richard Tarrant aptly describes as a "series of daring daylight robberies" of the *Aeneid*.[96] Alessandro Barchiesi describes Ovid's approach to his sources as "surgical": the poet "selects the most favourable point" of his source, "cuts into it, then closes it back up without leaving a trace."[97] His technique demonstrates his passion for the contact points between alien texts, and between his texts and those of other authors. Such a technique is not characterized by authorial anxiety, necessarily, but rather by an appreciation of intertextual contradictions.[98]

Although perhaps less subtle than Ovid's "traceless" intertextuality, Statius's approach to Virgil is likewise rooted in open imitation accompanied by contrast and concealment, and I will examine this relationship in more detail in chapter 1. Scholars including Karla F.L. Pollmann and Randall T. Ganiban, among others, have usefully discussed Statius's reinterpretation of the *Aeneid* in the *Thebaid*, a work developed out of Virgil's epic "in a negatively contrasting way." Despite his heavy debt to Virgil, Statius acknowledges his debt to Virgil only once, in the final lines of the poem.[99] (In this regard, his strategy can shed light on Lydgate's singular mention of Chaucer at the end of the *Siege of Thebes* [line 4501], a work that offers itself as auxiliary to the *Canterbury Tales*.)[100]

In Roman poetry, then, we witness narratives being transmitted according to practices of misreading and obfuscation, manoeuvres subsequently noted by writers such as Macrobius and Seneca the Elder. In studies of Roman poetry, moreover, we find scholars who, while still attentive to positive signs of influence, are invested in also detecting allusions that take these other forms, and in contextualizing these practices in broader literary traditions. (And here I must mention my debt to Rita Copeland, who defines translation as, at its core, antagonistic, and suggests that medieval hermeneutics take from ancient rhetoric the ideal of "oratorical discourse as a form of aggressive rivalry with a source or an opponent."[101] Although my own project looks at authorial erasure and manipulation as a literary trope – as evidence of convention and affinity rather than antagonism – Copeland's ideas were nevertheless fundamental to the development of my book, which treats intertextual manoeuvres that *seem* antagonistic, even if they are not.) Such an understanding of the relationship between poet and source as at times characterized by manoeuvres including erasure and dissimulation *as well as* similitude is at the root of many classical studies on intertextuality. For these scholars, "intertextuality" is more than a record of individual citations – more, indeed, than a Kristevian "mosaic of quotations."[102] Instead, it is a very "means for writing literary history": "Intertextuality divulges not merely how texts situate themselves in relation to others and thereby define traditions into which they inscribe or subtract themselves, but offers a window from which to look toward 'the production of the text and the figure of the author.'"[103] Providing insight into the past, intertextuality is also a lens for examining ongoing traditions. It can tell us not only *what* Chaucer has read, but also how he was read by subsequent poets. When it comes to Chaucer, who often manipulates and conceals his sources, and who is attuned to both the poetry and poetics of his predecessors, extending our analysis of his intertextual practices beyond positive textual echoes is not only advantageous but also necessary.

Barchiesi offers a metaphor for intertextual engagement, taken from Ovid's *Tristia* (I.1.105–20), which I have found particularly helpful. He imagines a library full of volumes in dialogue – "books" that "communicate with each other."[104] This image presents intertextuality as something diachronic as opposed to unilateral; it reminds us that allusion can "reanimate" previous works.[105] These "speaking volumes" cohabitate: they develop not only by way of imitation and repetition but also in and through conversation.[106] While this fantasy of books in dialogue may not describe how literature is generated in real time, it nevertheless characterizes how poets often *present* themselves in relation to a literary tradition. (The distinction between these two points can be illustrated, for example, by Petrarch's borrowings from Augustine's writings, on the one hand, and by his representation of Augustine as his Socratic interlocutor in the *Secretum*, on the other.) While temporal relationships inevitably determine which authors engage with what texts and when, poets do not always heed the dictates of time and space in their retrospective construction of authorial ancestries. Rather, they regularly portray themselves as part of a transhistoric literary cohort, brought into being by the reception and repetition of poetry and poetic tropes. It is in the act of perpetuating recognizable strategies of authorial engagement that poets make a "broader reflexive statement" (to return to my Barchiesian epigraph), insisting on their place within a literary tradition.

This book is thus profoundly indebted to theories of intertextuality and allusion from scholarship on Roman poetry. Seeking patterns of erasure and manipulation – or modes, rather than only evidence, of allusion – I illuminate networks of intertextuality that have previously remained hidden. The aim of my project, generally speaking, is to uncover patterns of intertextual engagement in Chaucer's poetry that, while open, remain unacknowledged, as previous scholars have done with respect to the writings of Roman poets. Nor do I see this process as an end in itself; rather, I read Chaucer's poetry as part of the broader European tradition that Chaucer aspired to join, through the reception and treatment of his textual models. In this regard, investigating Chaucer's sources can tell us more than simply what Chaucer read what day and where. This process can also shed light on transnational modes of reading taking place over centuries, originating long before Chaucer, and presumably (though this book takes as its final ambit the fifteenth century), continuing long after his death. In methodology and so much else, I am thus indebted to the scholarly works of Wallace, who saw in Chaucer "ambitions of European magnitude,"[107]

Ginsberg, Edmondson, and Clarke, and, like them, I seek to write literary history outside of single national traditions and across post-medieval borders.

My study also builds on comparative works outside of Chaucer and Italian scholarship, most especially (but hardly limited to) David Rollo's brilliant analyses of intertextuality and artifice in the French tradition,[108] Marilyn Desmond's careful tracing of adaptations of the Dido and Criseyde narratives,[109] and Sylvia Federico's and Dominique Battles's explorations of the literary traditions of Troy and Thebes, respectively.[110] Like these scholars, I excavate narratives from their point of origin through the late Middle Ages – nearly every chapter starts with a discussion of texts from Roman antiquity and concludes with an analysis of fifteenth-century poetry. In each case, I have found that I can trace networks of intertextuality across languages, centuries, and genres, because authors reiterate their predecessors' very modes of intertextual commentary in order to forge what appears, at least retrospectively, to be an authorial tradition.

To demonstrate the value of this approach, I will return once more to Chaucer's Ovidian misreading of the *Aeneid* in the *Legend of Dido*. In this example, we have evidence of a superficial reading of Chaucer's poetics of intertextuality at our disposal, in Douglas's shocked response to his "mastir's" bad intertextual manners:

My mastir Chauser gretly Virgill offendit.
All thoch I be tobald hym to repreif,
He was fer baldar, certis, by hys leif,
Sayand he followit Virgillis lantern toforn,
Quhou Eneas to Dydo was forsworn.
Was he forsworn? Than Eneas was fals –
That he admittis and callys hym traytour als.
Thus wenyng allane Ene to have reprevit,
He hass gretly the prynce of petis grevit.[111]

Douglas is taken aback by Chaucer's seemingly antagonistic interpretation of the *Aeneid*. Why does Chaucer announce his intention to follow Virgil's example only to narrate a version of the story in which Aeneas betrays Dido? Such a narrative derives not from Virgil's poem but from *Heroides* 7, Ovid's scathing revision of *Aeneid* 4, in which pious Aeneas is reimagined, through Dido's eyes, as cowardly and cruel. While he recognizes the boldness in his reproof of Chaucer, therefore, Douglas insists that Chaucer was "far baldar" in his treatment of his source.

Read in isolation, Chaucer's disingenuous claim to follow Virgil's example certainly *seems* to offer a challenge to his predecessor's authority. But would Virgil really have been "offended" by the *Legend of Dido*? Probably not, because the author of the *Aeneid* himself manipulated his textual models to reinvent the Carthaginian queen. As Petrarch laments in a letter, Virgil transformed the historical Dido from a woman who "died out of zeal for chastity" into one who yielded to a "wanton love."[112] What textual fidelity did Chaucer (or for that matter, Ovid) owe the *Aeneid* when Virgil *himself* fabricated his material?

Chaucer in fact signals his participation in a tradition of misreading Virgil in the opening lines of the *Legend*. His claim to follow Virgil's lantern recalls an episode from Dante's *Commedia*. Explaining that Virgil's words functioned as a lantern that illuminated his path to Christianity, Dante's Statius performs a "salvific misreading" of the fourth *Eclogue*, which shone a light on his path to Christianity that Virgil himself could not see: "Facesti come quei che va di notte, / che porta il lume dietro e sé non giova, / ma dopo sé fa le persone dotte" ("You did as one who walks at night, who carries the light behind him and does not help himself, but instructs the persons coming after" [*Pg* XXII.64–9]).[113] This episode from the *Commedia* has further resonance in Statius's own poetry. In the epilogue to the *Thebaid*, Statius asks his epic to follow reverently in the footsteps of the *Aeneid*, in what constitutes the first and only mention of Virgil's poem in his entire work:

> vive, precor; nec divinam *Aeneida* tempta,
> sed longe sequere et vestigia semper adora.
> mox, tibi si quis adhuc praetendit nubila livor,
> occidet, et meriti post me referentur honores. (12.810–19)

> Live, I pray, and do not essay the divine *Aeneid*, but ever follow her footsteps from afar in adoration. Soon, if any envy still spreads clouds before you, it shall perish, and after me you shall be paid the honors you deserve.[114]

Here, Statius "eschews open rivalry" with Virgil to "[wager] on time as the medium of both fame and vindication," as Edwards notes, "den[ying] outright envy only to introduce poetic competition."[115] Statius's words of praise for Virgil contain an allusion to Aeneas's forgotten wife, Creusa, trailing behind her husband as the two flee Troy ("et longe servet vestigia coniunx" [*Aen.* 2.711]). In Statius's silent appropriation of these words, we "glimpse the revisionary poet stalking his source, marking its steps, and measuring the distances still unfulfilled between them."[116]

More than a mere statement of attribution, Chaucer's insistence that he will follow Virgil's lantern is thus an allusion to a very mode of allusion, in which declarations of tribute conceal (or perhaps signal) misreadings of

Virgil's poetry. Following Ovid on not only narrative but also intertextual terms – that is, in his infidelity to Virgil's account of Dido – Chaucer wrenches the *Aeneid* from its author's influence in a way that shows him emulating previous poets who did the same.[117] Yet it is difficult if not impossible to discern the ways in which Chaucer is emulating his sources' modes of authorial engagement without first excavating the origin and development of these traditions, something this study hopes to do. Looking merely at textual echoes, that is, we witness only one dimension of Chaucer's attribution of the *Legend* to Virgil. From this perspective, Chaucer's treatment of his author seems "bold" and antagonistic. By examining a pattern of Virgilian misreadings, however, we see Chaucer distorting the *Aeneid* in a way that aligns him with not only Ovid, his ultimate source, but also Dante, Statius, and even Virgil.

Retelling "Olde Stories": Chaucer's Boccaccian Poetics

This book has five chapters, all of which begin with the question of why Chaucer omits mentioning his debt to Boccaccio. Accordingly, my focus is on narratives in which Chaucer relies on yet never names his vernacular source. Since it is predominantly in the proems, prologues, epilogues, and commentaries of works that episodes of authorial self-inscription take place, the bulk of my readings concentrate on the frame of the *Canterbury Tales* and the paratexts of its sources. Following the order of the *Canterbury Tales*, the first three chapters discuss the "Knight's Tale," the "Clerk's Tale," and the "Monk's Tale," outlining the ways in which Chaucer develops the poetics of his classical and Italian predecessors in order to align his writings with theirs. In my fourth chapter I turn to *Troilus and Criseyde*, discussing Chaucer's invention of Lollius and a tradition of Trojan artifice. My final chapter on Lydgate's *Troy Book* and *Fall of Princes* examines the ways in which Chaucer's intertextual poetics are recognized and carried out in the fifteenth century. By showing how Lydgate adopts Chaucer's strategies of artful allusion, though he uses them in his own way, I inscribe both authors within a genealogy of poets who respond to one another by developing their predecessors' mode of intertextual engagement.

Chapter 1, "Literary Patricide in the Legend of Thebes," uncovers a pattern of authorial erasure in narratives of Thebes from antiquity to the fifteenth century, following this pattern through the works of Statius, Boccaccio, Chaucer, and Lydgate. Chaucer's occlusion of Boccaccio's influence in the "Knight's Tale" under the premise of translating "olde stories" is not (or not only) a historicizing manoeuvre, anchoring his narrative to authority and antiquity, as has previously been argued. Rather, Chaucer is perpetuating a trope of erasure learned from Boccaccio himself, who likewise camouflages his debt to his source in the *Teseida* under the premise of translating an anonymous old book. As for why these authors erase their sources, they do so in order to participate in a tradition of authorial usurpation practised by the Latin epic poets, and with the full intention (indeed, hope) that this strategy will be detected by future readers. Killing their authorial fathers in anticipation of being erased by their literary heirs, it is from an Oedipal series of erasures and resurrections that these poets understand their legacies emerging.

Chapter 2, "Restoration through Translation in the 'Clerk's Tale,'" moves from erasure to misreading as an intertextual manoeuvre. Looking beyond the "Clerk's Tale" to its Latin and Italian antecedents, Petrarch's *Historia Griseldis* and Boccaccio's *Decameron* X.10, I excavate an ongoing – albeit unidirectional – debate on language and style, in which Chaucer, Petrarch, and Boccaccio use the Griselda story as the metaphoric stage upon which to deliver their argument. Initiating this debate is Dante, whose ideas in the *Convivio* and *De vulgari eloquentia* are, as I argue, crucial to our understanding of the narrative's origins and trajectory. Not only does Boccaccio's story of Griselda exemplify Dante's argument on the elegance and significance of the Florentine *volgare*, but Griselda's innate virtue also mirrors the natural and unaffected charms of the mother tongue. Both the vernacular and Griselda are, moreover, superior to their more illustrious counterparts. Feigning ignorance of the underlying importance of Dante and his linguistic arguments to *Decameron* X.10, and adorning both Griselda and her narrative in extravagant dress, Petrarch translates Boccaccio's novella into Latin. He further adds rhetorical flourishes to the work, such as a lengthy proem tracing the path of the River Po. In doing so, he transforms Boccaccio's language, style, and audience so that they no longer resonate with Dante's ideas. In response, Chaucer wields Petrarch's intertextual methodology like a cudgel against its author. He uses the "Clerk's Tale" to argue for the importance of his own mother tongue, English, and to reject the "termes," "colours," and "figures" of Petrarch's translation (IV.16). Even while he attributes the story to Petrarch, by redressing Petrarch's *Historia* in the vernacular and aiming it at women and unlettered folk, Chaucer restores the tale to its Boccaccian state and purpose.

My third chapter looks beyond Chaucer's immediate source for the "Monk's Tale," the *De casibus virorum illustrium*, to a tradition of triumphal poetry that, I argue, informs Boccaccio's creation of this work. Although warning us repeatedly about the transience of earthly goods, the *De casibus* also contains an appeal to earthly glory, its lesson of fame's ephemerality contested over the course of the poem with stories of famous men and women that have lasted for centuries. Chaucer, as I show, incorporates

Boccaccio's ambivalent approach to glory in the "Monk's Tale." Despite his repeated assertion of the transitory, tragic nature of human existence, the Monk does not, at last, present fame as necessarily fleeting. Instead, he shows that ruin and defeat are temporary, whereas glory has the potential to be eternal. Retelling stories that have been preserved over the years by poets, he regales his fellow pilgrims with catalogues of worldly accomplishments and acquisitions. When these catalogues are committed to the page, I propose, they become poetic triumphs: written monuments of transient victories, memorialized by the author himself.

Chapter 4, "Myn Auctor Lollius: Chaucer and the Invention of Troy," locates Chaucer's creation of Lollius in the *Troilus* within an ongoing tradition of authors fabricating their textual authorities, a practice that, while not exclusive to the literary tradition of Troy, is especially prevalent in these narratives. Similar to how stories of Thebes involve patricide on both a narrative and intertextual level, stories of Troy both concern and exemplify fraud. With the supposed aim of distinguishing themselves from the epic poets, who they claimed were deceitful in their writings, medieval chroniclers of Troy feigned reliance on pseudo-Latin authorities or anonymous old books. But these oaths of textual and historical integrity were regularly interrogated, if not by the author himself then by his readers. This chapter will argue that by the time Benoît de Sainte-Maure writes the *Roman de Troie* in the twelfth century, the trope of the pseudo-ancient source had shifted its semiotic significance, and what began as a device to establish historical veracity developed into a veiled admission of artistic invention. Excavating a tradition of fabricated sources and ironic truth claims in the writings of Benoît de Sainte-Maure, Boccaccio, and Chaucer, I argue that these poets recognized fraud as the defining attribute of the Troy story. By appropriating the authenticating language and manoeuvres of medieval historiographers, meanwhile exposing these devices as spurious, they signalled the equally fictitious nature of their own writings on Troy. Thus foregrounding their literary artifice, they aligned their poems with the Trojan writings of Homer, Virgil, and Ovid, establishing for themselves an epic genealogy in the process.

My final chapter, "Chaucer through the Looking Glass: Lydgate's Chaucerian Poetics," turns from Chaucer's Italian poetics of intertextuality to Lydgate's reception of this poetics in the *Troy Book* and *Fall of Princes*. Although in many poems praising Chaucer as the superior poet, Lydgate consistently avoids identifying Chaucer as his source. Instead, in works that he presents as the immediate antecedents or continuations of Chaucer's poems, he returns to the Latin, French, and Italian sources that *precede* Chaucer, and in some cases to the very sources used by Chaucer himself. He also meticulously establishes the Latin and continental textual histories of these works at the expense of acknowledging Chaucer's writings, a move that many critics have interpreted as antagonistic. In the practice of minimizing Chaucer's influence, however, Lydgate modifies what I see as a recognizably Chaucerian poetics: if Chaucer translates Boccaccio without naming him, that is, then Lydgate praises Chaucer profusely, meanwhile understating or denying altogether his debt to Chaucer's poetry. By offering a distorted, yet recognizably derivative version of Chaucer's treatment of Boccaccio in these poems, Lydgate reveals an important, associative function of authorial elision, aligning himself with Chaucer even while refusing to credit him as a source.

Tropes of Engagement thus concludes by examining Chaucer through the looking glass of Lydgate's poetry, providing crucial evidence of Chaucer's intertextual methodology vis-à-vis Lydgate's imitation of it. At the same time, I suggest that much of what we have interpreted as confirmation of Lydgate's ineptitude, or as his awkward attempts at self-authorization, instead shows the poet developing strategies of authorial engagement appropriated from Chaucer's own writings. Offering a new understanding of Chaucer's literary milieu that includes not only his ancestors – contemporary and ancient – but also his descendants, this book recovers a model of Chaucer's intertextual engagement that resonates beyond his poetry, well into the fifteenth century.

Erasing, manipulating, and inventing their sources – emulating their predecessors' modes of authorial engagement as well as their poetry – the authors included in this study do not merely "borrow" from, "copy," or "imitate" one another, prompting a return to the question of what constitutes a source in their writings. Perhaps, using the yardstick of T.S. Eliot, Picasso, Stravinsky, and Banksy, this is what makes them great.

Chapter One

Literary Patricide in the Legend of Thebes

The "Knight's Tale" is a Middle English adaptation of the Italian *Teseida* (1339–40), yet nowhere in his poem does Chaucer identify either his source or its author, Boccaccio. While plenty of medieval writers borrow but do not properly attribute their material, Chaucer invents a false foundation narrative for his first Canterbury Tale. The Knight's opening words, "whilom, as olde stories tellen us" (I.859), suggest the existence of an ancient, written source.[1]

That Chaucer does not designate Boccaccio as his source has often been attributed to his desire to lend his writings more substantial authority.[2] As a recent author writing in a vernacular language, Boccaccio's name lacks the solemnity of a "Lollius," a "Corynne," or even an anonymous ancient text. Critics have generally agreed, therefore, that Chaucer invents these sources for the same reason that medieval historiographers feign reliance on ancient *auctores* while camouflaging signs of recent invention: to bolster the authenticity and credibility of his works.[3] I want to propose in this chapter that Chaucer's erasure of Boccaccio has a separate origin and purpose. I will suggest that Chaucer learns his aesthetic of erasure from Boccaccio himself, who playfully conceals his massive debt to Statius in the *Teseida* under the premise of translating an anonymous "hystoria antica," describing his story – with no small irony – as one "che latino autor non par ne dica" ("that a Latin author appears not to have told").[4] As for why Boccaccio and Chaucer erase their sources, they do so in order to participate in a tradition of authorial usurpation, practised by the Latin epicists and further developed by medieval authors of Thebes, the latter with the aim of establishing an epic genealogy for their poems. Unlike some medieval historiographers, then, who minimize signs of poetic licence in naming established *auctores*, Boccaccio and Chaucer call attention to authorial erasure as a literary trope, situating their vernacular poems in a classical tradition while suggesting their preeminence as modern poets writing in a new literary language.

But when Boccaccio and Chaucer erase their sources, who do they expect to notice? Questions of Chaucer's anticipated and actual reception have often framed the way we have discussed his engagement with his sources. Paul Strohm in particular reminds us to consider in any discussion of Chaucer's reception the poet's "consciousness both of an immediate audience ... and an audience of posterity."[5] It is this second audience for whom I think Chaucer conceals his source. To clarify, I do not believe that either Boccaccio or Chaucer expected all of his patrons and readers to pick up on the implications of this erasure. My point is far more specific: that in stories of Thebes, we consistently find authors erasing their primary sources and further taking steps to emphasize this performance of erasure. These authors erase, we might say, with their literary descendants in mind, the poets who will follow them, and who will invoke these same genealogical strategies to warrant their places in an ongoing literary tradition. To adopt Walter Ong's famous phrase, by erasing their sources, these authors "fictionalize" an audience receptive to their rhetorical strategies.[6]

And if there is something patricidal about this behaviour, there is also something suicidal about it, since Chaucer writes not only to efface Boccaccio but also to be effaced by a worthy successor, an ambition we will see gratified by Lydgate. It is from this Oedipal series of erasures and unerasures, of literary patricides and poetic resurrections, that Theban poets understand their authorial legacies emerging. Taking as their theme this "emblematic tale of internecine rivalry," they draw a parallel between the patricide of Oedipus and the erasure of their authorial father.[7] Chaucer, and Boccaccio before him, would thus seem to conceive of literary lineage in both a retrospective and prospective sense: in mimicking Boccaccio's intertextual poetics, Chaucer not only binds his work to a previous literary tradition but also takes steps to ensure his own perpetuity.

That we can trace a pattern of authorial obfuscation from antiquity to the Middle Ages, or from Virgil to Lydgate, as I will do in this chapter, speaks to the efficacy of this device. In resituating Chaucer's famous occlusion of Boccaccio within a genealogy of Theban erasure, I aim to add a new understanding of Chaucer's construction of an authorial self in relation to a literary tradition that includes not only his ancestors – contemporary and ancient – but also his descendants, in a way that other poets may have appreciated even if we have missed it.

Following in the Footsteps of Virgil from the *Thebaid* to the *Teseida*

To recognize the importance of Boccaccio's absence from the "Knight's Tale," we must therefore look backwards, not only to Chaucer's source for this work, the *Teseida*, but also to those writings that influenced Boccaccio in his creation of this poem. As we will see, Chaucer's silence toward his source is prefaced by a series of authorial erasures, most notably Boccaccio's failure to acknowledge his own textual model, Statius, in the *Teseida*. Both of these examples must, moreover, be considered in light of Statius's challenge to Virgil's authority in the *Thebaid* (although not an instance of erasure per se). What we find in writings on Thebes is a pattern of poetic suppressions, which, while they take variable forms, develop from and build on one another. Authorial patricide is enmeshed in the literary history of Thebes; it is as integral to the story as are the components of the plot.

In what follows, I will consider these instances of authorial patricide, beginning with Statius's treatment of Virgil in the *Thebaid*. While critics diverge on whether Statius's engagement with the *Aeneid* (and especially the *Aeneid*'s portrayal of imperialism) is critical or admiring, there is little argument on the extent of the work's significance to his poem: the *Aeneid* is "undoubtedly Statius' most important model."[8] Despite his massive debt to Virgil, however, Statius is conspicuously reticent with regard to his predecessor's influence, acknowledging the *Aeneid* only in the *Thebaid*'s epilogue. In these final lines of his poem, the poet implores his epic to endure in the shadows of the *Aeneid*, and to follow in Virgil's footsteps with reverence:

> Durabisne procul dominoque legere superstes,
> o mihi bissenos multum vigilata per annos
> Thebai? iam certe praesens tibi Fama benignum
> stravit iter coepitque novam monstrare futuris.
> iam te magnanimus dignatur noscere Caesar,
> Itala iam studio discit memoratque iuventus.
> vive, precor; nec tu divinam Aeneida tempta,
> sed longe sequere et vestigia semper adora.
> mox, tibi si quis adhuc praetendit nubila livor,
> occidet, et meriti post me referentur honores.

> My *Thebaid*, on whom I have spent twelve wakeful years, will you long endure and be read when your master is gone? Already, it is true, Fame has strewn a kindly path before you and begun to show the new arrival to posterity. Already great-hearted Caesar deigns to know you, and the studious youth of Italy learns you and recites. Live, I pray; and do not attempt the divine *Aeneid*, but ever follow her footsteps from afar in adoration. Soon, if any envy still spreads clouds before you, it shall perish, and after me you shall be paid the honours you deserve.[9]

There is little in these lines themselves to suggest their author's insincerity. Yet Statius's admiration of the *Aeneid* skews ironic when we consider his overall engagement with Virgil throughout his poem. In light of his heavy debt to his predecessor, it is striking that he mentions the *Aeneid* once, and only at the very end of his work.

To be sure, evaluating Flavian standards of citation according to contemporary expectations seems like a futile task. We can hardly assume that authors from antiquity will cite their sources diligently, nor can we level charges of deliberate obfuscation against them when they fail to do so. In this case, however, the tardiness of Statius's acknowledgment of the *Aeneid* was significant enough to be remarked upon by Petrarch in the fourteenth century. In a fictional letter to Homer (*Familiares* XXIV.12 [1360]), a text I will return to later in this chapter, Petrarch apologizes to the Greek poet for Virgil's refusal to name him. Other poets acknowledge their debt to Homer, Petrarch points out, yet Virgil, who borrows so flagrantly from Homer's epics, does not.[10] Attempting to justify Virgil's silence, Petrarch directs Homer to the *Thebaid*. Despite Statius's extensive borrowing from Virgil in this epic, "illic tamen bona fide totum grati animi debitum benemerite persolvit Eneydi" ("it was [only] at the close that he openly and in good faith paid the full debt of his grateful mind to the *Aeneid* text"). It is plausible that Virgil, too, intended to praise Homer at the end of the *Aeneid*, Petrarch suggests, but that he died before being able to do so. Petrarch's explanation for Virgil's silence is, of course, facetious; it only draws his reader's attention to a trope of authorial obfuscation, practised by both Virgil and Statius, and which Petrarch himself perpetuates in his treatment of Dante, a point I will return to subsequently. At this juncture, what this letter reveals is that Statius's delayed attribution of Virgil was extraordinary even to early readers.

Statius's words of praise for the *Aeneid* are also not without their barbs. In the process of denying any rivalry between his own and Virgil's work, Statius recycles the language Virgil gives to Aeneas as he relates the loss of his wife Creusa. His words, "sed longe sequere et vestigia semper adora," mirror Virgil's, "et longe servet vestigia coniunx" ("and let my wife follow our steps at a distance").[11] Statius's echo of the *Aeneid* at the precise moment he announces its sovereignty over his poem complicates just such a gesture of humility. Rather than credit Virgil for this material, Statius silently absorbs the language of the *Aeneid* into the fabric of his work, insinuating a desire to match Virgil, maybe even to move beyond him, as Aeneas moves beyond Creusa, as an archetype in verse.[12] As Robert R. Edwards remarks, in the "image of his poem's reverently trailing behind the *Aeneid* ('longe sequere')," we may discern "the revisionary poet stalking his source, marking its steps, and measuring the distances still unfulfilled between them."[13]

Equally important are the words that follow. Statius observes that fame is transient, passing from one poet to the next, and he consoles his *Thebaid* that "tibi si quis adhuc praetendit nubila livor, / occidet, et meriti post me referentur honores" ("if any envy still spreads clouds before you, it shall perish, and after me you shall be paid the honours you deserve").[14] Statius imagines that time will grant him due honour and fame, even if, at present, he must pay lip service to the *Aeneid*, an admission that undermines his previous claim of Virgil's preeminence.[15] In the glare of this proviso, the grandeur of the *Aeneid* appears to stem from the temporary favour of the masses, and not from its intrinsic worth.

If we look outside the *Thebaid*, we find an even more explicit challenge to Virgil's poetic authority. Statius concludes an ode from the *Silvae* by claiming that his *Thebaid*, "Multa cruciata lima / temptat audaci fide Mantuanae / gaudia famae" ("Tortured by much filing, attempts with daring string the joys of Mantuan fame").[16] Here Statius discharges his epic from the "etiquette of deference" to the *Aeneid* that we saw at play in the earlier work.[17] Instead, he manipulates his words from the epilogue to the *Thebaid*, "nec tu divinam *tempta*," to imply a new relationship between himself and Virgil in which both poets stand on equal footing: "*temptat* Mantuanae famae" – attempt Virgilian fame. A second ode addressed to his father reflects a similar ambition. Statius writes, "magniloquo non posthabuisset Homero, / tenderet aeterno [et] Pietas aequare Maroni" ("Piety perhaps would have accounted me not inferior to mighty-mouthed Homer and striven to match me with immortal Maro [Virgil]").[18] Tempering his pride in his poetry with a father's expected indulgence of his son, Statius places himself on par with the poetic exemplars of Western civilization. It would seem that his earlier prostration before Virgil in the *Thebaid* was at least partly ceremonial, since in these odes Statius vies for equivalence.

Statius's engagement with Virgil thus develops from a posture of deference to one vying for equivalence. At the same time, the allusive backdrop of certain phrases – "nec tu divinam *tempta*" ("*temptat* Mantuanae famae"); "sed longe sequere et vestigia semper adora" ("et longe servet vestigia coniunx") – complicates even his words of praise for his predecessor, implying that while Virgil is preeminent now, Statius will perhaps some day overtake him. We witness a similar modulation in Boccaccio's treatment of Statius. In the *Filocolo* (1336–8), Boccaccio elevates Statius as the premier poet of war.[19] In the later *Teseida*, however, which takes the *Thebaid* as its primary source, he does not mention his predecessor at all, feigning reliance instead on an "hystoria antica." Boccaccio's treatment of Statius is thus inconsistent, which in itself is not so significant. That it is inconsistent in a way that mirrors Statius's earlier treatment of Virgil is, however, quite striking, because it suggests that Boccaccio borrows not only Statius's Theban material but also his poetics of intertextuality. We discover in both the *Thebaid* and the *Filocolo* that "poets can engage in artistic rivalry even as they praise their predecessors and models."[20] What is more, we find that poets can deploy strategies of authorial erasure and occlusion as acts of homage.

In his final farewell to the *Filocolo*, Boccaccio cautions his "piccolo libretto" not to aspire to match Virgil in verse, nor Lucan and Statius in poems of war, nor Ovid in works of love, nor Dante in vernacular poetry.[21] The role of his little book, Boccaccio suggests, is to follow behind these authors as a "minor servant":

> Ché, con ciò sia cosa che tu da umile giovane sii creato, il cercare gli alti luoghi ti si disdice: e però agli eccellenti ingegni e alle robuste menti lascia i gran versi di Virgilio ... E quelli del valoroso Lucano, ne' quali le fiere arme di Marte si cantano, lasciali agli armigeri cavalieri insieme con quelli del tolosano Stazio. E chi con molta efficacia ama, il sermontino Ovidio seguiti ... Né ti sia cura di volere essere dove i misurati versi del fiorentino Dante si cantino, il quale tu sì come piccolo servidore molto dei reverente seguire.
>
> For since you were created by a humble youth, it is not for you to seek out higher places. So leave the great verse of Virgil to the excellent wits and vigorous minds ... And those verses of mighty Lucan, in which the fierce arms of Mars are sung, leave them to martial knights, along with those of Statius from Toulouse. And whoever loved with great purpose, let him follow Ovid of Sulmona ... And do not be concerned to aspire to be where the measured verses of the Florentine Dante are sung, whom you ought to follow very reverently as a minor servant.[22]

This passage reflects a range of Boccaccio's epic and vernacular influences, from Statius and Ovid to Dante. The *Commedia* is perhaps the most recognizable model, with Boccaccio replacing the image of the pilgrim stalking behind his epic predecessors in *Inferno* IV with that of his physical book following humbly behind a similar succession of poets as their "piccolo servidore." In the *Filocolo*, Dante is the sole vernacular poet in a lineup of ancients. By naming him alongside Virgil, Lucan, Statius, and Ovid, Boccaccio places Italian poetry on the same level as Latin epic, a bold move that insists on the importance of both his own and Dante's work.

But Boccaccio also modifies the figures that comprise Dante's *bella scuola*, removing Homer and Horace to make room for "tolosano Stazio." Statius is not found among the epic poets in *Inferno* IV. Instead, we encounter him in *Purgatorio*, where Statius attributes both his conversion to Christianity and his poetic ability to Virgil. Again, artistic inspiration is described metaphorically, with the image of one poet walking behind another:

> Facesti come quei che va di notte,
> che porta il lume dietro e sé non giova,
> ma dopo sé fa le persone dotte,
> quando dicesti: "Secol si rinova;
> torna giustizia e primo tempo umano,
> e progenïe scende da ciel nova."
> Per te poeta fui, per te cristiano. (*Pg* XXII.64–70)

> You did as one who walks at night, who carries the light behind him and does not help himself, but instructs the persons coming after, when you said: "The age begins anew; justice returns and the first human time, and a new offspring comes down from Heaven." Through you I became a poet, through you a Christian.[23]

While Dante fabricates Statius's conversion, he does not invent the image of Statius trailing in the shadows of Virgil. For this, Dante borrows from the epilogue of the *Thebaid*, in which, as we have seen, Statius directs his poem to walk behind the *Aeneid* at a reverential distance, a passage Boccaccio, too, will evoke in his address to the *Filocolo*.

Boccaccio's farewell to the *Filocolo* thus combines Statius's address to his *Thebaid* with two passages from the *Commedia*, the first in which the pilgrim marches behind the great epic poets of antiquity, and the second (itself developed from the final lines of the *Thebaid*) in which Statius claims to walk in Virgil's footsteps. A nexus of intertextual poetics, this passage is a space where we may witness authors speaking to one another through the repetition of literary tropes. Since Statius betrays no outward interest in outpacing Virgil in the *Thebaid*, nor does Dante divulge an apparent rivalry with his epic ancestors, Boccaccio would seem to use these lines to place himself in a tradition of poets paying homage to their literary models by describing the physical act of walking behind them, in their footsteps. Yet both Statius's and Boccaccio's declarations of meekness are at odds with their ultimate presentation of themselves as poets of equal or superior rank in relation to their predecessors. What is more, these displays of modesty become increasingly mediated as we contextualize them within a larger literary tradition of allusive usurpation.

Whereas in the farewell to the *Filocolo* Boccaccio praises his authorial ancestors, establishing a Latin and vernacular foundation for his Italian poem, in the *Teseida* he appears more invested in concealing his literary debts, especially to Statius, than in enumerating them. Although he develops his Theban narrative "scene by scene, in open imitation of the main action of Statius's *Thebaid*," as David Anderson has shown, Boccaccio claims to translate the *Teseida* from an anonymous, pseudo-ancient source.[24] This is a curious and indeed prominent obfuscation: in the Middle Ages, Statius was the preeminent authority on Thebes. As Dominique Battles points out, whereas the Troy legend "came to medieval readers through a number of sources, the legend of Thebes derived from Statius alone."[25] We need only look to the *House of Fame* for evidence of this: eight poets hold up the glory of Troy, yet Statius alone bears the weight of Thebes (III.1460–3). Instead of capitalizing on his source's epic authority, however, Boccaccio obscures his debt to the *Thebaid* altogether.

As though to highlight Statius's absence, Boccaccio exaggerates the novelty of his poetic endeavour. In the prologue, he claims to be the first author to translate his "antichissima hystoria" out of what he suggests is a Greek source ("Prologue," 15).[26] He stipulates that his story is one that a Latin author has not told ("che latino autor non par ne dica" [I.2]), a passage he glosses with the words, "non è stata di greco translatata in latino" ("it has not been translated out of Greek into Latin" [I.2, gloss]). He will therefore take this ancient narrative and translate it into the Florentine vernacular and verse: "in latino volgare e per rima" ("Prologue," 15).

In this passage, Boccaccio positions himself as a mediator between Greek literature and the vernacular, a role the poet will take great pride in assuming later in his life, and one he uses, as James C. Kriesel claims, to distinguish his poetic achievement from those of his contemporaries.[27] Nor are his claims here entirely disingenuous: Boccaccio draws on myriad Greek authors in the *Teseida*, including Antimachus of Colophon, Accius, Naevius, Euripides, and Homer. Because his primary source is *Latin* and not Greek, however, his statement of novelty has the effect of minimizing Statius's influence on both his poem and the literary tradition of Thebes. At the very least, his claim of primacy is an exaggeration. At most, it can be read as a conspicuous attempt to undermine (or even to assume) Statius's role in the European Middle Ages as chief Latin/*latino volgare* authority on Thebes.

At the close of the *Teseida*, Boccaccio emphasizes his novelty for the second time. Addressing his book, he declares himself "first" to sing of war in the Italian vernacular, doubling down on this claim in the gloss:[28]

> Poi che lle Muse nude cominciaro
> nel cospecto degli uomini ad andare,
> già fur di quelli i quai l'exercitaro
> con bello stilo in honesto parlare,
> et altri in amoroso l'operaro;
> ma tu, o libro, primo a llor cantare

di Marte fai gli affanni sostenuti,
nel volgar latio più mai non veduti. (XII.84)

> Since the Muses began to walk naked in the sights of men, there have already been those who have employed them in fine style for moral discourse – and others have enlisted them in the service of love. But you, my work, may be seen as the first ever to have them celebrate the performance of martial feats in the vulgar tongue.[29]

Because he is first, Boccaccio is worthy of praise among other poetic luminaries. He suggests, "Et perciò che tu primo col tuo legno / seghi queste onde, non solcate mai / davanti ad te da nessuno altro ingegno" ("And since you first with your boat cleave these waves never before plowed by any wit"), perhaps you will be placed "tra gli altri d'alcuno honor degno" ("among others deserving of some honour") (XII.85). Notably, these other worthies remain unnamed in both the text and commentary.

Readers have long recognized that Boccaccio's assertion of primacy in the *Teseida* responds to Dante's call for an Italian poet of arms in *De vulgari eloquentia*. Listing the three subjects worthy of poetic treatment as love, virtue, and arms, Dante notes that Cino da Pistoia has written on love, and himself on virtue, yet "arma vero nullum latium adhuc invenio poetasse" ("As for arms, I find that no Italian has yet treated them in poetry").[30] Boccaccio steps forward to fill this vacancy in his Theban poem, transposing his vision of a vernacular trinity onto the pantheon of literary giants to whom he paid homage in the *Filocolo*. Where Virgil, Statius, Lucan, and Ovid once reigned, now stand Dante, Boccaccio, and Cino, with Boccaccio claiming the title of martial poet for himself. In making this move, however, Boccaccio also departs from the *De vulgari eloquentia*. If Dante presents himself as one of a small number of poets writing on worthy subjects in the Florentine *volgare*, then Boccaccio acknowledges only his own Italian vernacular achievement. Presenting the *Teseida* as first in its class among an anonymous majority, he privileges his accomplishment over even those of his Italian peers.

Still, Boccaccio does not dispense with his humble façade from the *Filocolo* entirely in the *Teseida*. Should it find itself in illustrious company, he tells his poem, "honorerai / come maggior ciaschedun tuo passato, / materia dando ad cui dietro ài lasciato" ("honour as greater those who have gone before you, thus setting a precedent for those you leave behind" [XII.85]) – advice that reprises his command to the *Filocolo* to "follow reverently" behind his models. Yet in this advice lurks the hint of a retraction. Not only do his predecessors again remain unnamed here, but, as with Statius's insistence in the *Thebaid* that time will grant him and his characters due fame, Boccaccio insinuates that he will eventually rise to a position of prominence. His language is that of generational progression: by treating other books as elders, he will set a precedent for subsequent poets, who will at a later point keep pace behind *him*. Like Statius before him, Boccaccio identifies a pattern of allusive usurpation, and he develops Statius's move to overtake Virgil in the *Thebaid* by expunging Statius from his succession of literary models in the *Teseida*. Literary fame, Boccaccio implies, is at least partially a textual construction, achieved through the open imitation and appropriation of past literary models, and memorialized by later poets' participation in similar patterns of homage and ascendancy. Boccaccio cements Statius's position within an authorial lineage and articulates his own future in that same lineage with a single poetic gesture.

I Will Be the First to Sing What Has Been Sung Before: Revolutions of Primacy in Antique Poetry

By insisting on the novelty, or "firstness," of the *Teseida*, especially in relation to a Hellenic past, Boccaccio invokes another refrain associated with *translatio studii* and *translatio imperii*, in which Latin poets announce their primacy as translators of Greek culture and then crown themselves with the laurel. In the proem to the third *Georgic*, for example, Virgil declares himself first to bring the poetic muses from Greece to Italy:

> Primus ego in patrium mecum, modo vita supersit,
> Aonio rediens deducam vertice Musas;
> primus Idumaeas referam tibi, Mantua, palmas.
>
> I first, if life but remain, will return to my country, bringing the Muses with me in triumph from the Aonian peak; first I will bring back to you, Mantua, the palms of Idumaea.[31]

Paradoxically, Virgil's claim of firstness recapitulates Ennius's earlier declaration that it was *he* who first brought the Greek Muses to Italy, as Lucretius reports in *De rerum natura*:

> Ennius ut noster cecinit, qui primus amoeno
> detulit ex Helicone perenni fronde coronam
> per gentis Italas hominum quae clara clueret.
>
> As our own Ennius sang, who first brought down from pleasant Helicon a chaplet of evergreen leafage to win a glorious name through the nations of Italian men.[32]

Later in the work, Lucretius echoes this assertion – only this time with regard to his *own* firstness ("et hanc primus cum primis ipse repertast / nunc ego sum in patrias qui possim vertere voces" ["and I myself am now found the very first to be able to describe it in our own mother tongue"]).[33] In *Odes* III.30, Horace claims the same achievement for himself: he was first to bring Greek song to Italy ("princeps Aeolium carmen ad Italos" [10–16]), he suggests, for which we should crown him with the laurel.[34] And although he reverses the standard direction of *translatio* from Greek to Latin, Boccaccio resorts to a version of this trope in his defence of Greek poetry in Book XV of the Latin *Genealogie deorum gentilium* (1350–75).[35] He boasts of his role as first in *restoring* the study of Greek and Greek sources to Italy, having brought the scholar Leonzo Pilato to his home to aid him in the lengthy production of his compendium:

> *Fui equidem! Ipse insuper fui qui primus meis sumptibus Homeri libros et alios quosdam Grecos in Etruriam revocavi,* ex qua multis ante seculis abierant non redituri. Nec in Etruriam tantum, sed in patriam deduxi. *Ipse ego fui qui primus ex Latinis a Leontio in privato Yliadem audivi.* Ipse insuper fui qui, ut legerentur publice Homeri libri operatus sum. Et, esto non satis plene perceperim, percepi tamen quantum potui.
>
> *It was I, in fact! And I too was the first who, at my own expense, called back to Tuscany the writings of Homer and of other Greek authors*, whence they had departed many centuries before, never meanwhile to return. And it was not to Tuscany only, but to my own city that I brought them. *I, too, was the first to hear Leontius privately render the Iliad in Latin*; and I it was who made arrangements for public readings from Homer. And though I did not understand Homer any too well, I got such knowledge of him as I could.[36]

Looking back to his predecessors' earlier declarations of firstness, each poet relies on, yet undermines, his textual models. As Stephen Hinds says of the *Georgics*, while on the one hand "Virgil's claim to be first is 'authorized' by its association with Ennius' claim," on the other hand "the Ennian precedent can be argued precisely to disqualify the Virgilian claim," since only one poet can be first.[37] Virgil's recycling of Ennius's words thus binds his work to a literary tradition at the same time as it calls attention to his own imposture, for if we admit the allusion then we concede the lie. While apparently self-abnegating, this formula of referential self-promotion tells us something about how Hellenizing revolutions operate in Roman poetry, as Hinds explains: "they operate through a revision of previous Hellenizing revolutions, a revision which can be simultaneously an appropriation and a denial."[38] Through the percussive repetition of a literary trope, in other words, a poet can at once invoke and subvert the authority of his models. Like the various versions of the phrase "Good poets imitate, great poets steal," discussed in this book's Introduction, borrowed assertions of firstness inevitably implicate those poets who came before, *even when those poets remain unnamed.*

Boccaccio's claim in the Envoy of the *Teseida* to be "first" to translate Greek culture into the *latino volgare* relies, then, on a recognizable primacy topos, which petitions its earlier models even as it overturns those models. By nominating himself first martial poet to compose in the *latino volgare*, Boccaccio invokes without naming Ennius, Virgil, Lucretius, and Horace, all of whom had already claimed the title of first Latin poet to bring Greek culture to Italy before staking their claim to the laurel. At the same time, Boccaccio uses his Envoy to glance back at the coterie of epic poets that he praised in the *Filocolo*: Statius and Lucan for poems of war, Ovid for elegiac verse, Dante for vernacular writings, and Virgil for general excellence. In the *Teseida*, however, he evacuates these posts of their former occupants. Identifying "gli altri" who came before him, he does not specify who these others *are*, exactly. At the completion of his literary odyssey Boccaccio, too, reaches for the laurel:

Et però che i porti disiati
in sì lungo peleggio già tegnamo,
da varii venti in essi trasportati,
le vaghe nostre vele qui caliamo,
e le ghirlande et i don' meritati,
con l'ancore fermati, qui spectiamo,
lodando l'Orsa che con la sua luce
qui n'à condocti, ad noi essendo duce. (XII.86)

And since we have already reached the harbour we yearned for during this long voyage, sped there by various winds – we here furl our roving sails and having dropped anchor here await the garlands and gifts that are our due, while praising the Bear whose light has led us here acting as our guide.[39]

His poetic enterprise now paramount, Boccaccio portrays himself as both first and alone. The new Statius in a poem where Statius is never named, he is the first to sing of war in the *latino volgare*, and the first vernacular poet to translate this story of Thebes out of Greek. With nothing to pay homage to but the laurel crown, and no one at this point to keep pace behind but the North Star, Boccaccio demands more for his *Teseida* than Statius dared apportion to his *Thebaid*. Whereas Statius couches an argument for equivalence in the verses of his poetry, in the *Teseida*, Boccaccio claims poetic dominion.

A Tradition of *Fingere* in the *Teseida* and the *Genealogie Deorum Gentilium*

Hidden beneath a seemingly benign statement of subservience or a declaration of firstness lies a rhetoric of allusive usurpation that allows authors to gesture at a prior literary tradition while declaring those poets who comprise that tradition antiquated. Boccaccio suggests his movement beyond a Statian model by evoking Statius's earlier treatment of Virgil, praising Statius in one poem only to erase him from a second, and claiming his novelty as a vernacular translator of Greek culture in the language of previous poets. In the glosses to the *Teseida*, Boccaccio flags his Theban poetics of intertextuality in a new way.[40] He incorporates lengthy summaries of the *Thebaid* as a commentary on his narrative, yet he attributes this material not to Statius but to a tradition of poetic fictionalizing.

Indeed, much of Boccaccio's engagement with Statius's epic takes place in the commentary accompanying his poem. In these paratextual spaces, Boccaccio can position the *Thebaid* as the handmaiden to his work by suggesting that it explicates key moments in his poem's plot. In Book I, for example, Boccaccio uses the *Thebaid* to justify Theseus's decision to lay siege on the Amazons. He insists that the same forces motivating the main action of Statius's epic likewise spur his characters to combat. Theseus is already enraged by reports of Amazonian women murdering men, we are told, when he notices Tydeus's shield affixed to a tree:

> Marte tornava allora sanguinoso
> dal bosco dentro al qual guidati avea,
> con tristo agurio del re furioso
> di Thebe, l'aspra schiera, e sì tenea
> lo scudo di Thydeo, il qual pomposo
> della vittoria, sì come potea,
> ad una quercia l'aveva appiccato
> cotal qual era, ad Marte consecrato. (I.14)

> Mars returned, bloody, from the forest into which he had guided, under the evil omen of the mad king of Thebes, the harsh host, and that forest held the shield of Tydeus, where, arrogant with his victory, he had hung it, as well as he could, to an oak tree and consecrated it to Mars.

This description of the shield of Tydeus, nailed to a tree, comes from *Thebaid* II.704–26.[41] Statius describes how Tydeus makes an envoy to Eteocles, slaughters fifty of his men, and then nails his shield to a tree as a warning to other potential adversaries. But Boccaccio makes no mention of Statius or the *Thebaid*. Instead, in the gloss accompanying this passage, he claims that his explanation of the shield of Tydeus is his *own* poetic invention, and that he includes it to establish a connection between Tydeus's valour and Theseus's indignation. The poet, "vuole … mostrare, poeticamente fingendo, qual fosse la cagione che movesse Theseo contra le donne amazone ad fare guerra" ("wants to demonstrate, poetically fictionalizing, what the provocation was that moved Theseus to make war against the Amazon women"; I. 14, gloss). This provocation is, as it turns out, Tydeus's envoy to Eteocles.

Shortly after this spurious confession, Boccaccio attributes a second passage from the *Thebaid* to poetic fictionalizing. He claims that the temple of Mars is housed in the frigid mountains of Thrace to accommodate the god's hot temperament. Boccaccio derives his description of Mars's Temple from *Thebaid* VII.34–42, where, on Jupiter's orders, Mercury makes an unpleasant journey to the seat of this frozen shrine. Once again, he does not credit this material to Statius; instead, he ascribes it to the fiction of the ancients:

> Scrivono fingendo i poeti che lla casa di Marte, dio delle battaglie, sia in Tratia, a piè de' monti Riphei. Alla quale fictione volere intendere … che l'ira et il furore s'accende più fieramente e più di leggiere negli uomini ne' quali è molto sangue, che in quegli ne' quali n'è poco. (I.15, gloss)

> Poets fictionalize that the house of Mars, God of battles, is in Thrace, at the foot of the Riphaean mountains. This fiction is to be understood to mean that … wrath and fury are more fiercely and easily ignited in men in whom there is much blood than in those in whom there is little.

Boccaccio appears to perform an important function of the glossator here. Modelling his scholia on academic commentaries that accompany works such as the *Thebaid*, he draws out and develops key ideas that remain opaque in the text, and articulates the intent of the author.[42] As Alastair Minnis notes, in the *Teseida*, "techniques of exposition traditionally used in interpreting 'ancient' authorities are being used to indicate and announce the literary authority of a 'modern' work."[43] By treating his poem as worthy of exegesis, Boccaccio accords it a gravity and reverence typically reserved for the Bible and Latin epics.

In the *Teseida*, however, the glosses do not so much explicate the contents of the poem as crib the *Thebaid* without crediting it as an influence. (Nowhere is this more evident than in the gloss to Book II, stanza 10, in which Boccaccio summarizes Statius's epic point by point before insisting – misleadingly – that this material is essential to our understanding of his poem. The author "intende di dimostrare come Arcita e Palemone vi pervenissero [ad Attene]. Alla quale cosa fare, gli conviene toccare la guerra stata tra Ethiocle e Pollinice, et quello che di quella adivenne"; "intends to demonstrate how Arcita and Palamone came there [to Athens]. To do this, he should touch on the war between Eteocles and Polynices, and that which followed"). Despite Boccaccio's protestations to the contrary, however, Tydeus's envoy to Eteocles clarifies very little with regard to Theseus's whereabouts prior to his invasion of Scythia; Mercury's journey to the temple of Mars sets up the Duke's imprisonment of Palamone and Arcita in only the most oblique way. Neither of these passages derives from poetic inventions. Rather, they are both hijacked unceremoniously from Statius's epic. Far from being critical to our understanding of the *Teseida*, they appear wholly extraneous to Boccaccio's poem.

But while they explain little with regard to his work, Boccaccio's Statian glosses provide important insight into his intertextual poetics. On the one hand, by suggesting that the events that set the cogs of the siege of Thebes in motion likewise spur his characters to action, Boccaccio anchors his *Teseida* to the *Thebaid* by way of teleological necessity. Rendered anonymous, yet still recognizable (at least to Boccaccio's more learned readers) as the poet's source for his Theban material, Statius is denied the status and tribute typically accorded a reputable *auctor*. Instead, Boccaccio treats him like an anonymous commentator, whose words expound on and serve the primary text.[44] On the other hand, by attributing his Statian material to his own and others' poetic fictionalizing, Boccaccio inscribes himself in a tradition of epic fabrication.[45] *Fingere* in this context implies not only authorial agency but also innovation, both of which are antithetical to the historiographer's cause.[46] We could not ask for a clearer indication that the "hystoria antica" is not merely an authenticating device than Boccaccio's emphasis on poetic invention in the glosses.

Boccaccio's celebration of poetic fictionalizing in the *Teseida* anticipates his later defence of poetry in the encyclopedic *Genealogie*.[47] In the fourteenth book of this treatise, completed under the guidance of Pilato, Boccaccio justifies the value of fiction before the *vulgus ineptum* and imperious censors alike.[48] First vindicating poetry against claims that it is unprofitable, insignificant, and immoral, he suggests that innovation is the very foundation of his craft. Certainly, poets invent stories, he grants, but they do so in the service of a greater truth. Drawing on Dante's *Epistle to Cangrande*, he advises his patrons and readers to look beyond the beautiful veil of the letter of the word for more profound meaning.[49] Such an expository approach, called *integumentum*, appears to endorse poetry by privileging its allegorical capabilities at the expense of the literal. But Boccaccio does not limit his defence of poetry to its underlying potential. On the contrary, he emphasizes the importance of the literal and historical sense as well.

Indeed, the "veil" of poetry is itself worthy: it is pleasing and restorative, with fables offering those overwhelmed by adverse fortune a form of consolation: "Qui iocosis confabulationibus recreent animos tigatos."[50] Beyond their ability to delight and console, fables also convey truth. David Lummus has discussed how Boccaccio's treatment of ancient myth is founded on his understanding of the veracity and historicity of these narratives.[51] Lummus uses Boccaccio's treatment of Perseus killing the Gorgon as an example. Here, Boccaccio appears to apply the fourfold method of interpretation to this story, moving from the literal to the allegorical to the moral to the anagogical:

> Perseus Iovis filius figmento poetico occidit Gorgonem,
> et victor evolavit in ethera. Hoc
> dum legitur per licteram hystorialis sensus prestatur. Si moralis
> ex hac lictera queritur
> intellectus, victoria ostenditur prudentis in vicium et ad virtutem
> accessio. Allegorice
> autem si velimus assumere, pie mentis, spretis mundanis deliciis,
> ad celestia elevatio
> designatur. Preterea posset et anagogice dici per fabulam Christi
> ascensum ad Patrem,
> mundi principe superato, figurari. Qui tamen sensus et si variis
> nuncupentur nominibus, possunt tamen omnes allegorici appellari.

> Perseus, the son of Jupiter, killed the Gorgon in the poetic fiction, and, victorious, he flies up into the air. When one reads this in the literal sense, it offers historical meaning. If one seeks a moral understanding from a reading, it reveals how the prudent conquer vice and accede to virtue. If we wish to treat it allegorically, it means that by spurning earthly delights the pious mind ascends to the heavens. In addition, an anagogical interpretation would say that the fable reconfigures the ascension of Christ to the Father after overcoming the ruler of the world. These interpretations, although labeled differently, could all be called allegorical.[52]

Although Boccaccio gestures at the fourfold method of interpretation, however, he does not employ it. Rather, he *inverts* the hierarchical structure of the *integumentum* by valuing the literal sense most highly.[53] His primary method of interpretation is, in this regard, euhemeristic:

> For Boccaccio … mythic narrations are directly traceable to an original historical moment, making them in effect narratives that unveil the historicity of their creation. Like biblical narration, myths are true historical narratives. So,

> by calling mythic meaning "polisemum" and by offering a fourfold reading of Perseus's struggle with the Gorgon, Boccaccio is expanding the integumental interpretative practice to include truth on the literal and historical level. He is in effect attributing a literal truth to the fictional narratives.[54]

Boccaccio, then, commends poetry for poetry's sake, celebrating his (and others') role as a fabricator. Fables and myths are more than just pleasing stories, justifiable only in their capacity to soothe and divert the reader. They can also be true historical narratives, akin to "biblical narration."[55] The process of innovation is, in this case, noble and praiseworthy. In the *Genealogie*, and, arguably, across his writings, "human acts of creating [are] given priority at the center."[56]

To further demonstrate the value of poetry, Boccaccio invents an etymology for the word "fable" that is rooted in the idea of a shared community of invention: "'Fabula' igitur ... a 'for, faris' honestam sumit originem, et ab ea 'confabulacio,' que nil aliud quam 'collucucio' sonat" ("the word *fabula* has an honorable origin in the verb *for*, *faris*, hence 'conversation' (*confabulatio*), which means only 'talking together' (*collocutio*)").[57] Boccaccio offers an example from the Gospel of Luke, in which two disciples spoke together, and Christ himself came to walk with them. Boccaccio concludes that if it is a sin to compose stories (*fabulari*), then it is a sin to converse (*confabulari*), which, he adds, only the biggest fool would admit.[58]

Boccaccio makes a particular case for the value of epic poetry.[59] Of the four kinds of *fabula*, he explains,

> Species vero tercia potius hystorie quam fabule similis est. Hac aliter et aliter usi poete celebres sunt ... Et hec si de facto non fuerint, cum communia sint esse potuere vel possent.

> The third kind is more like history than fiction, and famous poets have employed it in a variety of ways ... If the events they describe have not actually taken place, yet since they are common, they could have occurred, or might at some time.[60]

Naming Homer and Virgil among the "famous poets" who have employed this style of historical writing, and adding Christ himself to the list ("my opponents need not be so squeamish – Christ, who is God, used this sort of fiction again and again in his parables!"), Boccaccio celebrates poetry that takes on the guise of historical reality.[61] On a grander scale, he makes an argument for *fingere* as the common act connecting poets across history through the shared process of "confabulation."

Boccaccio's repeated characterization of events from the *Thebaid* as the result of his own or other poets' fictionalizing enables him to mark his debt to Statius while at the same time minimizing this debt, an approach to a classical past that Lee Patterson has described as an "emulation and exorcism" of one's sources.[62] While he fails to attribute his Statian material to its author, his description of this material as fiction is, I think, an affiliating gesture: Boccaccio positions himself and Statius among a genealogy of confabulators. The process of literary invention is honourable – even godlike. It is, moreover, justifiable vis-à-vis a poetic standard: his predecessors made up stories in the service of a larger historical truth, and so, too, shall he.

Lest we fail to notice the many signs of the *Thebaid*'s influence on and erasure from Boccaccio's work, the poet dedicates a final tribute to his silenced source. Addressing his work as the "*Theseyda* di nozze d'Emilia," a Latinate title reminiscent of the *Thebaid*, and the closest Boccaccio comes to naming his epic model in the poem,[63] Boccaccio announces in a concluding sonnet that it will bring him "in ogni etate fama immensa" ("immense fame in every age," *Teseida*, *Riposta delle Muse*). This final address recalls Statius's farewell to his *Thebaid* – "iam ... praesens tibi Fama benignum stravit iter coepitque novam monstrare futuris" ("Already ... Fame has strewn a kindly path before you and begun to show the new arrival to posterity")[64] – at the same time as it challenges it. Like claims of primacy, declarations of literary immortality can be both revived and countered by a usurping heir. Boccaccio's pronouncement of his *Teseida*'s everlasting fame not only evokes the silenced *Thebaid*, in which Statius predicts his own eternal glory, but it also influences how we interpret Chaucer's subsequent elision of Boccaccio, which, as I will demonstrate, is meant to revisit Boccaccio's earlier erasure of Statius. In his challenge to his predecessor, Boccaccio perpetuates a tradition of authorial patricide, and thus sets in motion the course of his own literary exile. Reproducing this manoeuvre by concealing Boccaccio's influence under the pretence of translating "olde stories" (the English equivalent of Boccaccio's "hystoria antica"), Chaucer corroborates Boccaccio's place in this tradition, and so offers himself as his ideal reader.[65]

The Silenced Author of Chaucer's "Knight's Tale"

In his encounter with the *Teseida*, Chaucer witnesses Boccaccio erase Statius under the premise of translating a fabricated ancient book. Unlike other writers that Chaucer may have observed doing something similar, however, Boccaccio introduces his "hystoria antica" at the precise moment at which acknowledging Statius as his principal source would be entirely apt, even desirable: his account of the siege of Thebes and its aftermath, for which he draws on the *Thebaid* so extensively, and with such frequency, that we cannot ignore its influence. Instead of capitalizing on the *Thebaid*'s very real authoritative clout, however, Boccaccio implies the *un*-reliability of Statius's epic by treating it as other writers treat their more dubious material: he buries his debt to it beneath the assertion that he is translating an anonymous ancient source. Chaucer, I argue, mimics and develops this trope of erasure. There is a distinct progression from Statius, who presents Virgil as his superior in the *Thebaid* yet implies his own equivalence in the *Silvae*; to Boccaccio, who names Statius as the exemplary poet of arms in the *Filocolo* only to omit all mention of him in the *Teseida*; to Chaucer, who sustains his erasure of Boccaccio throughout his poems, despite relying on him repeatedly as his principal source.

Yet Chaucer would appear unsatisfied with simply perpetuating a device found in the works of his predecessors. He reveals a further interest in recovering Boccaccio's silenced source from the *Teseida* by celebrating Statius as the predominant authority on Thebes. While not exclusive to the "Knight's Tale," this manoeuvre is most conspicuous in this work, in which Chaucer indicates the imposing influence of the *Thebaid* from the start.[66] Nearly all of the authoritative manuscripts of the "Knight's Tale" include a passage from *Thebaid* XII, detailing Theseus's triumphal return home after conquering the Amazons, as a gloss to the first segment:

> Iamque domos patrias, Scithice post aspera gentis
> Perlia, laurigero [subeuntem Thesea curra
> laetifici plausus missusque ad sidera vulgi
> clamor et emeritis hilaris tuba nuntiat armis.]

> And now Theseus drawing near his native land in laurelled car after fierce battling with the Scythian folk [is heralded by applause and the trump of warfare ended].[67]

With this reference to the *Thebaid*, Chaucer signals his deviation from Boccaccio, whose *Teseida*, though saturated with allusions to Statius's epic, at no point includes a direct citation of the text. In the *Thebaid*, these lines mark the introduction of Theseus, a figure who remains peripheral to the main action of the poem even as he plays a necessary role in its conclusion. As Chaucer himself will do, Statius all but forgoes mention of Theseus's whereabouts prior to his battle with Creon, referring to the Amazonomachy only in passing, in his description of the hero's triumphal return home.[68] Boccaccio, by contrast, devotes the first two books of the *Teseida* to Theseus's attack on Scythia, his marriage to Hippolyta, and finally his assault on Creon. This passage thus contains the kernel from which Boccaccio develops the opening of his poem. In beginning with these lines, Chaucer reveals the hidden inspiration behind Boccaccio's *amplificatio*, evoking both the original context of Theseus's journey to Thebes and Boccaccio's elaboration of this storyline.[69] Perhaps in the spirit of restoration, he folds the excess material back into its Statian proportion, a mere footnote to a chapter on Theban history.[70] Choosing Theseus's return home for his starting point, Chaucer relegates the Amazonomachy to the figurative margins of his poem – as Boccaccio did, quite literally, with the contents of the *Thebaid*. He then declares the battle (and, obliquely, the first two books of the *Teseida*) extraneous.

If Chaucer follows Statius in beginning his story after the conquest of the Amazons, then he is unique in showcasing this material before he discards it. Feigning reliance on ancient source texts – "whilom, as olde stories tellen us" (I.859) – he launches into an account of the Duke's Scythian interlude, describing

The grete bataille for the nones
Bitwixen Atthenes and Amazones;
And how asseged was Ypolita,
The faire, hardy queene of Scithia;
And of the feste that was at hir weddynge;
And of the tempest at hir hoom-comynge. (I.879–84)

The sum of this story, the Knight implies, is of little consequence. He casually dismisses this prefatory material as "to long to heere" (an amusing assessment, considering that the final detail of this summary, the "tempest at hir hoom-comynge," is Chaucer's own invention) before elaborating on the things he would have said, were it not for the time constraints of his journey. "I *wolde* have toold yow fully ... How wonnen was the regne of Femenye," he insists for a second time (italics added; I.865–6). Although the Knight flouts the structural integrity of the *Teseida* by omitting the poem's beginning, however, he hardly gives the rejected portion a quiet burial. Rather, in first presenting and then retracting his offer to speak of the siege against the Amazons, Chaucer calls attention to the restructuring of his source, rendering the very things he deems unnecessary conspicuous by their absence.[71]

Having opened his story with a passage from the *Thebaid* and then justified his truncation of the *Teseida* based on the shortness of time, in the second part of the "Knight's Tale" Chaucer takes his erasure of Boccaccio to a whole new level. He names "Stace of Thebes and these bookes olde" as his source for a scene deriving from the *Teseida*, in which Emilia/Emelye goes to the Temple of Diana to pray:

Smokynge the temple, ful of clothes faire,
This Emelye, with herte debonaire,
Hir body wessh with water of a welle.

But hou she dide hir ryte I dar nat telle,
But it be anything in general,
And yet it were a game to heeren al.
To hym that meneth wel it were no charge,
But it is good a man been at his large.
Hir brighte heer was kembd, untressed al;
A coroune of a grene ook cerial
Upon hir heed was set ful fair and meete.
Two fyres on the auter gan she beete,
And dide hir thynges, as men may biholde
In Stace of Thebes and thise bookes olde. (Italics added; I.2281–94)

Chaucer follows the *Teseida* rather closely here, embellishing his source only in the Knight's hesitancy to provide the specifics of Emelye's ritual, and in his attribution of the episode to "Stace."[72] Still, Chaucer's reference to Statius is not the outright falsification that it would seem: Boccaccio himself derives the details of Emilia's ritual from the *Thebaid*. In Statius's account, the prophet Tiresias attempts to conjure Apollo in order to learn the outcome of the war (*Thebaid* IV.416–73).[73] When these initial efforts fail, Tiresias warns Apollo that he is not above invoking darker forces:

Ne tenues annos nubemque hanc frontis opacae
spernite, ne, moneo: et nobis saevire facultas.
scimus enim [et] quidquid dici noscique timetis
et turbare Hecaten (ni te, Thymbraee, vererer)
et triplicis mundi summum, quem scire nefastum.
illum – sed taceo: prohibet tranquilla senectus.

Do not, I warn you, do not condemn my thinning years and the cloud upon my darkened brow. I too have means to be cruel. For I know whatever you fear to be spoken or known. I can harry Hecate, did I not respect you, Lord of Thymbra, him too, highest of the triple world, whom to know is blasphemy. Him – but I hold my peace: tranquil age forbids.[74]

At this point, Manto interrupts her father, as the earth opens to reveal a scene from the underworld. Among these phantoms are figures from myth in varying states of horror and despair: Semele holding her womb; Agave in a state of Bacchic frenzy, chasing her son Pentheus; Actaeon, horns protruding from his brow, fighting off the hounds that still tear at his limbs; and Niobe, madly tallying the bodies of her dead children. Finally, the old Theban King Laius arrives, with a neck wound marking the patricide of Oedipus, to prophesy that Thebes alone will survive this bloody war.

These visions, each more frightening than the last, set the tone for the final books of the *Thebaid*, in which the siege grinds toward its inevitable, tragic conclusion. As the model for Emilia's ritual in the *Teseida*, however, the episode is strikingly inappropriate.

Clearly a transgressive figure, Tiresias is a curious prototype for Emilia. Nevertheless, Boccaccio develops this scene of horror and necromancy into one of piety and devotion; if Tiresias is arrogant and impetuous, then Boccaccio's Emilia sacrifices "più divotamente" ("most devoutly," VII.70) of all three who made offerings to the gods. Pious and reverent, she displays not only respect for Diana but also an acceptance of her fate, asking the goddess,

> Se ' fati pur m'ànno riservata
> ad giunonicha legge sottostare,
> tu mi dèi certo aver per iscusata,
> né dèi però li miei prieghi schifare. (VII.83)

> If the Fates have nonetheless determined that I must submit to Juno's law, you ought surely to grant me pardon and not for that reason reject my prayers.[75]

Sacred though they may be, however, Emilia's rites retain the prior taint of necromancy. This is in part due to Tiresias's invocation of Hecate, and in part because of Statius's own literary models for this scene. In his commentary on the *Thebaid*, which we know Boccaccio consulted while writing the *Teseida*, Lactantius Placidus notes numerous allusions in this episode to necromantic rituals from Virgil's *Aeneid*, Ovid's *Metamorphoses*, Lucan's *Pharsalia*, and Seneca's *Oedipus*. This allusive backdrop makes it all the more difficult for us to accept Boccaccio's insistence on Emilia's piety, because her actions follow a long line of occult behaviour. What is more, by modelling her devotion on a necromantic ritual, Boccaccio makes himself complicit in Tiresias's original trespass, conveying by proxy what is "wrong to know." As though in response to its dreadful legacy, the Knight pares down this episode to a minimum, adding fearfully that "how [Emelye] dide hir ryte *I dar nat telle*" (although it is no doubt a "game to heeren al!")[76] It is as though he wishes to distance his tale from its transgressive origins as much as possible. Perhaps as a point of compromise, the Knight directs us to "Stace of Thebes and thise bookes olde" for the specifics of how Emelye "dide hir thynges." And while we will not discover the niceties of Emelye's ritual in the *Thebaid*, we do find its root, and, accordingly, the identity of Boccaccio's "old book," in Tiresias's original trespass.

Naming the ultimate source of his source but not his immediate author, Chaucer participates in a game of intertextual leapfrog, further associating Statius with the phrase under which Boccaccio concealed him in the *Teseida*, "thise bookes olde." This mention of Statius in a passage that he translates from the *Teseida* demonstrates the extent to which Chaucer has enhanced a trope of erasure learned from his predecessors. In reviving Boccaccio's silenced author in the figure of "Stace," summoning him from the dead as Tiresias summoned Laius, Chaucer renders this device more conspicuous, more metapoetic, than it appeared in previous forms, unmistakably showing the tradition of occlusion from whence he came.

Still, I suspect that Chaucer got the idea of crediting a Boccaccian passage to "Stace" from an episode in *Teseida* VI, in which Boccaccio likewise passes over his immediate source in favour of naming an earlier model. This manoeuvre is relatively muted in the *Teseida*, and has heretofore gone unnoticed. Boccaccio describes the arrival of many noblemen to the amphitheatre in which Palamone and Arcita will fight, and among these men is Idas the Pisan ("Yda piseo," VI.52). As Boccaccio explains in the glosses, the character of Idas is based on Virgil's description of Camilla (*Aeneid* VII.808–11): "della leggereza che qui pone l'autore che avea questo Yda, scrive Virgilio di Camilla, et quindi fu tolto ciò che qui se ne scrive" ("of the swiftness that the author here attributes to Idas, Virgil writes of Camilla, and therefore what is written here is taken from him," VI.53, gloss).[77]

Boccaccio's attribution of this passage to Virgil in the glosses constitutes his sole explicit mention of an ancient poet in the entire *Teseida*. It is, however, crucially, a *false* attribution, because the figure of Idas the Pisan is original to Statius, not Virgil.[78] Recently crowned with an Olympic wreath, Idas is a fearsome competitor in the games of *Thebaid* VI, triumphing over Parthenopaeus in the first footrace (550–645). Boccaccio clearly invokes this figure, dwelling on Idas's recent triumph in the Olympic games, and describing his exploits in the race (*Teseida* VI.52–3). Yet no scholar has thought to look beyond Camilla for a textual model, because Boccaccio names Virgil as his source.[79]

But while Virgil is not Boccaccio's source, he *is* the source of his source: Statius models his character Idas on Virgil's Camilla. Not only does Idas possess qualities reminiscent of the Amazonian warrior – Idas, for example, runs as fast as a speeding arrow (*Thebaid* VI.596–7), and Camilla can outrun the wind (*Aeneid* VII.806–7) – but also the games of *Thebaid* VI are modelled on Virgil's description of the athletic tournament in *Aeneid* V, as Lactantius Placidus reports.[80] In naming Virgil, then, Boccaccio brings to the surface of his poem a Virgilian archetype that remained unacknowledged by Statius. In doing so, he both excavates and perpetuates a tradition of authorial erasure in his work. Given how closely these authors were reading each other, it seems likely that Boccaccio was aware of Statius's obfuscation of his debt to the *Aeneid*, and that he names Virgil as his source for Idas so as to playfully allude to this manoeuvre, a manoeuvre that is deployed, as

I have argued, for the sake of being recognized and repeated. What is more, it appears that Chaucer amplified this tradition of authorial erasure in the "Knight's Tale": if Boccaccio discreetly credits Virgil for a figure taken from the *Thebaid* in the glosses to the *Teseida*, then Chaucer closely translates a passage from the *Teseida* before misattributing it twice – first to Boccaccio's occluded author "Stace," and second to the precise English equivalent of the phrase Boccaccio used to conceal this debt, "thise bookes olde."

To be sure, the consideration and humour that Chaucer puts into obscuring Boccaccio's influence suggests that he anticipated an audience that would recognize the intricacies of his intertextual poetics. I imagine that it was Chaucer's anticipation of just such an audience that led him to connect his erasure of Boccaccio in the "Knight's Tale" to his similar occlusion of Boccaccio in other works, most notably the *Troilus*, which I discuss in chapter 4. Rather than recycle the name assigned to him in the *Teseida*, "Penteo" (IV.3), Chaucer gives the exiled Arcite the alias of "Philostrate," his silenced Boccaccian source for the *Troilus*.[81] Perhaps it is no accident that (Ph)Filostrato(e)/Arcite is quite literally "buried" by the end of the work, with Mars, Boccaccio's patron god of the *Teseida*, enlisted to guide his soul home (I.2815), and a "coroune of laurer grene" placed on his brow (I.2875). This final detail – the laureation of Philostrate – may even be Chaucer's way of paying homage to his occluded author without explicitly naming him. In the epilogue to the *Troilus*, moreover, Chaucer repurposes the envoy from the *Filocolo* to praise those very poets (with the exception of Dante) that Boccaccio directed his poem to walk behind. Unceremoniously ousting Boccaccio from his own line-up of authors to make room for the exiled "Stace," Chaucer instructs his "litel bok" to kiss the steps of Virgil, Ovid, Homer, Lucan, and Statius (V.1786–92), usurping Boccaccio's position as the "sixth of six" poets.[82]

But it is not Boccaccio's role as "poet of arms" that Chaucer covets. In fact, he suggests in the *Troilus* that he would prefer *not* to sing of war.[83] It is rather Boccaccio's status as an intermediary poet – the vernacular arbiter in a line-up of ancients – that Chaucer seeks to assume, and by doing so to establish his place in an epic tradition. It is worth dwelling on why Chaucer removes not only Boccaccio but also Dante from his succession of literary models, severing Boccaccio's connection to the illustrious *latino volgare*. This second elision makes room for a new vernacular poetics – an *English* poetics. Although the *Troilus* is developed from an Italian model, Chaucer stresses the very Englishness of his poem:

> And for ther is so gret diversite
> In Englissh and yn writyng of oure tonge,
> So prey I God that non myswrite the,
> Ne the mysmetre for defaute of tonge;

And red wherso thow be, or elles songe,
That thow be understonde, God I biseche! (V.1793–8)

In a business where being "myswriten" is an occupational hazard, Chaucer no doubt intends his appeal for comprehension to be taken literally, but his plea for his book to be "understonde," "whereso thow be [read], or elles songe," also announces "oure tongue" as a literary language – a language that is accessible and coherent to all.[84] Chaucer then directs the *Troilus* for correction to his English counterparts, "moral Gower" and "philosophical Strode," casting aside the Latin poets and their "corsed olde rites" (V.1856, V.1857, V.1849).[85] In a poem in which the principal source receives no mention, the importance of this dedication cannot be overemphasized.[86] Naming himself poet of love (V.1769), Gower composer of moral works (V.1856), and Strode author of philosophy (V.1857), Chaucer changes Dante's three literary subjects appropriate for writing in the vernacular to love, virtue, and reason, removing not only Boccaccio but also the entire genre of martial poetry from this list. The effect of this dedication is to establish an English equivalent of the Italian *tre corone*.

Anchoring his *Troilus* in a classical past yet ultimately suggesting the primacy of a new vernacular literature, Chaucer attempts in one poem what Boccaccio enacted in two. After elevating a standard of ancient literary models in the *Filocolo*, Boccaccio suggests a corresponding vernacular literary tradition in his poem of Thebes, evoking the memory of his epic predecessors in their absence. For his part, in the epilogue to the *Troilus*, Chaucer develops an intricate web of allusions to his Italian forbears, Dante and Boccaccio, incorporating references to the *Commedia*, the *Filocolo*, the *Filostrato*, and the *Teseida* in a span of less than one hundred lines. Far from acknowledging his literary debts, however, he removes the names of Dante and Boccaccio from his succession of authorial influences, asking his work to follow in the footsteps of the classical *auctores*, "Virgile, Ovide, Omer, Lucan, and Stace," instead. Finally, Chaucer looks forward to an English posterity, inviting his friends, patrons, and readers to receive – and in Gower's and Strode's cases, to correct – his work. He thus parades his literary models before us, but in a way that requires our attention to the prevalence of his poetry in relation to previous writings, even those writings he refuses to acknowledge as among his influences.

Go, Little Quire

It remains to be shown that Chaucer is participating in a tradition of authorial erasure, and not merely imitating Boccaccio's treatment of Statius. I will therefore conclude this chapter by looking at two additional examples of literary patricide, the first in the writings of Chaucer's near contemporary, Petrarch, and the second in the poetry of Lydgate. The first example, which I raised briefly at the start of this chapter, concerns Petrarch's famous silence toward Dante in his writings. This instance occurs outside of the series of interconnected works on Thebes, and so is not illustrative of the trope of Theban patricide that I have identified. Nevertheless, it bears consideration because it corroborates what I have argued is poets' motivation behind perpetuating this trope: to position themselves within a genealogy of erasure, and to locate their works within an illustrious tradition of epic poetry.

In *Familiares* XXI.15 (1359), Petrarch responds to Boccaccio's suggestion that perhaps his frequent recommendation of Dante rankled with the older poet by denying that he is jealous of any man, including Virgil and Homer, but especially not Dante, who writes for idiots in taverns and squares ("ydiotas in tabernis et in foro").[87] In this letter, Petrarch gestures toward Dante multiple times, but he never once refers to him by name. This is standard behaviour for Petrarch, who, despite engaging with Dante consistently in his poetry, avoids mentioning him throughout.[88] As Giuseppe Mazzotta notes, were it not for his reluctance to name Dante, there would be nothing in this letter leading us to doubt Petrarch's sincerity with regard to his lack of envy of Dante's achievements.[89] Not long after this exchange, however, Petrarch makes abundantly clear that his silence toward Dante is far from arbitrary. On the contrary, it bespeaks his profound understanding of authorial erasure as a literary trope.

In a separate letter addressed to the deceased Homer, *Familiares* XXIV.12 (1360), Petrarch defends Virgil for neglecting to mention the Greek poet anywhere in his writings, drawing us "irresistibly ... to the implied homology" between these two instances of authorial erasure.[90] Petrarch concedes that Virgil's behaviour does, on the surface, appear extraordinary. Lucan, Flaccus, Ovid, Juvenal, and Statius all acknowledge their debt to Homer, while Virgil, overladen by the weight of Homer's spoils, does not.[91] Nor is Virgil consistent in his ingratitude. Indeed, he courteously mentions other poets, including his contemporaries, Varus and Gallus, something he would hardly have done if he were truly possessed by jealousy, as Petrarch suggests. Still, Petrarch cautions Homer not to draw the obvious conclusion, that Virgil's refusal to name the Greek poet constitutes a deliberate attempt to undermine Homer's authority. Instead, he asks Homer to give Virgil the benefit of the doubt. What happens next is rather remarkable: Petrarch offers Homer a clearly false explanation for Virgil's silence, deflecting rather than engaging in a legitimate conversation on authorial borrowing and occlusion. He claims that Virgil was reserving for Homer a place of honour in his poetry, but unfortunately died before he could grant him this tribute:

> Posuiesset, michi crede ... nisi mors impia vetuisset. Licet autem alios ubi occurrit atque ubi commodum fuit annotasset, tibi uni, cui multo amplius debebat, non fortuitum sed certum certoque consilio destinatum reservabat locum. Et quem reris, nisi eminentiorem cuntis atque conspectiorem? Finem ergo preclarissimi operis expectabat, ibi te suum ducem tuumque nomen altisonis versibus laturus ad sidera.

> He would have done so, believe me ... were it not that death interfered. Though he mentions others where it is opportune and convenient, for you alone, to whom he was much more indebted, he was reserving a special place selected after careful consideration. And what was this, do you suppose, if not the most prominent and distinguished place of all? He thus was waiting for the end of his outstanding work, where he intended to exalt your name to the heavens as his guide in sonorous verses.[92]

To substantiate this claim, Petrarch points to the *Thebaid* as an example. As Virgil took Homer as his source, so too was Virgil chosen by Statius as a model for the *Thebaid*, and yet Statius did not acknowledge Virgil until the very end of his work: "nec tamen ingenue ducem suum nisi in fine poetici itineris recognovit" ("yet he did not openly acknowledge him as his guide except at the end of his poetic journey").[93] Of course, Statius's mention of Virgil at the end of his epic belies a complicated program of erasure of his own, as we have seen, and Petrarch acknowledges this in his phrasing ("illic tamen bona fide totum grati animi debitum benemerite persolvit Eneydi" ("it was [only] at the close that he openly and in good faith paid the full debt of his grateful mind to the *Aeneid*"). Rather than support his case in defence of Virgil, then, by invoking the *Thebaid* as an example Petrarch aggravates any cause for Homer's resentment. He implies that Virgil's silence was not only deliberate but also recognized and perpetuated by a successor.

Petrarch uses his letter to Homer to establish a clear precedent for his reluctance to name Dante, and so to align himself with a classical tradition of occlusion. He implies a correlation between himself and Virgil, and between Dante and Homer, all the while emphasizing the distinct implications of his own situation: still among the living, Petrarch's silence toward Dante cannot be explained – however ironically – by an early death.[94] This is not to suggest that Petrarch's distaste for Dante's vernacular poetics was disingenuous, or that he lacked an "all too real desire to ... eclipse [Dante] and cancel his presence" (a topic I will pursue in my next chapter), but rather that he relied on a preexisting trope of erasure to act on these propensities.[95] In other words, Petrarch solicits our attention to a notable example of erasure from a classical past to corroborate his own silence. In doing so, he affiliates himself with his literary predecessors, meanwhile suggesting that his erasure of Dante is intentional.

Petrarch's letter to Homer establishes that poets rely on one another not only for material but also for modes of authorial engagement, one of this book's larger arguments. As Petrarch petitions an example of literary occlusion from antiquity to gloss his silence toward Dante, so Chaucer erases Boccaccio using Boccaccio's own poetics of intertextuality, expanding on a device adapted from his predecessors to render this erasure both recognizable and multifaceted. But *Familiares* XXIV.12 sheds light on more than Chaucer's silence toward Boccaccio in the "Knight's Tale." It also provides a lens through which we can interpret Lydgate's later treatment of Chaucer and his poetry, an engagement that, as many scholars have noted, often seems to straddle the line between slavish imitation and antagonism. We need look no further than the *Siege of Thebes*, Lydgate's added Canterbury Tale, to find the fifteenth-century poet establishing Chaucer as a model while obfuscating his influence. Writing his poem as a preface to the "Knight's Tale," Lydgate restores the material contained in the first two books of the *Teseida* to the *Siege*, material Chaucer had dismissed as "to long to heere." At the end of the *Siege*, moreover, where his narrative should intersect with the Knight's, Lydgate indulges in a little *occupatio* of his own, summarizing the parts of the story he *would* have told, if they did not fall beyond the scope of his narrative. It is only here, at the conclusion of his work, that Lydgate directs us to his "mayster Chaucer" (4501) and the beginning of the "Knyghtys Tale" (4524) for those details he deems extraneous.[96] Alluding to Chaucer throughout his work, Lydgate does not actually mention his "mayster" until the end of the *Siege*, a manoeuvre that looks back, perhaps, "to not only Chaucer's poetics of intertextuality but also Statius's."[97]

Lydgate's reluctance to name Chaucer prompted A.C. Spearing to propose that the "implicit claim of the *Siege*" is that "Lydgate *becomes* the father whose place he usurps."[98] But we can take Spearing's claim still further: Lydgate uses a trope of erasure readily available to him in the poetry of his predecessors to silence his English predecessor. His treatment of Chaucer in the *Siege* evokes Oedipus's murder of Laius, Virgil's refusal to name Homer in the *Aeneid*, Statius's deferred acknowledgment of Virgil in the *Thebaid*, Boccaccio's elision of Statius in the *Teseida*, and, most proximately, Chaucer's erasure of Boccaccio throughout his works. What is more, Lydgate appears to mirror Chaucer's strategy of omission/restoration of Boccaccio/Statius in the "Knight's Tale" by naming "Bochas" no less than seven times in the *Siege*, and in each instance as his source or authority. Lydgate thus resurrects Chaucer's buried *auctor* from the "Knight's Tale" at the same time as he puts his comparative silence toward Chaucer in high relief.[99]

Lydgate experiments with a strategy of elision elsewhere, naming Chaucer among a succession of illustrious poets in the *Fall of Princes* only to erase him from a similar catalogue in the *Life of Saint Alban and Saint Amphibal.* Openly alluding to the epilogue of the *Troilus* and its literary antecedents in the *Fall of Princes*, Lydgate identifies Chaucer as the most excellent of his literary predecessors:

I nevir was acqueynted with Virgyle,
Nor with the sugryd dytees of Omer
Nor Dares Frygius with his goldene style,
Nor with Ovyde, in poetrye moost entieer,
Nor with sovereyn balladys of Chauceer
Which among alle that euere wer rad or songe,
Excellyd al othir in our Englysh tounge.[100]

Although Lydgate would seem to exempt himself from this pantheon of great authors by denying any affiliation with its members ("*I nevir was acqueyted with ...*"), in "endorsing Chaucer's claim as the 'first' poet of stature to 'kiss' Parnassan steps" (a passage that reframes Chaucer's desire to kiss the steps of his epic models), Lydgate "firmly enters his own 'poetry' into this extraordinary company" with what Christopher Cannon rightly describes as only "ostensible modesty."[101] But Lydgate takes this strategy of self-authorization one step further in the *Life of Saint Alban and Saint Amphibal.* In a passage that again looks back to the ending of the *Troilus*, he names a similar succession of authors, only this time he omits *Chaucer* from the list. He claims that he lacks the poetic skills of Lucan, Virgil, Homer, Cicero, and Petrarch, whose aureate footsteps he hopes to follow. The implication is that now it is Lydgate who is sixth of these six great authors, and Lydgate who excels "al othir in our Englysh tounge":

I nat acqueyntid with Musis of Maro,
Nor with metris of Lucan nor Virgile,
Not sugrid ditees of Tullius Chithero,
Nor of Omerus to folwe the fressh stile,
Crokid to climb over so hih a stile,
Or for to folwe the Steppis Aureat
Off ffranceis Petrak, the poete laureat.[102]

Chaucer's omission from this sequence of authors is underscored in the following line, in which Lydgate invokes the *House of Fame* to honour these great poets: "The golden trumpet of the hous of ffame, / ... / Hath blowe ful few the knyhtly mannys name."[103] Presented without attribution, this reference to the *House of Fame* may show Lydgate cheekily complying with Chaucer's narrator's request in this same poem to remain anonymous. After witnessing Lady Fame's arbitrary dispensation of either glory or slander to her petitioners, a cowering "Geffrey" refuses to identify himself when questioned, so that "no wight have my name in honde" (III.1877).[104] At the same time, this second allusion to Chaucer's poetry only reminds readers of his absence from Lydgate's curated genealogy of predecessors.

Nor is this the first time that Lydgate excises Chaucer from a catalogue of his authorial models. In the *Mumming for the Mercers of London*, Lydgate names a succession of six poets: Cicero, Macrobius, Virgil, Ovid, Petrarch, and Boccaccio (29–33). Lydgate's lineage includes Boccaccio, but it overleaps Chaucer, an omission that Maura Nolan has read as Lydgate's attempt to suggest his unmediated relation to a European poetic tradition.[105] But perhaps, in light of Chaucer's naming of Statius but not Boccaccio, and Boccaccio's naming of Virgil but not Statius, more central to Lydgate's purpose than the tradition Nolan has identified is a trope of authorial erasure. Such an interpretation may not accord with our perception of Lydgate as a poet plagued by anxiety, more likely to follow Chaucer slavishly than to exploit his poetics. But it would suggest that Lydgate deeply understood the significance of Chaucer's refusal to name Boccaccio, and that he relied on a trope of erasure so as to affiliate his poems with those of his predecessors, a point I will argue more expansively in chapter 5. This perspective dovetails with the increasing scholarly impulse to see Lydgate as a canny, even playful, interlocutor of his English and Italian sources.[106] At the very least, the repeated acts of erasure committed by (and performed upon) Statius, Boccaccio, Chaucer, and Lydgate – acts, we might say, of literary patricide – remind us that authorial occlusion need not always signify a poet's concern over his source's inadequacy. Instead, erasure can be used strategically, to indicate the active tradition from whence we came, and which will continue long after we depart.

Chapter Two

Restoration through Translation in the "Clerk's Tale"

In Jorge Luis Borges's short story "Pierre Menard, Author of the *Quixote*," the narrator, a literary critic, celebrates the titular character for a profound achievement.[1] Menard has replicated *Don Quixote*, having produced "a number of pages which coincided – word for word and line for line – with those of Miguel de Cervantes."[2] It is a revelation to compare the original work with Menard's version of it, the narrator insists. Cervantes, for example, includes the following observation: "truth, whose mother is history, rival of time, depository of deeds, witness of the past, exemplar and advisor to the present, and the future's counselor."[3] This line fails to impress the narrator – it is "mere rhetorical praise of history."[4] When Menard writes this line, however, the narrator is astounded by its new implications:

> History, the *mother* of truth! – the idea is staggering. Menard … defines history not as a *delving into* reality but as the very *fount* of reality. Historical truth, for Menard, is not "what happened"; it is what we *believe* happened. The final phrases – *exemplar and adviser to the present, and the future's counselor* – are brazenly pragmatic.[5]

Once bombastic, these words have become bold and evocative in Menard's *Quixote*. Context has changed their very significance. Context also changes style: the archaic prose of Menard suffers from a certain affectation. Not so with respect to Cervantes, who handles "with complete naturalness" the Spanish of his time.[6]

"Pierre Menard" raises the question of whether imitation, translation, and transcription can reproduce an original work, and to what extent authors owe this effort of replication to their sources. While, on the one hand, his praise of Menard's innovation is comical, since Menard's task is one of repetition, on the other hand, the narrator is quite right to emphasize the difference between the two works. In the time that has passed since Cervantes wrote the *Quixote*, things *have* changed. As Sergio Waisman observes, "the same text, the same utterance, can never have the same meaning twice. Better yet: texts accumulate meaning through changes and shifts in time and space, so that with each displacement their potentiality expands."[7]

In Borges's fiction, this displacement is minimal. We are led to believe that the language, form, narrative, and characters remain identical in both works. Still, the renovated text takes on a completely new meaning: "Not for nothing have three hundred years elapsed," as Menard observes, "freighted with the most complex events. Among those events, to mention but one, is the *Quixote* itself."[8] But what happens when the shift in time and space between a text and its reproduction is relatively severe? And what transpires, as this chapter will ask, when an author exploits this potential for displacement, generating new meaning from an old text by untethering the original work from its linguistic and ideological moorings?

Such an experiment is realized, as I suggest, in the "Clerk's Tale." Chaucer's Clerk of Oxenford poses as a *fides interpres* of his source, the *Historia Griseldis*, Petrarch's Latin translation of the final story from Boccaccio's *Decameron*. Although faithful to his source on a literal level, by changing the work's language, audience, and style, Chaucer dramatically modifies Petrarch's authorial ambitions, offering a version of the Griselda story that aligns more closely with Boccaccio's original novella than with Petrarch's translation of it. In this case, the distance between text and reproduction is acute. Even more than Menard, who ostensibly transcribes passages from Cervantes's *Quixote* to the letter yet still generates a completely new work, the poet demonstrates that adherence to a text's literal sense does not ensure fidelity to its underlying meaning. On the contrary, as we see in first Petrarch's and then Chaucer's translation of the Griselda story, amending a narrative's form alters its significance, particularly when the languages involved in this transformation (Latin [*gramatica*], Italian, and English [vernacular]) stand on unequal footing with regard to perceived authority and status.[9]

Whereas in my last chapter, then, I discussed how, for Chaucer and Boccaccio, to fictionalize (*fingere*) is a divine act – something to be celebrated rather than concealed, a notion that privileges the superficial form of poetry as much as its allegorical potential – this chapter shows authors elevating the importance of the allegorical at the expense of the literal. Peering "beneath the veil" (*sub integumento*) of Chaucer's translation of Petrarch's Latin, we discover how capricious and malleable Griselda really is. Change her clothes and you change her nature, Chaucer shows, a lesson that dramatically contradicts the character's steadfast virtue in the story.

As before, however, to appreciate Chaucer's treatment of his source in the "Clerk's Tale" we must look beyond this immediate relationship and consider a larger tradition of authorial engagement, beginning with Dante's influence on the *Decameron*. Boccaccio, as we will see, uses his poem to imply his affiliation with a community of vernacular writers and especially Dante. Responding to Dante's call to poets to write elegant works in the vernacular, he directs his work to an audience of beautiful ladies, maintaining, in the tradition of the *Vita nuova*, that he *had* to write in Italian because he was beholden to his female readers.[10] In his translation of the Griselda story, however, Petrarch undercuts Boccaccio's efforts, eliminating the very features of the *Decameron* that aligned its author with Dante and vernacular poetry. While Petrarch retains the narrative's basic components, such as the characters and plot, he extracts *Decameron* X.10 from its larger framework and translates it into Latin, radically transforming Boccaccio's vision for his poem by removing both its intended audience of a vernacular literary community and its implied female readers. At the same time, Petrarch rescripts the narrative as a spiritual allegory, suggesting that Griselda's metaphorical significance, and not her literal trappings (in this case, her vulgar/*volgare* exterior), should be prioritized.

By translating the Griselda story back into a vernacular language, Chaucer thus deploys Petrarch's poetics of translation against him. He redirects the narrative to an audience of women and unlettered men, responding to the Host's (and, incidentally, Dante's) appeal to the *volgare*'s universality. Largely devoid of the superfluous "termes," "colours," and "figures" of the rhetor's toolkit, the "Clerk's Tale" has more in common both ideologically and linguistically with its Boccaccian archetype than it does with its Petrarchan source. At the same time, Chaucer refocuses our attention on Walter's cruelty, challenging our ability to read the Marquis and the trials he imposes on Griselda allegorically. In the "Clerk's Tale," it is the literal sense that prevails.

In some ways, then, the "Clerk's Tale" is less of a translation than a restoration, because it brings us closer to the Boccaccian original than Petrarch ever desired to reach. But of course, true restoration – a return to an original state – is hardly possible, something Menard's *Quixote* makes exquisitely clear, with a facsimile of Cervantes's novel offered to readers as a completely new work. So too does the "Clerk's Tale" bear the inevitable marks of change in time and space. These marks – we might call them the scars of translation – ensure that Chaucer can no more "restore" the work to its Boccaccian form than Walter can keep his promise to Griselda to repay what he has stolen from her: "intendo di rendere a te a un'ora ciò che io tra molte ti tolsi" ("I now intend … to restore to you in a single instant that which I took from you little by little").[11] As Kara Gaston notes, Walter's deception lies in his lack of attention to time: even as he returns her children to her, he nevertheless "consumes twelve of Griselda's years with little concern for their value."[12] Time, as it turns out, "is exactly what Gualtieri fails to repay."[13] Writing decades after Boccaccio, and in a different country and language, Chaucer is likewise unable to bridge the temporal gap between his tale and its textual archetype. Nor does he appear to *want* this process of restoration to be seamless, something he perhaps points to by incorporating a detail borrowed from the French translation of this tale: Griselda's ill-fitting former garments. Her "old coote," which Walter permits her to wear on her journey home, no longer fits, a reminder that the woman who returns after twelve years is not the same as the one who left.[14] Patient Griselda may be "defined by" her "changelessness," as Gaston affirms, but her exterior transforms over time.[15]

So too does the Griselda narrative transform with each retelling. Even as he undoes many of the changes that Petrarch made to Boccaccio's narrative, Chaucer suggests that in their new English garments, as part of the *Canterbury Tales*, certain features of the *Decameron* are now ill fitting. For one thing, he no longer requires the pretence of composing for lovely ladies to write in the vernacular. Indeed, part of the originality of the *Canterbury Tales* lies in the variety of not only genres and styles but also implied audiences – there is a range of writings for diverse folks diversely to read.[16] It is also English rather than Italian that the "Clerk's Tale" champions, with a serial widow from Bath petitioned ultimately (albeit ironically) as an authority and exemplum. Finally, the "Clerk's Tale" benefits from the prestige of its Latin model even as Chaucer translates the story into English, capitalizing on his work's status as a vernacularization of an authoritative text.[17] As Alison Cornish has discussed, translation from Latin into the vernacular could effectively "dignif[y] the 'lesser' language, first by writing it and then by making it the medium of discourse."[18] English in particular "became the status language at the end of the fourteenth century by means of developing itself as a medium of translation from other languages that already possessed extensive literary traditions," such as Latin, writes Janet Coleman.[19] For Chaucer, in this regard, there is a distinct advantage to translating Petrarch's version of Griselda that extends beyond restoring the tale to a vernacular language. That is to say, with his translation, Chaucer grounds the "Clerk's Tale" in an academic, textual tradition.

Dressing Griselda: Boccaccio's *Decameron* and Its Dantean Roots

Petrarch may well have been the author to recognize in Griselda's "re-clothing" a "parable of translation," but it is Boccaccio who first develops this story as a linguistic allegory.[20] The final novella from the *Decameron*, about a cruel Marquis testing his poor yet virtuous wife, dramatizes

Dante's argument from the *De vulgari eloquentia* on the greater nobility of the vernacular over Latin.[21] Although impoverished, Griselda possesses an innate virtue that makes her superior to her more illustrious counterpart. She is in this respect like the *volgare* itself, which, compared to Latin, lacks longevity but is nevertheless more dignified. As Dante explains, there are two kinds of languages, the vernacular and the *gramatica*. Of these two kinds of languages, the vernacular is the nobler, "tum quia prima fuit humano generi usitata; tum quia totus orbis ipsa perfruitur, licet in diversas prolationes et vocabula sit divisa; tum quia naturalis est nobis, cum illa potius artificialis existat" ("first, because it was the language originally used by the human race; second, because the whole world employs it, though with different pronunciations and using different words; and third because it is natural to us, while the other is, in contrast, artificial").[22]

While Griselda is an example of how people born into poverty can still behave morally, her husband demonstrates that a gentle upbringing does not necessarily foster a corresponding gentility of spirit. The narrator of *Decameron* X.10 is quick to remind us that "nelle povere case piovono dal cielo de' divini spiriti, come nelle reali quegli che sarien più degni di guardar porci che d'avere sopra uomini signoria" ("celestial spirits may sometimes descend even into the houses of the poor, whilst there are those in royal palaces who would be better employed as swineherds than as rulers of men").[23] In this regard, the relationship between husband and wife not only mirrors that of the *volgare* to Latin, as explained in the *De vulgari eloquentia* – she/the vernacular, is nobler, even though he/the *gramatica* is of higher status – it also corroborates Dante's theory of *gentilezza* from the final book of the *Convivio*.[24] As Dante writes, "È gentilezza dovunqu'è vertute, / ma non vertute ov'ella" ("Nobility resides wherever virtue is, / But virtue not wherever there's nobility").[25] Moreover, we witness in these two arguments a connective thread: just as a person does not have to have to possess an illustrious heritage in order to behave gently, so a "language does not have to be ancient (like Latin) to be noble," because "through careful cultivation it can fulfil its great potential" and "achieve perfect literary nobility."[26] "Virtue" in both a linguistic and social context is achieved by merit and not heritage, an argument Dante makes in the *Convivio* and then revisits in the *De vulgari eloquentia* "in an affirmation of the worthiness of the Italian language."[27]

If Dante's *Convivio* provides the philosophical foundation for Griselda's virtue born in poverty, then *De vulgari eloquentia*, in which the precepts of what would ultimately become *Stilnovism* are famously established, is in many ways the subtext underlying Boccaccio's decision to write in the Florentine *volgare*. The vernacular is, as Dante argues, a universal tongue, even if in Italy it takes various and corrupted forms. It does not require formal instruction: we learn our mother tongue by instinct: "nature" provides a knowledge of this tongue to everyone, "non tantum viri, sed etiam mulieres et parvuli" ("not only men, but also women and children").[28] Latin, by contrast, is "artificial" and *un*natural to us. It can, however, be acquired by people from various years and geographical areas, because its rules are fixed and do not change with time or according to region. Dante notes,

> Hinc moti sunt inventores gramatice facultatis; que quidem gramatica nichil aliud est quam quedam inalterabilis locutionis identitas diversis temporibus atque locis. Hec, cum de comuni consensu multarum gentium fuerit regulata, nulli singulari arbitrio videtur obnoxia et per consequens nec variabilis esse potest. Adinvenerunt ergo illam, ne, propter variationem sermonis arbitrio singularium fluitantis, vel nullo modo, vel saltem imperfecte antiquorum attingeremus auctoritates et gesta, sive illorum quos a nobis locorum diversitas facit esse diversos.
>
> This was the point from which the inventors of the art of grammar began; for their *gramatica* is nothing less than a certain immutable identity of language in different times and places. Its rules having been formulated with the common consent of many peoples, it can be subject to no individual will; and, as a result, it cannot change. So those who devised this language did so lest, through changes in language dependent on the arbitrary judgement of individuals, we should become either unable, or, at best, only partially able, to enter into contact with the deeds and authoritative writings of the ancients, or of those whose difference of location makes them different from us.[29]

But because acquisition of the *gramatica* is possible only through the process of lengthy and dedicated study, it is available only to some individuals, and not to women or children. Dante thus contrasts the illusory universality of the *gramatica* with the true universality of the illustrious vernacular, which is available and instinctive to everyone.[30]

Dante's insistence on the nobility of the vernacular is founded on his assurance that everyone, everywhere, is born with the ability to acquire it, if in various forms. These two tenets, the vernacular's naturalness and universality, form the basis of Boccaccio's justification for the language and style of the *Decameron*, which takes place at the opening of Day IV. Putting himself on mock trial against his would-be detractors, Boccaccio defends his "novellette … le quali non solamente in fiorentin volgare e in prosa scritte per me sono e senza titolo, ma ancora in istilo umilissimo e rimesso quanto il più si possono" ("little stories … which bear no title, and which I have written, not only in the Florentine vernacular and in prose, but in the most homely and unassuming style it is possible to imagine").[31] To explain these choices, the narrator points repeatedly to his primary purpose: he writes for women in love, with the hope of distracting them and soothing their hearts.[32] Despite this noble goal, Boccaccio laments that his critics have thought it unseemly for him to take pleasure in writing for such an audience. Others, assuming a posture of greater profundity,

> hanno detto che alla mia età non sta bene l'andare omai dietro a queste cose, cioè a ragionar di donne o a compiacer loro. E molti, molto teneri della mia fama mostrandosi, dicono che io farei più saviamente a starmi con le Muse in Parnaso che con queste ciance mescolarmi tra voi.

> have said that it is not good for a man of my age to engage in such pursuits as discussing the ways of women and providing for their pleasure. And others, showing deep concerns for my renown, say that I would be better advised to remain with the Muses in Parnassus, than to fritter away my time in your company.[33]

By way of an answer to such criticism, Boccaccio insists that by serving women he is simply obeying the dictates of Nature, since from childhood he has loved them. His critics must therefore be ignorant of "i piaceri né la vertú della naturale affezione" ("the strength and pleasure of natural affection").[34]

To bolster his argument, Boccaccio tells the story of Filippo Balducci, a heartbroken widower who chooses to isolate his son from the perils of love until he is eighteen years old. Upon first laying eyes on women, the boy is immediately and instinctively drawn to them. If a youth can have such a strong reaction to women, despite being shielded from them until adulthood, then how can anyone expect him, who has loved women all his life, to resist doing their bidding, Boccaccio wonders. Far from apologizing for writing for ladies, he decides to strive even harder to please them:

> Ora più che mai mi vi disporrò, per ciò che io conosco che altra cosa dir non potrà alcuno con ragione, se non che gli altri e io, che v'amiamo, naturalmente operiamo; alle cui leggi, cioè della natura, voler contrastare troppo gran forze bisognano, e spesse volte non solamente invano ma con grandissimo danno del faticante s'adoperano.

> Henceforth I shall redouble my efforts towards that end, secure in the knowledge that no reasonable person will deny that I and other men who love you are simply doing what is natural. And in order to oppose the laws of Nature, one has to possess exceptional powers, which often turn out to have been used, not only in vain, but to the serious harm of those who employ them.[35]

It is its very *naturalness*, then, that imbues the vernacular with vital importance for Dante. Boccaccio merely extends this argument to his service to *le donne.* It is also *natural*, he suggests, for him to write for women, since as a child he was inclined to love them. It is also *natural* for him to write in the vernacular, since it is the language to which his readers, since birth, have been inclined. A slave to his passions, Boccaccio is bound by "the laws of Nature," a force so powerful that he is unable to resist it.

Clearly, Boccaccio's "rhetoric of philogyny" has weighty linguistic implications.[36] A popular device among a community of poets composing in the *volgare*, the female reader provided a plausible explanation for choosing the vernacular over the *gramatica*. Following Dante in the *Vita nuova* (XXV.6), these poets maintained that they *had* to write in Italian, because they were beholden to their beloveds, who did not know Latin.[37] In most cases, however, these women were a refined patina for the actual readers of these works, a coterie of educated, polyglot males. We might suspect, along with Cornish, that "all this supposed talk to women … is really to impress other men, and then only an elite among them."[38] This is not to say that Boccaccio's female reader was completely imaginary – on the contrary, as scholars including Elena Lombardi have discussed, she may well have had a historical counterpart in *Trecento* Italy.[39] In the context of a nascent *Stilnovism*, however, she is more literary device than dedicatee; "real," but also "unrealistic."[40] The relationship between cause and effect as Boccaccio characterizes it in the *Decameron* would seem in this regard to be inverted: rather than write in Italian for the sake of women, the poet fictionalizes a female audience to justify writing in Italian.

Beyond providing the excuse of necessity, the female reader gave vernacular poetry an air of dignity. In his fourteenth-century commentary on Guido Cavalcanti's "Donna me prega," Dino del Garbo details the weighty implications of the term *la donna*:

> Et nota quod significanter dixit *Donna*, ut ostenderet quod ista petitio est iusta cui debet satisfacere, cum esset potens in satisfaciendo. In hoc enim verbo ostenditur quod petitio est iusta ratione illius qui petit: nam tunc est petitio iusta cui satisfieri debet ratione illius qui petit, quando petens cognoscit illud quod petit et quando qui petit est persona digna … etiam attribuitur mulieri digne; nam illud nomen attribuitur mulieri honeste: mu[lier] enim meretricia non dicitur donna. Et maxime attribuitur hoc nomen mulieri que est proles alcuius familie, que non est animo viliter nata: unde dignitatem habet ex honestate et ex prole generationis sue.

And note that he says, significantly, *donna* to show that this request is a just one, which must be satisfied if possible. With this word he shows that the request is just by reason of the person who asks; for a request is just by reason of the person requesting when that person knows what he or she is asking and when the person requesting is a worthy person ... This term is used for a worthy woman; for that name is applied to an honest woman since a prostitute is not called *donna*. Above all, this name is used for a woman who is the daughter of some family of no mean birth, whence she has worthiness because of her virtue and because of whose child she is.[41]

As Dino explains, a poet's expressed servitude to a woman is ennobling, since he is seen to be doing the bidding of a worthy person. Merely by directing a work in the vernacular toward her, an author can raise the perceived status of both the language and the text. As Cornish observes, "the nobility of a female audience turns vernacularization around from popularization to rarefaction and refinement: a virtuoso demonstration of the power and beauty of the native language."[42]

The female reader also granted poets access to a literary community – the same polyglot elite they supposedly set their sights beyond by writing in the vernacular in the first place. For Dante, whose love poems in the *Vita nuova* were circulated and discussed among men, his "lyric beloved" permits him to address Guido Guinizelli in the *Purgatorio* as "il padre mio" (XXVI.97), and to write "across time and space" to a "collective us of a readership ... 'coloro / che questo tempo chiameranno antico [those who shall call this time ancient] (*Pr* XVII.120).'"[43] Boccaccio also uses his sworn service to *le donne* to construct an authorial genealogy. Responding to Dante's call for eloquent works in the vernacular with the *Decameron*,[44] he authorizes his (prose) literary vision by naming himself alongside a trio of vernacular poets.[45] As an old man who writes for *le donne*, he finds himself in very good company, he says, for so too do "Guido Cavalcanti e Dante Alighieri già vecchi, e messer Cino da Pistoia vecchissimo."[46] In this case, Boccaccio wields his vulnerability as a badge of honour; he scripts a "false stance of humility in relation to the ranks of other stilnovist poets."[47] Using his posture as an old man in the service of women to bind himself to his predecessors and contemporaries writing in a sweet new style, he provides us with a clear sense of where his literary allegiances lie.

Boccaccio's professed service to women is therefore mutually advantageous. He writes for their pleasure, and they enable him to fulfil Dante's lofty injunction to write for the masses, while simultaneously elevating the vernacular, generally, and his work in particular.[48] Developing a concordance between Dante's philosophical and linguistic arguments in the *Convivio* and *De vulgari eloquentia* and his own work, he positions himself alongside Guido Cavalcanti, Dante, and Cino da Pistoia, all the while legitimating his use of the vernacular in the most practical of terms, as articulated by Dante in the *Vita nuova*: so that his audience will understand what he says. The *Decameron*, a "Galeotto" indeed, is thus the ideal go-between for Dante's lay audience and Boccaccio's implied readership.[49] Significantly, it is precisely this aspect of the *Decameron* – its status as a noble work in the eloquent yet accessible Florentine *volgare* – that Petrarch eliminates through translation.

Undressing Griselda: Petrarch's *Historia Griseldis*

The *Historia Griseldis* is the culmination of much time and labour. Writing in response to a now-lost letter from Boccaccio counselling him to engage more in leisurely activities, Petrarch takes it upon himself to translate *Decameron* X.10 into Latin, the sole instance of this direction of translation in his literary career.[50] Not only is the work of this translation arduous, as Petrarch himself suggests, but also the process of conveying the *Historia Griseldis* to his friend is met with multiple obstructions. The text of his translation is so covered with erasures that Petrarch prepares to transcribe it a second time in fair copy. As K.P. Clarke observes, "this is a picture of a text far from easy to produce; it is the result, instead, of much rethinking, rewriting and correcting."[51] Ultimately, a friend undertakes the task of recopying the text for him, leaving the author free to write an accompanying response to Boccaccio's letter.[52] This response (*Seniles* XVII.2), along with the fair copy of his translation (*Seniles* XVII.3), would reach Boccaccio only after Petrarch's death.

While he takes care in crafting his translation, Petrarch makes little attempt to replicate his Boccaccian source. He justifies the changes he makes to *Decameron* X.10 by referring to Horace's advice in the *Ars Poetica* against translating too faithfully, "Nec verbum verbo curabis reddere fidus interpres" (133–4): "Historiam tuam meis verbis explicui, uno alicubi aut paucis in ipsa narratione mutatis verbis aut additis" ("I have told your story in my own words, or rather changing or adding a few words at some points in the narrative").[53] Beyond superficial changes to the narrative, Petrarch also rescripts the novella as a biblical allegory, minimizing Walter's cruelty in order to lay the groundwork for his final lesson: that the Job-like Griselda is exemplary in her unbending adherence to her husband's – that is, God's – will. Whereas the narrator of *Decameron* X.10, Dioneo, describes Walter as notable not for his munificence but for his mad bestiality ("matta bestialità"),[54] Petrarch turns our focus to Griselda as a paragon of Christian virtue. As he announces at the close of his translation,

> Hanc historiam stilo nunc alio retexere visum fuit, non tam ideo ut matronas nostri temporis ad imitandam huius uxoris patientiam, que michi vix

imitabilis videtur, quam ut legentes ad imitandam saltem femine constantiam excitarem, ut quod hec viro suo prestitit, hoc prestare Deo nostro audeant.

I decided to tell a story in another language not so much to encourage the married women of our day to imitate this wife's patience, which to me seems hardly imitable, as to encourage the readers to imitate at least this woman's constancy, so that what she maintained toward her husband they may maintain toward our God.[55]

Perhaps because of his emphasis on the overarching moral lesson of the *Historia Griseldis*, it is easy to overlook the amendments Petrarch makes to the story's form itself.[56] Bookending a nearly two-decade correspondence between the two friends on the status of the vernacular, Petrarch's Griselda undergoes a change in dress so dramatic that it modifies Boccaccio's original tenor and purpose for his work.[57] Although he insists that his aim in translating *Decameron* X.10 is only to make it noble and fully pleasing, Petrarch uses *Seniles* XVII.3 to argue for the superiority of Latin over the Italian *volgare*. At the same time, he methodically undoes Boccaccio's efforts in the *Decameron* to align himself with Dante and his contemporaries. As we will see, nearly every change Petrarch makes to *Decameron* X.10 undercuts Dante's arguments on the elegance and importance of literature in the vulgar tongue. Nearly every criticism he levels at his friend's work can be traced back to Dante's ideas. Transforming not only the novella's moral but also its superficial form so that it no longer resonates with Dante's vernacular mandate, he eliminates the *Decameron*'s language, audience, and connection to Dante in one fell swoop.

Petrarch begins *Seniles* XVII.3 by informing Boccaccio that he has come across the *Decameron*. He claims not to have read the work, because it was written in the vernacular for the masses and is overly long: "Librum tuum, quem nostro materno eloquio … vidi. Nam si dicam 'legi,' mentiar, siquidem ipse magnus valde, ut ad vulgus et soluta scriptus oratione" ("I have seen the book [*Decameron*] you produced in our mother tongue … If I were to say I have read it, I would be lying, since it is very big, having been written for the common herd and in prose").[58] Petrarch concedes that the shortcomings of the work are not entirely Boccaccio's fault, because the poet likely published the *Decameron* when he was rather young ("iuvenis").[59] He repeats this speculation moments later, only more assertively, when he blames the *Decameron*'s infelicities on, among other things, the poet's youth: "siquid lascivie liberioris occurreret, excusabat etas tunc tua, dum id scriberes, stilus, ydioma, ipsa quoque rerum levitas et eorum qui lecturi talia videbantur" ("if anything met my eye that was too frankly lewd, your age at the time of writing excused it – also the style, the idiom, the very levity of the subject matter and of those who seemed likely to read such things").[60] The poem's final novella offers an exception to his general disapproval: Petrarch claims to enjoy this piece so much that he sets about translating it into Latin immediately, so as to make it available to those ignorant of the Tuscan vernacular.

Couching his critique of the work in expressions of friendship, Petrarch's remarks are deceptively casual.[61] Indeed, almost every statement he makes in these lines either contradicts or exploits Boccaccio's description in the *Decameron* of himself, his poem, and his audience. In the first place, the Florentine vernacular in which Boccaccio composes his poem is not, as Petrarch suggests, the spoken dialect of the uneducated masses, nor is it the "materna locutio" of Dante's *De vulgari eloquentia.*[62] It is, rather, a distinctly literary language, and one that both Petrarch and Boccaccio helped to create. A sophisticated tongue, the Florentine vernacular had already overcome the "resistance of consistent immigration from the countryside to the city" by the end of the thirteenth century and "been employed for over a hundred years in extensive writing of all genres," according to Alfredo Stussi.[63] As Mirko Tavoni explains, the standardized literary language we now know of as Italian largely became so "by imposing itself on the vernaculars of other Italian cities, thanks primarily to the prestige of the great Florentine writers of the *Trecento*, especially Dante himself, but also Petrarch ... and Boccaccio."[64] In the *Decameron*, Boccaccio even charts this evolution, giving us an "elaborate image of this fascinating phase of standardization and expansion during which characteristic archaic traits of phonology and morphology coexist alongside signs of nascent development."[65] The language of the *Decameron* is the product of both study and refinement.

As for the work's style and idiom, which Petrarch dismisses as low, the *Decameron* is technically virtuosic. In McWilliam's words, it is "elegant to a fault," and "more than worthy of stylistic comparison to any vernacular prose works [including those of Dante] which had preceded [it])."[66] Although Boccaccio himself describes his style as humble and unassuming ("umilissimo e rimesso"), this statement is likely made more on account of the author's false modesty than as a genuine reflection on his work. What is more, these words look back to his *Accessus* to the *Esposizioni sopra la Comedia di Dante*, in which he similarly refers to Dante's style as "umile e rimesso."[67] Again, we find Boccaccio adopting a "poetics of humility" to align himself with Dante.[68]

If Petrarch takes Boccaccio's self-deprecating remarks too literally in his dismissal of the *Decameron*'s style as low, then in his account of his friend as young he rejects Boccaccio's words entirely. As we recall, Boccaccio opens the fourth day of his poem by complaining that his critics have found it unseemly for a writer of his age to spend so much time trying to please young ladies. He then describes himself as an old man toiling in the company of the "vechissima" ("very old") Cino da Pistoia, Guido Cavalcanti, and Dante Alighieri. Petrarch echoes Boccaccio's double insistence that he is advanced in years by describing him twice as a young man, a contradiction that may appear at first unimportant.[69] But by suggesting that the *Decameron* was produced in Boccaccio's youth, Petrarch severs his friend's fabricated affiliation with Dante and his contemporaries on the basis of their mutual senescence. More importantly, Petrarch correlates the composition of the *Decameron* to his own youthful experimentation in Italian.

Although ultimately vocal in his distaste for it, Petrarch himself read and wrote poetry in the vernacular. As he recalls to Boccaccio in *Familiares* XXI.15 (1359), he delighted in Italian poetry as a boy. Still, he worried about his own impressionable nature, and so did not read the *Commedia* for fear that his youth would render him a slavish and reluctant follower of Dante:[70]

> Stilo deditus, vulgari eloquio ingenium exercebam; nichil rebar elegantius necdum altius aspirare didiceram, sed verebar ne si huius aut alterius dictis imbuerer, ut est etas illa flexibilis et miratrix omnium, vel invitus ac nesciens imitator evaderem.

> I too was devoted to the same kind of writing in the vernacular; I considered nothing more elegant and had yet to learn to look higher, but I did fear that, were I to immerse myself in [Dante's], or any other's, writings, being of an impressionable age so given to indiscriminate admiration, I could scarcely escape becoming an unwilling or unconscious imitator.[71]

Petrarch expresses pity for the author of the *Commedia*, whom he sees as throwing his words before the "ydiotas in tabernis et in foro" ("idiots in the taverns and squares").[72] He wishes to rescue Dante from the masses mangling his poetry, but, short on time, concludes, "nunc quod unum restat, queror et stomacor illius egregiam stili frontem inertibus horum linguis conspui fedarique" ("I can only express my reprehension and disgust at hearing them befouling with their stupid mouths the noble beauty of his lines").[73] Petrarch goes so far as to claim that the mere occurrence of hearing Dante's Italian verses read aloud by these individuals was enough to provoke him to switch to Latin.

Petrarch recalls a similar experience with regard to his own vernacular writings. He describes hearing the poetry he composed as a youth mangled by the masses: "In his ipsis paucis que michi iuveniliter per id tempus elapsa sunt, vulgi linguis assidue laceror, indignans quodque olim amaveram perosus"

("A few pieces that slipped from my youthful pen are constantly being mangled by the multitude's recitation, something that is so vexing as to make me hate what I once loved").[74] Rather than bring him pride or a sense of accomplishment, the experience of listening to his works read in public makes him feel helpless, as though he has lost control of them. In *Seniles* V.2 (postdated 1366 but likely written in 1364), Petrarch refers again to this feeling of dispossession. The poems of his youth, now dispersed, belong to the multitude, a realization that prompts him to turn away from the vernacular toward Latin:

> Intellexi tandem molli in limo et instabili arena perdi operam meque et laborem meum inter vulgi manus laceratum iri. Tanquam ergo qui currens calle medio colubrum offendit, substiti mutavique consilium iterque aliud, ut spero rectius atque altius, arripui; quamvis sparsa illa et brevia, iuvenilia atque vulgaria iam, ut dixi, non mea amplius, sed vulgi potius facta essent, maiora ne lament providebo.

> I finally came to realize that it was a waste of effort to build on soft mud and shifting sand, and that I and my work would be torn to shreds by the hands of the mob. Thus, like the runner who stumbles upon a serpent in the middle of the path, I halted and changed my mind, taking another pathway that I hope will be straighter and higher; although those brief and scattered vernacular works of my youth are no longer mine, as I have said, but have become the multitude's, I shall see to it that they do not butcher my major ones.[75]

In contrast to the "soft mud and shifting sand" of the vernacular, Latin seemed to him both durable and copious.[76] This language is "the root of our arts and the foundation of every branch of knowledge" ("radix artium nostrarum et omnis scientie fundamentum").[77]

Petrarch's letters detail his decisive rejection of the vernacular as an adult, and his choice to eschew Dante's writings for fear of slavishly imitating them. He describes coming to see his writings in the *volgare* as the wasted efforts of his youth, and their audience as ignorant and crude. Of course, this disdain is somewhat dissimulated: Petrarch continued to write and revise in the vernacular late into his life.[78] Nor, it would seem, did he successfully avoid reading Dante. As commentators going back as far as Bernardino Daniello can tell us, the influence of the *Commedia* on Petrarch's poetry was extensive.[79] Nevertheless, Petrarch's repudiation of Italian as the language of one's youth, the masses, and – most notably – Dante, recurs throughout his correspondence with his friend, converging in *Seniles* XVII.3, which he writes shortly before his death. While for Boccaccio, Italian was a refined tongue, appropriate for communicating with delicate ladies and fellow poets writing in the vernacular alike, for Petrarch, it was the passing fancy of his youth and the medium of the uneducated masses. The common denominator for both authors is Dante, the impress of whose Italian poetry Petrarch feared, and whose verses he heard mangled by the "ydiotas" in taverns and squares. If as a boy he found himself in danger of following Dante's path, then as an old man Petrarch appears determined to save his friend from a similar threat.[80] Still a youth (or so Petrarch insists), Boccaccio has time to turn away from the false allure of the *volgare* and pursue more serious scholarly endeavours. Revisiting a connection between his boyish infatuation with Dante and poetry written in the vernacular for the masses, Petrarch strips Griselda of her vulgar exterior and redresses her in noble Latin. In the process, he claims Boccaccio as his own disciple.

As Boccaccio explains at the start of *Decameron* IV, he is an old man in Nature's thrall, unjustly lambasted by critics for his amorous ambitions. In his letter to Boccaccio, and as a means of justifying the poem's low style and audience, Petrarch refers twice to his friend's youth, signalling his blatant disregard for Boccaccio's earlier account of himself. But nowhere is this disregard more obvious than in his description of Boccaccio's readers, where he contradicts Boccaccio's most fundamental claim for his poem: that it is composed for a group of beautiful ladies, for the sake of easing their hearts. Admittedly, Boccaccio's assertion is itself overblown – he writes in a refined Florentine vernacular for a community of other Italian poets. But Petrarch feigns ignorance of not only Boccaccio's implied readership of lovely ladies but also the *Decameron*'s target audience of educated men. Employing the same term he used in *Familiares* XXI.15 and *Seniles* V.2 to scorn the uneducated masses mangling his and Dante's vernacular poetry, he insists in *Seniles* XVII.3 that the *Decameron* is written "*ad vulgus*" – for the multitude.[81]

This is no mere lexical coincidence. A polyglot poet moving in the same intellectual circles as Boccaccio, Petrarch would have recognized the Dantean origins – and thus the hint of irony – behind his friend's claim to write in the *volgare* as a service to women. Without an audience of female readers, Boccaccio's excuse for choosing the vernacular evaporates, and with it his carefully curated association with *Stilnovism*. By substituting Boccaccio's *bellissime donne* for the *volgo*, then, Petrarch calls a bluff on his friend's superficial justification for choosing Italian, meanwhile ignoring his actual reasons for doing so. At the same time, he makes strikingly clear that his critique of the *Decameron* extends beyond the poem itself to its sociolinguistic roots in Dante's writings.

To be sure, Petrarch's abhorrence for the wide appeal of the vernacular is in earnest, leading Amy Goodwin to argue that "it is neither Italian nor Italian readers per se that Petrarch objected to but the broad democratic reach of Italian."[82] But his primary concern in *Seniles* XVII.3 is less the breadth of the *Decameron*'s readership than his friend's allegiance to Dante. In fact, later in the letter Petrarch boasts that by translating the story into Latin he will *increase* its potential audience to include those ignorant of Italian: "Subito talis interloquendum cogitacio supervenit, fieri posse ut nostril [eciam] sermonis ignaros tam dulcis historia delectaret" ("Suddenly, in the midst of talking, I was struck by the idea that maybe such a sweet story would appeal also to those who do not know our language").[83] At least geographically, of course, Latin *could* reach a broader audience than Italian. However, this audience was limited to educated men. It is for this reason that Dante elevates the vernacular over the *gramatica* in *De vulgari eloquentia*, because unlike Latin, it is available to all: "nature" gives everyone the ability to converse in the *volgare*, "non tantum viri, sed etiam mulieres et parvuli" ("not only men, but also women and children").[84] Petrarch does not refute Dante's arguments on the superiority of the vernacular directly. On the contrary, he appropriates them in *Seniles* XVII.3, but to make the opposite point. If Dante elevated the *volgare* on the basis of its universality, that is, then Petrarch suggests that Boccaccio's Tuscan dialect is exclusive and delimiting. What is more, he claims that Griselda can transcend her regional fetters by donning Latin garb.

In a separate letter to Boccaccio, *Seniles* XVII.4, Petrarch illustrates this point in practical terms. He relates the experience of sharing the *Historia Griseldis* with two friends, one from Verona and the other from Milan. Although ignorant of the Tuscan dialect, these men have no trouble understanding the story in Latin. What is more, they read (or attempt to read) Petrarch's translation aloud.[85] The *gramatica* takes on the role of the vernacular here, in the sense that it is a mode of (oral) communication among distant friends. In the same text, Petrarch claims to have learned that his earlier letters, including his translation, never reached Boccaccio. He blames the border guards stationed between Padua and Venice, who no doubt obstructed their passage. Perhaps these "donkey-eared" men are only following orders, Petrarch considers, yet he suspects something more sinister: "Illud nichil excusat, quod, siquid in literis ipsis inveniunt quod aures asininas mulceat, solebant quidem in transcibendo tempus terere et nuntios detinere; nunc crescent licentia, ut digitis suis parcant, abire illos iubent sine literis quodque gravissimum tedii genus est" ("What is inexcusable is that if they find anything in the letter to flatter their donkey ears, some used to spend time copying it and detain its messengers, but now, with growing wantonness, to spare their fingers they order them to leave without the letter").[86] A lesson to be learned here is that regional variance – among languages, between borders – is intellectually stifling, with even native speakers of Italian unable to communicate with one another in their mother tongue, or through epistolary exchange.

Dante himself addresses this variability in his treatise, lamenting the proliferation of languages from one stock as a sign of man's Babylonian decline.[87] It is for this reason that he takes a genealogical approach to locating what he judges to be the most illustrious tongue – the Tuscan dialect – and sets before himself the task of tracing how one language became many in the hope of discovering their common origin.[88] Despite this diversity among vernaculars, Dante remains clear: of the two kinds of languages, the *volgare* is nobler than the *gramatica*, "first, because it was the language originally used by the human race; second, because the whole world employs it, though with different pronunciations and using different words; and third because it is natural to us, while the other is, in contrast, artificial." Petrarch follows Dante – and, for that matter, Boccaccio – in prioritizing accessibility while defending his choice of language. At the same time, he conveniently ignores the crux of Dante's argument: that the vernacular is superior because it is available to *all*, whereas the *gramatica* is known only by a select few. Thus, whereas Petrarch claims to widen the story's scope by translating it into Latin, he fails to mention that in doing so he *removes* a key demographic from its potential readership: women.[89] Unsurprisingly, this is the precise demographic for whom Dante and Boccaccio claimed to write.

Indeed, in Petrarch's Latin academy, "women are not invited."[90] The *Historia Griseldis* is aimed specifically, and unapologetically, at learned men. Not only does Petrarch reclothe the story in Latin, a language available only to the most educated, but he also uses his commentary on the narrative to repeatedly gender his readers male.[91] We saw an example of this in *Seniles* XVII.4, where Petrarch appeals to Boccaccio with promises of a different audience, free from regional boundaries. Although geographically diverse, this new audience is biologically homogenous, composed, by design, of men. In his concluding remarks on the tale, we find Petrarch again using the pretence of inclusively to exclude women. Whereas Boccaccio claimed (albeit facetiously) to write the *Decameron* for an audience of women, for the sake of soothing their lovelorn hearts, Petrarch insists that his story is a model of constancy for *all.* As he notes in a passage discussed above, he chose to retell this story "not so much to encourage the married women of our day [matronas nostri temporis] to imitate this wife's patience, which to me seems hardly imitable, as to encourage the readers [legentes] to imitate at least this woman's constancy, so that what she maintained toward her husband they may maintain toward our God." As Cornish observes, "*Matronas* are clearly opposed to *legentes*" here, "so that Petrarch has turned [the *Historia*] into a story for male readers – *literati.*"[92]

Similarly, whereas Boccaccio emphasized Griselda's singular nature, asking readers, "chi avrebbe, altri che Griselda, potuto col viso non solamente asciutto ma lieto sofferir le rigide e mai più non udite pruove da Gualtier fatte?" ("who else but Griselda could have endured so cheerfully the cruel and unheard of trials that Gualtieri imposed upon her without shedding a tear?"),[93] Petrarch aligns Griselda with Old Testament patriarchs, such as Abraham and Job.[94] He further claims that the patience she exhibits is comparable to the steadfast virtue shown by the best of mankind. Far from being singular among women, Griselda stands among the *viris constantibus* as an exemplum among men: "Abunde ego constantibus viris ascripserim, quisquis is fuerit, qui pro Deo suo sine murmure patiatur quod pro suo mortali coniuge rusticana hec muliercula passa est" ("I would number among the men overflowing with constancy whoever would suffer without a murmur for his God what this little peasant woman suffered for her mortal husband").[95]

Through his translation itself, therefore, Petrarch changes the language as well as the supposed readership of the tale, removing women and unscholarly folk from its reception. In his remarks on his translation, moreover, he scorns a paradigm of vernacular universality, criticizing the *volgare* and its advocates, all the while rewriting Boccaccio as a misguided youth who would soon outgrow his infatuation with both Dante and the vernacular, a portrait in stark opposition to Boccaccio's description of himself as a seasoned old man in the company of Dante and his contemporaries. Finally, Petrarch feigns ignorance of Boccaccio's fabricated female audience, all the while flagrantly curating an audience of educated men. At the same time, he inverts Dante's arguments from the *De vulgari eloquentia* to advocate for the inclusivity of Latin, suggesting that he is extending Griselda's reach by translating her out of the vernacular. In spite of these changes, Petrarch insists that Boccaccio alone remains the source, and point of origin, for the *Historia Griselda*:

> Ego rem tuam tibi non alteri dedicandam censui. Quam quidem an mutata veste deformaverim an fortassis ornaverim, tu iudica. Illic enim orta, illuc redit: notus iudex, nota domus, notum iter, ut unum et tu noris et quisquis hec leget, tibi non michi tuarum rationem rerum esse reddendam.
>
> I decided to dedicate your work to you, not to anyone else. Whether I have deformed it or, perhaps, beautified it by changing its garment, you be the judge – for it all began there, and it goes back there; it knows the judge, the house, the way – so that you and whoever reads this may be clear on one point: that you, not I, must render an account of your words.[96]

In these lines, Petrarch implicitly likens his return of the translated text to Boccaccio with its vestment changed to Griselda's circular journey.[97]

Translated, redressed, and trundled back and forth between male authorities, Griselda is an ideal metaphor for the physical text's translation and transmission. As Carolyn Dinshaw suggests, in this story, "translation takes place on a feminine body," both literally and metaphorically, "it is a masculine hermeneutic gesture performed on the woman, on the text."[98]

Dinshaw refers to the preface of Saint Jerome's translation of Eusebius's *Chronicle* as an earlier example of this correlation between translation and the female body. In a passage Dante invokes in the *Convivio*, Jerome laments that certain readers "Superficiem, non medullam inspiciunt, ante quasi vestem orationis sordidam perhorrescant, quam pulchrum intrinsecus rerum corpus inveniant" ("Looking at the surface, not the substance, shudder at the squalid dress before they discover the fair body which the language clothes").[99] Suggesting that his translation is the "squalid dress" that mars the outward beauty of the original text, Jerome nonetheless maintains that the work's underlying *sensus* – the precious kernel beneath the vulgar husk – remains unchanged.[100] It would follow that one must discover the text *en déshabillé* to adequately appraise its value. In his letter to Boccaccio, Petrarch too invokes this Heironymian precedent, likening the act of translation to the dressing and redressing of a woman. Yet he hardly describes this performance in terms of cloaking a "noble body" in "squalid dress." On the contrary, analogous to Walter's exchange of Griselda's rude vestments for beautiful clothing, Petrarch insinuates that it is his Latin translation that is ennobling, while Griselda's original vernacular dress was shabby. At the same time, he exploits his ostensibly subordinate function as the translator of the work.[101] Acutely aware that the attribution of authorship bears the accompanying burden of responsibility, Petrarch insists that because he has changed the mere surface and not the substance of the tale, Boccaccio remains solely accountable for what is written: "Quisquis ex me queret an hec vera sint, hoc est an historiam scripserim an fabulam, respondebo illud Crispi: 'Fides penes auctorem', meum scilicet Iohannem 'sit'" ("Whoever asks me whether it is true, that is, whether I have written a history or just a tale, I shall reply with the words of Crispus, 'Let the responsibility fall on the author'... namely my Giovanni").[102] Such a transference of the burden of authorship onto Boccaccio must have rankled with the younger poet. Extracted from its original context and redressed in a new form, the *Historia Griseldis* undercuts much of what Boccaccio hoped to accomplish with his work. In the end, Petrarch's insistence that the work still belongs to Boccaccio, despite its altered state, only serves to emphasize the obvious: it no longer does.

Redressing Griselda: Chaucer's Translation of Petrarch

The final section of this chapter considers how Chaucer uses his translation of the *Historia Griseldis* to redress the linguistic, stylistic, and moral emendations that Petrarch first made to *Decameron* X.10, recycling his source's poetics of intertextuality to use against him. Chaucer's Clerk remarks on two separate occasions that he learned the story of Griselda from "Petrak" (IV.31, IV.1147), a statement corroborated by Chaucer's subsequent close reliance on Petrarch for the body of his tale. Yet the looming silence of Boccaccio's original version, along with Chaucer's repeated refusal to credit Boccaccio with anything, borrowed or not, makes this attribution seem suspicious. Still, scholars have scoured the "Clerk's Tale" for signs of the presence of *Decameron* X.10, with little to show for their efforts.[103] Textual evidence of Boccaccio's original version remains regarded by even the most optimistic critics as slight, and the work has largely been relegated to the status of hard analogue – albeit with a "relevance greater than any other."[104] Most readers agree that Petrarch's translation of *Decameron* X.10 serves as Chaucer's primary source. Others accept J. Burke Severs's claim that Chaucer also relied on an anonymous French translation of Petrarch, *Le livre Griseldis.*[105]

I will suggest that it is not in vague and verbal echoes that we see the spectre of the *Decameron* in the "Clerk's Tale," but in Chaucer's methodical undoing of the editorial changes that Petrarch first made to *Decameron* X.10.[106] Restoring the tale to its original function as a paragon of vernacular excellence vis-à-vis Dante's *Convivio* and *De vulgari eloquentia*, Chaucer mounts a seemingly laudatory but ultimately damning commentary on Petrarch's abilities as a translator. Not only does he reject Petrarch's Griselda as a viable example for women, insisting that both she and her author represent obsolete models of authority, but he also aligns his friend with a method of writing useless to anyone but an elite few, and with a brand of rhetorical superfluity that stands in stark contrast to Dante's advice on stylistic embellishment. Finally, Chaucer redirects Petrarch's initial purveyance of authorial responsibility onto Boccaccio back toward Petrarch himself at the same time as he sets up the *Historia Griseldis* for rigorous critique.

Seniles XVII.3 thus sheds light on Chaucer's subsequent approach to translation in the "Clerk's Tale," because it shows Petrarch relying on Boccaccio as a source even as he subverts Boccaccio's intentions for his poem.[107] Both Petrarch and Chaucer translate their source – in Chaucer's case, translates him *closely* – while manipulating that source's linguistic priorities by extricating the work from its original context and redressing it in a new form. I think Chaucer recognized and was delighted by Petrarch's backhanded accreditation of the *Historia Griseldis* to Boccaccio, and that he correspondingly enters into their "community of literate play."[108] Attributing his vernacular translation twice to "Petrak," Chaucer inserts himself into an ongoing conversation on the proper language and style in which to write.[109] The tradition in which he participates is thus one of *writing backwards* to his author. This is not to say that he expected the deceased Petrarch to read his translation (as Petrarch obviously did with Boccaccio). Rather, Chaucer grafts his name onto a genealogy of poets from the position of an outsider, so as to create an illustrious foundation for his vernacular tale. Whether he imagines this strategy will be appreciated by the individual patrons and readers of his poetry is secondary, at least to my thinking, to the larger question of how Chaucer wishes to be perceived by posterity in relation to a larger literary tradition. And by writing to his sources, Chaucer can shape his own authorial ancestry, painting a picture of a literary lineage to which later readers can bear witness. It is this idea of a poetic pantheon, crystallized in the process of retrospection, which I believe Chaucer had in mind when he responded to Petrarch's redressing of *Decameron* X.10.

Whereas Petrarch performed a "Horatian translation" of Boccaccio's work, liberally adjusting the style and content of *Decameron* X.10 as he saw fit, the "Clerk's Tale" is a fairly literal rendition of the *Historia Griseldis*.[110] Nevertheless, Chaucer ensures that the Clerk's assessment of both Petrarch and his tale as "worthy" erodes as the narrative progresses, in spite of – in some instances *because of* – his fidelity to his source.[111] This unravelling of Petrarch's status as an authority begins before the Clerk opens his mouth, when Harry Bailey first asks him for a story:

> Telle us som murie thyng of aventures.
> Youre termes, youre colours, and youre figures,
> Keepe hem in stoor til so be ye endite,
> Heigh style, as whan that men to kynges write. (IV.15–18)

The Host makes amply clear that he wishes to hear a simple yet entertaining story – one "that we may understonde" (IV.20) – rather than an elaborate yarn, puffed up with stylistic embellishments. His request echoes the Eagle's similar disparagement of rhetorical devices in Book II of the *House of Fame*. Explaining the science of sound to his thickheaded passenger, the Eagle suggests that even Geffrey, "a lewed man," should be able to follow his logic, since he has explained everything in a clear and straightforward manner. Ironically, the Eagle expresses this claim to clarity in a passage replete with rhetorical flourishes, such as the anaphoric repetition of the possessive, "of":

Telle me this now feythfully,
Have y not preved thus symply,
Withoute any subtilite
Of speche, or gret prolixite
Of *termes* of philosophie
Of *figures* of poetrie,
Or *colours* of rethorike? (*HF* II.848–59; italics added)

James R. Andreas suggests that the "inescapable," "oft forgotten conclusion" of the Eagle's words is that "raw speech is the *datum* of the poet, speech unrefined, unamended, unpolished, not carefully crafted rhetoric and the poetic refinement of the schools."[112] In both the *House of Fame* and the "Prologue to the Clerk's Tale," then, clarity is the thing that will catch the conscientiousness of men as "lewed" as Geffrey and as literal-minded as the Host.[113] Tacitly reconstructing Dante's unlearned reader from the *De vulgari eloquentia* in the form of the Canterbury pilgrims, Chaucer puts his Clerk in the position where he must modify his bookish source in order to address his present company. The Canterbury fellowship includes, after all, an innkeeper, a miller, and all manner of tradesmen – those very men and women in the shops and public squares whom Petrarch repudiated in *Familiares* XXI.15. Of course, whereas Boccaccio elevated Italian over Latin by claiming to write for an audience of aristocratic women, making "an axiom of an oxymoron: the vulgar … nobler" and the "mother tongue … superior to the tongues learned in school," Chaucer uses his translation to bolster the nobility of his *own* mother tongue, English, and to develop it as a literary language.[114] Indeed, he translates the story into a language and style that "*signif*[*ies*] clarity," and that is "easily comprehensible, whereas Latin is not."[115]

The Host implies that "termes," "colours," and "rhetoric" only muddle a man's speech. He asks the Clerk to avoid "heigh style, as whan that men to kynges write" (IV.18), and to speak plainly. The Clerk responds that he will tell a story written in "heigh style" by Petrarch, a man who "enlumyned al Ytaille" with his "rhetorike sweete" (IV.33, 32), and then launches into a proem that "with heigh stile [Petrarch] enditeth" (IV.41). At first blush, the Clerk's reply to the Host seems to be in blatant disregard of his wishes, since he twice recalls the "heigh style" and rhetoric that the Host rejects as unsuitable. But in fact, the Clerk fulfils his narrative obligations to the letter: by translating Petrarch's words *out* of the *gramatica* and *into* English, a vulgar, non-literary tongue, he obeys the

Host's request for a tale that common folk can understand. What is more, with the exception of the comical and thoroughly anti-Petrarchan Envoy, the "Clerk's Tale" is decidedly *un*-rhetorical. As Charles Muscatine suggested over fifty years ago, although written in rhyme royal, it possesses a "fine astringency, an austerity, that will not appeal to ... the extravagant taste."[116] Chaucer's repeated association of Petrarch with "heigh style," "termes," "colours," "figures," and "rhetorike sweete" thus serves only to distance his *auctor* from the work at hand, all the while aligning Petrarch with a method of writing useless to anyone but a precious few.

Following Chaucer's subtle mockery of Petrarch's style in the Prologue, in the first lines of the Tale the Clerk translates and then criticizes a rhetorical proem of Petrarch's own invention. Whereas Boccaccio began *Decameron* X.10 by discussing the figure of Walter, Petrarch adds an extensive proem to his translation, in which he grandly maps out the various regions of Italy according to the path of the River Po, beginning in the west and moving to the Adriatic Sea:

> Est ad Italie latus occiduum Vesulus, ex Appennini iugis mons unus altissimus, qui vertice nubila superans liquido sese ingerit etheri, mons suapte nobilis natura, Padi ortu nobilissimus, qui eius e latere fonte lapsus exiguo, orientem contra solem fertur mirisque mox tumidus incrementis brevi spatio decurso non tantum maximorum unus amnium sed "fluviorum" a Virgilio "rex" dictus, Liguriam gurgite violentus intersecat, dehinc Emiliam atque Flaminiam Venetiamque disterminans, multis ad ultimum et ingentibus ostiis in adriaticum mare descendit.

> On the western side of Italy there is a very high mountain of the Apennine chain called Monviso, whose summit, piercing the clouds, rises into the pure ether, a mountain famous for its size, but even more as the source of the Po which, flowing from a tiny spring from its side, moves toward the rising sun, and soon swollen by amazing tributaries over a short downward course, becomes not only one of the greatest streams, but is called "the king of Rivers" by Virgil [*Georgics* 1.482]; with its strong current, it divides Liguria, then separates Emilia, Flaminia, and Venetia, and finally empties with many huge mouths into the Adriatic Sea.[117]

The Clerk also includes these lines, faithfully guiding us through the regions of Italy as his author did before him.

> But forth to tellen of this worthy man
> That taughte me this tale, as I bigan,
> I seye that first with heigh stile he enditeth,

Er he the body of his tale writeth,
A prohemye, in the which descryveth he
Pemond and of Saluces the contree,
And speketh of Apennyn, the hilles hye,
That been the boundes of West Lumbardye,
And of Mount Vesulus in special,
Where as the Poo out of a welle small
Taketh his firste spryngyng and his sours,
That estward ay encresseth in his cours
To Emele-ward, to Ferrare, and Venyse. (IV.39–51)

Although he translates the proem into English, the Clerk's distaste for these lines is apparent. Attributing this prefatory material to "Petrak," who "enditeth," "wriyteth," "descryveth," and "speketh" it before him, our Clerk is merely rehearsing what originated from "his sours," following his narrative's movement like the path of the River Po. What is more, he ultimately dismisses this proem as "a long thyng were to devyse," adding,

Trewely, as to my juggement,
Me thynketh it a thyng impertinent
Save that he wole conveyen his mateere. (IV.52–5)

The Clerk's characterization of the proem as too long may parody Petrarch's earlier assertion that he did not read all of the *Decameron* because it was "very big." His rejection of the proem as a thing "impertinent" (irrelevant) is likewise significant, because it recalls not only Petrarch's critique of Boccaccio's low style but also Dante's instruction on stylistic embellishment. In both the *Convivio* and *De vulgari eloquentia*, Dante emphasizes the importance of writing clearly and embellishing appropriately, comparing the act of adorning a text to the dressing and undressing of a woman. In the *Convivio*, he praises the vernacular for its ability to express in simple terms "[gli] altissimi e novissimi concetti" ("the loftiest and the most unusual conceptions").[118] Likening them to a lady who is overdressed in finery, he then scorns "le accidentali adornezze" ("the accidental adornments") found in ornate verse:

> Sì come non si può bene manifestare la bellezza d'una donna, quando li adornamenti dell'azzimare e delle vestimenta la fanno più ammirare che essa medesima. Onde chi vuole ben giudicare d'una donna, guardi quella quando solo sua naturale bellezza si sta con lei, da tutto accidentale adornamento discompagnata: sì come sarà questo comento, nel quale si vedrà l'agevolezza delle sue sillabe, le *proprietadi* delle sue costruzioni e le soavi orazioni che di lui si fanno.

> Just as the beauty of a woman cannot be perfectly expressed when the adornment of her preparation and apparel do more to make her admired than she does herself. Therefore, if anyone wishes to judge a woman justly, let him look at her when her natural beauty attends her, unaccompanied by any accidental *adornment*, so it will be with this commentary, in which the smoothness of the flow of its syllables, the *appropriateness* of its constructions, and the sweet discourses that it makes will be seen.[119]

Here, cloaking a noble idea in superfluous rhetoric is akin to hiding a lovely lady beneath extravagant apparel. Both are inappropriate means of embellishment, because they conceal the simple beauty of the thing they ought to adorn.

Dante revisits this analogy between appropriate embellishment and attire in *De vulgari eloquentia*. In this work, the lady of the *Convivio* becomes a beast, disguised as another animal or tricked up in fancy finery:

> Et ubi dicitur, quod quilibet suos versus exornare debet in quantum potest, verum esse testamur; sed nec bovem epiphyatum, nec balteatum suem dicemus ornatum, ymo potius deturpatum ridemus illum; est enim exornatio alicuius convenientis additio.

> And as for my remark that anyone should embellish his lines as much as he can, I declare that this is true; but we would not call an ox well-adorned if it were dressed up to look like a horse, or a sow if it wore a sword-belt – rather, we would laugh at their disfiguring get-up, for true adornment consists in the addition of something *appropriate*.[120]

If embellishment is the addition of something appropriate for Dante, then inappropriate embellishment is, by contrast, like an "ugly woman swathed in gold and silk": "turpis mulier si auro vel serico vestiatur."[121] Her very adornments emphasize, rather than conceal, her flaws.

Dante's description of a poet's verse in terms of a woman's clothing echoes inversely Jerome's earlier reference to his translation as the "squalid dress" cloaking the "noble body" of his source. Whereas Jerome cautions his readers to look beyond the rude encasing that is his translation to the kernel of wisdom within, however, Dante puts the onus on the writer to embellish his work in an appropriate manner, stressing the importance of linguistic simplicity. Following his own instructions, he assures readers of the *Convivio* that his commentary on the individual *canzone* will be written in the vernacular, rather than in Latin, and in "rima aspr'e sottile" ("harsh and subtle rhymes").[122] Nor will his verses contain superfluous adornment, since that would hinder his desire to express himself with the utmost clarity.

Dante's comparison of excessive rhetorical flourishes to a preening pig or an overdressed woman adds a layer of complexity to the literal and literary costuming, performed by a series of authors, on Griselda and her tale. Whereas Petrarch sees his translation as ennobling – a luxurious covering that enhances the narrative's appeal – Chaucer portrays the content/unadorned body of the narrative as *itself* noble, and its Latin dress as unsuitable for his pilgrim audience. Simple yet beautiful, naked yet radiant, the English "Griselde" is text unencumbered, like the naturally beautiful woman of the *De vulgari eloquentia*. At the same time, the Clerk appears to follow Dante's tutelage when he pares down Petrarch's rhetorical additions to a minimum, adjusting his language and style to ensure that his fellow pilgrims "may understonde what [he] seye[s]" (IV.20). Indeed, his appraisal of Petrarch's proem as prolix and superfluous reads like an apology to the Canterbury fellowship for including material so *inappropriate* to the occasion, and so out of sync with the sparseness of the tale itself.

Nor is the Clerk's remark palliated by his further observation that the purpose of Petrarch's proem appears to be to "conveyen his mateere" (IV.55). If anything, this addendum reminds us of Petrarch's more serious failure as a translator – that he has shirked his duty as the conduit for his source's *materia* in favour of freely changing and embellishing Boccaccio's story throughout. The Clerk's commentary on the rhetorical prologue beginning the *Historia Griseldis* is therefore critical on an intertextual level, for it evokes not only Petrarch's yawning lament at the prodigious length of the *Decameron* but also Dante's words of instruction on appropriate embellishment. Following on the heels of the Host's rejection of the very brand of "heigh style" with which Petrarch is repeatedly associated, it suggests Chaucer's general repudiation of his source's performance as a translator. Petrarch's "rethorike sweete" has no place in the "Clerk's Tale," where "heigh style" is sifted for its function and deemed "impertinent."

After dismissing him as an unfit authority on matters of language and style, Chaucer questions the rectitude of Petrarch's ethics. Like Boccaccio's repeated solicitations to *le donne*, the Clerk interrupts his narrative regularly to address his audience, with the intention of condemning Walter's persistent testing of Griselda: "som men preise it for a subtil wit," he claims, but "as for me, I seye that yvele it sit / To assaye a wyf whan that it is no nede" (IV.459–61). At a later point, the Clerk questions his female readers directly about Walter's behaviour: "but now of wommen wolde I axen fayn, / If thise assayes myghte nat suffise?" (IV.696–7). With each narrative intrusion censuring Walter's actions, the Clerk moves farther away from his Petrarchan source and its moral conclusion. It is as though he suggests that the work, possessing a life of its own, resists his interpretation of it. This is perhaps most evident in the final lines of his tale, for whereas Petrarch concludes his translation by turning Griselda into an exemplum among men, advising all of his readers to emulate her constancy in the face of adversity, the Clerk follows Boccaccio in emphasizing her *singularity*.[123] He reminds us that "it were ful hard to fynde now-a-dayes / In al a toun Grisildis thre or two" (IV.1164–5). Women nowadays bend and break like alloyed metal. For the Clerk, Griselda's behaviour cannot – and, more importantly, *should* not – be imitated. His "storie is seyd nat for that wyves sholde / Folwen Grisilde as in humylitee" (IV.1142–3), he suggests. This, too, has a precedent in the *Decameron*, although Boccaccio suggests that it is Walter, and not Griselda, who is an unworthy exemplum. Dioneo condemns Walter's brutality before cautioning us against his bestial course, "la quale io non consiglio alcun che segue" ("which I do not recommend that anyone follow").[124] He later speculates, as we have seen, that "there are those in royal palaces who would be better employed as swineherds than as rulers of men."

In his narrative asides, Dioneo expresses less admiration for Griselda's unnatural behaviour than horror at Walter's "matta bestialità." So, too, does the Clerk, who, after interrogating Walter's persistent testing of his wife, instructs women to prevent what happened to Griselda from happening to them.[125] "O noble wyves, ful of heigh prudence," he warns, "lat noon humylitee youre tonge naille" (IV.1183–4).

> Lat no clerk have cause or diligence
> To write of yow a storie of swich mervaille
> As of Grisildis. (IV.1185–7)

The Clerk's plea for an end to further renditions of the Griselda story perhaps reflects his distaste for his story's moral message. While he reiterates Petrarch's command to read Griselda's deference to her husband allegorically, as a call for patience in the face of adversity (IV.1145–6), the Clerk seems barely able to perform this exegetical exercise himself. In the end, he not only cautions us against her level of persistence but also goes so far as to commend us to his Canterbury rival, the Wife of Bath (IV.1170), comically counselling the "archewyves" in attendance to "stondeth at defense" against tyrannical men (IV.1195), and to give their tongues free rein to "clappeth as a mille" (IV.1200). As ironic as the Clerk's expressed solidarity with wives – both noble and arch – may be, paired with his earlier address to the "wommen" in attendance, it recalls Boccaccio's original deference to a readership composed of ladies. His conclusion thus looks back to Boccaccio's *Decameron* at the same time as it unravels Petrarch's redirection of the narrative to men versed in the *gramatica*. If the *Historia Griseldis* is an Everyman parable for every man, then the "Clerk's Tale" gives voice to all women, from Griselda to the Wife of Bath.

Chaucer's privileging of the bawdy Alisoun of Bath as a more plausible model for female readers recalls Dioneo's fantasy of a different ending, in which Griselda responds to her husband's trials by leaving him for another man. It would have served Walter right if his wife, "Fuor di casa, l'avesse fuori in camiscia cacciata, s'avesse sí a un altro fatto scuotere il pilliccione che riuscito ne fosse una bella roba" ("Driven from her house in a shift, had found some other man to shake her skin-coat for her, earning herself a fine new dress in the process"), Dioneo suggests.[126] While Petrarch takes Dioneo's words as his cue to intercept Griselda on her way back to Walter, clothe her in the robes of Latin rhetoric, and cast her as a Christian martyr, Chaucer interprets Boccaccio's suggestion more literally. Indeed, he seems to have these lines in mind when he encourages women to bind their husbands "in jalousie," for so "thou shalt make hym couche as doth a quaille" (IV.1205–6). Such advice is the final nail in the coffin of Petrarch's Griselda, who, as Chaucer is quick to remind us, "is deed, and eek hire pacience" (IV.1177). One suspects that she and her patience are buried with their twice-named author, Petrarch, who, with his "rhetorike sweete," once "enlumyned al Ytaille of poetrie" but is now *also* "deed and nayled in his cheste" (IV.32–3, IV.29).[127]

Chaucer's abrupt interment of Petrarch, his heroine, and her crowning virtue has the two-pronged effect of declaring Petrarch and his Griselda obsolete while simultaneously parodying Petrarch's earlier depiction of Boccaccio as an impetuous youth and the *Decameron* as a juvenile exercise in the vernacular. Chaucer mires both Petrarch and his Griselda in Italian soil. If Boccaccio is a child, he seems to suggest, then Petrarch is a corpse. The Clerk's glowing epitaphic description of Petrarch as the man who once "enlumyned *al Ytaille*" – and with his *poetry*, no less – is also deceptively innocuous, since it recalls Petrarch's role as a vernacular poet. That in his Italian verse Petrarch could and did appeal to a more socially diverse demographic was hardly lost on him. As we have seen, he laments to Boccaccio that his disenchantment with the vernacular was prompted largely by the unpleasant experience of hearing his verses sung by the multitude.[128] He further uses this story as an opportunity to distinguish himself from Dante, reminding Boccaccio that whereas *he* grew out of his youthful infatuation with the vernacular, Dante did not: "Quod illi artificium nescio an unicum, sed profecto supremum fuit, michi iocus atque solatium fuerit et ingenii rudimentum" ("What was for him, if not his only occupation, surely his principal one, was for me mere sport, a pastime, a mental exercise").[129]

Boccaccio made repeated attempts to convince his friend of Dante's merits, even sending him a copy of the *Commedia*, and inviting him to participate in his celebration of Dante in *Ytalie iam certus honos*, but to no avail. Petrarch's distaste for the author and his followers continued into his final years.[130] But if in life Petrarch scorned Dante, in death, he was regularly associated with him. Together, Dante, Petrarch, and Boccaccio have come to be seen as Italy's *tre corone*, a vernacular pantheon that Boccaccio himself was instrumental in constructing.[131] In a final poem honouring his recently deceased friend, Boccaccio even immortalized Petrarch alongside the very poets he spurned in life: "Or con Sennuccio e con Cino e con Dante / vivi, sicuro d'eterno riposo" ("Now, with Sennuccio, Cino, and Dante, you live, sure of eternal repose").[132]

By committing him to eternal fellowship among Cino da Pistoia and Dante, those same writers with whom Boccaccio aligned himself in the *Decameron*, as well as Petrarch's friend, the Florentine poet Sennuccio del Bene, Boccaccio seemingly requites Petrarch for his ongoing mockery of the vernacular and its proponents. Yet he also anticipates the great irony of Petrarch's legacy: that this classicist supreme would be remembered primarily for his Italian verse. That the Clerk, too, commemorates Petrarch as a vernacular poet, writing him a eulogy of sorts as the great illuminator of Italy, could bespeak Chaucer's profound understanding of the complicated dynamic between Petrarch and Boccaccio, and of Boccaccio's precarious position as the self-appointed disciple of two vastly different thinkers.[133] At the very least, it indicates that Chaucer, like Petrarch, felt little remorse when it came to translating his *auctor* as well as his work. For after nailing Petrarch away in a chest marked "Italian poet," Chaucer resurrects an English model of Griselda alongside a standard of female sexual autonomy, putting the lady back on the pedestal where she reigned, however instrumentally, for the length of the *Decameron*. Petrarch, conversely, is rejected on linguistic, stylistic, and moral grounds, left, as Boccaccio was before him, the unwilling author of a text that no longer speaks for him.

While I have briefly illustrated how Chaucer reverses Petrarch's emendations to *Decameron* X.10, leaving his author "Petrak" responsible for the shortcomings of a work that is no longer in his possession, there is still much to be said on the subject of Chaucer's use of translation as a subversive mode of commentary, both in the "Clerk's Tale" and in his poetry as a whole.[134] For Chaucer, the process of acknowledging his literary models is neither clear cut nor wholly complimentary. His cited *auctores* represent only a fraction of those with whom he engages, and, as I have suggested in this chapter, belie his engagement with a literary trajectory that extends beyond the progenitor of Griselda's narrative to her ideological roots in Dante's writings. Chaucer's apparent misreading of his Petrarchan source can point us in this regard toward works with which the *Historia Griseldis* is in conversation, and which should also be considered among the matrix of the poet's textual influences. Put otherwise, we must look beneath Griselda's smock to find the act of redress that ultimately reveals her true ancestry, a genealogy that turns out to be extensive and illustrious at that. With Dante, Boccaccio, Petrarch, and Chaucer among her literary progenitors, one thing is certain: Griselda need not be ashamed to return to her father's house.

Chapter Three

Power in Flux: Chaucer's Triumphal "Monk's Tale"

Exegi monumentum aere perennius
regalique situ pyramidum altius,
quod non imber edax, non aquilo impotens
possit diruere aut innumerabilis
annorum series et fuga temporum.
non omnis moriar multaque pars mei
vitabit Libitinam; usque ego postera
crescam laude recens, dum Capitolium
scandet cum tacita virgine pontifex

[I have created a monument more lasting than bronze
and loftier than the royal structure of the pyramids,
that which neither devouring rain, nor the unrestrained North Wind
may be able to destroy nor the immeasurable
succession of years and the flight of time.
I shall not wholly die and a greater part of me
will evade Libitina [Goddess of Death]; continually I,
newly arisen, may be strengthened with ensuing praise so long
as the high priest climbs the Capitoline with the silent maiden]

Horace, *Ode* III.30[1]

Iamque opus exegi, quod nec Iovis ira nec ignis
nec poterit ferrum nec edax abolere vetustas.
cum volet, illa dies, quae nil nisi corporis huius
ius habet, incerti spatium mihi finiat aevi:
parte tamen meliore mei super alta perennis
astra ferar, nomenque erit indelebile nostrum,
quaque patet domitis Romana potentia terris,
ore legar populi, perque omnia saecula fama,
siquid habent veri vatum praesagia, vivam.

[And now my work is done, which neither the wrath of Jove, nor fire, nor sword, nor the gnawing tooth of time shall ever be able to undo. When it will, let that day come which has no power save over this mortal frame, and end the span of my uncertain years. Still in my better part I shall be borne immortal far beyond the lofty stars and I shall have an undying name. Wherever Rome's power extends over the conquered world, I shall have mention on men's lips, and, if the prophecies of bards have any truth, through all the ages shall I live in fame.]

Ovid, *Metamorphoses* XV.871–9[2]

On the one hand a series of exempla, on the other a catalogue of famous men and women from throughout history, the "Monk's Tale" would appear at once to condemn and propagate human glory. Telling tales of woe, the Monk parades before us a pageant of illustrious individuals. He preserves the names of his subjects – and of the poets who write of them – by reiterating their stories and thus memorializing their lives. In this respect, the Monk celebrates human achievement even as he denounces its transience, juxtaposing the temporary misfortune of his subjects against their more lasting literary fame, made possible by poets themselves.

This chapter will discuss the "Monk's Tale" as a form of perennial monument: a shrine to enduring memory in a world defined by flux. The Monk draws on our collective cultural knowledge of famous individuals, the very "remembraunce" of which defies his assertion that worldly things are all fleeting (VII.1989).[3] By recording the lives of rulers, heroes, and poets for posterity, he reveals, if in spite of himself, that glory can last centuries, transcending death, this world, and its temporary defeats – that words can be, as Horace insists in the *Exegi monumentum*, more permanent than bronze. While, for poets, the threat that a work may be lost or forgotten is always imminent, by recollecting a tradition of literary greatness – a pantheonic ancestry to which later writers could attest – Chaucer, I will suggest, creates the impression of a lasting and communal literary fame, distinct from the fleeting individual victories and falls of his subjects. Even as the Monk laments the transience of Fortune, his tale itself acts as a policy against extinction. Though men can be overthrown by Fortune without warning, and fame can melt with the seasons like ice, poets are able to thwart this process by inscribing the names of the mighty in their writings, tacitly petitioning future authors to do the same.[4]

The Monk's repeated assertion of the transitory, tragic nature of human existence – a Boethian maxim he attaches to each portrait, regardless of whether or not it applies[5] – has, however, obscured the Tale's cautious promotion of *gloria* from its readers, many of whom have dismissed this work as a dull and repetitive collection of sad stories.[6] Chaucer's notable debt to

Boccaccio's Latin prose treatise, *De casibus virorum illustrium* (begun c. 1355), in which the narrator intersperses his stories of famous individuals falling with moralizing asides about the illusory nature of worldly goods, has further skewed our reception of the tale along more sombre lines. Yet, as I will argue in the opening sections of this chapter, before turning to the "Monk's Tale," Boccaccio's treatment of worldly fame in the *De casibus* is itself highly ambivalent. While reminding us repeatedly that the human condition is to fall, the narrator also suggests in several places that a certain type of glory is virtuous and desirable. What is more, glory of this kind has the potential to provide both poets and their subjects with literary immortality, such as Ovid claims for himself in the final lines of the *Metamorphoses*: "Wherever Rome's power extends over the conquered world, I shall have mention on men's lips, and, if the prophecies of bards have any truth, through all the ages shall I live in fame."

I will further argue that the *De casibus* reflects Boccaccio's longstanding meditation on the rewards of worldly reputation, the seeds of which are planted in his earlier poetic triumph, the *Amorosa visione* (c. 1342–3), and cultivated in epistolary exchanges on the subject with his friend and *magister*, Petrarch. The *De casibus*, a Latin treatise written in prose, is, of course, a vastly different work from the *Amorosa visione*, an ekphrastic dream vision of triumphal processions, written in the Florentine vernacular and in Dantean *terza rima*. Still, these differences have overshadowed important thematic and structural parallels between the two texts, so that these similarities have largely gone unstudied.[7] Both works concern, for example, the individual's thraldom to Fortune vis-à-vis his attachment to worldly goods, and are organized according to the rotation of Fortune's wheel. Both texts further demonstrate Boccaccio's persistent interest in the poet's capacity to create, maintain, or withhold the reputations of his literary subjects. Finally, both the *Amorosa visione* and the *De casibus* espouse a view of worldly goods as inconsequential, potentially transient, yet also highly *desirable*, a seemingly contradictory perspective that Boccaccio carries forward from the poetic triumph to the Latin treatise. Reading these works together thus illuminates Boccaccio's ambivalent attitude toward worldly fame in the *De casibus* especially, which has so often been read by scholars of English literature as a prototype for tragic exempla in the Middle Ages and early modern period.[8] As we will see, Boccaccio's outlook on worldly fame in the *De casibus* is far more nuanced than the narrator's moralistic asides would suggest. Rather than insist unequivocally on the transience of all earthly things, the author advocates for renown as an escape from death, his lesson on glory's ephemerality contested over the course of the work.

To this end, I will claim that the *De casibus* resembles a triumphal procession – five of which are described consecutively in the *Amorosa visione* – but from a different narrative perspective. That is, with a focus on the conquered, rather than the ascending triumphator. The treatise is organized, as Simone Marchesi observes, as a series of visions "depicting in a triumph-like scenario a vast array of historical figures who march before the meditating author and lament their suffering."[9] It is also helpful to imagine the *Amorosa visione* as a processional *De casibus*, with each new triumphator depicted at the moment of victory, or on the upward swing of Fortune's wheel. (Such a view is particularly applicable to the poem's final procession, Fortune's Triumph, which Todd Boli rightly describes as an "embryonic version" of the *De casibus*.)[10] Taken together, the two works form a unit. Boccaccio uses the *Amorosa visione* and the *De casibus* to explore the *full* cycle of Fortune's wheel through opposing genres: triumph and moralizing treatise. It is important to note, however, that neither of these works wholly celebrates or condemns worldly glory. Rather, the *Amorosa visione* and the *De casibus* espouse a profoundly ambivalent view on the status of man's pursuit of fame, an ambivalence that is, as we shall see, rooted in the Roman triumph itself.

A ceremonial procession from antiquity, in which a laurelled general would ascend to the capitol while the citizens of Rome gathered, watched, and feasted, the Roman triumph exemplified and honoured martial primacy.[11] The triumphator would enter the city on a horse-drawn chariot led by his captives. The procession began in the Campus Martius, moved through the forum, and ended in the Temple of Jupiter on Capitoline hill. It was a spectacle that stood, in Zygmunt G. Barański's words, "as a *topos* for Roman authority and greatness."[12] Still, the triumph was as much a reminder of one's own mortality as it was a celebration of preeminence. A fleeting event commemorating short-lived conquest, it performed in real time the flux and pageantry of Fortune's wheel. The triumph was a "joyful procession, but it was also a melancholy one," as Robert Payne observes, because the victor knew that "men cannot attain these heights without incurring the wrath of the gods."[13] In the rare occurrence that he forgot this lesson, however, built into the Roman triumph were reminders of the transience of good fortune, so that the "very ceremony which glorified military victory and the values underpinning that victory also provided a context within which those values could be discussed and challenged," writes Mary Beard.[14] For example, an attendant would crown the triumphator and declare him a god-king before uttering the phrase, "'Remember that you are a man,' to avert the enmity of the fates and to remind the triumphator that victory and life were passing gifts of Fortune."[15] The captives also served as a warning to everyone watching that the mighty, too, shall fall. Arranged so that the most formidable among them were the most prominently displayed, the prisoners were both the spoils of battle and a possible vision into the victor's future. Indeed, even as he celebrated his martial preeminence, every victor knew that preeminence was itself a temporary state, and that "those who triumph today *may one day be triumphed over*."[16]

Beard uses Donatello's bronze statue of David to illustrate the triumph's attention to a cycle of victory and loss. At first glance, the statue shows a victorious David with his foot on the head of the slain Goliath. But closer inspection reveals a triumphal procession: on Goliath's helmet, Cupid rides a chariot in celebration. Invoking the Roman triumph as a visual shorthand for victory's transience, Donatello points to the "transitory nature of triumphal glory: Goliath who blazoned the emblem of the triumph on his armor is now himself the victim of his triumphant successor."[17] By using the image of a Roman triumph, Donatello would seem to suggest that David will also fall, as will the individual witnessing the sculpture.

There is yet another element of Donatello's *David* to consider. The cycle of transience the artist conveys is *fixed*, frozen in sculptural form. Instead of representing *one* victor, therefore, Donatello can simultaneously represent *three* – Goliath, David, and Cupid – levelling time's progression by constructing multiple temporalities at once. In this regard, while insinuating that worldly power is transient and that the human condition is to fall, Donatello also obstructs or at least slows the fleeting nature of victory by converting it into art. At the same time, he transforms victory from a solitary to a shared experience.

The complex and ambivalent legacy of the Roman triumph is, as I will argue, evident in both the *Amorosa visione* and the *De casibus*, in which Boccaccio portrays man's ascent to *and* fall from victory, with an emphasis on the former or the latter, respectively. In the *Amorosa visione*, Boccaccio exalts victory while demonstrating that it does not last, and in the *De casibus*, he chronicles our inevitable demise while registering the virtues of immortal glory. In both works, Boccaccio suggests that it is the artist/poet's prerogative to convert fleeting victory into enduring glory by portraying the stories of famous men and women in his works. Whether they are commemorated at the top or bottom of Fortune's Wheel, that is, the subjects of these works have already to an extent transcended the vicissitudes of Fortune by having their stories immortalized for posterity by the author. In what follows, I will discuss this immortalizing ambition – what I will refer to hereafter as a work's triumphal poetics – in Boccaccio's writings before identifying it as a feature of the "Monk's Tale." Although warning us of Fortune's transience in both the *Amorosa visione* and *De casibus*, Boccaccio also comments on the poet's power to generate immortality by archiving the names of the famous in his works. What is more, Chaucer appears to recognize this effort in Boccaccio's writings, and he perpetuates it in the Monk's portraits of mighty men.[18]

Poetic Glory in the *De casibus virorum illustrium*

The *De casibus*, which Boccaccio wrote in two versions, has a seemingly clear purpose: it is a moralizing treatise in nine books about the devastating effects of Fortune on mankind.[19] Insisting in the introduction that all worldly goods are temporary, Boccaccio suggests that his work will function as a corrective to contemporary princes, whose pride he hopes to check by showing them examples of powerful men and women who have been brought low by God (or, as these princes call God, Fortune) throughout history. Interspersed among these examples are moral asides and inducements toward virtue, a common theme of which is the transience of worldly things. Good fortune, Boccaccio insists, is fleeting. Power, beauty, wealth, and especially glory must fade. Time consumes our memory on earth, a message the narrator repeats throughout his work:

> Quot iam dudum imperatores incliti, quot illustres phylosophi, quot insignes poete, quot etiam plurimi summa cum difficultate suis seculis meruere laudes, quorum – ne reliqua dicam – nomen etiam in tempore consumptum est adeo ut nulla penitus ex eis sit memoria apud nostros?
>
> How many once-celebrated emperors, how many illustrious philosophers, how many preeminent poets, indeed, how many others earned, with the greatest difficulty, praise in their own age – let me not say the rest! – whose name has in time been so consumed that there is absolutely no memory of them among us?[20]

There are, he concludes, too many names to count. Like fire, water, and the steel of the sword, time lays waste to all things (I.5). The predictably negative effects of the cycle of Fortune should be sufficient to deter anyone from investing their hopes in a different outcome. As Marchesi notes, "Clear-mindedly framed as a systematic debunking of any illusory trust in earthly success, Boccaccio's treatment of history ... does not seem to need any theological underpinning. If history already proves *ad abundantium* (if not *ad nauseam*) a moral point, there seems to be no need to go beyond it to find meaning."[21] In Boccaccio's treatise, all the mighty must fall. Nobody is beyond, or immune from, Fortune's devastating reach.

Still, the narrator of the *De casibus* does not claim comprehensiveness in his catalogue of Fortune's casualties. Many names will be missing from his survey, he explains, but only because it would be impossible to include them all. For the sake of concision, therefore, he selects only the most illustrious:

> [E]xemplis agendum ratus sum eis describere quid Deus omnipotens, seu ut eorum loquar more Fortune, in elatos et fecerit ... Sed ex claris quosdam

clariores excerpsisse sat erit, ut, dum segnes fluxosque principes et Dei iudicio quassatos in solum reges viderint. Dei potentiam, fragilitatem suam, et Fortune lubricum noscant, et letis modum ponere discant, et aliorum periculo sue possint utilitati consulere. (Proem, 6–7)

I decided I ought to describe with examples what Omnipotent God (or, in their language, Fortune) can and will do to the lofty ... But it will be enough to have selected only the most illustrious from among the famous, so that when they [contemporary rulers] see princes sluggish and frail, as well as kings crushed onto the ground by the judgement of God, they might know the power of God, their own fragility, and the instability of Fortune, and they might learn to put a limit to their own joys, and from the dangers of others they might be able to look out for their own good.

In basing his selection on degree and extent of fame – opting to recite the stories of only the "most illustrious ... among the famous" – Boccaccio introduces a paradoxical element to his work, while at the same time insinuating an important distinction between the spoken and written word (and perhaps between the narrator and the poet). Although his narrator laments the impermanence of worldly goods, using his stories of fallen individuals as cautionary examples, Boccaccio counters this assertion of glory's transience by recollecting – even *preserving* – the fame of the figures he mentions. The *De casibus* thus operates as an archive of human glory even as its narrator insists that glory does not last.

If the work functions as a shrine to the memories of renowned individuals, moreover, then the narrator himself appears to change his mind about the significance of fame. While in Book I he classifies it as vain and fleeting, at the start of Book VIII he suggests the opposite: that glory can make man immortal. In a parodic inversion of Boethian logic – parodic because the conclusion is not that earthly fame should be abandoned as an end, but rather that it should be pursued with renewed vigour – the narrator, afflicted by lethargy, asks himself why he strives for renown, when all things in this world come to pass:

Quid veterum monimenta revolvens tam assiduo vexaris labore cum a nemine inpellaris? Ex antiquorum ruinis, ex cineribus infortunatorum, novis literulis extorquere conaris famam atque protelare dies nomenque tuum desideras. O insana cupido! Adveniet hora, et iam est, que te a rebus mortalibus eximat, que corpusculum conterat tuum ... Quid, oro, cum nil ex momentaneis rebus amplius senties, etiam si orbis totus ore pleno nil aliud preter nomen tuum cum laude cantet, absens, honoris aut voluptatis assummes? (VIII.1)

> Why do you vex yourself so tirelessly, rereading the tomes of the ancients, when no one compels you to do so? Do you yearn to extend both your days and your name by a reputation acquired in scribbling anew about the ruin of the men in history? Oh, what an insane desire! The hour will come, and it already is here, that will free you from mortal concerns [and] that will waste away your little body … What, I ask, will you feel when there is nothing left of these brief moments – even if with full mouth the entire world sings with praise nothing other than your name, what honor and pleasure will you obtain?

Nearly overcome by sloth, Boccaccio is greeted by a vision of Petrarch, whom he hails as the most famous man in all of Italy. Appropriately, Petrarch appears crowned with an evergreen laurel, the ultimate sign of his undying glory. Addressing Boccaccio as "ociorum professor egregie" ("famous Professor of Laziness" [VIII.1]), Petrarch berates the younger poet for rejecting earthly fame as transient, and for abandoning his quest for glory:

> Fama, quam tu paulo ante damnabas, tanquam bonum a cunctis mortalibus exoptata est. Que cum variis perquiratur viis, non nisi per virtutem acquiritur. Quam si quis damnet, virtutis exercitium damnet necesse est … Hec brevissimum mortalis vite tempus facit amplissimum et, quasi vita alia, defunctorum posteritati meritos testatur honores. (VIII.1)

> The fame that you condemned a little while ago is actually a great benefit, longed for by all mortals. Although it is sought after in various ways, it is not acquired except through virtue. If anyone condemns fame, he must [thus] condemn the practice of virtue … [Fame] makes the very brief span of mortal life very long, and, as if she gave us another life, she bears witness for posterity to the deserved honors of the dead.

Urging Boccaccio to pursue fame, and so to follow in the footsteps of their literary ancestors, Petrarch insists on the worthiness of glory: "ut, tanquam preteriti labore suo profuere nobis, sic et nos nostro valeamus posteris, ut inter peremnia nostrum scribatur nomen ab eis, ut famam consequamur eternam" ("so that just like those who came before us benefitted us with their labor, so too might we by our labor be influential to our successors, so that our name might be written by them among the immortals, so that we might achieve eternal fame" [VIII.1]). He cautions the younger poet, "Non ergo negligenda est, non ocio calcanda, non tanquam inane et superfluum detestanda, sed propter Deum totis exquirenda viribus est" ("renown must not be neglected, nor stifled by idleness, nor yet despised as useless or superfluous, but rather sought after with all your strength, according to God's will" [VIII.1]). Rather than something temporary, fame is the highest of all goods, which will lead to a kind of literary immortality among a pantheon of other great poets.

Petrarch's command to Boccaccio to pursue glory and renown appears out of place in a treatise purportedly decrying fortune's ephemerality, so that we might be inclined to read his message ironically.[22] But Petrarch's lesson is not as inconsistent with the work's overall outlook on fame as it may at first seem. In the first place, Boccaccio's portrait of Petrarch as a *vir illustribus* is entirely consistent with his treatment of him elsewhere. In one of two explicit mentions of his *magister* in the *Genealogie deorum gentilium* (1350–75), for example, Boccaccio includes a lengthy passage in praise of the "viribus preclarissimi viri," Francesco Petrarch, whom he recalls commending to the king.[23] Boccaccio then recounts how the king's emissary responds that while he has not met Petrarch in person, he has heard plenty about him, whose fame has not only spread throughout Cyprus but also reached the heavens.[24] As Mazzotta notes, this anecdote "may be a simple touch of elegant diplomatic rhetoric," and yet it "brings to the surface an issue central to the *Genealogy* and to Petrarch: fame, which crystallizes the will of the self to transcend time and its ruptures."[25]

In his biography of Petrarch, Boccaccio again emphasizes his friend's earthly fame, which lives on after his death. In this work, he eschews "the obligatory ascetic values of the *contemptus mundi* that made it fairly impossible to attribute to the category of fame a prominent place in biographic writing."[26] Instead, he "revive[s] the concept of fame and glory from Roman antiquity," drawing on "assertions of Roman poets like Hor ace, Ovid, or Propertius, who had expressed their conviction that their writings would be read by posterity and that they had erected for themselves everlasting monuments, more endurable than bronze statues or the Egyptian pyramids."[27] This notion of a virtuous fame – one that has the potential to give us new life, even to extend our "brief span" on earth, and which is within the reach of poets – was vital for Petrarch, forming the basis of many of his works, including the *Africa* and *De viris illustribus.*[28] The possibility of achieving glory of this kind was also fundamental to his epistolary writings, such as his correspondence with Boccaccio, which began in 1351 and ended only with Petrarch's death.[29] In the first letter addressed to Boccaccio in the *Seniles* (I.5), for example, Petrarch advises his friend to live well and avoid sin. As part of this instruction, he quotes Virgil's *Aeneid* on the brevity of life and man's quest for fame: "stat sua cuique dies, breve et inreparabile tempus / omnibus est vitae; sed famam extendere factis, / "hoc virtutis opus" ("Each has his day appointed; short and irretrievable is the span of life for all: but to lengthen fame by deeds – that is valour's task").[30] He then qualifies this as sound advice, especially when fame is achieved through the pursuit of virtue, rather than sought after as an end in itself. In a letter to his friend Laelius (*Familiares* XIX.3), Petrarch similarly distinguishes between the glitter and "inani dyademate" ("hollow diadem") of false glory and the weighty value of honourable fame, which is held up by worthwhile achievements and a virtue of spirit.[31] While the former is a vain and insignificant endeavour, the latter, Petrarch insists, is a most worthy pursuit.

Even as Petrarch flouts the didactic message laid out in the introduction of the *De casibus*, then, his role in the treatise is not ironic. On the contrary, Boccaccio appears to promote a particularly Petrarchan ideal of *gloria* here, a concept of eternal fame that "proposes to create a society of gifted initiates across centuries," in David Wallace's words.[32] Simply by having Petrarch come to him in a vision, Boccaccio invests in the reality of such a society. He alludes to corresponding scenes of eidolopoeia from works including Ennius's *Annales* (c. 200 BCE) and Petrarch's *Africa* (unfinished at the time of Petrarch's death in 1374), in which a poet is visited in a dream or a vision by his literary forbears, who then predict his ultimate greatness.[33] These visions are self-authorizing: the poet declares his preeminence vicariously, through the mouths of his predecessors. But they are also strategic insofar as they enable the poet to determine his own authorial lineage and fashion his literary pedigree accordingly.

In a particularly freighted nexus of allusion in Petrarch's *Africa*, for example, the Roman poet Ennius recounts to Scipio Africanus how the figure of Homer appeared to him in a dream. At first, Ennius laments that he is the sole author to sing of Scipio's greatness (Books VII–IX of the *Annales* focus on the Second Punic War), since he sees himself as unfit for such a task.[34] But Ennius finds great comfort in his conviction that the future will bring a poet, worthier than he, who will relate Scipio's triumphs in high style.[35] Ennius believes this, he goes on to explain, because Homer came to *him* in a vision to foretell the birth of this glorious poet, who is none other than Petrarch. According to Homer, Petrarch will write a Latin epic called the *Africa*, in which he will praise Scipio in a work worthy of Scipio's accomplishments. Homer marvels at Petrarch's brilliance and ambition: "Quin etiam ingenii fiducia quanta, / Quantus aget laudum stimulus" ("How great will be his faith in his own gifts! How strong the love of fame that leads him on" [IX.236–7]). He then predicts Petrarch's laureation, an honour Petrarch will receive for the *Africa*, equating this act with the making of a Roman triumph:

> seroque triumpho
> Hic tandem ascendet Capitolia vestra, nec ipsum
> Mundus iners studiisque aliis tunc ebria turba

Terrebit quin insigni florentia lauro
Tempora descendens referat comitante Senatu. (IX.237–41)

At last in tardy triumph he will climb the Capitol. Nor shall a heedless world nor an illiterate herd, inebriate with baser passions, turn aside his steps when he descends, flanked by the company of Senators, and from the rite returns with brow girt by the glorious laurel wreath.

Petrarch uses these scenes of prophecy to construct his genealogy indirectly, ventriloquizing his literary lineage through the mouths of his predecessors. Relying on the figures of Homer and Ennius to forecast his greatness, he creates the illusion that it is these famous poets who have elected him as their descendant, when in fact it is Petrarch who chooses them as his ancestors.

Nor is this the sole instance in the *Africa* in which Petrarch divines his excellence vicariously. Ennius's dream of Homer corroborates an earlier episode in the epic, in which Scipio the Elder visits his sleeping son, Scipio Africanus, to speak of Petrarch. Addressing the young general, Scipio the Elder explains that as Ennius recounted their labours in the *Annales*, so too will Petrarch tell their story in the *Africa*. Petrarch will be for their fame an "Ennius alter" ("second Ennius" [II.443]), but he will also outshine his Roman predecessor, since he will provide Africanus with the "ultimate praise he deserved."[36] Petrarch thus presents himself as Ennius's disciple at the same time as he insinuates his own authorial predominance.[37] Heir to Ennius's poetic subject, Petrarch will usurp his predecessor in excellence.[38]

It is not only Ennius's subject matter that Petrarch recuperates here. Both this scene and its parallel, Ennius's vision of Homer, also allude to (and to an extent usurp) an early scene from the *Annales*. Ennius begins his work by declaring that Homer had visited *him* in a dream to claim him as his reincarnate – to appoint him as a second Homer ("Homerus alter," the title by which Ennius is known to later poets), a linguistic formula that Petrarch then adapts and applies to himself ("Ennius alter").[39] Of course, Petrarch mines Ennius's Homeric prophecy to his own advantage. Since Ennius was a conduit for the dead Homer in the *Annales*, he must play this role again in the *Africa*, but with one key difference: whereas in the *Annales* Homer foretells the glory of Ennius, in the *Africa* the prophecy of greatness concerns Petrarch alone. But there is also a memorializing function to Petrarch's allusion. By the time Petrarch is writing, the *Annales* really were lost, existing for Petrarch only in fragments. By recalling Ennius's dream, even for the sake of honouring himself and not Ennius, Petrarch thus revitalizes the fragmentary epic, making Ennius "live and speak again" through his own Latin prose.[40]

I have discussed these episodes of eidolopoeia in some detail to demonstrate that Petrarch's visit to Boccaccio in the *De casibus* draws on and develops a rich tradition of poets fabricating their own authorial inauguration, a literary device that appears mutually advantageous for both the "modern" poet writing and his authoritative ancestors.[41] On the one hand, the poet authorizes his work by suggesting that he is part of an illustrious literary lineage, and that he is as good as, if not superior to, his predecessors. On the other hand, these ancient writers are resurrected by their literary progeny, their works recalled to memory by later poets. Although superficially a scene of comic remonstration, with the narrator scolded by a severe interlocutor, Petrarch's visit in the *De casibus* has an authorizing effect similar to that of the corresponding scene in the *Africa*, as I suggest, because Boccaccio uses this episode to induct himself and Petrarch into a pantheon of literary excellence. The figure of Petrarch even refers to his own and Boccaccio's *mutual* ancestors ("those who came before *us*"), marking both men's positions in an authorial lineage that binds them to one another, and to past and future poets.

Indeed, this process appears to be the very mechanism generating literary fame in the first place. Poets carry forth the names of their predecessors, inscribing themselves in a literary genealogy to which posterity can bear witness, with the understanding that this process may in turn bring them fame as well. In the *De casibus*, the figure of Petrarch accordingly recognizes the communal impetus to preserve the fame of one's predecessors.[42] As he explains to Boccaccio, poets praise great authors including Homer, Aristotle, and Cato as though they were present, with the hope that later writers will memorialize *them* in a similar fashion: "id quod illi suscipiunt a nobis, nos labore nostro apud futuros posse suscipere credimus; et sic futuram gloriam spirantes anticipamus" ("that which they receive from us, we believe that we will be able to gain among those who come after us; and so, while we live, we anticipate future glory" [VIII.1]). In this case, Petrarch's advice to the weary Boccaccio also acts as an entreaty: he urges Boccaccio to facilitate the propagation of their mutual fame, just as Petrarch had revivified the name of Ennius in his *Africa*. At the same time, by contributing in this tradition of dream/vision inauguration (and so invoking its previous models for our consideration), Boccaccio implies that Petrarch also risks having his epic overshadowed by a literary successor: as the *Annales* give way to the *Africa* (at least according to Petrarch), so too might the *Africa* be eclipsed by Boccaccio's lengthy Latin work.

Were it only Petrarch singing the merits of fame in the *De casibus*, it would be possible to dismiss his words as aberrant in a treatise for the most part condemning the vanity of worldly goods. But the figure of Petrarch only echoes what Boccaccio himself insists upon in the poem: that when accompanied by virtuous motives the quest for fame is not only free from sin, it actively counters it.[43] In Book III, Boccaccio claims that poets earn the right to wear the evergreen laurel because poetry alone has the capacity to transcend life's mutability, and that ancients gave them this wreath in testimony of their "eternal powers" ("virtutis eternum" [III.14]). In his encounter with Lady Fortune in Book VI, Boccaccio applies this maxim to his own situation. Suggesting that he writes in order to make his name eternal, he asks Fortune to propagate his renown long after he is dead, so that his name will not disappear with his body:

> Verum ne dum et ego ipse dissolvar, nomen meum sepulcro una cum corpore detur et ferarum ritu ... queso supplex ut tua gratia ceptum secundetur opus et quod obscurum presentibus nomen meum est tuo illustratum fulgore clarum apud posteros habeatur. (VI.1)

> But lest when I myself am gone my name be given to the tomb together with my body, and in the manner of wild beasts ... A suppliant, I pray that by your grace this work I have undertaken might find favor, and my name – which is unknown at present – by your brilliance might be held as brightly famous among the future generations.

Though earlier condemning her for her changeability, Boccaccio now appeals to Fortune as an agent in his quest for immortality, asking her to preserve his fame for all of time. What is more, Fortune *agrees* to these terms: she confirms for Boccaccio his lasting greatness, predicting his notoriety in times to come among glorious poets from history: "quin et Certaldum tuum et tuum nomen inter clara veterum nomina numerentur" ("Indeed, your name and that of your Certaldo will be numbered among the famous names of antiquity" [VI.1]).[44] Like Petrarch's advice to Boccaccio, Fortune's words to the author suggest that fame offers a kind of antidote to this world's transience. The very process of having one's story told provides temporary immunity from Fortune's spinning wheel.

For all of the narrator's sententious remarks on the vanity of worldly things, then, the *De casibus* evinces a profoundly divided approach to fame. The narrator no doubt recognizes, and fears, Fortune's frailty. The figures he encounters demonstrate that no amount of worldly power or goods can stave off our eventual mortal downfall. At the same time, Boccaccio implies that poets have the ability to counteract our inevitable demise by telling and retelling the stories of great individuals. They are, in Mary C. Flannery's apt words, "powerful trespasser[s] on Fortune's turf."[45] In the *De casibus*, Boccaccio provides a second life to the fallen individuals whose names and stories he archives, and in doing so he creates out of his treatise a monument "more permanent than bronze." Even as he insists on the ephemerality of good fortune, he presents fame as an escape from this cycle of transience.

Before the Falls: The Roman Triumph, *Tropaea*, and a Tradition of Triumphal Poetry

If seemingly incompatible with the didactic thrust of his treatise, Boccaccio's approach to fame as a means of escaping mortality is fundamental to a tradition of triumphal art and architecture. The ancient Romans had a practice of commemorating triumphal processions with memorials and arches. Called *trophee* or *tropaea* (singular: *tropaeum*), these objects were the spoils of war, or the more permanent markers of a transient victory: they converted fleeting conquests into enduring monuments to fame.[46] A tour of Rome and its surrounding areas offers a glimpse of the importance of these monuments to the history of this region. Triumphal arches, carvings, and memorials adorn the city.[47] Yet these physical structures built in honour of triumphal processions were only part of a larger approach to preserving the victor's glory. Equally important to this "process of memorialization" were the written accounts of these processions, created by biographers, historians, and poets.[48] Like their physical counterparts, these triumphal texts prolonged mortal accomplishments by fixing them in time, thereby keeping the ember of the victor's memory alive.[49] They were, in this regard, themselves a form of *tropaeum*, in that they shared with triumphal structures the aim of memorializing a moment of victory. As Beard notes, discussing Pompey's lavish triumphal procession of 61, "for all the undoubted importance of the memorials in marble, bronze, and gold," "It was writing, more than anything else, that inscribed the occasion in Roman memory; it was recalled, rethought, and resignified through the tales of Pompey's biographers, the poetic imagination of Lucan, the sometimes grinding narratives of ancient historians, the encyclopedic curiosity (and moralizing fervor) of the elder Pliny, and more."[50] Indeed, precisely because triumphs are momentary, it is "in the interests of the sponsors to ensure the memory lasts, to give the fleeting spectacle a more permanent form."[51] One way of safeguarding these memories was by commissioning art and architecture, crafted out of durable metals and heavy stones. Another approach was to generate written records of triumphal processions, which have the potential to outlast even physical monuments.

Sometimes, these two methods of extending the glory of the triumphator would be combined. Many triumphal arches contain inscriptions detailing the accomplishments of the victor, thus serving as a visual and textual reminder of his enduring excellence. A monument known as the

Fasti triumphales, for example, records the names and titles of every known triumphator from the beginning of the history of Rome.[52] Although today this monument survives only in fragments, having been excavated in pieces in the mid-sixteenth century, the names of more than two hundred triumphant generals (as well as the names of the people or places they conquered) remain visible. Victory, preeminence, triumph – all the provenance of the individual – are celebrated in this text-object as *communal* attributes, with each conqueror exalted among other conquerors. In this regard, the *Fasti triumphales* memorializes both individual conquest and shared fame. It shows victory passed like a baton from one conqueror to the next, a process that does not detract from the glory of the individual.

But to the victor and not the sculptor go the spoils. Monuments devoted to honouring triumphs, like the *Fasti triumphales*, were more often than not unattributed. It is for this reason that Beard warns us against assuming them to be "neutral documentary records" of historical moments, since "texts inscribed in stone rarely blazon their authors."[53] The same is true of triumphal accounts penned on softer surfaces. Many written records, particularly those composed by officials or administrators, remained anonymous. In accounts of triumphs written by poets, however, we find the opposite. When Virgil, Horace, Propertius, and Ovid adapt the Roman triumph to verse, the identity of the author becomes paramount – as significant as, if not more significant than, the subject of the procession himself. For these poets, the genre of the triumph is not only a mode of praising others but also a vehicle for self-promotion. Certain features of the procession – the grandeur of the ceremony and subject, the rituals devoted to honouring preeminence, the display of once glorious, yet now defeated prisoners – proved the ideal platform for showcasing (or, at least, proclaiming) one's poetic predominance. (And it is no accident that the practice of appointing oneself "first" in the language of previous poets, a phenomenon I explore in chapter 1, often accompanied these poetic triumphs, such as we see in Virgil's *Georgics*, below.) Thus while the poetic triumph "attracted imitators" because it "allowed a dazzling display of knowledge of the past while celebrating some cause or person in an epic key," as Aldo S. Bernardo writes, in certain cases, the victorious subject was ancillary to the author's message of self-congratulation.[54]

In the proem to the third *Georgic*, for example, Virgil announces his intent in a new poem to commemorate Caesar's triumphs, but he uses this opportunity to celebrate primarily his own poetic conquest:

Primus ego in patriam mecum, modo vita supersit,
Aonio rediens deducam vertice Musas;
primus Idumaeas referam tibi, Mantua, palmas

et viridi in campo templum de marmore ponam
propter aquam, tardis ingens ubi flexibus errat
Mincius et tenera praetexit harundine ripas.
in medio mihi Caesar erit templumque tenebit.
illi victor ego et Tyrio conspectus in ostro
centum quadriiugos agitabo ad flumina currus.
cuncta mihi, Alpheum linquens lucosque Molorci.
cursibus et crudo decernet Graecia caestu.
Ipse caput tonsae foliis ornatus olivae
dona feram.

I, first, if life but remain, will return to my country, bringing the Muses with me in triumph from the Aonian peak; first I will bring back to you, Mantua, the palms of Idumaea, and on the green plain will set up a temple in marble beside the water, where great Mincius wanders in lazy windings and fringes his banks with slender reeds. In the midst I will have Caesar, and he shall possess the shrine. In his honour I, a victor resplendent in Tyrian purple, will drive a hundred four-horse chariots beside the stream. For me all Greece will leave Alpheus and the groves of Molorcus, to compete in the foot race and with the brutal boxing glove. My brows graced with leaves of cut olive, I myself will award the prizes.[55]

Virgil's description of Caesar "in the midst" is overwhelmed by references to himself as a victor: "I, first … first I," "I, a victor … in Tyrian purple … For me all Greece … will leave." As Philip Hardie observes, Virgil the "triumphant poet … sing[s] of victorious, triumphant [Caesar]," and both "earn fame, glory and eternal name" in the process.[56] While on the surface in praise of Caesar, this passage honours predominantly Virgil himself.[57]

In the *Africa*, Petrarch invokes the triumph to a similar end: he transitions from celebrating the glory of Scipio Africanus to praising himself. Having celebrated the triumphs of both Scipio and Ennius in Book IX, Petrarch describes his 1341 laureation as a third procession. Announcing his "similar crown, like site, and glorious name," he honours himself alongside Scipio Africanus and Ennius as a fellow triumphator, who will give and receive eternal glory for immortalizing the deeds of his subject.[58] In the process, as James Simpson observes, he binds "state power and poetic enterprise" together in the "single motif of the triumphal laurel that crowns both imperial victor and poet."[59] Nowhere is a poet's exploitation of the Roman triumph as a means to praise himself more blatant.

Still other poets abandon the pretext of a triumphal subject nearly altogether. In the *Elegies*, Propertius grants a triumph to his elegiac muse, which is brought into being by his own poetic genius. He describes a grand procession in which Fame elevates him while his Muse rides victorious:

> Me Fama levat terra sublimis, et a me
> nata coronatis Musa triumphat equis,
> et mecum in curru parvi vectantur Amores,
> scriptorumque meas turba secuta rotas.

> Soaring Fame uplifts me from the earth, and the Muse that is born of me triumphs with garlanded steeds; with me in the chariot ride little Loves, and a throng of writers follows behind my wheels.[60]

Using the procession as a metaphor for his relationship to his poetic predecessors, Propertius refers to previous writers scornfully, as prisoners who hang at his wheels.[61] These poets serve as his literary ancestors: on the one hand, they set a precedent of excellence for Propertius to follow. On the other hand, they are also his rivals – the former conquerors of a near or distant past, who must clutch at his wheels in defeat.[62]

There is thus a profoundly self-authorizing element to the writing of poetic triumphs. Poets were keenly aware of the immense power they wielded as the guardians and propagators of fame, and they invoked the triumph to showcase this power. After describing the triumphal procession of his muse, Propertius even reminds readers that it is the writer who grants fame in the first place. Comparing himself to Homer, he asks who would have heard of Troy, were it not for the author of the *Iliad*. Who would know of Hector, whose body was dragged three times around the walls of Ilium?[63] Juxtaposing the collapse of an empire with the rise of Homer's prominence, Propertius recognizes that our knowledge of Troy is contingent on the poet who sang of it. But whereas Troy was reduced to ashes, Homer has found his reputation grow with time, his fame only escalating in death.[64] In what one scholar has described as a "self-congratulatory fantasy," in which the "topos of glory … allows poets to prolong their existence through the memory of posterity,"[65] Propertius concludes that Rome will likewise praise him long after his demise, his glory and name immortalized by his words.[66]

In the prologue to the *Polycraticus* (1156–9), John of Salisbury likewise attributes the fame of great individuals to the labours of writers. In a passage that interprets even the Holy Scriptures as a kind of *tropaeum*, or an apostolic record of human glory, he compares these "monimenta scriptorium" to triumphal arches:

> Quis enim Alexandros sciret aut Cesares, quis Stoicos aut Peripateticos miraretur, nisi eos insignirent monimenta scriptorum? Quis apostolorum et prophetarum

> amplexanda imitaretur uestigia, nisi eos posteritati diuinae litterae consecrassent? Arcus triumphales tunc proficiunt illustribus uiris ad gloriam, cum ex quibus causis et quorum sint, inpressa docet inscription. Liberatorem patriae, fundatorem quietis, tunc demum inspector agnoscit cum titulus triumphatorem ... indicat Constantinum. Nullus enim umquam constanti gloria claruit, nisi ex suo uel scripto alieno. Eadem est asini et cuiusuis imperatoris post modicum tempus gloria, nisi quatenus memoria alterutrius scriptorum beneficio prorogatur.
>
> Who would know of Alexander or Caesar, or would respect the Stoics or the Peripatetics, unless they had been distinguished by the memorials of writers? Whoever would have followed the footsteps of the cherished apostles and prophets, unless they had been consecrated for posterity in the Holy Scriptures? Triumphal arches advance the glory of illustrious men whenever inscriptions explain for what cause and for whom they have been erected. It is only because of the inscription on a triumphal arch that the onlooker recognises that Constantine ... is proclaimed liberator of his country and founder of peace. No one would ever be illuminated by perpetual glory unless he himself or someone else had written. The reputation of the fool and the emperor is the same after a moderate period of time except where the memory of either is prolonged by the beneficence of writers.[67]

It is the record of his deeds and not his deeds themselves that distinguishes the emperor from the fool, John of Salisbury suggests. It would follow that the author determines who is made glorious and who dies without consequence; who is memorialized as a triumphator and who as a captive. In other words, authors determine not only *if* we are remembered but also *how* we are remembered.

The accomplishments of great men and women would die with their bodies were it not for the physical and written records of their deeds. The author thus holds a pivotal place in the history and creation of triumphal monuments. But precisely because heroic actions can be memorialized in art and text, neither the downward turn of Fortune's wheel nor the inevitability of death is entirely tragic. Rather, an individual's defeat may precipitate his glory; in such cases, death is an apotheosis of sorts. Time, which in life destroys all things, can have the inverse effect at the moment of our demise, increasing rather than shrinking our glory.

Boccaccio's Triumphal Poetics: The *Amorosa visione*, Textual Monument

I have dwelled on the triumph and its history so as best to convey the significance of Boccaccio's choice to compose the *Amorosa visione*, to which I will now turn, as a series of triumphs. The narrator of the poem witnesses murals depicting famous poets, heroes, and generals from antiquity as prisoners in five triumphal processions: Wisdom, Fame, Wealth, Love, and Fortune. He spends the majority of the poem marvelling at the first four triumphs – an "ecstatic admiration" that may reflect, as Vittore Branca suggests, Boccaccio's adolescent yearning for worldly things: these processions "exalt precisely the goods to which he has most anxiously aspired in his youth."[68] The final procession, by contrast, displays the consequences of such desires. Outfitted as a conqueror, Fortune rides on a chariot behind her prisoners, an impressive group of famous men and women from throughout history, whom she made glorious and then brought low.

The fifth and final Triumph of Fortune thus functions as a partial reversal of the first four processions, which concern and for the most part celebrate worldly goods. As a reminder of the brevity of their former state, many of the figures we encounter in the earlier processions even reappear as prisoners in Fortune's Triumph. While fearsome, however, this procession never quite overshadows the redemptive power of worldly pursuits, and especially fame, as promoted in the earlier four triumphs. Certainly, the narrator's love of earthly things is presented by Boccaccio as problematic and overweening. (Nor should it surprise us when this figure remains largely unfazed by Fortune's Triumph, moving promptly from this scene to the garden of earthly delights.) But the poet suggests that the voices opposing this perspective, such as the moralizing guide, are equally erroneous and limited. As Juan Pablo Gil-Osle notes, the guide's "lack of … authority, as well as weakness, accumulate in order to present [her] as an un-authorized voice of virtue."[69] Fortune's dominance is likewise circumscribed, in this case by the form of the poem itself. We have already seen how the genre of the triumph showcases the fleeting nature of conquest. From its origins in ancient Rome, the spectacle celebrated individual greatness while reminding us that every victor falls. As a poem made up of triumphs, the *Amorosa visione* likewise operates on the assumption that every procession – even Fortune's – is necessarily transient. As all conquerors must fall, so too must Fortune submit to a force more powerful even than she, which in the *Amorosa visione* is the poet himself.

To this end, I will suggest that the *Amorosa visione*, like the *De casibus*, reflects Boccaccio's profound ambivalence on the subject of worldly goods, an ambivalence that was integral to the original Roman triumph. I will further argue that Boccaccio composes the *Amorosa visione* with an acute sense of the poet's capacity to archive worldly glory. Using Fortune's Triumph to warn readers that nothing worldly lasts, he also levies a powerful argument for writing as a potential avenue to immortality. Fixing the memory of his subjects textually and visually on the page – writing their names, that is, and describing their triumphs through ekphrasis – he presents both victory and defeat as temporary. It is only through the intervention of the poet that either can last, since writers have the power to convert transience into durability by making *tropaea* out of triumphs.

Of course, by the time Boccaccio writes the *Amorosa visione* as a young man living in Florence, having recently moved from his beloved Naples, the genre of the poetic triumph had waned in popularity.[70] As these processions stopped being celebrated, there was a corresponding decline in the triumphal works honouring them. It was thus with a deliberately nostalgic eye to a classical past that Boccaccio attempted this form. Still, the *Amorosa visione* is a confusing and at times flustering work, and it has not been well received by critics.[71] In certain places, the poet indulges in florid descriptiveness. Elsewhere, he does little more than catalogue names. The poem is also constrained by its structure. Its fifty cantos are preceded by three sonnets, in which Boccaccio spells out in an acrostic (which Luigi Surdich describes as "artificiosissimo")[72] the principal letters of every *terzina* in the work. These acrostic sonnets provide – and perhaps even determine – a map to his poem.

If stylistically overwrought, however, as a philosophical meditation on fame and the poet's role in its creation, the *Amorosa visione* is nothing short of extraordinary.[73] A work motivated by movement, yet equally defined by stasis, it explores Fortune's wheel as a perpetual force that the artist/poet alone has the power to impede. What this means is that victory can be both transient *and* fixed; worldly goods can be both ephemeral *and* enduring. As not one but a series of triumphs, the poem captures the inevitable progression of time even as it freezes time in text, a paradoxical feature of *tropaea* that Boccaccio dramatically exploits. Indeed, the *Amorosa visione* revels in the brevity of conquest, reminding readers with each new procession that victory is a temporary state. At the same time, the poet enshrines this cycle of conquest in the lines of his poem, marking a clear distinction between transitory victory and a more enduring fame.

The *Amorosa visione* is thus a textual oxymoron – a static record of mutability. The poem operates as a mechanism against the very transience it displays, chronicling for posterity the names of its subjects, and fixing these names in history in the process. While to some extent, this could be said of every poetic (or artistic) representation of flux, Boccaccio takes particular pains to highlight the immortalizing function of his poem through ekphrasis. The narrator does not witness actual triumphal processions but rather artistic representations of them. What this means is that the full course of each triumph is ostensibly memorialized on the wall before he even appraises it. He sees figures who, though frozen in paintings, are so realistically rendered that they appear *still* to be engaged in the very activities that made them famous. Aristotle, sitting by himself in the Triumph of Wisdom, appears *still* lost in thought.[74] Troilus seems to be forever drawing closer to Criseyde (VII.30). Indeed, so vivid is the image of Dido, sword in hand, depicted next to Aeneas, that the narrator is frightened by her behaviour even from a distance (IX.7–10). Though these actions are part of a distant historical past, they appear as though ongoing in Boccaccio's poem.

Clearly a parody of Dante's pilgrim, the narrator is an impetuous pleasure seeker, who repeatedly rejects the moral inducements of his guide to pursue his own whims. He perceives the acquisition of worldly goods (with the possible exception of wealth, which is portrayed as base) as worthy. In the Triumph of Wisdom, philosophers including Plato, Galen, and Boethius muse contentedly in a pleasant green space; poets, among them Homer, Virgil, Ovid, and Dante, converse about the pleasures and joys of living (V.43). While alluding to Dante's Limbo for intellectuals, a space bereft of hope and joy, Boccaccio also overturns this model by presenting the prisoners of Wisdom as *happy*. In the process, he implies that knowledge itself is a fulfilling goal. In the Triumph of Fame, prisoners are commemorated not at the occasion of their fall but at the height of their glory, often enacting whatever it was that made them famous in the first place. Ulysses and Diomedes look to be still planning stratagems (VIII.29–30); Dido is ever on the edge of falling in love with Aeneas;[75] Julius Caesar, Octavian, and Pompey all appear together, adorned with beautiful weapons and armour, about to gain honour by entering into battle. Caesar is even crowned with that perennial sign of undying glory: the triumphal laurel (X.25–51).

In this regard, although Boccaccio borrows extensively from the *Commedia*, adopting, among other things, Dante's metrical scheme, concept of a dream vision, and expression of triumphs in terms of allegory, he also uses his poem to subvert Dante's lesson that worldly goods must be renounced on the path to spiritual salvation.[76] In an early scene parodying Matthew 17 and *Inferno* I, for example, the narrator is confronted with two doors: the first is narrow, at the top of a steep climb, and it looks to have never been entered. This door leads to salvation and eternal repose. The second door is broad and inviting, and sounds of revelry emanate from within. It promises its chooser worldly treasures. Inscribed above its arch are the words: "Ricchezze, dignità, ogni tesoro, / gloria mondana copiosamente / do a color che passan nel mio coro" ("Riches, dignity, every treasure, / worldly glory do I give abundantly to those who join my chorus" [III.16–18]). Merrily dismissing the supplications of his increasingly disheartened guide, who urges him to take the narrow virtuous course, Boccaccio starts without hesitation toward the wider portal: "Ora che siamo quasi nel sentieri, / andiam, vediamo questi ben fallaci" ("Now that we are almost on the path, / let us go, let us see these fallacious good things" [III.37–8]). It is as though he says along with Augustine, "God make me good, just not yet."[77]

It should hardly surprise us that the narrator rejects the stringent teachings of his guide, who is an amalgam of Dante's Virgil and Boethius's Lady Philosophy. She is a moralizing crank, who cannot distinguish between the false sheen of wealth and the enduring virtues of wisdom and glory. To her, all worldly things are equally bad, a perspective neither Boccaccio nor his narrator appears to share. It is little wonder that instead of heeding her instruction, the narrator wishes to pursue wisdom alongside great thinkers, contemporary and ancient, and fame alongside brave generals and heroes.

Indeed, of all the worldly goods celebrated in the *Amorosa visione* it is glory that is the most compelling. The narrator himself testifies to the posthumous fame of his subjects, often to the chagrin of his moralizing guide, such as we see in his encounter with Dante in the Triumph of Wisdom. Crowned, like Caesar, with the triumphal laurel, Dante is in the company of the epic poets with whom he had aligned himself in *Inferno* IV – Homer, Virgil, Ovid, Lucan, and Horace – and surrounded by a throng of admirers.[78] Boccaccio hails Dante as his "maestro" (a role Dante reserves for Virgil) and the "gloria de' Fiorentin" (VI.2, VI.14), from whom he takes every good thing. He expresses his wish to remain at the portrait of Dante, gazing forever on his image. This act will give him consolation, he claims, because it will confirm his belief that although Dante is dead – and too little honoured while alive – "vivrà la fama [sua], e ben saputa" ("[his] fame will live on, and well recognized" [VI.13]). As Kathryn McKinley rightly notes, "this mural, above all, is not one the author Boccaccio wishes to be consigned to the moral scrap heap."[79] Yet the guide rejects his desire to remain there. In a passage echoing Beatrice's admonition of Dante, devastated by the sudden departure of Virgil (*Pg* XXX.57), she asks, "Che più miri? forse credi / renderli col mirar le morte posse? ("Why do you gaze more? Do you believe perhaps you can render him back his dead powers by staring?" [VI.23–4]). In the *Commedia*, Beatrice's words remind Dante of his poem's larger Christian mandate: as Sylvia Huot points out, they represent the "pilgrim's experience of learning to give up his attachment to worldly things," an experience that involves "wean[ing] himself from his dependence on the pagan poet Virgil."[80] In the corresponding scene from the *Amorosa visione*, however, the priorities are reversed, and it is precisely Boccaccio's attachment to Dante that amplifies both poets' fame. The scene calls to mind two corresponding tableaux: first of Dante, laurelled and triumphant among the great poets of antiquity. The second is of Boccaccio, gazing reverently at his maestro and aligning himself with the poet in the process. Boccaccio's recollection of Dante's fame thus leads to the proliferation of his and Dante's memory, even if this experience undermines Dante's lesson in the *Commedia* that, relative to heaven's eternal movement, glory is insignificant.[81]

It is not only the narrator of the *Amorosa visione* who is limited by his appetite for worldly goods here. His female guide is also constrained by her rejection of it. The narrator's dismissal of her words is just and swift:

> Donna, tu non sai
> neente perché tal mirar m'aggrata
> costui cui miro, ché se tu il sapessi
> non parleresti forse sì turbata. (VI.30–3)

> Lady, you know nothing of the reasons why it pleases me to look on him I contemplate; if you knew them, maybe you would not speak so disconcertingly.

Echoing Virgil's admission of inadequacy in the *Commedia*, "Quanto ragion qui vede, / dir ti poss'io; da indi in là t'aspetta / pur a Beatrice, ch'è opra di fede" ("As much as reason sees here, I can tell you, beyond that, you must wait for Beatrice, for it is a matter of faith" [*Pg* XVIII.46–8]),[82] Boccaccio's guide acknowledges her limitations. "Veramente se tu il mi dicessi," she concedes, "nol saprei me" ("Truly if you were to tell me why, I would not know any better" [VI.34–5]). Despite her Beatrice-like insistence on the futility of earthly fame, she would seem more closely aligned in this passage with Dante's Virgil, since her ideology constrains her discourse and is ultimately rejected by the poet.[83] As Huot notes, Boccaccio gives us a protagonist who is "in many ways an 'anti-Dante,'" and "in so doing [he] raises the questions we always had about Dante but were afraid to ask: Can human love really lead to the beatific vision? Must we abandon the human … in order to write good love poetry?"[84] And, we should add, can fame truly make man immortal? Implicitly answering in the affirmative to this last question, Boccaccio pursues courses of action that were presented in the *Commedia* yet circumvented, since Dante could follow them only obliquely in the poem he wished to write. Whereas Dante moves toward heavenly salvation, and is even scolded by Beatrice for looking back at Virgil, Boccaccio dangles a precisely pagan form of poetic immortality before his readers as a worthy endeavour, one that is supplementary if not an alternative to Christian salvation.[85] What is more, he suggests that it is through writing that one can generate and achieve this sought-for end.

Thus if the Triumph of Fortune casts a pall over the poem's otherwise celebration of worldly goods, it is only a temporary one. Instructing the narrator to banish his longing for these things, his guide prepares him in advance for the suffering he will witness: "Ogni mondan valor vedrai conquiso / in termine assai brieve" ("You will see every earthly good conquered in a very short time" [XXXIII.85–8]). She assures him that this destruction is the consequence of the fickle ways of Fortune: "con mirabile voltare / dona a costui a quell'altro levando, / come vedi un salir, l'altro abassare" ("with marvelous turning, [Fortune] gives to one what she takes from another, as you see one rise, you see another fall" [XXXIV.10–12]). The narrator is momentarily frightened by her message, to the point where he considers changing his course (XXXVII.22–42). But while "a conversion seems to … tak[e] place," it is deferred in favour of the prospect of future pleasures – the narrator moves blithely from Fortune's procession to the garden of earthly delights – and so, as Robert Hollander notes, "one need only read on a bit to see how insubstantial are the traveler's claims to virtue."[86]

To his guide's wheedling protests – she pleads with him to turn back to the path of virtue – the narrator responds with disdain:

A te che face
l'entrar là dentro ed un poco vedere?
Or veggio ben che tu ogni tuo parere
vuo' pur seguir in ciascheduna cosa
e fai quel che tu vuoli a me volere. (XXXVIII.1–2, XXXVIII.4–6)

What does it do to you if I go in there and see a little? Now I see well that you want me to follow your own opinion in everything and make me want whatever you want.

Certainly, the narrator's remonstration with his guide here is satirical. Whereas Dante's pilgrim learns to let go of his worldly desires, the narrator of the *Amorosa visione* becomes increasingly frustrated by his guide's intentions to save him, to the point where he dismisses her entirely in favour of following his own whims. Still, I think the guide's inability to convince the narrator of Fortune's dominion operates on a level beyond parody. Perhaps the narrator fails to be persuaded of Fortune's tyranny because he (and for that matter, we) has already witnessed the limits of her authority. If nothing worldly lasts, we must ask, then why does the poet present us with so much evidence to the contrary?

Indeed, the *Amorosa visione* testifies to the stabilizing potential of earthly goods on multiple levels. Although the order in which he presents these processions would suggest the ultimate conquest of Fortune over the triumphs of Wisdom, Fame, Wealth, and Love, for example, the poet ultimately shies away from recommending one triumph as predominant over the last. Instead, the narrator witnesses what appears to be an infinite cycle of victors, rejoicing in the glory and renown of those involved in each spectacle. What becomes clear by the final procession is that the triumph form is motivated by precisely the kind of transience that the guide attributes to Fortune ("she gives to one what she takes from another …"). Because *trionfi* depend, both structurally and historically, on an ongoing cycle of victory and defeat, moreover, by portraying her as a triumphator, Boccaccio suggests that Fortune, too, will be conquered. One of many in the poem, her triumph is necessarily fleeting, fated to be cut short by an impending victor.

A second and more pervasive reason that Fortune's power is limited in the *Amorosa visione* is that the poem itself functions as a textual monument. Much like that early Roman record of triumphators, the *Fasti triumphales*, it archives the names and glory of the figures from all five processions. In spite of the guide's insistence to the contrary, then, Fortune cannot possibly "destroy" or "take away" the worldly fame granted to the figures in the poem because Boccaccio has already given it to them. The names (and, as we are told, the images) of the glorious have already been recorded by the poet, witnessed by the narrator, and further embedded in the readers' minds. As Boccaccio demonstrates in this work, and as Chaucer will suggest in the *House of Fame*, a poet's inscription of the names of the famous is a mechanism – if not a foolproof one – for prolonging their glory.

By having his narrator ignore his guide's words of warning, then, Boccaccio seems to be demarcating the very real limits of Fortune's influence in his poem, a work in which poets hold more power than the Goddess. The *Amorosa visione* explores in this regard the intersection of transient victory and long-lasting fame, and the ways in which poets have the power to convert one into the other. Victory is a fleeting and solitary achievement, wholly dependent on the defeat of others. Fame, by contrast, which sometimes develops from victory, is both communal and durable. Fame depends on other people, and especially poets, who play an integral role in the creation and maintenance of reputation. Thus while Boccaccio does not fully endorse the perspective of his narrator, who is utterly enamoured of worldly pleasures and gives little thought to his own salvation, he appears equally opposed to the guide's rejection of this view. She cannot perceive the value and potential of fame – its very real ability to prolong our lives – and so does not align with the poet's vision. If we learn anything from the *Amorosa visione* it is that a virtuous life does not always preclude the experience of rewards on earth. Rather, Boccaccio seems to suggest, these transient goods can lead to more lasting ones.

To conclude this lengthy section on Boccaccio's triumphal poetics in the *De casibus* and *Amorosa visione*, I have argued that while these works contain explicit denunciations of worldly goods, they also instruct readers on the value of enduring glory, propagating a thoroughly pagan belief that fame can make man immortal. Telling stories of famous men and women, Boccaccio offers renown as an exception to our inevitable march toward mortality, an attitude he develops in the *Amorosa visione* and carries forward in the *De casibus*. Examining the latter work through the lens of the former thus reveals important correspondences between the two, such as the author's longstanding interest in writing as a form of triumphal monument. We further see that the *De casibus*, with its constant rotation of glorious individuals having first their victories and then their falls recorded, is a kind of triumphal procession, but with a focus on the downward, as opposed to upward, spin of Fortune's wheel. Nor does Boccaccio's shift in focus correspond to a less vigorous pursuit of fame in the *De casibus*. On the contrary, this treatise functions as an impassioned plea to future writers for remembrance. An archive of prominent figures from Boccaccio's past and present, it requires its readers to reflect on each portrait of famous men and women as part of a larger literary tradition, and on its creator as part of a genealogy of illustrious poets. Fame engenders more fame, and we are perpetuated in the memories of others.

Chaucer's Eternal "Monk's Tale"

In what follows, I will suggest that the "Monk's Tale" appeals to readers as a petition for immortal glory in a world defined by flux, an idea for his poem that Chaucer appears to derive from the *De casibus* and perhaps even the *Amorosa visione*.[87] Although repeatedly lamenting the vanity of mortal things, the Monk does not, in the end, present fame as fleeting. Instead, he shows that ruin and defeat are only temporary, whereas glory has the potential to be eternal. Retelling stories that have endured for centuries, he regales his fellow pilgrims with catalogues of worldly accomplishments and acquisitions. When these catalogues are committed to the page, I propose, they become poetic triumphs: written monuments of transient victories, memorialized by the author himself.

To this end, Chaucer highlights his own role as an archivist of fame by presenting himself as a compiler of *tropaea*. Within the fiction of the *Canterbury Tales*, he is transcribing his fellow pilgrims' oral narratives: he "moot reherce / hir tales alle, be they better or werse" (I.3173–4). When we encounter these stories, however, we read them as text. If we are bothered by one tale, we can always "turne over the leef and chese another" (I.3177). There are thus two chronological vectors at play in the "Monk's Tale," each of which promotes a vastly different lesson regarding the potential longevity of earthly fame. While for the Monk and his fellow pilgrims, his portraits of men and women who "endeth wretchedly" vanish into thin air with the Knight's interruption, for the reader, they remain fixed on the page, textual evidence of these figures' enduring reputations, which have withstood the ravages of time.[88] From this perspective, not only has the Knight misread the Monk's narrative by dismissing it in favour of tales of those who "abideth in prosperity" (VII.2777) – since "abide" is precisely what these individuals have done – but so, too, have we, puzzling for centuries over how an "outridere" who "lovede venerie" (I.166) and other fine things can have such a dismal outlook on earthly things.[89]

Of course, this interpretation of the tale contradicts a theory of the narrative provided by the Monk himself, who attempts to control the reception of his words along the lines of genre. Organizing his portraits according to the motif of Fortune's transience, the Monk insists that he will narrate a series of "tragedies," which he defines as stories of men who fall from "heigh degree" to low:

Tragedie is to seyn a certain storie,
As olde bookes maken us memorie,
Of hym that stood in greet prosperitee,
And is yfallen out of heigh degree
Into myserie, and endeth wrecchedly. (VII.1373–7)

But the Monk promises a narrative payoff that never materializes, defining the generic parameters of his tale only to flout the very rules that he sets for himself. Despite his rigorous attention to form, that is, his tale never wholly corresponds to his description of it as tragic, nor does it appear governed at every instant by an arbitrary Lady Fortune.[90] Indeed, in many portraits, Fortune plays no role at all. Of Lucifer we are told that he is immune to the whims of Fortune, since "Fortune may noon angel deere" (VII.1001). Lucifer falls only because of his wicked behaviour: "from heigh degree … fel he *for his synne*" (VII.2002; italics added). The portrait of Adam does not contain a single reference to Fortune. The Monk insists that it is Adam's "misgovernaunce" that precipitates his fall from "hye prosperitee" (VII.2012–13). Sampson is brought to ruin because of his mistress Delilah's betrayal; the lesson to be learned is not of Fortune's transience but rather of woman's untrustworthiness. The Monk concludes this portrait with a warning:

Beth war by this ensample oold and playn
That no men telle hir conseil til hir wyves
Of swich thyng as they wolde han secree fayn,
If that it touche hir lymes or hir lyves. (VII.2091–4)

Husbands must be careful what they reveal to their wives, he counsels. Lady Fortune, however, receives no mention.

In still other portraits, the lesson of Fortune's impermanence appears as though arbitrarily pasted onto what would otherwise be a tale of victory.[91] The Monk celebrates his subjects' heroic and military conquests, expounding for many lines on their excellence before turning at last to their fall. We are treated to a dazzling report of Sampson's physical achievements. "This noble almyghty champioun," without a weapon "save his handes tweye, / ... slow and al torente the leoun" (VII.2023–5). After killing the lion, "thre hundred foxes took Sampson for ire, / And alle hir tayles he togydre bond" (VII.2031–2). At last, "a thousand men he slow eek with his hond, / And hadde no wepen but an asses cheke" (VII.2037–8).

The first half of Hercules's portrait similarly catalogues its hero's labours, accumulating his physical feats like trophies on display.[92]

He slow and rafte the skyn of the leoun;
He of Centauros leyde the boost adoun;
He Arpies slow, the crueel bryddes felle;
He golden apples rafte of the dragoun;
He drow out Cerberus, the hound of helle;
He slow the crueel tyrant Busirus
And made his hors to frete hymn flessh and boon;
He slow the firy serpent venymus;
Of Acheloys two hornes he brak oon;
And he slow Cacus in a cave of stoon;
He slow the geant Antheus the stronge;
He slow the grisly boor, and that anon;
And bar the hevene on his nekke longe. (VII.2098–2110)

In his narrative of Nebuchadnezzar, the Monk marvels at the King's indescribable glory, splendour, and riches:

The myghty trone, the precious tresor,
The glorious ceptre, and roial magestee
That hadde the kyng Nabugodonosor
With tonge unneth may discryved bee.
He twyes wan Jerusalem the citee;
The vessel of the temple he with hym ladde.
At Babiloigne was his sovereyn see,
In which his glorie and his delit he hadde. (VII.2143–50)

Before Fortune turns against him, Caesar, too, ascends to heights of glory through his great wit, vigour, and deeds:

By wisedom, manhede, and by greet labour,
from humble bed to roial magestee,

up roos he Julius, the conquerour,
That wan al th'occident by land and see. (VII.2671–4)

In these instances, the Monk illustrates the *full* rotation of Fortune's wheel: his heroes climb to heights of power before being brought low on account of numerous factors – a rival, their own folly, or the recklessness or deceit of a loved one. Rather than "tragedies" as the Monk defines them, these narratives of those who abide "in greet prosperitee" before descending "into myserie" seem to follow the narrative arc of a poetic triumph, since they begin with a description of a famous figure's ascent. While eventually narrated, the demise of each subject, a fall that every conqueror must eventually face, is described only briefly. (The Monk, like the Knight, seems to prefer stories of good fortune to those of devastation.) A mere footnote to a larger story of heroic exploits, this fall is a small price to pay for lasting notoriety, the brevity of defeat paling in comparison to the scope and duration of worldly renown.

Chaucer heightens our impression of the rewards of reputation by stripping the *De casibus* of its moral framework.[93] According to Boccaccio, as we recall, the *De casibus* contains stories of only the most famous, so that when contemporary princes see these individuals brought low they will recognize their own weakness and change their wicked ways. Although the Monk consistently laments the far-reaching arm of Lady Fortune, he does not claim to do so for the sake of edifying his contemporaries. In the absence of a clear didactic ambition, however, his portraits of famous individuals are just that: stories of men and women who have reaped acclaim, or at least recognition, for their memorable deeds and great wealth. We are regaled with reports of Caesar's martial successes, the high nobility and worth of Peter of Spain, and the royal majesty of Antiochus. Of Holofernes we are told that never was there a captain or a king who put more reigns in subjection. Never was any man stronger nor had a greater reputation in his time. Alexander is introduced with similar words of praise:

Comparisoun myghte nevere yet ben maked
Bitwexe hym and another conqueror;
For al this world for drede of hym hath quaked. (VII.2639–41)

Even Nero, though he "were as vicius / As any feend," is described in superlative terms (VII.2463–4). According to Suetonius, he had this "wyde world" in "subjeccioun, / bothe est and west, [south], and septemtrioun" (VII.2466–7). Reminiscent of the "General Prologue," in which every figure is "parfeet" in his field, these descriptions suggest a celebration of mortal accomplishment rather than a lament on the transience of good fortune. We are reminded over and over that reputation outlives individual victories and falls, surpassing these events in significance.

The Monk himself fixates on the enduring fame of his subjects, counting on our familiarity with the stories he tells.[94] He begins his portrait of Alexander by emphasizing its very "commonness":

> The storie of Alisaundre is so commune
> That every wight that hath discrecioun
> Hath herd somewhat or al of his fortune.
> This wyde world, as in conclusioun,
> He wan by strengthe, or for his hye renoun. (VII.2631–5)

What makes Alexander's story so common is his "hye renoun" itself. In other words, the Monk celebrates Alexander for being famous – for having his story sung in the far corners of the world.[95] Nor does Alexander's eventual defeat detract from his glory; rather, he remains fixed in our memories at the height of his power. What we recall about this mighty conqueror – what we repeat about Alexander over and again – is the story of his fame itself, a fame that outlasts his eventual fall.

The portrait of Hercules likewise features abundant praise of the hero's reputation – and we should not forget that it is Hercules who stands alongside Alexander on the shoulders of Lady Fame (*House of Fame* III.1413). The Monk begins with a call to praise:

> Of Hercules, the sovereyn conquerour,
> Syngen his werkes laude and heigh renoun;
> For in his tyme of strengthe he was the flour. (VII.2095–7)

So great is the glory of Hercules that it extends long after his death, with his reputation eclipsing that of any man since time began. His name is sung throughout this "wyde world":

> Was nevere wighte, sith that this world bigan,
> That slow so manye monstres as dide he.
> Thurghout this wyde world his name ran,
> What for his strengthe and for his heigh bountee,
> And ever reawme wente he for to see. (VII.2111–15)

The final lines of Hercules's portrait, warning us to "beth war, for whan that Fortune list to glos, / Thanne wayteth she her man to overthrowe" (VII.2140–1), do little to palliate the exaltation of worldly fame pervading the overall account. Rather, the Monk's description of the range and duration of his reputation seems as though designed in response to arguments that glory is fleeting. While eventually the memory of Hercules might fade, this day will not come as long as his story is told.

Even as he labours to categorize his portraits as stories of men and women brought low by the close of their lives, the Monk thus unravels his own efforts by showing that not all earthly things are transient, and that fame, particularly when it is generated by poets, can last for centuries. As written records of fleeting victories, these narratives owe as much – at least conceptually – to a tradition of triumphal poetry as they do to a tragic Boethian precedent. Some of the Monk's subjects, like Nebuchadnezzar and Balthasar, and Pompey and Caesar, even succeed one another historically as well as textually, giving the impression of a real and ongoing procession of victors. Perhaps it is with a vision of successive triumphators in mind that the Monk depicts Caesar and Pompey as victors of equal strength and valour, who are both targeted unjustly by Fortune. He laments how "to thise grete conqueroures two / Fortune was first freend, and sithe foo" (VII.2722–3). To this end, he describes each figure's ascent to power separately, beginning with Caesar ("Up roos he Julius, the conquerour") before turning his attention to his predecessor, Pompey, "that of the Orient hadde al the chivalry / As fer as that the day bigynneth dawe." In a way, then, the *De Julio* contains not one but two portraits, since the Monk interrupts his treatment of Caesar to describe Pompey's military career: "But now a litel while I wol biwaille / This Pompeus, this noble governour / Of Rome, which that fleigh at this bataille" (VII.2687–9). At the moment when he must relate Pompey's defeat, however, the Monk shifts his focus again, this time back to Caesar, to celebrate his victorious return to Rome.

So insistent is the Monk on presenting Pompey's fall as Caesar's victory that he defies his purported source to award Caesar a Roman triumph. Hailing the new conqueror's arrival, he declares, "to Rome ageyn repaireth Julius / With his triumphe, lauriat ful hye" (VII.2695–6), before "recomend[ing]" us to "Lucan" as a source (VII.2720). Lucan, however, does not give Caesar a triumph in the *Pharsalia*. On the contrary, he insists that civil war yields no triumphs, because nobody profits when countryman fights against countryman ("bella geri placuit nullos habitura triumphos" [1.12]).[96] But the Monk cares little for textual fidelity. Nor, it would seem, does he have the temperament for telling tragic stories. Taking an epic notorious for violence, destruction, and civic unrest, he *converts* it into a poetic triumph, commemorating Pompey and Caesar together in a single textual monument. If in life these two were bitter rivals, in death their enmity is elided in the final parity of a posthumous fame.

Of all the stories in his "celle" (VII.1971–2), it is Zenobia's in which the Monk reveals the extent of his triumphal poetics. Together with the *De Julio*, this portrait features one of two triumphal processions in the "Monk's Tale" (and we should not forget the correlation between military and authorial glory in poetic triumphs, nor the historic precedent of authors using the martial accomplishments of their subjects to exalt themselves).[97] Like many of the vignettes in the tale, Zenobia's portrait is predominantly celebratory in tone and content. The Monk spends the vast majority of the 127 lines that make up his account (the longest in his tale) praising the queen for her rise to power. He describes her prowess in battle, bravery, and gentility, all of which he claims to have read about in earlier writings, on account of Zenobia's great fame:

Cenobia, of Palymerie queene,
As writen Persiens of hir noblesse,
So worthy was in armes and so keene
That no wight passed hire in hardynesse,
Ne in linage, ne in oother gentillesse. (VII.2247–51)

The Monk admires Zenobia's figure ("of hir shap she myghte nat been amended" [VII.2254]), athleticism – she can outwrestle any young man, "were he never so wight / ther myghte no thyng in hir armes stonde" (VII.2267–8) – and chastity: she "kepte hir maydenhod from every wight; / To no man deigned hire for to be bonde" (VII.2269–70). When she marries Odenathus, this union only adds to her glory. Together, Zenobia and her husband make a formidable pair:

They conquered manye regnes grete
In the orient, with many a fair citee,
Apertenaunt unto the magestee
Of Rome, and with strong hond held hem ful faste,
Ne nevere myghte hir foomen doon hem flee. (VII.2313–17)

When Odenathus dies, Zenobia continues to dominate in battle: she "mightily / the regnes held" (VII.2326–7). The Monk catalogues the many kings, rulers, and generals over whom she triumphs. These include the Emperor of Rome, Claudius (VII.2335), the Roman Galien (VII.2336), and every Armenian, Egyptian, Syrian, and Arabian soldier that she fights (VII.2337–40). This survey of warriors indicates Zenobia's superior competence in battle while locating her within a sequence of victors throughout history. She is part of a triumphal tradition, a genealogy of illustrious men and women whose fame is durable even if their individual victories are transient.

It is only after celebrating her many successes that the Monk alludes to Zenobia's fall. Still, he directs us *outside* of his narrative – to his "maister" Petrarch – for the details of this conquest:

> How that al this proces fil in dede,
> Why she conquered and what title had therto,
> And after, of hir meschief and hire wo,
> How that she was biseged and ytake –
> Lat hym unto my maister Petrak go,
> That writ ynough of this, I undertake. (VII.2321–6)

By pointing us to Petrarch, the Monk seems to suggest either that he does not *want* to narrate Zenobia's fall or that this event is outside the purview of his portrait, both of which are at odds with his desire to tell tragedies. Instead of dwelling on "hire wo," he deflects narrative accountability for the story of "how that al this proces fil in dede," focusing instead on Zenobia's many successes.

When the Monk can no longer forestall narrating her defeat, he flouts the tragic parameters of his tale again, shifting his focus from captive to captor. As he does in the *De Julio*, he makes the new victor, Aurelian, the grammatical and narrative subject of his account:

> Aurelian, whan that the governaunce
> Of Rome cam into his handes tweye,
> with his legions he took his weye
> Toward Cenobie, and shortly for to seye,
> He made hire flee, and atte laste hire hente,
> And fettred hire, and eek hire children tweye,
> And wan the land, and hoom to Rome he wente. (VII.2351–2, VII.2354–8)

The effect of this shift is striking: the Monk records Aurelian's conquest instead of Zenobia's defeat, a change in perspective underscored by his description of Aurelian in terms similar to those he had previously applied to Zenobia. As Zenobia was a "myghty" and "worthy" queen, so too is Aurelian a "grete Romayn" (VII.2361).

Even as a prisoner, Zenobia is honoured. The Monk relates how she is crowned "after hir degree," gilded, covered in jewels, and made to walk before her captor's chariot as the spoils of his triumph: "Biforen his triumphe walketh shee" (VII.2363). Leading the ceremony, attired as a queen, she adds luster to Aurelian's procession by virtue of her excellence. Chaucer draws on ancient Roman custom here. Triumphators had a practice of adorning their most illustrious prisoners in gold and finery, and positioning them at the front of their processions for all to see. Indeed, these captives were a vital component of the ceremony: preeminent in their own time, they set a standard of excellence for later conquerors to follow. The Greek historian Zosimus, for example, describes how Aurelian placed Zenobia at the front of his procession after conquering Palmyra. A regal prisoner, ornamented with gold and accompanied by attendants, she was so laden with treasure that she required assistance in carrying it.[98] Of course, such opulence could not "help but raise questions about exactly who was the star of the event," as Beard observes, which set an obstacle in the path of victors intent on highlighting their own preeminence.[99] While "glamorous and impressive prisoners were powerful proof of the splendor of the victory achieved," there was a danger in putting these qualities on display, because "the more impressive they appeared, the more likely they were to steal the show and to upstage the triumphing general himself." In triumphs led by gilded, illustrious prisoners, in other words, there was always the potential for "slippage between victor and victim."[100]

Whereas the spectacle of a Roman triumph could celebrate only one individual at a time, however, poetic triumphs can glorify communal fame. These works showcase victory's transience without lamenting that transience, because the question of who is the winner or loser depends only on our perspective – on where we choose to look – like the experience of gazing upon Donatello's *David*. Poetic triumphs can thus inhabit, and even exploit, this "slippage" Beard describes between victor and victim. For example, Chaucer can celebrate the glory of Zenobia before turning to her conqueror, Aurelian, using his triumphal procession to illustrate the transfer of victory from one individual to the next. Such a manoeuvre points to his profound understanding of the poetic triumph's capacity to celebrate multiple individuals at once. Minimizing the distance between captor and captive, Chaucer levels temporary hierarchies in the interest of recording power in flux.

Chaucer's description of Zenobia as an illustrious captive, leading Aurelian's triumphal chariot, reinforces both her and her captor's excellence even while it showcases the queen's defeat. In this way, the Monk celebrates what appears to be a continuum of victors, extolling the martial accomplishments of Zenobia before praising Aurelian for his conquest over Palmyra. The attention and focus with which he treats Zenobia's many military successes mean that her ultimate fall – briefly (and, it would seem, unwillingly) rendered – does not detract from her glory. Rather, preeminence shifts from one conqueror to the next on only a nominal level, with the vestiges of greatness remaining with the defeated queen long after we have moved on to her conqueror's procession. In poetic triumphs, as in Chaucer's poem as a whole, we can always transfer our attention to an earlier or a later episode of conquest. We can always "turne over the leef and chese another tale."

Not only does the portrait of Zenobia contain a triumphal procession, then, but it also unfolds like one, with the Monk recording his subjects' consecutive victories, which together resolve themselves into a kind of communal fame. Celebrating Zenobia for her rise to power, when it comes time to narrate her defeat, he shifts his focus from the queen to her victor, immortalizing both in a state of collective splendour. Of course, as a "myghty man" in his own right (VII.1951), the Monk has a vested interest in memorializing his subjects.[101] His focus on their heroic exploits is perhaps even aspirational: should he, too, fall, he may yet be remembered by a great poet. Nor do I think it is a coincidence that Chaucer has the Knight, the mightiest of the Canterbury pilgrims, interrupt the Monk's narrative. With this interruption, Chaucer draws his reader's attention to the connection between the Monk's alleged "tragedies" and the Knight's "gladsom" story of a "povre" man "wex[ing] fortunat" (VII.2776–7), which begins, as we recall, with a gloss referencing Theseus's triumphal procession ("Iamque domos patrias, Scithice post aspera gentis Perlia, laurigero.")[102] We should also note that it is the Monk who was supposed to follow, or "quite" the Knight in the storytelling competition. The Knight's interruption thus lends a cyclical quality to the *Canterbury Tales*. Perhaps this work was never meant to be read as linear – as a pilgrimage from the Tabard Inn to Canterbury, with a single victor at the end, that is – but rather as a rotation of infinite conquests and falls. Perhaps Chaucer conceptualized the *Tales* as a cycle of triumphs, with the Knight's interruption spinning us back to the bottom of Fortune's wheel, where we will witness its upswing anew.

At the very least, the Knight's interruption reminds us that while his epic romance differs from the Monk's "tragedies" in form and perspective, both tales describe what is essentially a sequence of victory and defeat. Both, moreover, offer a similar lesson, as pronounced solemnly by Theseus at Arcite and Palamon's funeral-turned-wedding, that it is "best, as for worthy fame, / To dyen whan that he is best of name" (I.3055–6) because our existence is cyclical and transient: "Speces of thynges and progressiouns / Shullen enduren by successiouns, / And nat eterne" (I.3013–15). Like the Knight, the Monk reminds us of the great "remembraunce" we have of famous men and women, even while their individual downfalls and rivalries fade. Paling in comparison to their posthumous reputations, these specific ends and enmities appear insignificant, as mere footnotes to larger stories of glory and conquest. What we learn from the "Monk's Tale" is that falls, like victories, are only transient. In the best of cases, moreover, they give way to an enduring fame, a second life for both the author and his subject that can withstand the test of time.[103]

Chaucer's triumphal poetics thus extends beyond his memorialization of famous figures in the "Monk's Tale." He further incorporates the language and conventions of the triumph into his narrative, using the procession as a literary device with which to explore the relationship between poetry and fame, victor and captive, and spectacle and monument. What is more, our attentiveness to Chaucer's triumphal poetics provides possible answers to numerous inconsistencies in the "Monk's Tale" that have been noted by readers over the years.[104] I have already discussed how the Monk's worldliness, as described in the "General Prologue," appears far less aberrative when we consider his tale in terms of a poetic triumph. But scholars have also questioned the significance of the enigmatic Latin authority, "Trophee" (glossed in the Ellesmere as *tropaeum*), the Monk's attributed source for Hercules's establishment of pillars at each end of the earth: "At bothe the worldes endes, seith Trophee, / In stide of boundes he a pileer sette" (VII.2117–18). Although various candidates have been put forth for his identity, we have yet to reach a consensus on who this Trophee is, nor have we found a satisfactory explanation for his presence in the portrait of Hercules. When we consider the work's roots in a triumphal tradition, however, Chaucer's attribution of this material to "Trophee" makes abundant sense. In the Roman triumph, as we recall, the term *trophee/tropaea* (singular: *tropaeum*) signifies the "memorials to victory" erected in honour of the victor's ceremony.[105] The enduring markers of a transient spectacle, *tropaea* possess a commemorative function that we can ascribe to the "Monk's Tale" itself.[106]

What is more, the figure of Hercules is intimately tied to the ritual of the Roman triumph.[107] Tracing the hero's "historical and material associations" with this procession, Matthew P. Loar suggests that Hercules's name becomes a "metonym for Rome's Republican triumphal past."[108] Annalisa Marzano notes that "although the triumph was a ceremony linked above all with Iuppiter Optimus Maximus, Hercules was connected to the triumph from the early times of Rome."[109] Hercules's role in the triumph is not only ancient but also extensive. First, he was an integral part of the procession: victors would pass through the Forum Boarium, in which a bronze statue of Hercules – the *triumphalis* – was erected. Pliny the Elder explains that on the occasion of a triumph, this statue was arrayed in triumphal clothes.[110] On the way to the capitol, the triumphing victor would stop before the *triumphalis* and dedicate a portion of his spoils to the hero, a longstanding tradition in ancient Rome.[111] In the second and first centuries BCE, Hercules began to figure on triumphal coinage.[112] There also appeared a number of temples, dedicated to Hercules, which were stationed along the triumphal route, some of which hosted feasts following the procession.[113] By honouring Hercules as part of their triumphs, victors appealed to the hero as a fellow conqueror, who triumphed over so many others, even if he was eventually brought low by his wife.

According to some traditions, moreover, the Hercules celebrated along the triumphal route – the recipient of a portion of the triumphal booty – was an immortal god, his death at the hands of Deianira the impetus of his deification. Marzano traces the progression of Hercules from a figure associated with trade to one deeply linked to martial conquest, and sometimes even conflated with Mars himself.[114] This Hercules was "celebrated for his physical strength, which allowed him to overcome difficult tasks and to ultimately become a god."[115] The association of Hercules with invincibility and martial triumph has its origins in the Hellenistic period. In mid-Republican Rome, "the epithets of *Invictus* and *Victor* were introduced ... when the figure of Hercules primarily connected to traders was substituted with a god more directly connected to the sphere of war and victory in a 'Hellenistic' way."[116] Hercules, then, was essential to the Roman triumph, his name bound up with ideas of fame, victory, and even immortality. His statue, at which victors would lay down a portion of their spoils, was a highlight of the procession, and a feast was given in his honour. Chaucer's invocation of Trophee – the spoils or monuments of the Roman triumph – in his portrait of Hercules, a figure closely connected to the procession, is thus both thematically and historically appropriate. Indeed, the portraits in the tale function as trophies or *tropaea*, in that they provide a more permanent form to narratives of fleeting fortune, as well as a pointed reminder that fame is the domain of the poet.

Let us also consider the Monk's direction of his audience to Petrarch for the details of Zenobia's capture. Such a directive has confused readers, because, as has long been recognized, Chaucer relies on Boccaccio for this account, drawing on both *De mulieribus claris* and *De casibus* for his material.[117] F.N. Robinson, for example, has speculated that "why Chaucer refers here to Petrarch rather than to Boccaccio is unknown. From the fact that he never names Boccaccio it has been inferred that he attributed to Petrarch (or to Lollius) all the writings of Boccaccio that he knew."[118] To be sure, that Chaucer fails to identify Boccaccio as his source is hardly extraordinary – if anything (as Robinson notes), it is completely consistent with Chaucer's repeated refusal to name Boccaccio anywhere in his works. In this case, however, Chaucer's attribution of Zenobia's fall to "Petrak" points us toward Petrarch's *Trionfi*, a collection of six consecutive triumphs indebted primarily to the *Commedia* and the *Amorosa visione*.[119] In the fourth procession of his work, the *Trionfo della Fama*, Petrarch writes an account of Zenobia, who is a captive in Fame's opulent triumph. Here, the "slippage" between triumphal victor and prisoner is acute, with both Fame and Zenobia immortalized in splendour. As triumphator, Fame is embellished with gold and precious stones, and her head is crowned with laurel leaves. Zenobia, her illustrious prisoner, is equally honoured: Petrarch celebrates the Palmyrian queen as an example of unfading youth and enduring magnificence:

E vidi in quella tresca
Zenobia del suo onor assai più scarsa.
Bella era, e nell'età fiorita e fresca:
quanto in più gioventute e 'n più bellezza,
tanto par ch'onestà sua laude accresca;
Nel cor femineo fu sì gran fermezza
che col bel viso e coll'armata coma
fece temer chi per natura sprezza:
io parlo de l'imperio alto di Roma,
che con arme assalìo; ben ch'a l'estremo
fusse al nostro triumpho ricca soma. (*TF* II:107–17)

In the line I saw Zenobia, more jealous of her honor:
For she was fair, and in the flower of youth,
And all the more in beauty and in youth
To cherish honor is to merit praise;
And in her woman's heart was strength so great
That with her beauty and her armored locks
She brought dismay to men unused to fear
I speak of the imperial might of Rome
That she assailed in war – albeit at last.
She for our triumph was a wealthy prize.[120]

Petrarch's description of Zenobia reflects what Fabio Finotti perceives in the *Trionfi* as the poet's ambition to "collect the lives" of those figures "so illustrious that … their praises have been handed down" by generations of poets.[121] Zenobia is a trophy, or prize, for his narrative procession. Petrarch uses his triumph to "raise Zenobia from the captive's place of shame, endowing her with a share in the glory of the triumphator, who conquered her, and so revers[e] the customary direction of Fortune's wheel."[122] Her greatness also reflects back on Petrarch himself, extending the life of both poet and his subject in the process. It is Fame, according to Petrarch, who "trae l'uom del sepolcro e 'n vita il serba" ("saves man from the tomb, and gives him life" [*TF* I.9]).[123]

While not its textual basis, Petrarch's *Trionfo della Fama* is, I suspect, an important conceptual model for Chaucer's depiction of Zenobia in the "Monk's Tale." Marching at the front of Aurelian's procession, bejewelled, gilded, and wearing a crown, she reprises her role as a wealthy trophy for Petrarch's triumph. Chaucer's attribution of this material to Petrarch would seem in this regard neither arbitrary nor erroneous. On the contrary, it reminds us of the poet's singular capacity to freeze glory in time.[124] Should we follow the Monk's instructions and go read his "maister Petrak," who "writ ynough of this" matter, we learn the opposite lesson from that the mighty all fall. Instead, we witness a victor exalted in a state of perpetual youth and splendour at the hands of a poet.

But if poets can dispense fame then they can also deny it. While Chaucer's mention of Petrarch at the expense of crediting Boccaccio is not unusual in this regard, it is particularly poignant in the "Monk's Tale," which is, for all intents and purposes, an archive of names. Along with the *House of Fame*, it is the work that most fully explores the poet's ability to generate reputation.[125] In the *House of Fame*, the names of famous men and women are described as carved into a mountain of ice.[126] While some names have faded beyond recognition, "so unfamous woxe hir fame" (III.1146), other names are so clear and legible that they appear to have been written that very day. Fame, Chaucer seems to suggest, is utterly unpredictable, its tenure dictated by forces unknown to us. Chaucer's meeting with Lady Fame appears to confirm this perspective: witnessing her dispense glory, slander, and obscurity seemingly at random, Geffrey refuses to give his name when asked for it. Instead, he claims to want only anonymity: "Sufficeth me, as I were ded, / That no wight have my name in honde" (III.1876–7). This phrasing recalls Chaucer's experience of first entering Fame's house, where he learns that the glory of men is literally held aloft by poets. Statius holds up the fame of Thebes and Achilles on his shoulders; Homer, Dares, Dictys, Lollius, and "Englyssh Gaufride" bear up the fame of Troy; Virgil carries the glory of Aeneas; and Lucan holds the fame of Pompey and Caesar (III.1461–1502).

For all his emphasis on the fickleness of Lady Fame, however, Chaucer ultimately reveals that her power is an extension of the poet's, since he – and not she – decides who is named and who is unnamed in his work.[127] The prominence of certain names on the mountain of ice also suggests our potential for immortal glory, a potential that increases when these names are inscribed and reinscribed in new works. Like Propertius and John of Salisbury before him, then, Chaucer reminds us exactly how fame is propagated in the first place: it is poets who grant immortality, and who preserve the names of the glorious.[128] This is not to say that there is no element of chaos in the production of fame – works can be lost; names can be forgotten; wisdom can be mis/unattributed. While not everyone can achieve (or for that matter hold onto) fame, however, the poet can create a monument to reputation, staving off obscurity by memorializing his subjects in the lines of his work. Conversely, he can also *reserve* fame from others, increasing the likelihood that their names will be forgotten, like those "molte[d] away" on the mountain of ice. We can thus connect Chaucer's description of famous poets bearing up the glory of their subjects in the *House of Fame* to his retelling of well-known stories in the "Monk's Tale." If in the former it is Homer, Virgil, Ovid, Statius, and others who elevate the fame of ancient heroes and cities, then in the "Monk's Tale" Chaucer does this heavy lifting himself, sustaining the reputation of individuals like Sampson, Hercules, Alexander, Zenobia, Pompey, and Caesar even as the Monk decries worldly glory as ephemeral. We can similarly consider Chaucer's refusal to identify Boccaccio through the lens of the poet's prerogative to *withhold* fame. Blowing the horn of glory, "sklaundre," and anonymity in the "Monk's Tale," Chaucer disseminates good fame, bad fame, and, in Boccaccio's case, no fame at all.[129]

But as a *monumentum perennius*, the *De casibus* can withstand the erasure of its author. Omitted from the "Monk's Tale," Boccaccio reappears in Lydgate's translation of the *De casibus*, the *Fall of Princes*, as the work's most celebrated source, a restoration I will discuss in more detail in chapter 5.[130] Placing "Bochas" alongside Homer, Virgil, Petrarch, and Chaucer, Lydgate attests to the death-defying power of poetry, and of the *De casibus* in particular.[131] Were it not for writing this poem, Lydgate suggests, our memory would fade in passing ages (4.154). Nor does Lydgate imagine that Boccaccio was somehow oblivious to the worldly advantages accompanying poetic creation.[132] Rather, he claims that Boccaccio wrote the *De casibus* precisely for the sake of achieving glory: while recording the "fallyng of many conquerours," his author "Gan sharpe his penne, to his eternal fame, / Onli be writyng to geten hym a name" (4.164–8).[133] With his characteristic bombast, then, Lydgate reminds us of the durability of human reputation and the immortalizing authority of poets, lessons he claims to acquire from his reading of Boccaccio's treatise.[134] Still, the frankness of Lydgate's pursuit of glory in the *Fall of Princes* should not divert us from Chaucer's quieter appeal for the same end.[135] Although muted by his repeated definition of the work as tragic, Chaucer's insistence on the author's ability to outrun death – to check the continual rotation of Fortune's wheel, and to glorify his subjects and himself – is a constant and vital maxim in the "Monk's Tale." Fame's house may be built on a firmament of ice, but poems are lasting monuments to glory. And poems are stronger than bronze.

Chapter Four

Myn Auctor Lollius: Chaucer and the Invention of Troy

Quha wait gif all that Chauceir wrait was trew?
Nor I wait nocht gif this narratioun
Be authoreist, or fenyeit of the new
Be sum poeit, throw his inventioun.

– Robert Henryson, "The Testament of Cresseid"[1]

Detecting no mention of Lollius in the *Filostrato*, Chaucer's source for *Troilus and Criseyde*, Thomas Warton urged us roughly two hundred and fifty years ago to consider that Chaucer had access to a larger, fuller version of Boccaccio's poem than we have at present, one that is now lost. "Shall we suppose," he asks, "that Chaucer followed a more complete copy of the *Filostrato*? Or one enlarged by some officious interpolator?"[2] Indeed, a lost source would tidily explain Chaucer's substantial additions to the *Filostrato*, as well as his supposed reliance on Lollius, inconsistencies that otherwise baffle Warton, who admits that, while he has looked, he has failed to discover Chaucer's pseudo-Latin authority.

Warton's search for Lollius appears to be the product of a different scholarly era, analogous, perhaps, to the archaeological efforts of a generation of critics on a quest to find Keats's original urn. One is reminded of Keats's own remark, that "they are very shallow people who take everything literal."[3] But we have not entirely moved beyond a literal reading of Lollius. Although a few scholars, including Bella Millett, Barry Windeatt, and George Edmondson, advise readers to take Lollius as a literary joke or piece of deliberate artifice,[4] many others have put forth candidates for his identity.[5] The most prominent – and convincing – theory, popularized by George L. Kittredge and Robert A. Pratt, suggests that Chaucer came across a reference to "Lollius Maximus" in Horace's *Epistles* 2.1.[6] Assuming this Lollius to be an ancient authority on the Trojan War, and concerned with vesting his poem with an "air of truth and authenticity," Chaucer named Lollius to make his poem historically credible.[7]

To be sure, pretensions to narrative scrupulousness were frequent in the Middle Ages. Poets and historiographers alike camouflaged signs of recent invention beneath spurious assurances that they were translating faithfully from an ancient, written source, a practice that can be traced back to the sixth century BCE.[8] Geoffrey of Monmouth – perhaps the most famous practitioner of this manoeuvre – claims that his *Historia Regum Britannie* is translated from a *liber vetustissimus*, a very old book, containing all the deeds of the British kings (I.1). John of Salisbury conjures up a pseudo-classical and fictional source text, Plutarch's *Institutes of Trajan*, in the *Policraticus* (V.2). The *Ephemeris belli Troiani* and *De excidio Troiae historia*, written, respectively, in the fourth and either fifth or early sixth centuries CE, are offered to readers as the authentic diaries of Dictys Cretensis and Dares Phrygius, two soldiers who participated in the Trojan War. As we know now, Dares and Dictys are completely fictitious figures, invented by the authors of these pseudepigraphic texts.[9] Depending far more on his own invention than on his alleged source, Benoît de Sainte-Maure promises in his Old French *Roman de Troie* (c. 1155–60) to follow Dares's testimony. He insists that "Omer," having been born after the siege against Troy, inevitably misrepresents it. And although relying predominantly on Benoît's *Troie* as his source, Guido delle Colonne announces in the *Historia destructionis Troiae* (1287) that he will tell the true history of the Trojan War, as transcribed in the ancient works of Dares and Dictys. Following Benôit's example, he rejects the writings of Homer, Virgil, and the other pagan poets as no more than fiction and lies.[10]

While ubiquitous, however, claims of invented sources did not go unchallenged. Rather, as scholars such as Anthony Grafton, David Rollo, and Monika Otter have shown, they were regularly questioned and subverted, if not by the author himself then by his readers.[11] William of Newburgh objected so strongly to the *Historia Regum Britannie* that he devoted the entire preface of his *Historia Anglorum* to debunking Geoffrey's historical façade. A particular issue for William was that Geoffrey presented invented material as though it were corroborated by "immobili veritate" ("unshakeable truth").[12] Distinguishing Geoffrey's blatant fictions from what he describes as the more legitimate historical writings of Bede, William insists that, "quam petulanter et quam impudenter fere per omnia mentiatur nemo nisi veterum historiarum ignarus, cum in librum illum inciderit, ambigere sinitur" ("none except those ignorant of ancient histories can possibly doubt the extent of [Geoffrey's] wanton and shameless lying virtually throughout his book").[13] Rejecting the *liber vetustissimus* as inauthentic, he warns his readers that whatever Geoffrey wrote was a fiction, invented by himself or someone else, and motivated either by an "effrenata mentiendi libidine" ("uncontrolled passion for lying") or by a "gratia placendi Britonibus" ("desire to please the Britons").[14]

While singular in their tenacity, William's remarks are part of an ongoing conversation on the value and merits of fiction, and his response to Geoffrey is symptomatic of a growing scepticism in the Middle Ages toward pseudepigraphic writing.[15] This scepticism is, as we shall see, reflected in the literary tradition of Troy, in which the failure of truth and dominance of fiction are thematized. As spurious claims of authenticity accumulate, the trope of the pseudo-ancient source shifts its semiotic significance, I will propose, and what began as a device to establish historical veracity develops into a sign of authorial fabrication.[16]

Appropriating the historiographer's posture as the translator of a pseudo-ancient authority, Chaucer thus names Lollius not (or not just) to give his poem the illusion of historical validity, as scholars have previously supposed, but rather to foreground his literary invention, and to contextualize it within a tradition of fiction making – or what Boccaccio calls "confabulation."[17] In other words, Chaucer emphasizes the fictitiousness of the *Troilus* with a manoeuvre endowed with centuries of narrative fraud.[18] I further suggest that he learns and develops this manoeuvre from his sources: falsely claiming to translate the tragedy of Troiolo from a very old book, Boccaccio camouflages his debt to his more contemporary models, Benoît's Old French *Troie* and Guido's Latin *Historia*.[19] Benoît and Guido likewise feign reliance on ancient authorities in their writings on Troy. Although both claim to translate Dares and Dictys to the letter, neither does. Benoît invents the majority of his material, and Guido relies almost exclusively on Benoît.

To look back at the literary tradition of Troy, then, is to identify a tradition of artifice, a tradition composed of fabrications that divulge in one way or another their own fictionality. As the story of Troy moves between the *gramatica* and the vernacular, developing along the way from epic to historiography to romance, each author manipulates his source material, all the while fervently maintaining that his goal is to tell the truth. Excavating this tradition of open fabrication in the works of Benoît, Boccaccio, and Chaucer – each of whom discloses an ambition beyond merely replicating his source – I argue that these poets recognized fraud as the defining attribute of the Troy story,[20] by which I mean that they questioned the veracity of not only the Homeric but also the anti-Homeric accounts.[21] By appropriating the authenticating language and manoeuvres of medieval historiography, which were by this time charged with implications of fraud, they signalled the equally fictitious nature of their own writings on Troy, stories themselves centred on artifice. In doing so, they affiliated their works with the great but historically maligned Trojan narratives by Homer, Virgil, and Ovid, inscribing their names in a genealogy of epic poetry in the process.

Dynastic Fraudulence in the Troy Story: The *Roman de Troie*

The story of Troy came to the European Middle Ages by way of two literary traditions. Medieval readers could have learned about the fall of the city from the epic poetry of Homer, Virgil, and Ovid (although, for the most part, Homer's poetry was accessible in the Middle Ages only through Latinized versions of his work, like the *Ilias Latina*). Far more popular among medieval readers, however, were those works that comprise what is now referred to as the anti-Homeric tradition. Beginning with Dares's and Dictys's pseudepigraphical accounts, these texts leverage a kind of historical authority over the Trojan writings of Homer, Virgil, and Ovid on the basis of their supposed precedence. Since Dares and Dictys allegedly fought in the Trojan War, the compilers and translators of their diaries argue, their accounts of it are more authoritative than those of the epic poets, who lived and wrote after the city burned.

We see such a declaration in the *Roman de Troie*. Benoît makes exaggerated claims about the historical accuracy of his poem on the basis of the alleged truth of his source. He insists that because Dares fought in the Trojan War and recorded everything that he saw, his story, written in ancient Greek before Cornelius Nepos supposedly uncovered the text and translated it into Latin, offers a precise account of all that took place. After attesting to the truthfulness of his source, Benoît promises to translate Cornelius to the letter:

> Le latin sivrai e la letre,
> Nule autre rien n'i voudrai metre,
> S'ensi non com jol truis escrit.
> Ne di mie qu'aucun bon dit
> N'i mete, se faire le sai,
> Mais la matire en ensivrai.

> I shall follow the text of the Latin version faithfully; I wish to add nothing to it but what I find written there. I do not say that this will not include some clever additions of my own, if I am capable of doing so, but I shall follow my source material.[22]

This promise is strikingly insincere: Benoît elaborates handsomely on his source. By attesting to his fidelity, however, he raises serious questions about the accuracy of not only his own translation but also Cornelius's. Indeed, how can Cornelius (or a proxy claiming to be the first-century Roman scholar) be so certain of Dares's authenticity, having no assurance of it outside of Dares's own testimonial, and how can Benoît deliver an eyewitness account in a language and time twice removed from the original?

In fact, Benoît's pledge of textual fidelity echoes closely that made by Cornelius in *De excidio Troiae historia*. In a prefatory letter addressed to Sallust,[23] the translator-compiler explains that he unearthed an ancient diary, written in Dares's hand:

> Quam ego summo amore conplexus continuo transtuli. cui nihil adiciendum vel diminuendum rei reformandae causa putavi, alioquin mea posset videri. optimum ergo duxi ita ut fuit vere et simpliciter perscripta, sic eam ad verbum in latinitatem transvertere.
>
> I was very delighted to obtain it and immediately made an exact translation into Latin, neither adding nor omitting anything, nor giving any personal touch. Following the straightforward and simple style of the Greek original, I translated word for word.[24]

Cornelius insists that his fidelity to Dares is of the utmost importance, since Dares participated in the Trojan War and wrote an eyewitness account of all that he saw. It is on this basis that Cornelius proclaims that not only he, but we, too, can appraise his translation as truthful:

> ut legentes cognoscere possent, quomodo res gestae essent: utrum verum magis esse existiment, quod Dares Phrygius memoriae commendavit, qui per id ipsum tempus vixit et militavit, cum Graeci Troianos obpugnarent, anne Homero credendum, qui post multos annos natus est, quam bellum hoc gestum est.
>
> Thus my readers can know exactly what happened according to this account and judge for themselves whether Dares the Phrygian or Homer wrote more truthfully – Dares, who lived and fought at the time the Greeks stormed Troy – or Homer, who was born long after the War was over.[25]

Invoking his readers as adjudicators of the accuracy of the two Troy stories, Cornelius urges us to assess Homer's account as fiction and Dares's as truth. Moreover, he positions himself as the sole purveyor of historical fact.

While Cornelius claims to replicate Dares's firsthand experience to the letter, there is one crucial difference between the supposed testimony of Dares and Cornelius's translation of it. Even if we *were* to accept at face value Cornelius's statement that Dares was a real soldier who fought in the Trojan War (and we should not, and he did not), even if we believed that first-century Roman scholar Cornelius Nepos translated Dares's diary (R.M. Frazer, for one, dates the Historia to as late as the sixth century)[26] we are still left with the undeniable detail that unlike Dares, Cornelius did not, nor does he purport to, witness what he recounts, a realization to which the reader is inevitably drawn. True history was, and could only be, "told by those who had been present," in the words of David Ganz, and Cornelius lived many years after the war.[27] While he offers his work as historical, therefore, it can only be masquerading as such. By Cornelius's own estimation, historiographic truth depends on the written testimony of someone who was there to witness it.[28] Thus, as Rollo points out, "If Homer's work is historically untrustworthy because written after the event, then Cornelius' judgment of its untrustworthiness is untrustworthy for the same reason. He was no more a contemporary of Homer than Homer was a contemporary of the great army that assembled before Ilion."[29] The same logic applies to Benoît, who absorbs Cornelius's protestations of accuracy but from a further remove. Twice, Benoît positions himself as the personal guarantor of the *Troie*'s historical integrity, acquiring, or so it would seem, "the legitimacy of presence."[30] In the first case, Benoît writes of Homer that he was a "clers merveillos / E sages e esciëntos" ("wonderful cleric, wise and learned"),[31]

> Mais ne dist pas sis livres veir,
> Quar bien savons senz nul espier
> Qu'il ne fu puis de cent anz nez
> Que li granz oz fu assemblez:
> N'est merveille s'il i faillit,
> Quar onc n'i fu ne rien n'en vit.
>
> But his book does not tell the truth, for we know for certain and without doubt that he was not born until a hundred years after the great expedition was assembled. No wonder he failed, for he was never present there and never witnessed anything that happened.[32]

In the second instance, Benoît acts as character witness to the Trojan warrior, not only providing his reader with the everyday comings and goings of Dares, but also assuring us of Dares's honesty in recording exactly what he witnessed:

> Chascun jor ensi l'escriveit
> Come il o ses ieuz le veeit.
> Tot quant qu'il faiseient le jor

O en bataille o en estor,
Tot escriveit la nuit après
Icist que je vos di Darès:
Onc por amor ne s'en voust taire
De la verté dire e retraire.

Each day he would record exactly what he had witnessed with his own eyes. This Dares I am telling you wrote down that very night all the day's exploits in battle or in skirmish. He could not be deflected even by fidelity to his own people from saying and telling the truth.[33]

Benoît's posture of certainty in both cases, as though he were himself an eyewitness to the testimonials of Homer and Dares, discloses his fraudulence. As a vernacular writer active in the twelfth century, Benoît cannot possibly know "without doubt" that Homer told fictions, any more than he can guarantee that never on any account would Dares lie. To claim as fact that Dares wrote at night what he saw during the day, and in a most strained and awkward rhyme, "Tot escriveit la nuit après / Icist que je vos di Darès," only weakens his claims to truth.[34] Inevitably, we must acknowledge that Benoît is an unreliable witness to the story he tells for the same reason that Cornelius is unable to approximate Dares's firsthand experience: the degree of distance separating the translator from his alleged source is insurmountable. Like Aristotle's paradox of Achilles and the Tortoise, or Derrida's concept of *différance*, however small the variance between text and translation – however industrious the scribe or translator in his efforts to mitigate this gap – the breach separating an eyewitness account from its copy is always too great. The very trait in Dares with which Benoît identifies, therefore, "the trait by which he seeks to ratify his own work," is, as Edmondson observes, "The one thing that he can never imitate: Dares' now impossible position as eyewitness to the past. Any exact mirroring, then, is out of the question; Benoît can only aspire to a promise, the promise to let Dares' words be his guide in the writing of his own text."[35] But what if the impossibility of mirroring an eyewitness experience is precisely Benoît's point? Assuring us of Dares's (vis-à-vis-Cornelius's) truthfulness on the one hand, and of his own integrity as a translator on the other, Benoît intimates the fraudulence of the first assertion by advertising the illegitimacy of the second, resorting to rhetorical *inventio* for much of his material.[36]

This is not to say that *inventio* is inimical to the integrity of a translation. As Douglas Kelly explains, literary invention was common in both Latin and vernacular medieval writings, often co-existing with a kind of conceptual fidelity to one's source. The author would seek to reproduce if not what his source *actually* wrote, then what his source *would* have written, had he wanted to: "Literary fidelity to a source was not sought after, but infidelity was not the goal either. In the Middle Ages, invention is the art whereby a writer draws from antecedent material a new version that conforms to his, her, or a patron's conception of the material. Medieval writers termed this re-creation."[37] Kelly explores this kind of invention with regard to the character of Briseida. Barely present in Benoît's sources, Briseida plays a major role in the *Troie*, becoming, of course, the inspiration behind Criseida/Criseyde for Boccaccio and Chaucer.[38] Benoît, as Kelly explains, creates the romantic subplot involving Troilus and Briseida, but he does so according to established medieval practices of invention. As described by John of Salisbury in the *Metalogicon*, Bernard of Chartres advises that an author should embellish in good medieval measure, in the sense of "restraint, control, proportion – *modus*, *tenuitas*, and *quasi macies sermonis*"; they should be "slim ... delicate and finespun."[39] In situations where an author finds multiple, perhaps contradictory, sources, the new configuration of material that he offers should be an improvement, so that they, too, might be "imitable in turn" – "ad experimendam auctorum imaginem ... conscendere iubebat"; for Kelly, Benoît's invention is a "showpiece illustration of Bernard's technique, even though he wrote in the vernacular."[40] The *Troie* includes developments that "unfaithfully rehearse the source in order to recreate and thus render more faithfully the new author's idea," and it is imitated by not only vernacular but also Latin authors.[41]

Building on Kelly's point, I suggest that Benoît flaunts his artistic invention, in part to demonstrate the impossibility (for both himself and his sources) of conveying historical truth through translation, and in part to align himself with the epic poets, including but not limited to "Omer," who, although he does not tell the truth, is "sages e esciëntos." Distinguishing between the facts provided by Dares and Dictys and the fictions told by Homer, Benoît polarizes his literary predecessors along the axis of truth versus lies. No sooner does he establish this division, however, then he reveals it to be a fallacy, suggesting that all writing on Troy is mediated, and thus contrived.

Truth and Fiction in the *Filostrato*

Written in King Robert's Angevin court, where stylized art and lyric poetry were prized, the *Filostrato* celebrates medieval chivalry in a pagan world.[42] Although he sets the poem in classical Troy, and ostensibly translates it from an ancient text, Boccaccio relies on the twelfth-century vernacular *Roman de Troie*, a work that develops out of the apocryphal tradition of

Dares and Dictys. Whereas Benoît de Sainte-Maure seems keen to show how the prose historians deconstruct their own truth claims, meanwhile claiming to write "un histoire," Boccaccio presents the *Filostrato* as fiction from the start. Carrying over Benoît's pursuit of sifting truth from falsehood, he relies on a series of authorizing tropes to emphasize primarily his own poetic artistry. Offering his work as a consolatory fable, as opposed to a precise record of history, he draws our attention to the *Filostrato*'s origins in a tradition of epic fabrication, a tradition he will go on to theorize and defend in the *Genealogie deorum gentilium* (1350–75).

Boccaccio crafts the *Filostrato* as a courtly metaphor. Troiolo's pain is a "scudo" (shield) for his narrator's heartache, and Priam's Troy is a precursor to Naples under the rule of Robert the Wise.[43] As the eponymous narrator explains to his beloved Filomena, he translates this text in order to appease his sorrow, because the two situations – his own and Troiolo's – strike him as very similar. Lamenting his lady's absence, he claims that if we can give any faith to ancient sources, his life since her departure mirrors Troiolo's after Criseida left Troy.[44] To be sure, the singular difference between his story and Troiolo's is the latter's early success in love:

> È vero che, dinanzi alle sue più amare lagrime, in simile stilo parte della sua felice vita si trova, la quale puosi non perch'io disideri che alcuno creda che io di simile felicità gloriare mi possa – perciocché né mi fu mai tanto favorevole Fortuna né, sforzandomi di sperarlo, mel può in alcun modo concedere la credenza che ciò avvenga. (Proem, 30)

> It is true that before his most bitter misfortunes a part of the work deals in a similar style with the happiness he experienced – but I did not include this in order to give the impression that I myself can boast of gaining similar happiness, for Fortune has never granted such a favour to me, nor, even should I strive to hope for it, can I ever imagine it would be achieved.

The narrator nevertheless includes these happy moments for the sake of contrast. By bearing witness to the early joys of Troiolo, he insists, we will have a better understanding of the depths of his subsequent sorrows (Proem, 30–1).

Boccaccio's decision to bind his narrator's fate to Troy/Troiolo's would have been a familiar enough gambit to his readers. The Troy narrative was repeatedly used by Angevin poets and artists as an analogy for Naples's program of military expansion (or lack thereof), as Marilyn Desmond has discussed. Certain manuscripts even "situat[ed] the Angevin viewer within the city under siege," and so solicited a "readerly identification with the Trojans."[45] Invoked not only in origin stories but also as a warning against civic divisiveness, Troy provided a "key cultural site for Robert, as for several other projects of European expansion."[46]

To be sure, by positioning Troiolo as both Filostrato's tragic counterpart and a microcosm of Troy, Boccaccio invites our speculation on the fate of his beloved Naples, a city to which he felt both a literary and political allegiance.[47] By enabling Antenor's return, Criseida's disappearance precipitated both Troiolo's and Troy's fall. If Troiolo's story is at all prophetic, it would follow that Filomena's departure leaves Naples vulnerable as well. But Filostrato refrains from drawing out the political implications of this connection. Nor does he dwell on the broader historical significance of Troiolo's situation. Instead, he turns to Troy as an inspiration and starting point for his *private* account of heartache. Having resolved not to wallow in despair, he explains, "mutai proposto e pensai di volere con alcuno onesto ramarichio dare luogo a quella e uscita del tristo petto" ("I changed my mind and considered how through some dignified form of complaint I might provide the means for my grief-laden breast to be relieved of such sorrow" [Proem, 25]). He then begins to scour ancient sources, "per trovare cui io potessi fare scudo verisimilmente del mio segreto e amoroso dolore" ("to find which I could convincingly use as a shield for my secret and lovelorn suffering" [Proem, 27]).[48] It is Troiolo's story that he considers to be the closest to his own.

Seeking solace in the artistic rendering of Troiolo's experiences, Filostrato expresses himself "in someone else's story," in Kara Gaston's words, "and he emphasizes that the significance of the poem for him is as much tied up in its performance as in its initial composition."[49] The consolation he seeks from reading and writing is thus highly *personal*. The *Filostrato* has something in common with the *Decameron* in this regard. In both works, the narrator expresses that the purpose of his composition is to *soothe*. Filostrato finds solace in the act of writing, while the narrator of the *Decameron* writes to provide succour and refuge ("soccorso e rifugio") to women in love.[50] Of course, in the *Decameron*, a work composed, at least ostensibly, of "cento novelle, o favole o parabole o istorie" ("a hundred novellas, or fables or parables or stories"), Boccaccio's emphasis on the consolatory aspect of poetry is hardly striking.[51] In the *Filostrato*, however, such a focus clashes with the purported historical ambitions of Boccaccio's anti-Homeric sources. Although he ultimately reveals the impossibility of such tasks, Benoît, for example, announced his intention to write true history, translate his ancient Latin sources faithfully, and convey the rarely heard truth about the siege on the city, vis-à-vis Dares's and Dictys's firsthand accounts.[52] Among the many renditions of Troy available in various languages, the *Troie*, he insists, translates the only accurate version of this story into the French vernacular.

Boccaccio makes no such promises of historical accuracy in the *Filostrato*. Nevertheless, from the beginning of the work, he recycles Benôit's concern for sifting truth from falsehood, as well as his recourse to a pseudo-ancient source text. In the proem, Filostrato describes a popular debate among lovers at court: whether thinking of, talking about, or looking at his beloved would provide the greatest pleasure. He describes how his thoughts on this question have evolved. Whereas once he believed that thinking about his lady would deliver the most solace, confronted with her absence, he grasps how wrong this assumption was, exclaiming, "O stolto giudizio, o sciocca estimazione, o vano argumentare, quanto dal vero eravate lontani" ("Oh stupid judgment, oh foolish estimation, oh vain argument, how far you were from the truth" [Proem, 6]).

The answer to such a question is a matter of personal preference. Yet Filostrato frames it otherwise, as a mission for objective truth, which he can only discover through firsthand experience. Once deluded by "falso parere" ("false opinion"), he claims, "truth" prevailed over his muddled thoughts, which "amara esperienza" ("bitter experience") has made clear (Proem, 6). Now, he affirms to be true ("affermo ... esser vero" [Proem, 8]) that being able to witness his beloved's person offers the most consolation, something he failed to recognize in her presence, but nevertheless should have known. It is this revelation that leads the narrator to search old books for answers, and to come upon Troiolo's story in an unnamed "istoria antica."[53] In "leggier rima" and "mio fiorentino idioma," he decides to treat Troiolo's sorrows and his own in similar terms (Proem, 29).

Thus anchoring his poem in the pursuit of objective truth, the warrant of firsthand experience, and a spurious ancient source, Filostrato invokes a trifecta of historicizing devices.[54] No sooner does he employ these manoeuvres, however, then he casts doubt on their credibility. Embellishing his source in the language of deception – the story is a cover for his "segreto ... dolore" (Proem, 27) – Filostrato speculates at regular intervals "se fede alcuna alle antiche storie si può dare" ("if any faith may be given to the ancient stories" [Proem, 28]), "s'el non erra / la storia" ("if the account is not mistaken" [I.16]), or "se 'l ver dice la storia" ("if the account is true" [I.46]).[55] Indeed, he makes clear that the extent to which his sources do, or do not, tell the truth matters to him only insofar as the narrative functions as a metaphor for his personal heartache. He makes no attempt to assure us of his credentials as a reliable translator, nor does he advocate for the historical accuracy of his source.

Adding to our reasons for scepticism is that Boccaccio's source is not an "istoria antica" at all. Although it is unclear whether or not his contemporaries would have recognized this, Boccaccio relies predominantly on Benôit's vernacular *Troie*, while also consulting other works that comprise the anti-Homeric tradition.[56] Nor is Boccaccio faithful to his uncredited medieval sources. Instead, he intervenes in these writings with what Luigi Surdich has described as "estrema libertà," turning what in the *Troie* was a marginal episode – the romance between Briseida and Troilo – into the subject of his entire poem.[57] Filostrato is likewise unreliable.[58] He knows intimate details about his narrative while remaining ignorant of other key points,[59] questions the accuracy of his memory,[60] and describes certain events as "impossibile a dire" ("impossible to tell" [III.31]). When Criseida leaves Troy, Filostrato connects his failure as a translator with his inability to speak the truth. "Chi potrebbe giammai narrare appieno / ciò che Criseida nel pianto dicea?" ("Who could ever recount all that Criseida said in her grief?"), he asks, "Certo non io, ch'al fatto il dir vien meno, / tant'era la sua noia cruda e rea" ("Certainly not I, for her distress was so cruel and fierce that words fail to describe it" [IV.95]). Filostrato's confession prompts the question: in a story that has already been written, what, indeed, is beyond description? Filostrato is either diverging from his source or lying about it altogether, but either way we cannot trust him to convey his story faithfully.

In a twist of irony, whereas texts and oral testimony deceive in the *Filostrato*, divinely inspired prophecies and dreams, the sort of outlandish content for which medieval readers maligned Homer, convey the truth.[61] The wisdom of divine prophecy is intimated from the start of the poem, with Calcàs asking Apollo the outcome of the war. This request is articulated, like so much else in this poem, as a function of determining truth: Calcàs wishes to know "del futuro il vero" ("the truth about the future" [I.8]). Foreseeing Trojans slain and Troy burned, he defects to the Greek camp, leaving Criseida in enemy territory. The fulcrum of the poem's action, Calcàs's prophecy anticipates Troiolo's subsequent dream of Criseida's infidelity (and there is a structural symmetry to the twin downfalls of Troy and Troiolo, as foreseen in twin visions). Imagining Criseida with her heart routed by a boar, Troiolo grasps his dream's import immediately. He tells Pandaro that Criseida has been unfaithful: "ella ha altrui il suo amor donato ... / gli dii me l'hanno nel sogno mostrato" ("She has granted her love to someone else ... The gods have shown as much in a dream" [VII.26]). Troiolo's oracular sister, Cassandra, perceives the reason for her brother's heartache. She connects his suffering to the larger momentum of the Trojan War, predicting that accursed love will be the downfall of them all (VII.86). Troiolo rejects Cassandra's claim, insisting on her ignorance of the truth of the matter, and threatening to expose her as a fraudulent prophet (VII.90). In this case, however, Troiolo's repudiation of Cassandra only enforces the veracity of her words: doomed to tell the truth to an audience who will not believe her, Cassandra is the narrative antithesis of her brother, whose blind faith in Criseida leads to his beguilement.[62]

If prophecies and dreams reveal the truth in the *Filostrato* then oral and written correspondence – letters, oaths, and conversation – only obscure this reality.[63] (It is hardly surprising that the shrewd Calcàs cautions vigilance against such means of intelligence, claiming to rely on neither messengers nor private or public communications [IV.6]).[64] One reason for this occlusion of truth is the heavy mediation of all correspondence in the poem. Pandaro, a self-professed "mezzano," negotiates the better part of Troiolo and Criseida's interactions, in some instances relaying messages that either are excluded from the narrative or are altogether contrived. Pandaro also arbitrates the lovers' letters, prompting, at times even dictating, their content. When they do arrive, these letters are blotted with sympathy-inducing tears, sometimes to the point of unreadability.[65] (Indeed, the narrator himself sends a tear-stained letter to his lady, suggesting that he, too, participates in this ritual of textual manipulation.)

Beyond its constant mediation, language is itself fickle in the poem. As Criseida's affection for Troiolo wanes, her former oaths are no longer binding. For Troiolo, this is extremely difficult to comprehend. He wants Criseida's words to correspond to a singular, coherent truth, and when they do not, he rebukes not only Criseida but also her language for being deceitful:

> Io ti credetti, e spereva per certo santa esser la tua fede, e le parole essere un ver certissimo ed aperto più ch'a' viventi la luce del sole; e tu parlavi ambiguo e coperto, sì com'egli ora appar nelle tue fole, ché solamente a me non se' tornata, ma con altro uom ti se' inamorata. (VII.31)

> I trusted you, and firmly believed your pledge to be sacred and your words more constant and clear than the light of the sun is to men. Yet you were speaking deceitfully and insincerely as your falsehoods now seem to show – for you have not only failed to return to me but have given your love to another man.

Equally deceptive is the language of letters. Long after falling for Diomede, Criseida writes to Troiolo vowing to return. Pandaro urges Troiolo to respond:

> Però che s'ella non t'avrà 'n calere, non credo che risposta abbiam da lei; o se l'avrem, potrem chiaro vedere, per le scritte parole, se tu dei sperare ancor nella sua ritornata, o s'ella s'è d'altro uomo innamorata. Scrivile adunque, ché se ben lo fai, chiaro vedrem ciò che cercando vai. (VII.49–50)

> For if she no longer cares for you I do not think we shall get a reply from her; and if we do have one we shall be able to see clearly from what she writes whether you can continue to hope for her return, or whether she has fallen in love with someone else ... Write to her then, for if you do it properly, we shall find out for sure what you seek to know.

Pandaro's suggestion is not only misguided in its faith in the stability of the written word. It also serves as a warning to the reader to question textual authority, since *we* know Criseida's letters lie. By negative example, then, we are deterred from Troiolo-like gullibility, provoked by Boccaccio's use, and then repudiation, of fraudulent authorizing devices. Once Boccaccio reveals the unreliability of the written and spoken word, moreover, he invites us to read the *Filostrato* as fiction.

Even as he follows Benôit's example by employing recognizable warrants of his work's historical legitimacy, then, Boccaccio exposes the unreliability of his narrator, the speciousness of his ancient source, and the subjectivity of his personal experience. In the process, I suggest, he positions his work as not history but *fabula*. To be sure, fables are not empty lies for Boccaccio. On the contrary, they can contain *truths* (albeit not always historical truths). Placing between himself and his reader a patently fictional story about the origins of his work on Troy, he "esplora la possibilità dell'illusione del vero, che è l'insidioso passaggio che porta alla conquista di una terra nuova: la verità della *finzione* che si può leggere come una *storia*," in Elisabetta Menetti's words.[66] As becomes clear in the *Filostrato*, a text need not be historically precise for it to contain profundities. At the same time, a work of fiction can entertain and offer valuable consolation.

Filostrato's approach to his narrative anticipates in this regard Boccaccio's larger defence of poetry in the *Genealogie*, which I discussed in chapter 1. In this defence, Boccaccio upholds the value of fiction on the basis of these two qualities: its ability to convey truths and its capacity to console. He proposes a theory of poetry as *integumentum*. Adopting the Horatian precept that fictional works can both delight and benefit us, he insists that poetry is the beautiful veil that can conceal profound truths. Indeed, poetry is God-given, composed only by the rarest and most extraordinary of men. What is more,

> Huius enim fervoris sunt sublimes effectus, ut-puta-mentem in desiderium dicendi compellere, peregrinas et inauditas inventiones excogitare, meditates ordine certo componere, ornare compositum inusitato quodam verborum atque sententiarum contextu, velamento fabuloso atque decenti veritatem contegere.

> This fervor of poesy is sublime in its effects: it impels the soul to a longing for utterance; it brings forth strange and unheard-of creations of the mind;

> it arranges these meditations in a fixed order, adorns the whole composition with unusual interweaving of words and thoughts; and thus it veils truth in a fair and fitting garment of fiction.[67]

In this way, poetry is distinct from rhetoric: "mera poesis est quicquid sub velamento componimus et exponitur exquisite" ("for whatever is composed as under a veil, and thus exquisitely wrought, is poetry and poetry alone").[68]

Boccaccio further highlights fiction's restorative properties. Defending poetry against claims that it was unprofitable at best and immoral at worst, he writes:

> Fabulis fessis illustrium virorum circa maxima animis vires persepe restitute sunt, quod non tantum exemplo veteri, sed assiduis demonstrator. Cernimus enim principes, et maximis occupatos rebus, quasi rerum natura docente, post regnorum suorum sublimes dispositiones in melius, ut fessas in nervum revocent vires, convocare, qui iocosis confabulationibus recreent animos fatigatos.

> By fiction, too, the strengths and spirit of great men worn out in the strain of serious crises, have been restored. This appears, not by ancient instance alone, but constantly. One knows of princes who have been deeply engaged in important matters, but after the noble and happy disposal of their affairs of state, obey, as it were, the warning of nature, and revive their spent forces by calling about them such men as will renew their weary mind with diverting stories and conversation.[69]

Fables (*fabulae*) thus contain truths beneath an "exquisitely wrought" surface, and they console troubled minds. They are, in Lucia Battaglia Ricci's words, "non solo belle 'vesti' alleghoriche di piú o meno profunde verità: esse possono offrire a chi è travolto dall'avversa fortuna una qualche forma di consolazione."[70] (And it is difficult to avoid connecting Boccaccio's defence of poetry in the *Genealogie* to his defensive posture in the *Decameron*, or "sfuggire all'impressione che dietro questa 'difesa' della favole inventate dai poeti se celi l'esigenza di difendere il suo *Decameron* dagli attacchi di moralistici censori.")[71] But this secondary function of consolation means that even if they *do not* contain truths, fables still have value. As Glending Olson notes, "whatever sort it may be, whether it veils truth or not, fiction, like conversation, brings recreation and health to its audience."[72] It entertains and restores its readers.

Boccaccio's multifaceted endorsement of poetry as *integumentum* counters claims by Christian writers such as Augustine that truth cannot be found outside of the Bible and the teachings of the Church. As Robert Hollander observes, such an argument elevates fiction on the basis of its allegorical potential. It develops from a desire to associate poetry "with some form of exegesis, whether biblical or literary," and "is related to a continuing defensive posture on the part of medieval poets and interpreters of poetry which arises from the hostility of Fathers and Doctors of the Church to the approximate quality of the truth (read 'lies') of all fiction."[73] But it also priveleges the literal sense by valuing poetry's ability to console.[74] Equally important to Boccaccio's defence of poetry is the trans-temporal bond it offers authors. As I discussed in chapter 1, Boccaccio invents a spurious etymology for the term *fabula* so as to create for himself an eminent heritage: "'Fabula' igitur ... a 'for, faris' honestam sumit originem, et ab ea 'confabulacio,' que nil aliud quam 'collucucio' sonat" ("the word *fabula* has an honorable origin in the verb *for*, *faris*, hence 'conversation' [*confabulation*], which means only 'talking together' [*collocutio*]").[75] This explanation not only creates an illustrious derivation for fables, as he suggests, but it also makes the process of writing poetry a *collaborative* activity – Boccaccio even designates this process "confabulation" to express its communal nature. Writing fiction, he insists, is a collective pursuit.

To emphasize this last point, Boccaccio names Homer and Virgil (and even Christ!) among the famous authors of *fabulae*.[76] These authors write fictions that masquerade as histories, he suggests. Of the four kinds of *fabula*, "Species vero tercia potius hystorie quam fabule similis est. Hac aliter et aliter usi poete celebres sunt ... Et hec si de facto non fuerint, cum communia sint esse potuere vel possent" ("The third kind is more like history than fiction, and famous poets have employed it in a variety of ways ... If the events they describe have not actually taken place, yet since they are common, they could have occurred, or might at some time").[77] Singling out epic poetry for praise, Boccaccio contradicts the popular refrain in the anti-Homeric narratives, that Homer, Virgil, and Ovid told lies, even if their poetry was artful. Instead, he affirms that these works convey *truths*. Finally, he elevates invention as the unifying element binding poets together from antiquity to the Middle Ages, creating an illustrious precedent for his fabrications, from his historical romances to the *Decameron*.

For Boccaccio, then, the process of creating stories is profound, noble, consolatory, and genealogy building. Cloaking the *Filostrato* in "belle 'vesti' alleghoriche," he writes an account of Troy that undresses itself as poetry, thus aligning this work with the creative endeavours of Homer and his epic followers. Boccaccio does not contradict the denunciation, so popular in the Middle Ages, of Homer, Virgil, and Ovid as fictionalizers. Rather, he unmasks himself as a fellow fabricator in the *Filostrato* before arguing in the *Genealogie* that poetry can enshroud truths and offer consolation. Further rewriting the definition of *fabula* to encompass conversation through creation, he builds a figurative pantheon for himself and his predecessors, from Homer and Virgil to Christ.

Authority and Invention in *Troilus and Criseyde*

In Chaucer's Troy, the city and its inhabitants are doubly doomed. First, as Lee Patterson has shown, they fall because of a cyclical determinism rooted in Theban history.[78] The second reason is markedly Trojan: the city collapses on account of human artifice. Whether it takes the form of the deception of Sinon, the treachery of Antenor, or the (perceived) betrayal of Troilus by Criseyde, fraud is the common denominator binding together stories of Troy.

Accompanying this theme of fraudulence is a poetics of intertextual dissimulation. From the epics of Homer, Virgil, and Ovid to the apocryphal diaries of Dares and Dictys to the historiographies, romances, poems, and plays that develop from this anti-Homeric tradition, the authors of Troy habitually refuse to acknowledge or translate their sources faithfully.[79] At the same time (and in spite of their shared impulse to falsify their textual models), these authors are consumed by the pursuit of veracity. Beginning in the Middle Ages, poets and historiographers strove to distinguish their Trojan works from those of their epic predecessors by identifying themselves and their sources as singularly truthful. A repeated charge levied against Homer, Virgil, and Ovid in the medieval writings on Troy is, as we have seen, that the epic poets lie whereas Dares and Dictys tell the truth.

Fraudulence, then, accompanied by an emphasis on textual veracity, characterizes stories on Troy and their authors' poetics of translation, a pattern that Chaucer both picks up on and exploits in *Troilus and Criseyde*. The narrator himself "ne dar to Love" (I.16), yet he compensates for his lack of experience by promising to follow a reputable source, posing, like the medieval historiographers of Troy, as an unwavering translator of an authoritative ancient text. By the end of the poem, however, the narrator reveals the cracks in this façade.[80] While at first insisting on the importance of translating his "auctor Lollius" word for word, as the story proceeds he becomes increasingly suspicious of his fabricated source, eventually abandoning all pretence to textual fidelity altogether.[81] Lollius may not exist, in other words, but that does not stop the narrator from questioning or undermining him repeatedly. (The poet takes a different, though hardly more reverential approach to his actual source, Boccaccio's *Filostrato*, which he neither acknowledges nor follows dutifully; where possible and relevant, I will distinguish between the poet-Chaucer and the narrator-Chaucer.) After multiple promises of textual fidelity, the narrator's unwillingness or inability to translate his *auctor* distances the reader from both the poem and its supposed model, "complicat[ing] attempts to get back to authentic historical knowledge," in Gaston's words.[82] Unable to trust Chaucer, his poem, or his poem's alleged source, readers are left at a critical impasse. Like the Trojans, awoken in the middle of the night to their city walls breached, we are confronted with the knowledge that we have been duped by a vessel of fraud. While for the Trojans this is a wooden horse, for us it is the Troy narrative itself, from its inception a vehicle for literary and historical invention.[83]

Still, our awakening to this tradition of fraud is gradual. When he first introduces his source before the *Canticus Troili* in Book One, the narrator is confident in his author, and in his own ability to translate him faithfully. He insists that he will provide "naught only the sentence" of the *Canticus Troili*, "as writ myn autour called Lollius" (I.394–5), but also,

Save oure tonges difference,
I dar wel seyn, in al, that Troilus
Seyde in this song, loo, every word right thus
As I shal seyn; and whoso list it here,
Loo, next this vers he may fynden here. (I.396–9)

Chaucer cultivates a sense of immediacy, as though we ourselves hear Troilus sing. He guarantees a similar intimacy in Book Two, emphasizing his minimal role as a translator: "Of no sentiment I this endite, / But out of Latin in my tongue I write" (II.13–14). We must therefore "disblameth" him for any infelicities, for "as myn auctour seyde, so sey I" (II.17–18). Later in this book, Chaucer implies that Lollius recorded Criseyde's inner monologue: "and what she thoughte somewhat shal I write, / As to myn auctour listeth for t'endite" (II.699–700).

These pledges of fidelity should inspire confidence in Lollius, and perhaps they would, if Chaucer did not repeatedly highlight the failure of his efforts to translate closely. Despite claiming to convey both letter and sense of the *Canticus Troili*, for example, the narrator does neither, failing to communicate the words and meaning of his source. As has long been recognized (albeit presumably not by Chaucer's own original readers), Troilus's song is a translation of a Petrarchan sonnet. Although they sound similar, however, Petrarch's question, "s'amor non è, che dunque è quel ch'io sento?" is entirely different from that which Troilus poses: "if no love is, O god, what feel I so?" Petrarch asks if what he feels is love; Troilus asks if love exists.[84] While offering himself as a faithful scribe of the *Canticus Troili*, the narrator also notes that there is an important emotional connotation to Troilus's song that he does not grasp. He has never been in love, and so while he can attempt to convey the original text, he cannot possibly understand its significance. Thus, "of no sentement I this endite, / But out of Latyn in my tonge it write" (II.13–14). It is as though "love itself might remain untranslated," in Gaston's words, "a remainder of the past."[85] The narrator's concession speaks to the overall impossibility of recuperating the original version of the *Canticus Troili.*[86] Translation can only approximate firsthand experience, it can never duplicate it. Chaucer's promise to translate Criseyde's thoughts invites further scepticism, for how would Lollius know what Criseyde is thinking? Even if he were an eyewitness to her story, he could not read her mind. Either Lollius or Chaucer is inventing this episode, but either way it is fiction.

At first, the narrator seems to make a genuine attempt to translate his source text faithfully, only to find himself stymied by linguistic and emotional difference. Feeble though they are, these early efforts to present himself as a zealous translator of Lollius, and Lollius as a reliable witness to history, do not endure. As Troilus loses faith in Criseyde, the narrator loses faith in his source, and he abandons his initial vow to translate closely.[87] Although Benoît and Boccaccio specify that Criseyde is childless, for example, Chaucer claims to find nothing about this in his book: "wheither that she children hadde or noon, / I rede it naught," he insists, "therefore I late it goon" (II.132–3). (He feigns a similar obliviousness in his description of Criseyde, which is taken largely from Benôit and Joseph of Exeter. After describing her physical features, he writes, "I kan nat telle hire age" [V.826], a completely unnecessary admission, since nearly all of his sources are silent on this question.)[88] By maintaining his ignorance on a point so clearly articulated by his authors, Chaucer creates a textual crux out of nothing, positioning his invented source in contrast to his actual textual models. Like the pseudepigraphic Dares and Dictys, he offers an alternative to the dominant record of events, whose mere existence undermines the authority of earlier versions.

Chaucer splinters the literary tradition of Troy more dramatically elsewhere in the poem. When he declares his literary subject as the love between Troilus and Criseyde, he points us to Homer, or Dares, or Dictys for scenes of war:

> But how this town com to destruccion.
> Ne falleth naught to purpose me to telle,
> But the Troian gestes, as they felle,
> In Omer, or in Dares, or in Dite,
> Whoso that kan may rede hem as they write. (I.141–2; I.146–8)

On the one hand, in his choice of "or" instead of "and," Chaucer acknowledges that the writings of Homer, Dares, and Dictys are mutually unintelligible. We cannot read Homer (or in Chaucer's case, a Homeric, Latinized version of the Troy story) alongside the diaries of Dares or

Dictys without coming to an interpretive gridlock, since the latter insist that Homer told lies. On the other hand, by directing us to one or another author, and thereby encouraging us to turn a blind eye to this tradition of dissent, Chaucer glosses over the variance among his sources. He creates the impression not of textual disharmony but rather of homogeneity, "of an untroubled Trojan space – a place that has been emptied of its traitorous enemies, collectively known as history," in Sylvia Federico's apt phrase.[89] This is *occupatio* on a grand scale, the elision of political, historical, and textual conflict, and an elision that Chaucer compels us to confront in his very attempt to sweep it under the rug (it "ne falleth naught to purpose me to telle"). By advising us to read Homer or Dares or Dictys, he invites our attention to the fundamental incompatibility of his sources, whose lack of agreement belies the concept of a single, historical truth. At the same time, he performs the role of someone trying to hide this incompatibility from his readers in the service of presenting his and his sources' version of history as unilaterally true and uncontested.

In Book Three, Chaucer admits to tampering with his material. In one of the poem's largest departures from the *Filostrato*, he explains that there is no real need for him to translate Lollius literally. While some men would have him rehearse "every word, or soonde, or look, or chere," it would simply take too much time: "I trowe it were a long thyng for to here" (III.492; III.495). Nor is any author this meticulous, he suspects: "I have naught herd it don er this, / In storye non, ne no man here, I wene" (III.498–9). Although Chaucer is dubious, this is exactly what Benoît suggested Dares did ("each day he would record exactly what he had witnessed with his own eyes"), and what Benoît himself promised to do in the *Troie* ("I shall follow the text of the Latin version faithfully; I wish to add nothing to it but what I find written there … I shall follow my source material"). In proposing that no one records every detail, Chaucer thus undermines the entire medieval tradition of Troy, the supposed truth of which is premised on its authors' and translators' claims of point-to-point fastidiousness, at the same time as he calls attention to his own poetic artifice.

But even if he *did* want to be precise in his translation, which he does not, Chaucer makes clear that he could not possibly achieve this goal. As it turns out, Lollius omitted a lengthy letter, nearly half as long as the poem, because he did not want to copy it out: "ther was som epistle … / that wolde, as seyth myn autour, wel contene / Neigh half this book, of which hym liste nought write" (III.501–3). "How sholde I thanne a lyne of it endyte" (III.504), Chaucer contends, when Lollius failed to transcribe this letter in the first place? This admission prompts a deluge of similar confessions, all of which disclose either his own unreliability as a translator or Lollius's failure as a witness to history, and which demonstrate beyond a doubt that we are getting only a partial account of what occurred – or, according to Richard Utz, that this "fictionalizer has a personal interest in the story which makes him deviate from his supposed source."[90] When Pandarus invites Criseyde to dinner, swearing that Troilus is out of town, Chaucer tells us that Lollius did not feel like including what Criseyde thought in response (III.575–8). After Pandarus thrusts his hand down Criseyde's dress, a squeamish Chaucer passes over "al that which chargeth nought to seye" (III.1576). When his lovers go to bed, he concedes that he "kan nat tellen al, / As kan myn auctour" (III.1324–5).[91] And indeed, if we have a problem with these changes and omissions, we can respond to them how we like: "Doth therwithal right as youreselven leste" (III.1330). Later, the poet casually invites us to "encresse or maken dymynucioun / Of my langage" (III.1335–6), an offer to edit his poem that at this point should not surprise us.[92] By his own admission, Chaucer has been manipulating Lollius all along.

In the fifth book, Chaucer destabilizes our faith in the medieval tradition of Troy still further. Reminding us that he is the mere translator and not the author of what he finds, he prefaces nearly every narrative development with a statement of attribution. He notes that "the storie telleth us" (V.1037; V.1051), "I fynde ek in stories elleswhere" (V.1044), "as telleth Lollius" (V.1653), and "as men may in thise olde bokes rede" (V.1753). After crediting everything he transcribes to someone or something else – "the storie," "thise olde bokes," or the writings of Lollius – Chaucer expresses scepticism regarding this material. He wonders why, for example, he finds nothing in his sources on how long it took Criseyde to forsake Troilus, as though this omission – and the pocket of time it obfuscates – undermines their later attempts to defame her:

> But trewely, how longe it was bytwene
> That she forsak hym for this Diomede,
> Ther is non auctour telleth it, I wene.
> Take every man now to his bokes heede,
> He shal no terme fynden, out of drede.
> For though that he bigan to wowe hir soone,
> Er he hire wan, yet was ther more to done.

Thus directing us to our "bokes," the narrator suggests that we affirm for ourselves this dearth of evidence on the timeline of Criseyde's infidelity. At the very least, he will not follow his sources in slandering her without due cause:

> Ne me ne list this sely womman chide
> Forther than the storye wol devyse.

Hire name, allas! is punysshed so wide,
That for hire gilt it oughte ynough suffise (V.1087–9)

Statements like these position the narrator in direct opposition to the authors of "olde bokes," who, he suggests, either withhold or simply do not know vital information that could perhaps exonerate Criseyde. Yet rather than garner sympathy for his heroine, by claiming not to know how long it took her to forsake Troilus, the narrator casts doubt on his own reliability. As E. Talbot Donaldson points out, earlier in Book Five, the narrator offers this information *himself*, specifying that Criseyde abandoned plans to remain loyal to Troilus "er fully months two" (V.766).[93] Chastising his sources for their incompetence, he thus ends up implicating mainly himself. Should we heed his advice and "take … to [our] bokes," moreover, we discover that his authors agree on very little, not only with respect to the sequence of Criseyde's activities but also regarding the Troy story as a whole. Worse still, we learn that Chaucer has been lying about his sources all along.

The narrator's growing scepticism of his sources reaches its pinnacle when Criseyde succumbs to Diomede's advances. At this point, he makes a confession of ignorance that casts the credibility of previous authors into question, musing openly on whether or not they spoke the truth: "Men seyn – I not – that she yaf hym hire herte" (V.1050). These men say one thing, but he does not know if it is true. By refusing to disparage Criseyde along with his sources, the narrator abandons any pretence of translation, suggesting that we go elsewhere for this version of her story – we "may hire gilt in other bokes se" (V.1776). We will not, however, find it in his poem.

Having moved from a position of reverence for old books to the complete rejection of their wisdom, Chaucer untethers his poem from the moorings of a source. Even as he feels compelled to repeat the outcome of the story as he finds it written (as Troy must fall, so Criseyde must leave Troilus), he nevertheless questions everything leading up to this moment. Coming to the conclusion that not only Lollius but also "other bokes" are unreliable, he refuses to confirm that Criseyde fell in love with Diomede. Since this storyline originated in the medieval tradition of Troy, the implicit targets of Chaucer's scepticism here are those authors who reported Criseyde's faithlessness: Benôit de Sainte-Maure, Guido delle Colonne, and Boccaccio. It should hardly surprise us that at the close of his poem Chaucer directs his "litel bok" (V.1786) to "kis the steppes" of not these medieval authors of Troy, nor even his fabricated *auctor* Lollius, but rather the epic poets themselves:

Go, litel bok, go, litel myn tragedye,
Ther God thi makere yet, er that he dye,

> So sende myght to make in some comedye!
> But litel book, no makyng thow n'envie,
> But subgit be to all poesye;
> And kis the steppes where as thow seest pace
> Virgile, Ovide, Omer, Lucan, and Stace. (V.1786–92)

Chaucer's farewell to his poem is first and foremost a statement of association. As David Wallace observes, the poet uses this passage to articulate his literary allegiance to "those famous texts of antiquity which share his serious concern with the great themes of warfare, love, and moral virtue."[94] At the same time, "In placing himself sixth in a poetic confraternity of six, a grouping which extends from the pagan past to the Christian present, Chaucer is deliberately upholding a precedent established by Jean de Meun and then adopted within Dante's *Commedia* and Boccaccio's *Filocolo*."[95] But it is important to note the ways in which Chaucer not only upholds precedents set by his sources but also deviates from these examples. Recall that Benôit de Sainte-Maure and Guido delle Colonne denounced the epic poets, the latter lamenting "Tamen defectum magnorum auctorum, Virgilii, Ouidii, et Homeri, qui in exprimenda ueritate Troyani casus nimium defecerunt … et specialiter ille summus poetarum Virgilius, quem nichil latuit" ("the failure of the great authors, Virgil, Ovid, and Homer, who were very deficient in describing the truth about the fall of Troy … especially the highest of poets, Virgil, whom nothing obscures."[96] Chaucer, by contrast, directs the *Troilus* to prostrate itself before "all poesye," and to pay reverence to the very imprints of Homer, Virgil, Ovid, and others, as they walk in front of him. If the poet indeed "works hard" to "seem like a historian" in this work, as has been argued, then such a directive shatters this illusion.[97] Chaucer may chastise those "payens" and their "corsed olde rites" (V.1849), and marvel at the transience of "olde clerkis speche" (V.1854), but he also dismantles the historical apparatus upholding the credibility of his poem and ultimately entrenches it in a tradition of epic fabrication.

As I see it, Chaucer presents the Troy story as an exercise in Boccaccian confabulation: a multi-century-old piece of fiction, binding poets to one another from antiquity to his present. And if the *Troilus* is the vessel of this fabricated literary tradition, then Lollius – a self-negating symbol of authenticity – is its talisman. Despite his many protestations of textual fidelity, Chaucer has no intention of presenting Lollius as a legitimate source. Nor, for that matter, does he wield Lollius as a historicizing cudgel, whose Latin name and supposed antiquity will vest his work with some much-needed *gravitas*. On the contrary, Chaucer uses this figure to illuminate the fraudulence behind the medieval historiographers' practice of inventing sources. At first soliciting our confidence in Lollius, by the poem's end Chaucer has drained his fabricated source of all semblance of authority, drawing our attention to the collective textual fraud of Troy. Indeed, far from obfuscating Chaucer's artifice, Lollius *embodies* it.

An important precursor for such a figure is Dante's classically inspired "imagine di froda" ("image of fraud" [*Inf* XVII.7]), Geryon.[98] Symbolizing the very process of deception, Geryon has the face of a kind man, the patterned midsection of a serpent, and the tail of a scorpion, so that he can charm, distract, and then sting his victim. Upon encountering Geryon, Dante nearly remains silent, because he fears that this creature is too fantastical to be believed:

> Sempre a quel ver c'ha faccia di menzogna
> de' l'uom chiuder le labbra fin ch'el puote,
> però che sanza colpa fa vergogna;
> ma qui tacer nol posso; e per le note
> di questa comedia, lettor, ti giuro,
> s'elle non sien di lunga grazia vòte,
> ch'i' vidi per quell' aere grosso e scuro
> venir notando una figura in suso,
> maravigliosa ad ogne cor sicuro.

> To that truth which has the face of a lie a man should always close his lips as long as he can, since without fault it brings him shame, but here I cannot be silent; and by the notes of this comedy, reader, I swear to you – so may they not be empty of long grace – that I saw through that dense and dark air a figure come swimming upward, a cause for marvel to even the most secure of hearts.[99]

Dante poses as a truthteller here. He claims, like the medieval historiographers, that he in fact *sees* what he records – "Io vidi" – even if what he describes is hardly credible. Ironically, the poet's insistence on the truth of what is a blatantly invented episode forces us to recognize it as fiction. In Teodolinda Barolini's words, Geryon is "An outrageously paradoxical authenticating device, one that, by being so overtly inauthentic – so literally a figure for inauthenticity, a figure for 'fraud' – confronts and attempts to defuse the belatedness or inauthenticity to which the need for an authenticating device necessarily testifies."[100] Dante does not retreat from the fictionality of the *Commedia*, in other words. Instead, he swears on his poem as though it were the Bible, using Geryon "as the stake on which to gamble the veracity" of his vision.[101] We may perceive what Hollander has described as "an authorial wink" behind this episode: "I know you won't believe this (why should you? – I don't either), but the convention of my poem compels me to claim historicity even for such as Geryon."[102]

Contrary to Geryon, Lollius is *not* outrageously inauthentic. Old, Latin, and textual, he possesses all the trappings of a respectable source. Yet Chaucer, like Dante, writes a poem that compels him to claim its historical accuracy. And he, too, invents a figure to signal (if less glaringly) that his work is a fiction, first by asking us to place our trust in Lollius, and then by preventing us from keeping it there.[103] Systematically eroding his source's credibility, he thus destroys his poem's carefully constructed illusion of historical truth. Whereas for Boccaccio (as for Dante), poetry can conceal profound meaning beneath the veil of allegory – and so, advertising his artifice does not negate his work's exegetical potential – for Chaucer, I suspect a somewhat different ambition. What the poet makes clear in the *Troilus* (indeed, what he demonstrates as well in the *House of Fame*) is that poetry is *vital* to the immortalization of art and mankind, regardless of its literal or underlying truth. As we saw in chapter 3, poetry enables both authors and their stories to live once more, even if they survive vis-à-vis a tradition of authorial manipulation and invention.

Chaucer thus showcases his fiction-making for the sake of literary immortality. He emulates Boccaccio and Benoît in presenting his work as *fabula* masquerading as history, yet for the distinct purpose of creating a literary memorial. If Benôit deconstructs the truth claims of contemporary historiographers to show that the medieval tradition of Troy is itself a fiction, and Boccaccio exposes his work as allegorical in the service of defending poets and poetry, then Chaucer creates out of the *Troilus* a monument that is more lasting than bronze. It is a monument that he can bear up alongside Homer, Virgil, Dares, and even Lollius in the House of Fame, so that posterity will have his "name in honde."

In the *Testament of Cresseid*, Robert Henryson describes pulling *Troilus and Criseyde* from his bookshelf. He wonders if Chaucer, or some other author, fabricated the contents of this poem:

> Quha wait gif all that Chauceir wrait was trew?
> Nor I wait nocht gif this narratioun
> Be authoreist, or fenyeit of the new
> Be sum poeit, throw his inventioun.

Without dwelling further on the question, Henryson returns the *Troilus* to his shelf, trading it for a second text – this one anonymous – the contents of which relate Criseyde's "fatall desteny," and which is, presumably,

Henryson's source for the *Testament* itself.[104] Of course, this second tome does not exist. The substance of Henryson's *Testament*, detailing the course of Criseyde's life after Diomede abandons her, is entirely fabricated.

Henryson's blatant fictionalizing suggests that his scepticism regarding the historical integrity of the *Troilus* was not meant to disparage Chaucer. Rather, his remarks are consistent with what I have argued is a program of conspicuous artifice among authors of Troy, which entails the consistent revelation of collaborative invention, binding poets to one another as mutual curators of confabulated histories. Far from presenting his narrative as historically accurate, Chaucer advertises the contents of his poem as artifice, invoking and then undermining a series of authorizing devices. In the *Testament*, Henryson reveals his intricate understanding of Chaucer's Trojan poetics: not only does he cast doubt on the accuracy of the *Troilus*, but he also feigns reliance on his own version of Lollius – a spurious old tome – before adding a new narrative of Troy to the collection of previous fraudulent accounts.

Medieval poets "were able to play with fictionality as a matter of literary virtuosity, much as modern writers do," as Otter observes.[105] I would like to emphasize this word, virtuosity, as a marker of the wide-ranging textual deceptions perpetrated by authors of Troy. What if Benoît, Boccaccio, Chaucer, and even Henryson suspected that the diaries of Dares and Dictys were inauthentic, just as they assumed that Homer, Virgil, and Ovid made up stories? What if, in other words, from their perspective (as well as ours), the entire written legacy of Troy, and not only the works of those authors writing within a Homeric tradition, appeared fabricated? While Chaucer does not follow Boccaccio in penning his own treatise defending fiction and its makers, in its careful unravelling of oral and written truth, the *Troilus* functions similarly as a celebration of poetic innovation.[106] At the very least, by thematizing spuriousness – that is, by embedding signs of their own artifice within Trojan narratives of deceit (Criseyde's infidelity, the Trojan Horse, the fraud of Sinon, the treachery of Antenor) – Chaucer, Boccaccio, and Benoît align themselves with a tradition of poets who, instead of bearing witness to history, invented it. Exposing their works as fictions, they garnered if not historical then poetic authority, developing, through confabulation, the legend of Troy.

Chapter Five

Chaucer through the Looking Glass: Lydgate's Chaucerian Poetics

One of the most curious facets of Lydgate's poetry is the simultaneous omnipresence and absence of Chaucer. "Master" and "muse" in many of Lydgate's works, Chaucer is almost never his primary source. On the contrary, in some of Lydgate's most "Chaucerian" writings – that is, in the works that he presents as the immediate antecedents or continuations of Chaucer's poems, such as the *Troy Book*, *Siege of Thebes*, and *Fall of Princes* – Lydgate returns to the Latin, French, and Italian sources that precede Chaucer, and in some cases to the very sources used by Chaucer himself. He also goes to great lengths to establish the Latin and continental textual histories of these poems at the expense of crediting the influence of Chaucer and an English literary tradition, a move many critics have interpreted as antagonistic. Yet while Lydgate obscures Chaucer's role as a progenitor of his works, he praises Chaucer profusely in these same poems, emphasizing his predecessor's importance to an English literary tradition, if not to his own poetry. His treatment of Chaucer would thus seem to move between two contrasting poles: at the same time as he circumscribes his role in his writings, Lydgate hails Chaucer as the superior poet. Identifying him as the "cheeff poete off Bretayne," he situates his work in direct relation to – even as an extension of – Chaucer's poetry.[1]

Scholars have responded to Lydgate's ambivalent treatment of Chaucer with correspondingly ambivalent readings, for the most part placing Lydgate in the position of rival or sycophant. Nicholas Watson, Derek Pearsall, and James Simpson have pointed to a latent antagonism toward Chaucer in Lydgate's poetry.[2] Watson, for example, suggests that Lydgate treats Chaucer as a "challenge, a powerful and even threatening figure, some of whose authority [Lydgate] must annex as a vital part of [his] self-invention as [a] poet."[3] Pearsall argues similarly that Lydgate's "career, poem by poem, is a determined effort to ... surpass Chaucer in each of the major poetic genres that Chaucer had attempted."[4] A.C. Spearing and Seth Lerer, by contrast, interpret Lydgate's approach to Chaucer as deferential to the point of being childlike.[5] Lerer in particular delineates an aesthetic of inferiority in Lydgate's and other fifteenth-century poets' writings: "as children to the father, apprentices to the master, or aspirants before the laureate, those who would read and write after the poet share in the shadows of the secondary."[6]

Both of these approaches certainly help to explain many features in Lydgate's poetry, but insofar as they focus on Lydgate's relationship to Chaucer independent of a larger network of intertextual affiliations, they overlook an important way in which Lydgate engaged with Chaucer's treatment of his sources. As we have seen in the last four chapters, Chaucer consistently erases and mistranslates his predecessors, an approach to previous authors perhaps epitomized by his refusal to name Boccaccio anywhere in his works. Yet, as I have noted throughout this study, Chaucer's treatment of his sources draws on and develops extensive patterns of intertextual engagement. Virgil refrains from acknowledging his massive debt to Homer in the *Aeneid*, Petrarch makes a habit of not naming Dante, and Boccaccio invents ancient source texts to avoid crediting the influence of a range of authors, from Statius to Benôit de Sainte-Maure. Even as he erases and misreads their poetry, therefore, Chaucer in effect aligns himself with his authorial models by adapting their strategies of intertextual poetics.

We can identify a similar genealogical program in Lydgate's poetry. Although he praises his predecessor across his writings, Lydgate consistently avoids crediting Chaucer as a source, even where his imitation of Chaucer's poetry is undeniable. Yet in the course of minimizing Chaucer's influence, Lydgate modifies what I see as a specifically Chaucerian poetics: if Chaucer translates Boccaccio without naming him, then Lydgate pays ample tribute to Chaucer, meanwhile understating or simply denying his debt to Chaucer's poetry.[7] While elements of both the usurper and subordinate are evident in Lydgate's characterization of himself in relation to Chaucer, therefore, these elements must be read in light of analogous features we find in Chaucer's own writings.

This chapter will examine Lydgate's treatment of Chaucer accordingly, through the looking glass of Chaucer's earlier approach to intertextuality. In my analysis of two of Lydgate's massive Chaucerian works, the *Troy Book* (1412–20) and *Fall of Princes* (1431–9), I suggest that Lydgate draws clear parallels between his own poetics of intertextuality and Chaucer's, particularly those instances in which Chaucer erases Boccaccio.[8] Showcasing his suppression of his English predecessor, Lydgate aligns his treatment of Chaucer with Chaucer's earlier refusal to credit Boccaccio as a source. In the prologue to the *Troy Book* – a legend preoccupied, as we have seen, with questions of textual authenticity – Lydgate goes to great lengths to shape his illustrious literary ancestry, naming a series of credible authors whose example he will follow.[9] Although his use of the *Troilus* in this poem is considerable, he refuses to identify Chaucer among these sources – nor, indeed, until nearly a third of the way through his work – implicating Chaucer instead among a tradition of falsifying poets.

In the *Fall of Princes*, Lydgate names Chaucer almost immediately, celebrating him in the prologue as the "cheeff poete off Bretayne" (1.248). Despite this early display of regard for his English predecessor, however, Lydgate wholly elides mention of Chaucer's "Monk's Tale" in his careful delineation of his poem's textual history, positioning the *Fall* as the sole English translation of Boccaccio's *De casibus virorum illustrium* (begun c. 1355), which he repeatedly identifies as his primary source. Of course, there are other factors at play here, such as the question of national and linguistic prestige. There is no doubt, for example, that Lydgate's elevation of "Bochas" as his source for the *Fall* is symptomatic of the "new status Italian literature has acquired in England" from the fourteenth to the fifteenth century.[10] By the time Lydgate is writing, the *De casibus* had been translated from Latin into French and circulated widely in deluxe manuscripts. From his first titular rubric, Lydgate invokes what Guyda Armstrong describes as the "cultural capital" of this prestige text, proudly announcing that his book "is a 'Boccaccio,' with all that this signifies."[11] But the *De casibus* is not Lydgate's only – nor even his primary – source for the *Fall*. Instead, Lydgate relies on Laurent de Premierfait's French prose translation of Boccaccio's work. What is more, although the *Fall* replicates Chaucer's decision to write a version of the *De casibus* in English, Lydgate minimizes the significance of the "Monk's Tale" even as he praises Chaucer as a great poet. As in the earlier *Troy Book*, then, Lydgate's construction of an authorial genealogy involves the sublimation of previous authors' influence.

I think that Lydgate offers a distorted, yet recognizably derivative version of Chaucer's treatment of Boccaccio in these poems, and that, by doing so, he establishes his proximity to Chaucer. He demonstrates that he is capable of not only adapting Chaucer's writings, which we know he does as well, but also developing Chaucer's intertextual poetics. In other words, he camouflages Chaucer's influence and signals that this process of sublimation is something distinctly Chaucerian. At the same time, by making Chaucer's absence legible, Lydgate reveals an important, associative function of this elision, aligning himself with Chaucer even while neglecting to credit him as a source.[12] In the process of reading Lydgate reading Chaucer reading Boccaccio, that is, we can situate Lydgate among a pantheon of poets who, looking back to their literary models and forward to posterity, create their own legacy and fame.

Lineage and Legitimacy in the *Troy Book*

Genealogical strategies proliferate in the *Troy Book*.[13] A political commission by the Prince of Wales, later Henry V, and completed about eight years into his reign as king, this early work provides Lydgate with an opportunity to delineate imperial and literary lines of heredity, and thus to establish not only Henry's illustrious ancestry but also his own. Hailing his patron as one who "longe by successioun" will "gouerne Brutys Albyoun" (*Prol.* 103–4), Lydgate positions Henry as the true offspring of his father, Henry IV, "of knyghthood welle and spryng" (*Prol.* 96).[14] Indeed, Henry exhibits a similar honour and chivalry: "In euery part the tarage is the same, / Lyche his fader of maneris and of name" (*Prol.* 99–100).

After praising the noble lineage of his future king, Lydgate makes clear that he, too, derives from honourable stock. Situating himself as heir to the "true" history of Troy, originating with the diaries of Dares and Dictys, and standing in contrast to the lies told by Homer, Lydgate characterizes his subject as one "handed down in a literary tradition anchored and legitimized" by eyewitness accounts.[15] These authors who came before him severed the "verreie trewe corn … from the chaf" (*Prol.* 150–1) and compiled "the trouthe only" about Troy (*Prol.* 153), sparing their readers from deceit and negligence.[16] Describing his sources as elders and familial ancestors, Lydgate then aligns the practice of writing the true story of Troy with the process of imperial heredity. His predecessors bequeathed to him the stories of "thinges passed," so that "thorugh writyng thei be refresched newe" (*Prol.* 165–6). History, we learn, much like nobility, is handed down from one generation to the next:

> Of oure auncetrys left to vs by-hynde;
> To make a merour only to oure mynde,
> To seen eche thing trewly as it was,
> More bryght and clere than in any glas. (*Prol.* 167–70)

As Henry IV gave his name and royal qualities to his son, so too is the true history of Troy passed down, through the process of *translatio studii*, from first Dares and Dictys to the unnamed Benoît de Sainte-Maure, to his immediate source, Guido delle Colonne, and finally to Lydgate himself. Lydgate reserves the most praise for Guido, who "excellest by soureinte of stile" (*Prol.* 373), and whom he will attempt to follow most reverently, "as nyghe as euer I may" (*Prol.* 375). Equipped with this noble ancestry and mandate, Lydgate is both vessel and conduit of true history. He will write the *Troy Book* in "oure tonge" (*Prol.* 113), for Henry's sake (*Prol.*

110), and "y-writen as wel in oure langage / As in latyn and in frensche it is," so that "the trouthe we nat mys" (*Prol.* 114–16).[17]

Authorizing his work on account of the wisdom of his literary ancestors and his proximity to his patron, Lydgate thus uses his prologue to establish himself and Henry V as twin heirs to legitimate inheritances: the crown, in Henry's case, and the true story of Troy, in his own. As Henry will rule England "by successioun" after his father, usurper of Richard II's throne, so too will Lydgate translate the historical account of Troy's fall, as conveyed to him by his authorial models, and especially Guido, "sovereign" in style. The *Troy Book* has two analogous and, as Robert Meyer-Lee suggests, "idealized agents at its center: the prince who commissions it … and the translator who fulfills the commission."[18]

Parallel figures in more ways than one, Lydgate further insists that both men are responsible for importing Troy and its honourable ancestry to England, thereby restoring the glory of Brutus of Albion. Christopher Baswell observes that Lydgate presents Henry V as a "reverser of Trojan disaster who replicates its greatest power while avoiding its weakness."[19] For his part, Lydgate "insert[s] himself into the myth of restoration" by translating the Troy story into English and then presenting it to the man who has repeated Troy's triumphs.[20] He "encode[s] England as a mirror of Troy," and himself as a mirror of Henry.[21]

But establishing an implied homology between himself and Henry V affords Lydgate more than the opportunity to glorify his poetic endeavour and the Lancastrian dynasty. Lydgate also exploits this metaphorical affinity to comment on his relationship to his own deceased Ricardian predecessor, Chaucer.[22] Specifically, as we will see, he encourages us to interpret this relationship through the lens of Henry IV's usurpation and subsequent erasure of the previous king. By aligning himself with Henry, Lydgate positions himself as the ascendant sovereign poet of England – a status he implies is both his birthright and his due – at the same time as he suggests that Chaucer is his rightfully deposed and illegitimate predecessor. He cultivates this impression, moreover, by omitting both the former king, Richard, and the departed, preeminent "poet of Briteyne" (2.4687), Chaucer, from the parallel genealogies he articulates for himself and his patron.[23] Rich in names though it may be, with the absence of these two figures, the prologue provides only a partial snapshot of sovereign and literary English histories.[24]

To be sure, Lydgate's omission of Richard from Henry V's illustrious lineage would not have alarmed many of his readers.[25] On the contrary, this literary absence corresponded to a contemporary effort to eradicate Richard's memory in the political realm as well. As Alan S. Ambrisco and Paul Strohm note, the "crisis of legitimate succession" produced by the

Lancastrian usurpation pervaded every aspect of fifteenth-century political life.[26] Lacking stability and longevity, the reign of Henry IV and his descendants depended in part on their effacement of Richard's memory.[27] Eager to demonstrate the appearance of sanctioned power, the Lancastrians sought to expunge all record of the previous king's rule:

> [They] were unceasing in their efforts to erase Richard as a significant precursor. With respect to creative genealogy, the Lancastrians not only floated the Edmund Crouchback story, in which a son of Henry III with subsequent Lancastrian ties was said to have been barred from the throne by physical infirmity, but also built their claims by asserting … the virtues of other prominent Lancastrians such as John of Gaunt. Concurrently, Richard was demoted to that status of "a private person, sir Richard of Bordeaux, a simple knight," and, of course, paraded in shows of docility, spirited to prison in the remote north, starved, and finally displayed at a London funeral principally designed to show him really dead.[28]

But that Lydgate's omission of Richard would have been expected does not mean it would have gone unnoticed. If anything, precisely because the Lancastrians undertook the erasure of Richard's reign in full view of a public who knew better, Lydgate's subsequent elision of the usurped king could very well have served as a reminder of the precariousness of their claim to the throne. For that matter, Lydgate's praise of Henry IV as a "welle and spryng" of virtues, ruling England long "by successioun," has the potentially ironic effect of underscoring the very newness of his reign, since it glosses over the existence of his Ricardian predecessor. As Strohm rightly notes, Bolingbroke having "gained the throne only by *interrupting* 'successioun,'" and maintaining power despite the "superior claims of the Earl of March, Lydgate's dynastic argument would seem" – to his readers if not patron – "less than ideally secure."[29]

Lydgate exploits the visibility of Richard's absence to stage a parallel elision of his own Ricardian predecessor, providing a model for Chaucer's erasure that is both highly conspicuous and historically justifiable.[30] Although he does eventually praise him, and at various points, Lydgate excludes Chaucer from the genealogy of truthful authors provided in the prologue. Despite drawing considerably on the *Troilus* in his writing of the *Troy Book*, especially for the story of Troilus and Criseyde, he does not actually name Chaucer until nearly ten thousand lines into his poem (2.4679). At the same time, he implies that he is the first English author of the Troy story, offering to translate this narrative out of Latin and French into "oure tonge," so that "the trouthe we nat mys." But if Richard's absence could be rationalized on account of his obvious unpopularity during the Lancastrian reign, no such historico-political explanation exists for Lydgate's erasure of Chaucer, who was regularly invoked in the fifteenth century as an authorizing presence.[31] The *Troilus* was held in particularly high esteem. As Lee Patterson observes, the Troy narrative was a "legitimizing device" for unstable monarchies.[32] Prior to commissioning the *Troy Book*, and perhaps in the hopes of bolstering the perceived validity of the Lancastrian reign, Prince Henry ordered an ornate copy of the *Troilus* for his personal library.[33] Precisely because of Chaucer's prominence in the fifteenth century, however, it is hard to imagine that Lydgate's elision of his influence – on both his poem and the literary history of Troy – could have gone unnoticed. Rather, by suggesting that his own translation provides a necessary counterpart to the Latin and French historical accounts of Troy, meanwhile failing to acknowledge Chaucer among his authors, Lydgate implies that his poem gratifies a national demand for an English version of the Troy narrative, a demand that Chaucer's *Troilus* perhaps could have fulfilled but does not.

Were Chaucer merely omitted from Lydgate's catalogue of truthful sources, his absence could arguably be explained in terms of Lydgate's specific historiographic vision for his poem. Indeed, unlike Boccaccio's *Filostrato* and Chaucer's *Troilus*, Lydgate's poem does not focus on love. But Chaucer is implicated elsewhere in the prologue to the *Troy Book*, pointedly if indirectly, as part of a separate tradition of lying poets, and in a way that makes his absence from Lydgate's genealogy of legitimate authors all the more significant. In contrast to the credible Dares, Dictys, and Guido, Lydgate suggests, there are others who have propagated a false version of the city's fall. These writers "han the trouth spared / In her writing, and pleynly not declared" (*Prol.* 259–60). Following Homer, they transform history

Thorugh veyn[e] fables, whiche of entencioun
They han contreved by false transumpcioun
To hyde trouthe falsely vnder cloude
And the sothe of malys for to schroude. (*Prol.* 263–6)

Lydgate names three poets after Homer who perpetuate lies, beginning with Ovid, who "poetycally hath closyd / Falshede with trouthe" (*Prol.* 299–300), and Virgil, who is only in part "trewe of his writyng" (*Prol.* 305) on account of sometimes following "the tracys ... of Omeris stile" (*Prol.* 308). The final figure in this tradition of deceitful poets is none other than "Lollius," Chaucer's fabricated source for *Troilus and Criseyde*, who, Lydgate coyly notes, "eke" wrote of "this sege" (*Prol.* 309).[34]

We recall that Chaucer masked his close reliance on Boccaccio's *Filostrato* in the *Troilus* by claiming that he translated the invented Lollius word for word. By including Lollius among the fraudulent poets, then, Lydgate effectively tars Chaucer with the same brush: either Chaucer's source is a liar, or he is lying about his source. If we believe that Chaucer translated his author faithfully, then Lydgate's revelation of Lollius's fraudulence implicates Chaucer as well, since by Chaucer's own admittance, "as myn auctour seyde, so sey I" (*Tr.* II.18).[35] In this regard, by incorporating Lollius as the fourth figure in a genealogy of lying authors, Lydgate carves out a fifth spot for the unnamed Chaucer too, petitioning him implicitly as an extension of his spurious source. If, however, we reject – in this case rightly – Chaucer's assertion of fidelity to Lollius, then Chaucer is *still* a liar, and if not propagating "fables" then perhaps inventing them. At the very least, he is falsifying his source. In this respect, whether we confirm Lollius's illegitimacy or not, Lydgate implicates Chaucer in a tradition of fraudulent sources on Troy, as the fifth, unnamed author.

On the surface a tribute to his patron and ancestry, the *Troy Book*'s prologue thus delineates legitimate and illegitimate ancestries for both the crown and the literary tradition of Troy, with Henry and Lydgate usurping the stations of their spurious, unnamed predecessors. Richard is overthrown and delegitimized, first by the Lancastrians and then by Lydgate himself, who traces a genealogy of nobility from the earliest king of Britain, Brutus of Albion, to Henry IV to the Prince of Wales, excluding not only Richard but also his entire bloodline. Emphasizing the metaphorical proximity between the young Henry and himself, Lydgate then codes his erasure of Chaucer as a parallel dethroning of sorts. After identifying a lineage of reliable poets, consisting of Dares, Dictys, and Guido, he disparages the falsehoods of Homer, Virgil, Ovid, and Lollius, discrediting Chaucer by undermining his alleged source. Unlike the *Troy Book*, which translates the true history of Troy, the *Troilus* follows a fraudulent, perhaps apocryphal tradition. It is only right that its unreliable author should be displaced as "cheeff poete" of Britain, and that Lydgate, the poetic equivalent of his noble Lancastrian patron, be installed in his stead.[36] Implicitly likening his literary trajectory to Henry's inevitable path to the throne, Lydgate uses his prologue to align Richard's absence with Chaucer's. His patron will be the new king of England, and Lydgate, having stricken Chaucer from the record and exposed his illegitimate stock, will rule alongside Henry as its new sovereign poet.[37]

In light of his cultivation of an elaborate similitude between the Lancastrian usurpation of Richard and his own erasure and delegitimization of Chaucer, it is thus tempting to follow those critics who would read Lydgate's treatment of Chaucer as primarily antagonistic – i.e., as his genuine effort to outdo his illustrious predecessor (perhaps even as an early illustration of what Harold Bloom has called the "anxiety of influence").[38]

Indeed, Lydgate's refusal to name Chaucer while positioning himself as the sole English author of Troy appears to indicate what Watson describes as the poet's "ambitious competitiveness" with his absent source,[39] or, in Pearsall's words, his "inflated ambition": what Chaucer "did well, and for the first time in English poetry," Lydgate "must do better."[40] But there is a self-consciousness to Lydgate's poetics of intertextuality, which I am arguing is deliberately Chaucerian. By erasing Chaucer while usurping his role as English translator of Troy, that is, Lydgate is still, effectively, imitating him. Parodying the truth claims of the medieval historiographers, Chaucer, as we recall, insisted on Lollius instead of Boccaccio as his source for the *Troilus*. By refusing to acknowledge his debt to the *Troilus* while also maligning Lollius (and so, Chaucer) as fraudulent, Lydgate, I think, looks back to Chaucer's famous elision of the *Filostrato*, reinforcing his claim as Chaucer's literary heir by emulating his poetics.

The sheer length of the *Troy Book* and the time it took to write it also serve to complicate the simple competitive reading offered in earlier criticism, in that so much changed for both the poet and his patron from the work's commencement to its completion. In April of 1413, less than a year after Lydgate began his translation of the *Historia*, Henry V ascended to the throne. One of the first things he did in his capacity as king of England was to dig up the bones of his deposed uncle and rebury him with honours in Westminster. This reburial was, we may be sure, "a significant affirmation of continuity and hereditary legitimacy," and an important step toward publicly ameliorating the breech between his Lancastrian father and Ricardian uncle.[41] Perhaps offering himself once again as the metaphorical mirror of his patron, Lydgate performs a similar exhumation of Chaucer and the *Troilus* in the later books of his poem. Seemingly forgetting his promise to follow Guido "from point to point, lyche as [his] bokis seyn" (1.919), along with his earlier deprecation of Lollius as a liar, he turns to Chaucer as both master and source.

Indeed, although erased and discredited vis-à-vis the figure of Lollius in the *Troy Book*'s prologue, by the end of the second book, Chaucer develops into a person of great authority, jockeying with Guido for the position of Lydgate's "maister" (3.4255).[42] "Chefe poete / that euere was yit in oure langage" (3.4256–7) and magnifier of "oure tonge" (3.4242), Chaucer is the first "to reyne / The gold dewe-dropis of rethorik so fyne, / Oure rude langage only t'enlwmyne" (2.4698–4700). His verse the magnificent ruby on the copper ring of English poetry (2.4710), Chaucer is the English counterpart to the laureate Petrarch. Lydgate registers his "maister Galfride" in the House of Fame, "Amonge other in the higheste sete" (3.4255–6). At the conclusion of the *Troy Book*, Lydgate pays tribute to Chaucer in a new way, echoing Chaucer's submission of the *Troilus* to Gower and

Strode for correction by conveying his own poem to his master for similar improvement. Trusting that Chaucer will be lenient despite finding "ful many [a] spot" (5.3521), Lydgate describes his predecessor as equal parts genial and languid: "Hym liste nat pinche nor gruche at euery blot," he suggests, "Nor meue hym silf to parturbe his reste" (5.3522–3). In his final farewell to his poem, Lydgate adapts yet another recognizably Chaucerian manoeuvre: "Go, litel bok," he commands, and "put the in the grace / Of hym that is most of excellence" (*Env.* 92–3). Echoing not only his words "but also Chaucer's context of warning his poem to be true to its predecessors, Lydgate here conflates Chaucer with Henry as the one 'most of excellence,'" as Sylvia Federico observes. He would seem to "associate[e] his own poetic legitimacy not with his patron," nor even with his much-lauded source, Guido, but ultimately "with Chaucer."[43]

The beneficiary of his poem and praise, Chaucer is also, and increasingly, Lydgate's source for much of the *Troy Book*'s material. Despite identifying Guido as his authorial model, Lydgate regularly deviates from the *Historia*, and most of the changes he makes to this work align his poem categorically with Chaucer's.[44] As Baswell observes, Lydgate "repeatedly pulls [his] poem's focus to Chaucer as its source," replacing a "Latin model of rhetorical linguistic accomplishment ... with a native model of accomplished eloquence."[45] Some of these changes are structural or stylistic: Lydgate reduces Guido's *Historia* from over thirty books to a taut Chaucerian five (a move "presumably meant to recall" the *Troilus*), and mimics Chaucer's rhyme scheme from the *Canterbury Tales*.[46] Other changes are more narrative: Lydgate incorporates the romance of Troilus and Criseyde into his story of war, and he relies on Chaucer's poem as his subtext.

But it is especially in Lydgate's description of Criseyde that we see the extent of Chaucer's influence. Here, Lydgate goes beyond mere emulation to baldly appropriating Chaucer's words, incorporating a passage from *Troilus and Criseyde* directly into his own poem.[47] Finding himself without the language to describe Criseyde's beauty, Lydgate's pen stumbles. Struggling to follow the order of the *Historia* yet loath to commit the "highe foly" of attempting to improve on Chaucer's poetry, he must choose between "necligence" and "presumpcioun" (2.4692). In the end, rather than compete with Chaucer, he replicates Chaucer's portrait of Criseyde nearly to the letter. What is more, he prefaces this episode by echoing Chaucer's favourite (if ironic) declaration of inadequacy.[48] He will "procede" with Criseyde's description "yif I konne" (2.4721–2):

> Ther-to of schap, of face, and of chere,
> Ther myghte be no fairer creature

And Saue hir browes Ioyneden y-fere,
No man koude in hir a lake espien. (2.4738–9, 2.4748–9)

With a few minor exceptions, these lines are, as Pearsall first noted, identical to Chaucer's:[49]

Therto of shap, of face, and ek of cheere,
Ther myghte ben no fairer creature.
And, save hire browes joyneden yfeere,
Ther nas no lak, in aught I kan espien. (*Tr.* V.807–8, V.813–14)

Faced with the task of describing Criseyde in verse "yif I konne," Lydgate finds that he cannot, or at least not with his own words and imagery.

To be sure, absorbing the text of the *Troilus* directly into his poem is one way to avoid competition with Chaucer. But Lydgate's blatant emulation of the *Troilus* undermines his original promise to follow Guido's *Historia* "as nyghe as euer I may." Excessive in his recognition of Guido and miserly in his acknowledgment of Chaucer, Lydgate is neither faithful to nor candid about his textual models. Instead, finding himself "sette euene amyddes tweyne" (2.6912) – caught between two conflicting authors and narrative ambitions – he must forsake his historical source to follow his English "maister."[50]

Because Lydgate identified Lollius as spurious in the prologue, his turn to Chaucer complicates his earlier protestations of textual and historical fidelity. He is not only departing from Guido, but also doing so to follow a writer whose alleged source Lydgate has already dismissed as illegitimate.[51] Perhaps Lydgate has moved on from or changed his mind about the status of Lollius and the Homeric tradition by the time he borrows directly from the *Troilus*. Still, by emulating Chaucer, he places his readers in an interpretive gridlock. We can salvage Chaucer as a legitimate authority only by dismissing Lydgate's earlier assertion that Lollius is part of a spurious tradition. To do so, however, we must concede that Lydgate slandered Chaucer's source erroneously, an allowance that requires our judgment of Lydgate if not Chaucer as unreliable. Should we accept Lydgate's original claim that Lollius fabricated stories, by contrast, then it is Chaucer who is peddling fictions, and wherever Lydgate emulates Chaucer, he too must be disseminating false content. Either way we interpret his turn to Chaucer as a model, in other words, the credibility of the *Troy Book* is compromised. Substituting historical for poetical authority, Lydgate exposes himself as an unreliable witness to the events that took place during the siege of Troy, whose pretensions to truth are overblown.

Intriguingly, both of these actions – his turn to Chaucer as a source and the revelation of his own illegitimacy – reinforce Lydgate's desired kinship not with Dares, Dictys, and Guido, his alleged models from the prologue, but rather with the Homeric tradition of Troy. As I argued in the previous chapter, poets including Benoît de Sainte-Maure, Boccaccio, and Chaucer made spurious claims to legitimacy that operated at least in part as petitions to epic authority. By revealing their collective fraudulence – what Boccaccio calls "confabulation" – authors of Troy aligned themselves with Homer, Virgil, and Ovid even as they vocally condemned these poets for their lies. Lydgate's undermining of his own historical legitimacy similarly incriminates him among those authors whom he denounced in his prologue for inventing "vain[e] fables" under the guise of speaking truth: Homer, Virgil, Ovid, and Lollius. By drawing on the *Troilus* as a source, he thus positions himself, albeit tacitly, after Lollius and (by extension) Chaucer as the sixth and final poet in a lineage of confabulators. In doing so, he replicates Chaucer's genealogy of epic poets from the *Troilus* almost precisely, writing himself into an illustrious authorial succession while appropriating for himself the coveted "sixth of six" position.[52] That two out of six of Lydgate's fictionalizing poets remain unnamed only solidifies his connection to Chaucer. Bound together by their common strategies of erasure and invention, Lydgate offers himself as his master's disciple in not only poetry but also poetics, excluding Chaucer from the prologue only to appeal to him later as both authority and source.

Insofar as Lydgate's approach to his predecessor changes over the course of the *Troy Book*, our scholarly tendency to reduce Lydgate's treatment of Chaucer to one or another binary impulse – antagonism or deference – is thus not entirely helpful. To assess this treatment as purely laudatory on account of Lydgate's eventual praise and even emulation of Chaucer ignores Lydgate's earlier efforts to erase and delegitimize him. To interpret Lydgate's approach to Chaucer as merely hostile, however, reduces the poem to a very specific set of historical moments: the fall of Troy, Henry IV's usurpation of Richard II, and the date and time at which Lydgate begins his poem. Instead, written over the course of nearly a decade, the *Troy Book* illustrates a historical and literary gamut. As Richard was usurped by Henry only to have his bones reburied with honour by Henry's son, so too does Lydgate omit his Ricardian predecessor from his record of Trojan literary history only to resurrect him as both ancestor and source. After swearing fidelity to Guido, Lydgate unveils his reliance on not only the *Historia* but also the *Troilus*, implicating himself in the same tradition of authorial elision and invention that Chaucer evoked with his fabrication of Lollius. History, like poetry, repeats itself, a point Lydgate will make explicit in the repetitive and catastrophic portraits of the *Fall of*

Princes but nevertheless develops in the *Troy Book* in his presentation of erasure as both cyclical and derivative. It is this very cycle of usurpation and ascension, of erasure and primacy, which connects rulers and poets across time and space.

Lydgate's "Bochas" and Chaucer's *Fall of Princes*

In the *Fall of Princes*, Lydgate turns from the demise of a single city to the fates of the multitude. Following in the footsteps of his Latin and French sources, he records the stories of famous men and women from biblical antiquity to present day. As he did in the *Troy Book*, moreover, he indicates his desire to not only convey but also write himself into literary history.[53] The colophon provides Lydgate's name, where he is from, and why he translated the poem: the work is "translatid in to Inglissh bi Iohn Ludgate Monke of the Monastery of Seynt Edmundes Bury atte commaundement of the worthi Prynce Humfrey Duk of Gloucestre." In the opening lines, Lydgate emphasizes the provenance of the stories he tells, comparing his poem to a piece of pottery crafted out the broken pieces of previous authors' works. He explains that he will begin with the fall of Adam and end with the story of King John, who was taken prisoner in France by Prince Edward. Lydgate then praises the "diligence" (1.1) of the "noble translatour" (1.99), Laurent de Premierfait, who, in *Des cas des nobles hommes et femmes*, translated Boccaccio's *De casibus virorum illustrium* "in Frensh … Out of Latyn" (1.2–3). Finally, after praising Laurent for many lines, Lydgate turns his attention to Boccaccio. The original "auctour off this book" (1.141) Boccaccio was first in "Shewyng a merour how al the world shal faile" (1.159).

By starting with himself and moving backward to Laurent and Boccaccio, Lydgate establishes his name within a succession of poets lamenting the falls of noble men and women. He will translate his two "auctours," Boccaccio and Laurent, who, having written this work in Latin and French, left an opening for an English translation. The impression one receives is that Lydgate is "a writer's writer," as Meyer-Lee points out, "a learned poet self-consciously working in a long tradition" and "acknowledging his debts and sources."[54] "This is no silent translation," according to Armstrong, "but a deliberate remaking, a process where Lydgate gives every man his due."[55] The *Fall* is, as Lydgate's meticulous documentation of its textual history suggests, a kind of aggregate effort: it is the culmination of Boccaccio's *De casibus*, Laurent's *Des cas*, and Lydgate's own translation – of each author's creation and recreation of the work.

Yet, as at the start of the *Troy Book*, notably absent from Lydgate's catalogue of authors, translators, and sources are Chaucer and his "Monk's

Tale." As the immediate English precursor of the *Fall*, and itself a partial translation of Boccaccio's *De casibus*, the "Monk's Tale" should – or at least be expected to – receive mention in Lydgate's careful documentation of his poem's textual history. While not the basis for Lydgate's poem, the "Monk's Tale" stands behind the *Fall* as an important textual archetype, in the same way that the *Troilus* underlies the *Troy Book*, the "Knight's Tale" the *Siege of Thebes*, and the *House of Fame* the *Temple of Glass*. None of these Lydgatian poems rely on Chaucer as their primary or sustained source, yet, as previous scholars have noted, they are nevertheless developed in imitation of his writings.[56] Lydgate, however, excludes Chaucer and his "Monk's Tale" from the *Fall*'s literary lineage, positioning himself instead (and again) as the sole inheritor of a Latin and French tradition, and implying, by omission, that he alone has translated the *De casibus* into English.[57] If his poem is a vessel made from the broken pieces of his predecessors' writings, then this literary lineage suggests that none of these fragments are Chaucer's.

Whereas in the prologue to the *Troy Book* his refusal to recognize Chaucer's *Troilus* as a significant precursor takes on a distinctly historical dimension, in the *Fall*, Lydgate's motivations for erasing the "Monk's Tale" appear to be predominantly literary.[58] In addition to omitting Chaucer from his catalogue of authorial influences, Lydgate foregrounds his reliance on Boccaccio – Chaucer's original yet obfuscated source for the "Monk's Tale" – insisting that he will follow Bochas as closely as he is able. To be sure, Lydgate has ample reasons for identifying the *De casibus* as the *Fall*'s textual antecedent. For one, such a move enables him to capitalize on Boccaccio's status as an important and reputable source, a status that, as Armstrong notes, citing changing responses to the *Decameron*, has shifted since the time Chaucer was writing.

> At each point in his reception history, Boccaccio has been known for very divergent texts; and surprisingly, the work now perceived as his acknowledged masterpiece ... was not at all esteemed for the first two hundred years or so of his English reception. If translated texts provide evidence of an unmet need in the receiving culture, and are produced to fill a perceived gap in the reading life of the nation, they can be understood generally to represent a prestige import into English. The parameters by which this prestige is valorized, however, are highly variable, and change in different linguistic communities and time periods.[59]

Duke Humphrey's open fondness for Boccaccio's works no doubt also played a prominent role in Lydgate's praise of his Italian model.[60] (Armstrong documents Humphrey's "deeply rooted" interest in Boccaccio, an interest that led the Duke to patronize not one but two translations of the poet's works.)[61] Finally, medieval theory distinguishes between the roles of author and translator, and Lydgate's emphasis on Bochas as opposed to Laurent could simply reflect this division.[62]

Lydgate's Boccaccio, then, is not Chaucer's Boccaccio, nor should we expect the two English poets to cite their Italian source in a similar manner. At the same time, Lydgate's emphasis on Bochas can stem from more than one impulse. Perhaps Lydgate accentuates Boccaccio's influence to show his patron and readers his familiarity with Italian humanism, and to indicate his perception of Boccaccio (as opposed to Laurent) as his actual source. Neither of these ambitions is, moreover, in conflict with what I see as his desire to replicate Chaucer's poetics of intertextuality in his treatment of his sources.[63] In what follows, I will suggest that by accentuating Boccaccio's presence in the *Fall* at the expense of fully acknowledging his other debts – i.e., to his actual source, Laurent, or to his forerunner in translating Boccaccio's *De casibus* into English, Chaucer – Lydgate trains our focus on the Italian author as the progenitor of the *De casibus* tradition. What this means is that whether or not we recognized Boccaccio as Chaucer's original source for the "Monk's Tale," we are confronted with this information in the *Fall*.

At the same time as he increases the visibility of Boccaccio in his own poem, Lydgate draws our attention to Chaucer's erasure of Boccaccio across his poetry. Although not commenting on this erasure directly, he alludes to the illegitimacy of Chaucer's pseudo-Latin authorities from the *Troilus* and the "Monk's Tale," revealing that Chaucer's actual source for these works was Italian (a manoeuvre I will discuss later in this chapter). For Lydgate, I argue, the figure of Bochas is more than the author of the *De casibus* – more, still, than the poet occupying the shelves of Humphrey's library. He is also, and perhaps most significantly, Chaucer's unacknowledged source from the "Monk's Tale" and other works. As I will claim in this next section, Lydgate draws back the curtain from Chaucer's poetics of intertextuality. He indicates that Chaucer made a recurring practice of concealing the identity of his source, and then he reveals that this source is Boccaccio. Finally, Lydgate hints that his own exaggerated fidelity to Boccaccio and elision of Chaucer are connected. Minimizing his debt to Chaucer while excavating Chaucer's poetics of erasure, Lydgate thus illuminates a shared pattern of authorial dissimulation in both his and Chaucer's works.

But first, to suggest that Lydgate obscures Chaucer's influence in the *Fall* requires further explanation, because if Lydgate waited until nearly a third of the way through the *Troy Book* to name Chaucer, then in this later poem he praises Chaucer early and often.[64] After tracing the textual lineage of his poem in the prologue to the work, he pauses to lament the death of the "cheeff poete off Breteyne":

> But, o allas! who shal be my muse,
> Or onto whom shal I for helpe calle?
> My maistir Chaucer, with his fresh comedies,
> Is ded, allas, cheeff poete off Breteyne,
> That whilom made ful pitous tragedies;
> The fall of pryncis he dede also compleyne,
> As he that was of makyng souereyne,
> Whom al this land sholde off riht preferre,
> Sithe off oure language he was the lodesterre. (1.239–40, 1.246–52)

Although overtly praising Chaucer, this passage has the effect of downplaying the influence of Chaucer and the "Monk's Tale" on his poem. By this point in the prologue, Lydgate has finished acknowledging his literary debts, having recognized Laurent's French translation and named Boccaccio as his author repeatedly. In suggesting that Chaucer would be his "muse" – that is, if he were still alive – Lydgate thus marks a difference between the authorities whom he is translating and Chaucer. Boccaccio and Laurent, writing in other languages, allow Lydgate to position himself as a humble but useful translator. But if Chaucer has already written a version of the *De casibus* in English, what role is left for Lydgate as author? Indeed, what role does medieval literary theory permit someone like Lydgate, who, unless he offers himself as Chaucer's scribe or compiler, is in the position of retreading territory Chaucer has already walked? Either he must contend with the "Monk's Tale" as a prototype or ignore it altogether, and in doing so suggest that it is unworthy of attention. Stressing Chaucer's poetic and physical inertness, Lydgate appears to choose the latter. Chaucer is not only missing from Lydgate's genealogy of authors, but he is also *dead* – no longer capable of producing new works, or of holding court as the country's sovereign maker. While he has the potential to inspire, in other words, he can no longer create. Like Petrarch and his Griselda, who Chaucer reminds us in the "Clerk's Tale" are, in the first case, "deed and nayled in his chest" (IV.29), and in the second, "deed, and eek hire pacience" (IV.1177), Chaucer and his poem seem to function in the *Fall* as antiquated models that cannot, and perhaps should not, be emulated. They set an untenable standard, and are ultimately "impertinent" (IV.54).

Because Chaucer is dead, moreover, Lydgate can put his praise of the poet in the past tense without appearing overtly disingenuous. But his use of this tense can also be read to suggest that these laudatory expressions are no longer applicable. Chaucer "*was*" of "makyng" sovereign, and "*was*" the "lodesterre" of "oure langage," but "*is*," now, "ded, allas," leaving space for a new "cheeff poete off Breteyne." The expectation is that Lydgate himself will fulfil this position, a reading inevitably fortified by his characterization of the *Fall* as the direct English successor of the *De casibus* and *Des cas*. The form of Lydgate's praise further strengthens this impression. In charting the course of Chaucer's career – his rise and fall from sovereign poet to death – Lydgate positions Chaucer as one of his poem's literary subjects. Indeed, he gives Chaucer what is arguably the first portrait of his poem. Ascending to poetic excellence only to plummet to his death, Chaucer follows the pattern of Lydgate's other mighty exempla, who rise to great prominence before they fall, sometimes at the hands of a worthy successor. The tragedy of Laius, for example, is followed by the story of the son who killed him (1.3158–3653). Lydgate narrates the life of Julius Caesar immediately after he describes the fall of Pompey at Caesar's hands (6.2024–2819), and the story of Herod the Great is followed by an account of his sons, Herod Antipas and Herod Archelaus (7.78–312), who succeed their father in power. In these instances, Lydgate is following the order of his French and Latin models, yet this organizational strategy inflects how we read Chaucer's narrative arc as well. Lydgate's accounts of rulers, generals, and otherwise powerful men and women depict recurring shifts in power. Inevitably, the fall of one individual precipitates the rise of another, because the poem spins on the axis of Fortune's wheel. Chaucer's demise, like the deaths of other sovereigns – authorial or otherwise – creates a similar vacancy for a new chief poet, one that Lydgate suggests he will occupy. "Dante in Inglissh" (1.302), translator of a Latin and continental tradition, Chaucer is at least superficially made redundant by Lydgate, who expands Chaucer's Boccaccian narrative without fully crediting Chaucer for having written it first.

Buried within Lydgate's eulogistic remarks on Chaucer is also the poem's first reference to the "Monk's Tale." Chaucer once wrote "fresh comedies," and "whilom made ful pitous tragedies; / The fall of pryncis he dede also compleyne." Deceptively benign, this brief allusion to the "Monk's Tale" seems to highlight Lydgate's earlier omission of Chaucer and his work from his catalogue of sources. Instead of remedying this lapse by finally acknowledging the "Monk's Tale" as an important forerunner of the *Fall*, Lydgate couches this reference within a catalogue of other Chaucerian endeavours. What is more, he introduces Chaucer's narrative here in terms of its subject matter, and with the title of his own poem, as though it were derivative of his translation.[65] In doing so, he implies that Chaucer's poem has been subsumed beneath his literary enterprise. As yet another redaction of the *De casibus*, and an incomplete one at that, the "Monk's Tale" has no obvious utility or purpose –

to be sure, it does not even warrant its own name. Lydgate further appends to this description the term "also": "The fall of pryncis he dede also compleyne." This "also" could describe Chaucer's writing process, i.e., Chaucer made comedies and tragedies, *together with* a compilation of the falls of princes. Or, like Lydgate's praise of Chaucer in the past tense, it can be read another way, to indicate Chaucer's ancillary status. As in, Lydgate wrote the *Fall of Princes*, while "the fall of pryncis" Chaucer did "*also*" – in addition to Lydgate – complain.[66] Chaucer may have crafted a poem on this subject, in other words, but Lydgate is the first English author to treat this material with any real scope and gravity. In his introduction of his predecessor, Lydgate thus seems to acknowledge that Chaucer causes a problem for the tidy genealogy in which he has tried to place himself, and that he will address this problem by praising Chaucer as a poet while minimizing the significance of his poetry to his own work. In essence, this passage performs in miniature the problem of Chaucerian authority that plays out over several thousand lines in the poem.

If the prologue hints at a difficulty of Chaucerian antecedence, then in the body of his work Lydgate demonstrates what this problem is in practice – he does not want to retranslate Chaucer's sources, nor will he compile from the "Monk's Tale." Rather, with the obvious exception of the *De casibus* itself, whenever Lydgate is confronted with the prospect of rewriting a story that Chaucer has already told, he articulates a desire to change course, and to translate a different author entirely. He demurs from narrating the story of the Roman Lucretia, for example, because Chaucer, "cheeff poete off Bretayne" (2.979), has already written her tale in the *Legend of Good Women*, and "it were but veyn / Thyng seid be hym to write it newe ageyn" (2.1000–1). Although he proceeds with her account, Lydgate tells a version translated from the Latin prose *Declamatio* of Coluccio Salutati, whereas Chaucer relied primarily on Ovid's *Fasti*.[67] The story of Procne and Philomela presents a similar problem. Lydgate insists that to speak of the downfall of these sisters would be presumptuous, since Chaucer has bemoaned it elsewhere:

Ther pitous fate in open to expresse,
It were to me but a presumpcioun,
Sithe that Chaucer dede his besynesse
In his legende, as maad is mencioun,
Ther martirdam and ther passioun. (1.1793–7)

In this case, Lydgate turns his attention to Cadmus, seeing no point in attempting to improve on Chaucer's poetry.

Prior to narrating the story of Cleopatra, Lydgate finds that he must once again contend with a Chaucerian archetype. Chaucer described the queen's fate in the *Legend of Cleopatra*, and so her "tragedie" must be "set aside" (6.3620–1) There is, Lydgate explains, a "vanity" to reproducing Chaucer's textual labour:

> Thyng onys said be labour of Chauceer
> Wer presumpcioun me to make ageyn,
> Whos makyng was so notable & enteer,
> Riht compendious and notable in certeyn.
> Which to reherse the labour wer but veyn. (6.3627–31)

Although he later recounts Cleopatra's story at length, Lydgate makes clear that he does so only because Bochas recorded her untimely end first, and he is bound by the dictates and structure of the *De casibus*. To this end, the story of Zenobia presents a particular challenge. Although Chaucer already treated "hir pitous fall" in the "Monk's Tale" (8.671), a detail that at first discourages Lydgate from retelling it, his account is developed from Boccaccio's. For Lydgate, then, fidelity to his source necessitates replicating Chaucer's labour at least in part. In the end, he strikes a compromise: he will tell Zenobia's story, drawing on Boccaccio and Laurent for the narrative, yet he will provide only the essential details – "I will passe ouer, rehersyng but the grete" (8.672).[68] Indeed, to "passe ouer" narratives that Chaucer has already told appears to be a general rule for Lydgate. Whereas his Latin and continental authors are suitable for revision and translation, he indicates repeatedly that he is unwilling or unable to rework stories that Chaucer has already composed.[69]

In both the prologue and the body of the *Fall*, then, Lydgate circumscribes the role that Chaucer is allowed to play, refusing to permit Chaucer's verse to pervade, and potentially overshadow, his poem. So loath is he to replicate Chaucer's poetic endeavours that, with the exception of Boccaccio, whose influence Chaucer never acknowledges, Lydgate goes out of his way to avoid even retranslating Chaucer's sources. This is a drastically different approach to his predecessor, and to the dangers of poetic redundancy, from that in the *Troy Book*, where, faced with the option of rewording something Chaucer had already written, Lydgate inserted Chaucer's English directly into his poem. At the same time, his incessant need to call attention to the novelty of his translation – a novelty predicated on his resolve to avoid rewriting Chaucerian poetry – still points, at least initially, to Lydgate's desire to displace his predecessor as "cheeff poete off Bretayne." Although not "translating" Chaucer, he is still retranslating Chaucerian narratives, and so offering himself as Chaucer's substitute. As Elizabeth Scala notes, in displacing a source, a translation "appropriates its authority in the very act of replacing its language (and perhaps its meaning). This feat is accomplished only because displacement is never a fully completed transaction. The former text 'appears' and 'disappears' at the very moment a new one is produced."[70] While Lydgate is performing the opposite task to what Scala here considers (he does not translate Chaucer into a new language but rather provides new English translations of narratives Chaucer has already written), Scala's point still applies. Every time Lydgate insists on not following Chaucer, Chaucer's writing both appears and disappears as part of the *Fall*'s textual history. Like Heidegger's crossed-out inscription of "being" in *Zur Seinsfrage*, the deleted/absent text is not a "merely negative symbol"; rather, as Derrida reminds us, it is meant to be seen: "Under its strokes the presence of a transcendental signified is effaced while still remaining legible. Is destroyed while making visible the very idea of the sign. In as much as it de-limits onto-theology, the metaphysics of presence and logocentrism, this last writing is also the first writing."[71] Lydgate's approach to creating something original likewise "makes visible" the text that his own writing replaces. The Chaucerian precedent remains legible in the *Fall* even while being eschewed.

How, then, do we reconcile Lydgate's insistence that he is deferring to Chaucer's authority with his repeated attempts to position himself as Chaucer's literary substitute? It is once again Lydgate's poetics, if not his poetry, that complicates a comfortable reading of this performance as purely antagonistic. Even as he insinuates his role as Chaucer's usurper, Lydgate excavates a pattern of authorial dissimulation in his predecessor's poetry, demonstrating his familiarity with Chaucer's erasure of Boccaccio. By using Chaucer's elision of his vernacular source as the backdrop for his own apparent oversight of the "Monk's Tale" (which, for the immediate English precursor of the *Fall*, receives surprisingly little attention), Lydgate qualifies this treatment as a literary trope, isolating it to a certain extent from a primarily psychoanalytic reading.[72] While not necessarily uninhibited by desire, antagonism, or other such motivations, Lydgate's deliberate inattention to the "Monk's Tale" is on some level lateral to these concerns, because it is developed in imitation of previous examples of authorial erasure. Like the poet's "dullness" (which, as David Lawton has admirably shown, was a cultivated aesthetic in the fifteenth century), this device draws on a set of preestablished literary topoi, and further asks to be interpreted in light of them.[73]

Perhaps the most striking example of Lydgate's consideration of Chaucer's intertextual poetics can be found in the *Fall*'s prologue. Immediately following his delineation of the *Fall*'s textual history – a history from which the "Monk's Tale" is significantly absent – Lydgate includes an eighty-four-line catalogue of Chaucer's work, so that we can "yiue hym laude & glory / And putte his name with poetis in memory" (1.279–80).[74] The first poem he mentions, and further locates within an authorial tradition, is *Troilus and Criseyde*. In the *Troy Book*, as we recall, Lydgate criticized Chaucer's Lollius for being untruthful. Lollius was the final poet among those authors of Troy who "hyde trouthe falsely under cloude / And the sothe of malys for to schroude." In the *Fall*, however, Lydgate claims that Chaucer's source for the *Troilus* was not Lollius at all, but rather an Italian book called "Trophe." "In youthe," Lydgate explains, Chaucer

made a translacion
Off a boke which called is Trophe.
In Lumbarde tunge, as men may reede & see,
And in our vulgar, long or that he deide,
Gaff it the name of Troilous & Cresseide. (1.283–7)

Of course, Chaucer makes no mention in the *Troilus* of either a book or an author called Trophe. He does, however, name him in the "Monk's Tale," as we have seen, identifying this figure as his source for the portrait of Hercules.[75] "At bothe the worldes endes," the Monk notes, "seith Trophee, / In stide of boundes he a pileer sette" (VII.2117–18). Lydgate, then, substitutes one of Chaucer's spurious Latin authorities for another, and further qualifies this source as Italian, a complex, yet deeply revelatory misattribution.

At the very least, in claiming that Chaucer translates a "Lumbarde" text, Lydgate shows himself keenly aware that Chaucer's source for the Troilus was Italian and not Latin, despite Chaucer's own claims to the contrary. But this passage also serves as a literary palinode: in attributing the *Troilus* to Trophe, Lydgate looks back to, and retracts, his earlier identification of Lollius in the *Troy Book* as a historically real, if methodologically fraudulent, author.[76] Far from corroborating the existence of Lollius, this passage suggests that by the time he wrote the *Fall*, if not before, Lydgate thought of Lollius and Trophe as interchangeable. Since both figures appear in works in which Boccaccio is Chaucer's unacknowledged model, moreover, it seems likely that Lydgate discerned a larger pattern of authorial erasure across Chaucer's poetry – signalled, perhaps, by his feigned reliance on an invented Latin authority. Lydgate then cross-pollinates Chaucer's spurious sources, substituting Lollius for Trophe before unmasking Trophe as Italian, a manoeuvre that bespeaks his profound understanding of Chaucer's intertextual play.

In the *Fall*'s prologue, Lydgate calls a bluff on Chaucer's fictional Latin authors from the "Monk's Tale" and the *Troilus* and further indicates that

Chaucer's actual source for both works was Italian. In the remainder of the poem, Lydgate shows us who this silenced source really was, unmasking Boccaccio as the progenitor of the *De casibus* tradition, and so of Chaucer's translation as well as his own. All but ignoring his debt to Laurent following his initial mention of him in the prologue, Lydgate makes grand statements of loyalty to Boccaccio, promising to follow his *De casibus* in tone and substance ("aftir myn auctour lik as I may atteyne" [1.232]). "Bochas" is the "auctour off this book" (1.141) and "myn auctour for to sue" (1.230). The *Fall* is a translation of "the book of Bochas" (1.2), or, as it is called elsewhere, "the noble book off this Iohn Bochas" (1.423). Boccaccio is also Lydgate's narrator, a role he played in the *De casibus* as well. Boccaccio wrote himself into his poem as a character of sorts, who is visited in his study by shades. He has lengthy conversations with these subjects, enticing some with the rewards of fame and threatening others with slander.[77] Beyond these exchanges, Boccaccio engages with allegorical figures, such as Fortune, and exhorts his readers with moral asides. Instead of telling the *Fall* from his own perspective, Lydgate retains Boccaccio in his earlier role. Observing everything through the lens of this persona, he relates how Bochas opined against the pride of princes, for example, and how Fortune lectured Bochas in his study.

Lydgate's preservation of Boccaccio as his narrator would perhaps be less notable were it not an acute departure from his more immediate source. Laurent produced two translations of the *De casibus*, one in 1400 and the second in 1409, the latter of which appears to have been Lydgate's immediate source. In this 1409 retranslation, Laurent conflates his narrative voice with Boccaccio's, using the first person to narrate the falls of famous men and women.[78] By shifting to the third person, Lydgate produces a "fundamentally different work from its French predecessor," as Nigel Mortimer observes, since "we are told that figures present themselves before 'Bochas,' rather than seeing the complainants through the eyes of the musing poet."[79] In certain places, this shift in perspective has a clear political purpose, enabling Lydgate to distance himself from his sources and their anti-English sentiments. In his story of King John, for example, Boccaccio exhibits an obvious bias against the English, labelling them "inertissimis atque pavidis et nullius valoris homnibus" ("most weak and fearful men, lacking all strength").[80] Lydgate warns us of his author's prejudice in his own rendition, prefacing his story with the instruction to read Boccaccio's "narwe" interpretation with care:

> Thouh Bochas yaff hym fauour bi langage,
> His herte enclyned onto that partie,
> Which onto hym was but smal auauntage:

Woord is but wynd brouht in be envie.
For to hyndre the famous cheualrie
Of Inglissh-men, ful narwe he gan hym thinke,
Lefft spere and sheeld[e], fauht with penne & inke.
Thouh seide Bochas floured in poetrie,
His parcial writyng gaf no mortal wounde. (9.3162–70)

Gently admonishing Boccaccio for his partisan perspective, Lydgate reminds his readers that "euery cronicleer, / Sholde in his writyng make non excepcioun" and instead "Indifferentli conueie his mateere / Nat be parcial of non affeccioun" (9.3183–6). The effect of this advisory is that Lydgate emerges as a diligent translator of his sources, but also as one who is capable of recognizing their partiality.

Lydgate's shift from the first to third person has implications beyond the political. By prefacing each story with an account of what Bochas says or does, he directs our attention to Boccaccio as the original author of this work.[81] In this, he distinguishes his poem from not only the *Des cas* but also the *De casibus*, because whereas in the *De casibus* we experience everything as though through the eyes of Boccaccio, in the *Fall* we observe Boccaccio vicariously in his study. "Bochas" becomes an almost living presence in a work about the vicissitudes of earthly fame, his name carried forward in Lydgate's translation, and in our experience of reading it. As Jennifer Summit has shown, there is a monumentalizing – even stabilizing – quality to Lydgate's depictions of poets at work in their studies.[82] The poem builds a "memorial edifice" to spaces of reading and writing, and to the poets within them.[83] This process of memorialization becomes especially prevalent in Bochas's encounter with Petrarch, a scene from the *De casibus* that I discussed in detail in chapter 3. Lydgate preserves this episode with an important emendation. He translates into English Petrarch's entreaty to Boccaccio to write so as to make them both famous ("And for to make *our* names perdurable, / And *our* merites to putten in memorie" [8.176–7; italics added]). But after recording Bochas's vision of Petrarch, Lydgate adds a passage of his own. Having heard Petrarch's lesson, Lydgate describes how Bochas "Roos from his couche," his "feeblesse" and exhaustion overcome (8.186–7). It is at this point that Lydgate directs our focus to himself: "*I folwyng aftir*," though "fordullid with rudnesse,"

Mor than thre score yeeris set my date,
Lust of youthe passid [with] his fresshnesse;
Colours of rethorik to helpe me translate
Wer fadid awey: I was born in Lidgate,
Wher Bachus licour doth ful scarsli fleete,

My drie soule for to dewe & weete.
Thouh pallid age hath fordullid me,
Tremblyng ioyntes let myn hand to write,
And fro me take al the subtilite
Of corious makyng in Inglissh to endite. (8.190–200)

Lydgate, then, inserts a description of himself writing into this scene between friends. We imagine the poet composing in his study, his joints trembling with age. If in the *De casibus* we had the impression of Petrarch initiating Boccaccio into a pantheon of great poets, then in the *Fall* Lydgate adds his own name to Boccaccio's "virtual coterie" (to adopt R.D. Perry's useful term).[84] Positioning himself after Petrarch and Boccaccio, he demonstrates his intricate understanding of this episode as an opportunity – for first Boccaccio and now himself – to construct his literary ancestry retrospectively, through his emulation of previous poets.

This scene is only one of many episodes in the *Fall* that show Lydgate using his poem to generate glory for himself and others. Celebrating the "memorialising power of writing," these episodes demonstrate the care with which he names and venerates his predecessors.[85] He is well aware that "writyng" makes his authorial ancestors immortal, causing "poetis to recure / A name eternal, the laurer whan thei wan" (4.64–5). It is, as Mary C. Flannery observes, "these poets, the fame they bestowed upon others, and the fame they gained for themselves" that "form the backdrop for Lydgate's own ambitions. Lydgate sees and depicts himself as the textual arbiter of ... renown."[86] Flannery is quite right to highlight Lydgate's positioning of himself as Fame's arbiter, but it is worth noting that the "fame" Lydgate confers on his authorial predecessors is not distributed equally. Indeed, there is a notable difference between his depiction of Boccaccio as a dynamic hologram, capable of movement and speech, and his praise of the "dead" Chaucer – a "deadness" Lydgate stresses more than once. If his translation of the *De casibus* shows Lydgate making "olde thynges for to seeme newe," then his portrayal of Bochas in his study seems designed to bring the poet back to life, to make him in "name" if not in person "eternal," thereby reversing Chaucer's earlier efforts to erase him.

Identifying Boccaccio as his source and the Lombard Trophe as Chaucer's, Lydgate calls our attention to, emends, and perpetuates Chaucer's poetics of erasure, drawing a connective thread from his own elision of the "Monk's Tale" to his predecessor's earlier obfuscation of Boccaccio. Raising Boccaccio from the grave, he buries Chaucer and his poem, lamenting the death of England's "cheeff poete," meanwhile all but ignoring the precedent set by the "Monk's Tale." At the same time as he minimizes Chaucer's influence, however, Lydgate prompts us to read this practice as modelled on a preexisting trope of erasure. Illuminating and developing Chaucer's strategy of authorial dissimulation, he offers his poem as an extension of the "Monk's Tale" even as he insists on getting his inspiration elsewhere.[87]

It is thus by conspicuously overlooking Chaucer's translation of the *De casibus* in his delineation of the *Fall*'s textual history that Lydgate positions himself as Chaucer's disciple. Still, he does not hazard his readers' recognition of his Chaucerian poetics on our attention or perspicacity. As he did in the *Troy Book*, he inscribes this progression of influence directly into the poem, once in the prologue and a second time in an envoy, bookending his elision of Chaucer with guidelines for how we are to interpret this behaviour. In the prologue, Lydgate records a succession of five tragedians. Not only naming Boccaccio and Chaucer as his poetic models but also using them as such, he refashions the "sixth of six" lineups from the *Filocolo* and the *Troilus*, and so announces, as David Wallace suggests, his "highest poetic ambition: a desire to complete a sequence of poetic activity conjoining pagan antiquity and the Christian present."[88]

> Senek in Rome, thoruh his hih prudence,
> Wrot tragedies of gret moralite;
> And Tullius, cheeff welle off eloquence,
> Maad in his tyme many fressh dite;
> Franceis Petrak, off Florence the cite,
> Made a book, as I can reherce,
> Off too Fortunys, welful and peruerse.
> And Iohn Bochas wrot maters lamentable,
> The fall of pryncis, where he doth expresse
> How fro ther ioie thei fill in gret distresse;
> And semblabli as I ha[ue] told toforn,
> My maistir Chaucer dede his besynesse,
> Wherfore lat us yiue hym laude & glory
> And putte his name with poetis in memory. (1.253–9; 1.269–71; 1.274–5; 1.279–80)

First praising Seneca, Tully, and Petrarch, Lydgate stations Chaucer immediately after Boccaccio here, an arrangement Chaucer implied throughout his poetry but never articulated. Leaving the "sixth of six" position vacant, he situates himself implicitly after Boccaccio and Chaucer as the final author in a genealogy of tragic poetry.[89]

In an envoy to the poem, Lydgate includes a second catalogue of poets, only here he does not merely infer his own presence. Rather, he identifies himself as the final author writing in the *De casibus* tradition, following after Boccaccio, Petrarch, and Chaucer:

> My mayster had[de] nevir pere, –
> I mene Chauceer – in stooryes that he tolde;
> And he also wrot tragedyes olde.
> The Fal of Prynces gan pitously compleyne,
> As *Petrark* did, and also *Iohn Bochas*;
> Laureat Fraunceys, poetys bothe tweyne,
> Toold how prynces for ther greet trespace
> Wer ovirthrowe, rehersyng al the caas,
> As *Chauceer* did[e] in the Monkys Tale.
> But I that stonde lowe doun in the vale,
> So greet a book in Ynglyssh to translate,
> Did it be constreynt and no presumpcioun.
> Born in a vyllage which callyd is *Lydgate*,
> Be old[e] tyme a famous castel toun. (9.3419–32; italics added)

Lydgate positions himself directly after Petrarch, Boccaccio, and Chaucer in this lineage, a process of "self-canonization" that raises "at least the possibility that he embodies the [*De casibus*] tradition's ultimate fulfillment," as Larry Scanlon notes.[90] Indeed, the final poet is the best poet according to this literary device, and Lydgate assumes this position unapologetically. But Lydgate is staking out a claim to more than just a position in Chaucer, Boccaccio, and Petrarch's literary lineage here. He also offers himself as a literary critic. According to Perry,

> Included in the list of names and activities that formally constitute his virtual coteries is the poetic "I" that makes them possible. When Lydgate forms a virtual coterie, he arrogates to himself substantial agency over its members; he makes himself responsible for recording their relationships to each other and their actions.

As curator of this literary lineage, Lydgate proves himself instrumental to our perception of a chain of relationships. There are two "I's" represented in Lydgate's genealogy: the "I" who stands "lowe doun in the vale, / So greet a book in Ynglyssh to translate," and the scholarly "I," who brings to our attention textual borrowings that would otherwise remain hidden. Lydgate thus frames the *Fall* with two authorial genealogies, both of which locate him immediately after Boccaccio and Chaucer in a sequence of poetic emulation. The first genealogy implies his status as their authorial descendant, but the second insists on this title, and further makes explicit both his and Chaucer's literary debts.

Lydgate's emulation of Chaucer's language has long been recognized by scholars. The poet locates in his predecessor "an origin for English 'poetry,'" as Christopher Cannon has observed, invoking a set of "imitable linguistic objects in Chaucer's English whose subsequent use could make the writing of imitators excellent too."[91] But Lydgate's imitation of Chaucer extends beyond words, phrases, and other linguistic formulations, as I hope to have shown, to the very intertextual strategies Chaucer used to write himself into a literary tradition. Prompting us to read his treatment of Chaucer in the *Troy Book* and *Fall of Princes* through the looking glass of a Chaucerian poetics, he follows in Chaucer's footsteps even while erasing their imprints behind him. Whether he remained in his self-appointed position alongside Chaucer in a grand literary pantheon is, of course, a matter of ongoing scholarly debate. But in the words of Lewis Carroll's intrepid Alice, "at any rate, there's no harm in trying."[92]

Notes

Introduction

1 Barchiesi, "Future Reflexive," 352, reprinted in *Speaking Volumes*, 118.
2 Eliot, "Philip Massinger," in *Selected Essays*, 182.
3 Somewhat fittingly, the origins of this phrase are fiendishly difficult to locate. Steve Jobs (among others, including Banksy) has attributed this line to Picasso, but others have attributed it to Faulkner, Stravinsky, and even Voltaire. During the television program "Triumph of the Nerds" (1996), Jobs suggested, "Ultimately it comes down to taste. It comes down to trying to expose yourself to the best things that humans have done and then try to bring those things in to what you're doing. I mean Picasso had a saying he said good artists copy great artists steal. And we have always been shameless about stealing great ideas."
4 For Stravinsky's supposed utterance of these words, see Yates, *Twentieth Century Music*, 41.
5 In his visual rendering of this formula, Banksy crosses out Picasso and attributes the phrase to himself, making the very marks of his predecessor's erasure legible. You can find this image, under the heading "Inside," here: www.banksy.co.uk.
6 All quotations of Chaucer are from the *Riverside Chaucer*.
7 I follow John V. Fleming, *Classical Imitation and Interpretation in Chaucer's "Troilus,"* 190, among others, in rejecting Kittredge's claim that the *House of Fame* precedes the *Troilus*. We have no evidence of this timeline, and, as Fleming notes, there is "no compelling prima facie reason to deny to the *House of Fame* a degree of Chaucerian playfulness clearly present in his allusions to Lollius in the *Troilus*" (190). If anything, Chaucer's mention of Lollius among the great authors of Troy seems to suggest that Chaucer wrote the *House of Fame* after the *Troilus*, including his own invented source among these famous authors of Troy as a way of emphasizing their communal fraudulence.

See also Helen Cooper, "The Four Last Things in Dante and Chaucer." Cooper makes a case for 1384 as the date when Chaucer composed the *House of Fame*.

8 Many scholars have, however, raised the question of why Chaucer erases Boccaccio. In his notes on the "Monk's Tale," for example, F.N. Robinson, *The Works of Geoffrey Chaucer*, 855, speculates that "why Chaucer refers here to Petrarch rather than to Boccaccio is unknown. From the fact that he never names Boccaccio it has been inferred that he attributed to Petrarch (or to Lollius) all the writings of Boccaccio that he knew." Piero Boitani asks a series of general questions with regard to this erasure in his introduction to *Chaucer and the Italian Trecento*: "Why does [Chaucer] seem to attribute to Petrarch works written by Boccaccio; why does he never mention Boccaccio by name; and who is 'Lollius'?" (5). These are, he determines, "insoluble problems." N.R. Havely, *Chaucer's Boccaccio*, 12, suggests that Chaucer's erasure of Boccaccio is likely strategic, but does not elaborate on what kind of strategy Chaucer may have had in mind: "For someone who had visited Italy at least twice, and spent some time in Florence, to misattribute one or two of the works may be considered ignorance; but to disregard the authorship of the whole corpus begins to look like design." More recently, Karen Elizabeth Gross, "Chaucer's Silent Italy," has pointed out certain limitations of popular theories on Chaucer's erasure of Boccaccio, but she does not provide an explanation of her own for this treatment. Considering Chaucer's decision not to import certain features of his Italian inheritance, she concludes, "I realize I have not given an answer satisfactorily as to why Chaucer chooses not to use these ... Most likely we can never develop a satisfactory answer. But I believe it is more complicated than the assumptions that Chaucer was medieval and therefore misunderstood what the early modern Italians were doing, or that because Chaucer wrote in English he felt inferior about the abilities of his vernacular when compared to the rhetorical possibilities inherent in Italian, or even that England was different politically from the city states of Italy" (44).

9 Notable (and amusing) exceptions include Donald R. Howard, *Chaucer*, 193, who imagines an encounter between the two poets that went sour, the result of which was Chaucer choosing not to name his source. In this meeting Howard envisions, Chaucer "somehow felt himself demeaned, or condescended to, or disappointed – a meeting that he left with the uneasy feeling that he had met the great man at the wrong time, or had failed to put his best foot forward, perhaps a meeting in which his own embarrassment and diffidence had made him an unlikely and foolish-seeming companion – all this could explain why he admired Boccaccio's books but ignored the man himself." J.A.W. Bennett, "Chaucer, Dante, Boccaccio," 91, wonders if Chaucer acknowledges Petrarch but not Boccaccio because the latter name is "less

easily anglicized." A.C. Spearing's theory ("Classical Antiquity in Chaucer's Chivalric Romances," 61) is equally delightful: Chaucer "recognized the special value of this crucial model … and wanted to keep it to himself." J.W. Bright, "Chaucer and Lollius," suggests that Chaucer intends a punny reference to Boccaccio in the name Lollius. Boyd Ashby Wise (*The Influence of Statius upon Chaucer*, 67–8), offers that "Corynne," Chaucer's invented source for *Anelida and Arcite*, refers to Boccaccio's "wry face."

10 William E. Coleman, "The Knight's Tale," 109. See also Kathryn McKinley, *Chaucer's "House of Fame" and Its Boccaccian Intertexts*, 15, who notes that many scholars still "assum[e] that Chaucer did not know Boccaccio's name, perhaps because manuscript copies did not include it." McKinley directs our attention to Victoria Kirkham, *Fabulous Vernacular*, 133, who notes that, in many places, Boccaccio signed his works with not his surname but "Johannes de Certaldo."

11 Boitani, "The 'Monk's Tale,'" 69n35.

12 Robin Kirkpatrick, "The Griselda Story in Boccaccio, Petrarch, and Chaucer," 231. For this view, see especially J. Burke Severs, *The Literary Relationships of Chaucer's "Clerkes Tale."*

13 Early examples of this argument include Hubertis M. Cummings's PhD dissertation, "The Indebtedness of Chaucer's Works to the Italian Works of Boccaccio" (1916), and Willard Farnham, "England's Discovery of the *Decameron*" (1924). Peter Beidler, "Just Say Yes, Chaucer Knew the *Decameron*, esp. 25–6, provides a useful summary of the "pendulum swing" of scholarly opinion on this topic. Helen Cooper, "The Frame," 8, suggests that "the case against Chaucer's knowledge of the work is based on the lack of specific verbal parallels such as are characteristic of his borrowings from other works of Boccaccio's, notably the *Filostrato* and the *Teseida*. He never gives the impression of working extensively with a copy in front of him; he often uses a source other than Boccaccio even when he is telling a tale that also appears in the *Decameron*."

14 Douglas Bush, "Chaucer's 'Corinne'"; Lee Patterson, *Chaucer and the Subject of History*, 63n59; Walter William Skeat, in *Complete Works of Geoffrey Chaucer*, 1:531. For further theories on the possible identity of Corinne, see Vincent DiMarco's headnote to *Anelida and Arcite* in the *Riverside Chaucer* (991).

15 George Livingstone Hamilton, *The Indebtedness of Chaucer's "Troilus and Criseyde" to Guido delle Colonne's Historia Trojana*, esp. 55–7 and 150–4; Frederick Tupper, "Chaucer and Trophee"; Robert A. Pratt, "Chaucer and the Pillars of Hercules," 122–3; Oliver Farrar Emerson, "Seith Trophee," 143–4. See also Skeat, *Complete Works of Geoffrey Chaucer*, 2:liv–lvi, and my "'Trophee' and Triumph in the Monk's Tale."

16 This theory was first presented by R.G. Lantham, "Chaucer Note" (1868), and Bernhard Ten Brink, *Chaucer* (1870), but it gained traction with the

publication of George L. Kittredge's "Chaucer's Lollius" (1917). Kittredge's article was further corroborated by Robert Pratt, "A Note on Chaucer's Lollius" (1950), who provided specific manuscript evidence of scribes mistranslating Horace's "Lollius Maximus."

17 Fleming, *Classical Imitation and Interpretation*, 191, suggests that this kind of argument reduces Chaucer to a "dimwit." Fleming's own "small claim to originality," in his words, is his belief that Chaucer "could read Latin" (189).

18 Kittredge, "Chaucer's Lollius"; Minnis, *Chaucer and Pagan Antiquity*; David Wallace, *Chaucer and the Early Writings of Boccaccio.* Kittredge suggests that Boccaccio's *Filostrato* "would not answer, for the conditions of the problem required an ancient (or at least antique) personage, and preferably one who had written in a learned language" (49). Kittredge thus falls into both critical camps: he suggests that Chaucer believed Lollius to be a real author on the Trojan War, but that he named him to provide the illusion of historical authority.

19 Minnis, *Chaucer and Pagan Antiquity*, 23–4. See also his *Medieval Theory of Authorship*, 209–10. Here, Minnis suggests that Chaucer's commendation of the *Troilus* to Virgil, Ovid, Homer, Lucan, and Statius is intended to convey the poet's "dependen[ce] on 'ancient' literature ... The 'modern' writers who were his main sources (Boccaccio, Benoît, Petrarch) would not serve this purpose, so Chaucer did not acknowledge them, but ascribed material taken from their work to 'ancient' *auctores*. Chaucer did not much care what 'Omer, Dares and Dite' had actually said; he did not bother to verify the existence of his 'auctour Lollius': he wished to use the names of the *auctores*, to 'cash in' on their antiquity and *auctoritas*."

20 Wallace, *Chaucer and the Early Writings of Boccaccio*, 50.

21 Wallace, *Chaucer and the Early Writings of Boccaccio*, 50. More recently, Wallace repeated a version of this argument ("Chaucer's Italian Inheritance," 50): "both Ilario and Lollius are ... pious fictions, cultural ciphers expressive of a common commitment to revivifying an ancient past." The *Filostrato*, by contrast, "did not suit Chaucer admirably as a poetic source." Marilyn Desmond, "Chaucer and the Textualities of Troy," 244–5, espouses a similar view: "in constructing the textual fiction that the *Troilus* is a vernacular rendition of a Latin text, Chaucer's narrator claims a truth-value for his account. The fictional Lollius confers the same sort of authority on the *Troilus* that Dares confers on the *Roman de Troie*, since a vernacular text such as Boccaccio's *Filostrato* clearly lacked the *auctoritas* attributed to a Latin historical narrative."

22 Wallace, *Chaucer and the Early Writings of Boccaccio*, 152. The influence of Kittredge, Minnis, and Wallace on later scholarship has been immense. Even those critics who see Chaucer's invention of Lollius as a joke, intended to be recognized by his clever friends, follow these scholars in assuming that the poet's aim in naming him was first and foremost to authenticate or

historicize his poem. See, for example, Bella Millett, "Chaucer, Lollius, and the Medieval Theory of Authorship," 99, Barry Windeatt, *Troilus and Criseyde*, 40, and Fleming, *Classical Imitation and Interpretation*, 192.

23 For a recent and excellent study on the status of English in medieval England, see Christopher Cannon, *From Literacy to Literature*. See also the five essays in *The Idea of the Vernacular*, 311–78.

24 Minnis, *Medieval Theory of Authorship*, 110.

25 *LGW* III.924–6. See also *HofF*, I.378–9.

26 Gavin Douglas, "Eneados," *Prol.* 420. The situation was, moreover, as Sheila Delaney notes (*The Naked Text*, 194), "worse than Douglas acknowledges," because Chaucer not only conflates his sources in a way that exacerbates the differences between them but also, by suggesting that he will "folwe [Virgil's] lanterne" (*LGW* III.926), announces this manoeuvre with an allusion to an earlier misreading of Virgil's poetry from Dante's *Purgatorio*. I discuss this Dantean allusion in more depth later in the Introduction.

27 Alain of Lille (*De fide catholica contra haereticos* I.30 [*Patrologia latina* 210:333]) describes authority as having a waxen nose, capable of being bent in many directions to provide new meanings: "Sed quia auctoritas cereum habet nasum, id est in diversum potest flecti sensum, rationibus roborandum est." Minnis adopts this delightful metaphor across his writings; see, for example, *Magister Amoris*, 138, as well as *Fallible Authors*, 258 and 287.

28 Minnis, *Medieval Theory of Authorship*, 193, 198, and 208.

29 For Chaucer's construction of his authorial persona in relation to classical authority, see also Jamie C. Fumo, *The Legacy of Apollo*. Fumo argues that "Chaucer, perhaps more out of private experimentation than public vision, mythologized a new idea of authorship in English" (15). For Fumo, this construction of an authorial self involves looking to the figure of Apollo in myth: "By attending to Apollo's deeply ambivalent function in the construction of classical models of authority, and the reinforcement and transmutation of this ambivalence by medieval hermeneutic practices, we can more fully understand the complexity of Chaucer's attitude toward vernacular *auctoritas*, a structure of power that Chaucer both cultivated and denied" (11).

30 For a sustained study on Chaucer's Petrarchan borrowings, see William Rossiter, *Chaucer and Petrarch*.

31 Petrarch regularly lamented the consequence of making poetry accessible to the masses. In *Fam* XIII.7, for example, he complains of carpenters and farmers deserting their tools of trade to write poetry, and in *Fam* XXI.15, he recalls the horror of hearing Dante's *Commedia* read aloud in taverns and public squares. He suggests that this experience alone was incentive enough for him to switch to Latin. For the text of these letters, see *Le Familiari*.

32 For studies on Dante and Chaucer, see especially R.A. Shoaf, *Dante, Chaucer, and the Currency of the Word*; Howard H. Schless, *Chaucer and Dante*; Karla

Taylor, *Chaucer Reads the "Divine Comedy"*; Richard Neuse, "*Troilus and Criseyde*: Another Dantean Reading"; and Neuse, *Chaucer's Dante*. Other important studies include (but are hardly limited to) Boitani, "What Dante Meant to Chaucer"; Kirkpatrick, *English and Italian Literature from Dante to Shakespeare*, 24–79; Wallace, *Chaucerian Polity*; Warren Ginsberg, *Chaucer's Italian Tradition*; Suzanne C. Hagedorn, *Abandoned Women*; Susan Schibanoff, *Chaucer's Queer Poetics*, 99–152; John M. Fyler, *Language and the Declining World in Chaucer, Dante, and Jean de Meun*; and Havely, "'I Wolde … han Hadde a Fame.'"

33 Minnis, *Fallible Authors*, 23, suggests that the Wife of Bath's female body "fades into insignificance as her voice utters the most authoritative and compelling of statements, Dante, both poet and sage, being ostentatiously cited as a major source."

34 Minnis, *Translations of Authority in Middle English Literature*, 3.

35 Minnis, *Translations of Authority*, 3. Minnis further observes that while Dante does not spell this out in the *Convivio*, the entire concept of innate *gentilezza* can, "very easily, be appropriated in an affirmation of the worthiness of the Italian language" (3).

36 Minnis, *Translations of Authority*, 3.

37 Robert R. Edwards, *Chaucer and Boccaccio*, 11, considers Chaucer's erasure of Boccaccio in light of his treatment of his French sources. He very rightly points out that Chaucer's "silence over Boccaccio appears somewhat less anomalous when seen against his links to the French poets who proved equally decisive earlier in his career. Though Chaucer acknowledges Oton de Granson as the source for the balades he translates in the 'Complaint of Venus' (82), he marks his borrowings from Machaut and Froissart … only by internal allusion and citation within his poetry. This suggests that the issue is not vernacular writing or the shadow cast by accomplished contemporary writers; rather Chaucer's engagement is with the works themselves and the possibilities they bring to English poetry."

38 "By emphasizing Dante's vernacularity and Petrarch's Latinity, Boccaccio was highlighting … his unique authorial identity." James C. Kriesel, *Boccaccio's Corpus*, 4.

39 As Gross notes, "Chaucer's Silent Italy," 20, Boccaccio's early reputation was "just as much tied to his Latin works as Petrarch's was, in part due to his *De casibus virorum illustrium* and *Genealogiae deorum gentilium*." Ugo Foscolo, *Saggi di letteratura italiana*, 184, reminds us that Erasmus thought Boccaccio's Latin superior to even Petrarch's.

40 In his introduction to *The "Decameron" and the "Canterbury Tales,"* 14, Koff points out that Chaucer's not naming Boccaccio "has been used to keep the *Decameron* away from Chaucer, but not the *Filostrato* or the *Teseida* or *De casibus virorum illustrium*." He suggests that "the source of this

resistance to the *Decameron* as an influence on Chaucer lies" in connecting the "moral uncertainty" of the work "with a Chaucer who has, or should have values, and whose *Canterbury Tales*, though unfinished, *seems* to be reaching, despite its range and contradictions, for comprehensiveness, a stability of vision." Beidler, "Just Say Yes," 29, notes that "even in Italy," the *Decameron* "earned a reputation for immorality such that several early editions were seriously expurgated, as were virtually all the translations. The *Decameron* was placed on the Roman Catholic Index in 1563, but that banning probably increased the demand for the book." He adds that "so widespread was the conviction that Boccaccio's *Decameron* was a dangerously subversive document that it may be that Chaucer himself was reluctant to have his name associated with the 'immoral' Boccaccio's" (28).

41 Boccaccio writes, "Sane, quod inclitas mulieres tuas domesticas nugas meas legere permiseris non laudo, quin imo queso per fidem tuam ne feceris." The text of the letter is printed in Ginetta Auzzas and Augusto Campana's edition in *Tutte le opere*, 1:704–7 ("Epistole" XXII.19). Many critics have seen in this statement a renunciation of the *Decameron*, interpreting the author's warning to women not to read his words as an apology for his poem. Francesco Bruni, for example (*Boccaccio*, 43–59), suggests that the letter is written in earnest, initiating a misogynistic and anti-erotic phase of Boccaccio's writing, in which the poet derives inspiration from not *le donne* but the muses. Renzo Bragantini, "L'amicizia, la fama, il libro," 115, considers the letter in light of Boccaccio's intense consideration of his poems' readers. He observes in the epistle "un'ansia reale di Boccaccio sul destino della propria opera." Other scholars have, however, read Boccaccio's remarks more facetiously. Branca in particular (*Tradizione delle opere di Giovanni Boccaccio*, 2: *Un secondo elenco di manoscritti e studi sul testo del "Decameron" con due appendici*, 176) argues that Boccaccio has no intention of repenting for his work, and that his letter to Cavalcanti was meant as a joke. For a review of scholarly responses to the epistle, see Rhiannon Daniels, "Rethinking the Critical History of the *Decameron*." See also Daniels, "Boccaccio's Narrators and Audiences." Daniels herself makes the claim that Boccaccio is referring to not only the *Decameron* in the letter but the "whole of his vernacular output, which includes the *Decameron*" ("Rethinking the Critical History of the *Decameron*," 429).

42 On translations of Boccaccio in England, see Herbert G. Wright, *Boccaccio in England*, but especially Guyda Armstrong, *The English Boccaccio*. Piero Boitani, "Boccaccio in Western Europe," 10, makes the important point that while Christine de Pizan's *Cité des dames* is "fundamentally based" on Boccaccio's *De mulieribus*, the poet also "inserts into her collection ... novellas from the *Decameron*, such as those of Elisabetta, Sigismonda, and Griselda ... In other words, Christine sees no contrast between the moral, prehumanistic author of the *De mulieribus* and the freer, 'boccaccesque' writer

of the *Decameron*. For her, 'Bocace l'Ytalien' – whom, unlike Chaucer, she always mentions by name many times in the *Cité* – always is 'grant poete,' a title Chaucer had reserved only to the Dante of the Ugolino story."

43 I discuss Lydgate's (sometimes disingenuous) emphasis on Boccaccio as his author in the final chapter of this book.

44 See David Rundle, ed., *Humanism in Fifteenth-Century Europe*, and Rundle, *Renaissance Reform of the Book and Britain*. See also Boitani, "Boccaccio in Western Europe."

45 Timothy Kircher, "Boccaccio's Humanist *Brigata*," 36–7, begins his chapter by discussing Giannozzo Manetti's fifteenth-century biography of Boccaccio, in which Manetti is "at pains to showcase Boccaccio's Latin writings and no less his role as the *primus praeceptor* of Greek studies in Italy." He adds that "not only humanists from the late trecento onward, but also modern scholars, appear to have supported Manetti's emphasis on Latinity in the Quattrocento."

46 As quoted in Kircher, "Boccaccio's Humanist *Brigata*," 37.

47 Kircher, "Boccaccio's Humanist *Brigata*," 39, 41.

48 Stephen Hinds, *Allusion and Intertext*, 34, notes that the topos "invokes its intertextual tradition as a collectivity, to which the individual contexts and connotations of individual prior instances are firmly subordinate."

49 Harold Bloom, *The Anxiety of Influence*, 5, has identified what he sees as the common practice of poetic "misreading." He holds that "strong poets make ... history by misreading one another, so as to clear imaginative space for themselves." Bloom develops these ideas elsewhere, and especially in *A Map of Misreading*. "Influence," he suggests in this later study, "means that there are *no* texts, but only relationships *between* texts. These relationships depend upon a critical act, a misreading or misprision, that one poet performs upon another, and that does not differ in kind from the necessary critical acts performed by every strong reader upon every text he encounters" (3). My own theory differs from Bloom's for the obvious reason that it extends to Chaucer (Bloom begins his analyses with Milton, as influenced by Shakespeare), but also because it steps outside of a psychological framework as a means to analysing influence. Bloom sees literary allusions through the scrim of an inescapable, post-Freudian "anxiety," whereas I explore the idea of a self-conscious, conventional, cycle of allusive usurpation, in which a poet deliberately locates his place within a tradition of great poets by alluding to his precursor's prior positioning of himself within this tradition. This cycle of self-fashioning that I identify is distinct from a Bloomian anxiety, because it recognizes that the poet's mock humility is a posture, a posture that is undermined the moment we recognize its conventionality – its historical precedent – and with it the poet's strong sense of his own worth. In this regard, I agree with Gian Biagio Conte, *The Rhetoric of Imitation*,

27, who notes that Bloom "of course forgets the inexorable but essentially neutral meeting with a 'tradition' that both conditions and helps poetic expression. Tradition can be defined simply as poetic 'langue,' the simultaneous projection of literary models and codifications, a single organic body of once individual but now institutionalized choices, a system of rules and prescriptions."

50 "On a most general level," as Henry Spelman observes, *Pindar and the Poetics of Permanence*, 84, "intertextuality is related to the rhetoric of permanence."

51 For Chaucer and fame, see especially B.G. Koonce, *Chaucer and the Tradition of Fame*, Boitani, *Chaucer and the Imaginary World of Fame*, the collection of essays in *Chaucer and Fame*, and the first chapter of Mary C. Flannery, *John Lydgate and the Poetics of Fame*, 13–37.

52 Sarah Spense, "Felix Casus," 133.

53 For the "ludic" aspect of allusions, see Paul Lennon, "Ludic Language." Built into the word "allusion" is, indeed, a sense of play.

54 In Joseph Pucci's words, *The Full-Knowing Reader*, 46, "The etymology of allusion – *ad* plus *ludere*, literally, 'a playing to or toward' – well suggests the power and authority afforded the full-knowing reader in making the allusion mean. Play is, after all, the fundamental quality of allusive space."

55 *Sources and Analogues of Chaucer's "Canterbury Tales,"* ed. W.F. Bryan and Germaine Dempster (1941). (This work was preceded in 1872 by Frederick James Furnivall, Edmund Brock, and W.A. Clouston's *Originals and Analogues of Some of Chaucer's "Canterbury Tales."*) Robert M. Correale and Mary Hamel, editors of the more recently published *Sources and Analogues of the Canterbury Tales*, vii, have sought to provide an updated, revised, and expanded study of Chaucer's influences, the purpose of which was to "present the sources in the forms that Chaucer knew them, and where sources are unknown, to present the closest analogues of the tales in the forms with which Chaucer was presumably acquainted." See also *The Literary Context of Chaucer's Fabliaux*, ed. Larry D. Benson and Theodore M. Andersson, and Windeatt, *Chaucer's Dream Poetry*, xi. Peter Beidler has come up with five terms to help articulate the relationship between Chaucer's poetry and its literary antecedents. (For Beidler's explanation of these terms, see his "Just Say Yes" and "New Terminology for Sources and Analogues.") These terms are as follows: 1) the hard source, which refers to a work for which we have an "extant copy and that we know, from verbal similarities, character names, and plot sequences, that Chaucer used"; 2) the soft source, which refers to a work that Chaucer "almost certainly knew and probably remembered as he wrote"; 3) the hard analogue, which refers to a work that is "old enough in its extant form that Chaucer could have known it and that bears striking resemblances … to a Chaucerian work"; 4) the soft analogue,

which refers to a work that, "because of its late date or its remoteness from its Chaucerian counterpart, Chaucer almost certainly did not know"; and finally 5) the lost source, which refers to a "literary work that is not extant but that may have existed at one time." Many scholars in the field of Chaucerian source study have accepted Beidler's terms as comprehensive (see, for example, the essays contributed to the colloquium "The Afterlife of Origins," which includes Beidler's own essay ["New Terminology for Sources and Analogues"] as well as others applying his terminology. Although it is also worth quoting from Ruth Evans's amusing and incisive response to Beidler's matrix, "Textual Forensics," 264, which is also part of this colloquium: "source study has been figured primarily – and to its detriment – in forensic terms. Even 'hard' and 'soft' suggest not so much boiled eggs ... as degrees of punishment"). Certainly, Beidler's methodology (if not always his terminology) is descriptive of the sort of source-sleuthing practised by the *SA* contributors, past and present. Because Beidler's list limits its analysis to textual correspondences and plot sequences to which Chaucer clearly and straightforwardly alludes, however, it can only speak to the poet's engagement with works that are, quite literally, evident in his writing. Even with Beidler's new terminology, then, we still lack the vocabulary to describe influence when it presents itself in ways other than the most obvious.

56 In Bryan and Dempster's 1941 edition of *SA*, for example, Severs, in his entry on "The Clerk's Tale," 289, rationalized *not* including Boccaccio's *Decameron* X.10 among the literary influences on the "Clerk's Tale" on the basis that the parallels between the two works were "neither numerous nor important enough to be convincing." Even though it was the prototype for Chaucer's story of Griselda, then, *Decameron* X.10 was discounted as an influence simply because Severs was unable to draw positive parallels between Boccaccio's and Chaucer's texts. In Correale and Hamel's more recent edition of *SA* (2002), Farrell and Amy Goodwin ("The Clerk's Tale," 103) do include *Decameron* X.10 in their chapter on the "Clerk's Tale." Still, they struggle with determining the relationship of Boccaccio's narrative to Chaucer's work, using the positivistic language (and methodology) favoured by the contributors to *SA* to do so: "The evidence of Boccaccian influence on the language of the *Clerk's Tale* remains very slight, but the likelihood that Boccaccio's version – especially, perhaps, his conclusion – was present in Chaucer's memory as he worked on the *Clerk's Tale* gives the *Decameron* a relevance greater than that of any other analogue." Because we are faced with a dearth of "parallels" between these two texts, therefore, as with the previous edition, the importance of *Decameron* X.10 to Chaucer in this recent edition must remain indeterminate.

57 Studies of Chaucer's use of the *Decameron* are particularly plagued by this practice, with scholars at the ready with a red thread on a corkboard to

determine which precise manuscript Chaucer accessed and when. In a travelogue fantasy worthy of Donald Howard, for example, Frederick M. Biggs, *Chaucer's "Decameron" and the Origin of the "Canterbury Tales,"* speculates that "if Chaucer was offered or ordered a copy of the *Teseida*, might he not have asked for one of the *Decameron* as well? If so, manuscript 870 in the 1426 catalogue [of the books in the libraries of the Visconti brothers and co-dukes of Lombardy, Bernabò's library in Milan and Galeazzo II's in Pavia] is a possible candidate for its exemplar [probably in Galeazzo II's library in Pavia]." This is "a thick, one volume book on paper in Italian called the *Decameron* written by dottore Giovanni Boccaccio from the Florentine city Certalda, which begins 'Ogni cosa' and ends 'alcuna cosa giova laverlo leto Deo Gratias, amen.' With thick, flat clasps and fine bindings of rough, whitened red leather" (9).

58 Minnis, *Chaucer and Pagan Antiquity*, 9.
59 Minnis, *Chaucer and Pagan Antiquity*, 9.
60 Minnis, *Chaucer and Pagan Antiquity*, 9–10.
61 There is plenty of rich material on Chaucer's scribes. See especially Simon Horobin and Linne R. Mooney, "A Piers Plowman Manuscript by the Hengwrt/Ellesmere Scribe and Its Implications for London Standard English," Mooney, "Chaucer's Scribe," Alexandra Gillespie, "Reading Chaucer's Words to Adam," Mooney and Estelle Stubbs, *Scribes and the City*, Daniel Wakelin, *Scribal Correction and Literary Craft*, and Lawrence Warner, *Chaucer's Scribes*.
62 On Boccaccio's autographs, and his design of, and control over, the production of his works, see, for example Branca, "Copisti per passione, tradizione caratterizzante, tradizione di memoria"; Branca and Pier Giorgio Ricci, *Un autografo del "Decameron"*; Manlio Pastore Stocchi, "Su alcuni autografi del Boccaccio"; Branca, ed., *Boccaccio visualizzato*; Daniels, *Boccaccio and the Book*; Marco Cursi, *La scrittura e i libri di Giovanni Boccaccio*, especially the first chapter, as well as his "Authorial Strategies and Manuscript Tradition" and "Boccaccio architetto e artefice di libri"; Teresa DeRobertis et al., eds., *Boccaccio autore e copista*; Eisner, *Boccaccio and the Invention of Italian Literature*; Sandro Bertelli and Davide Cappi, eds., *Dentro l'officina di Giovanni Boccaccio*; Michelangelo Zaccarello, "Boccaccio as a Scribal Editor"; Victoria Kirkham, "A Visual Legacy (Boccaccio as Artist)"; and Anna Bettarini Bruni, Giancarlo Breschi, Giuliano Tanturli, "Giovanni Boccaccio e la tradizone dei testi volgari." According to Armando Petrucci, "Minuta, autografo, libro d'autore," the increase in complete and partial autographs of works in *Trecento* Italy was an effect of the revolt of authors against unfaithful scribes.
63 Hugh M. Thomas, *The Secular Clergy in England, 1066–1216*, 247, notes that "the loss of medieval manuscripts over the centuries has been staggering, and almost all books that survived did so *because* they were housed in

institutional libraries." For possible explanations for these losses, see, for example, David L. d'Avray, *Medieval Marriage*, 40–53. See also Uwe Neddermeyer, *Von der Handschrift zum gedruckten Buch*, 1:72–85, who estimates loss percentages based on the survival rates of incunabula.

64 Hagedorn, *Abandoned Women*, 174.

65 In the "Nun's Priest's Tale," Chauntecleer incorrectly translates the "sentence" of the phrase "*Mulier est hominis confusio*" to mean "Womman is mannes joye and al his blis" (VII.3163–6).

66 Immediately after announcing his "entente" in the "Retraction" – that "al that is written is written for oure doctrine" (X.1083), a wholly contradictory phrase – Chaucer revokes his "tales of Caunterbury, thilke that sownen into synne" (X.1085).

67 In her rendition of the story of Midas, for which she cites Ovid as her source, the Wife of Bath suggests that Midas's wife spreads the secret of his "asses erys two" (III.976). In the *Metamorphoses*, it is Midas's barber who blabs.

68 As Boitani notes ("'My Tale Is of a Cock'"), Chaucer makes it difficult for us to read this tale either literally *or* allegorically. The Nun's Priest's reminder that his tale is only "of a cok" seems to flout an exegetical interpretation. At the same time, his concluding advice is to read his narrative according to a new sense: "But ye that holden this tale a folye, / As of a fox, or a cok and hen, / Taketh the moralite, goode men. / … / Taketh the fruyt, and lat the chaf be stille" (VII.3438–40, VII.3443). We are thus told first to read the work literally, and then after to read it morally.

69 Chaucer repeatedly asks us not to blame him for the content of the *Tales*. See, for example, VII.960, I.726, and I.3185.

70 Wallace, *Chaucer and the Early Writings of Boccaccio*, 1–2. See also N.S. Thompson, *Chaucer, Boccaccio, and the Debate of Love*, 2–3, who roots our inability to establish the *Decameron* as a source for the *Canterbury Tales* to our overzealous positivism: "By adhering too closely to a 'source-hunting' approach, previous critics have been hampered by looking exclusively at individual links, and many connections have been missed."

71 Ardis Butterfield, *The Familiar Enemy*. See also Butterfield's more recent discussion of the limits of source study, "The *Book of the Duchess*, Machaut, and the Image of the Archive," 199–201. For Butterfield, the *Book of the Duchess* "epitomises why source study fails" (200). For the limitations of a source-study-centred approach to analysing Anglo-Saxon poetry, see, for example, Katherine O'Brien O'Keeffe, "Source, Method, Theory, Practice."

72 Butterfield, "The *Book of the Duchess*, Machaut, and the Image of the Archive," 199.

73 Butterfield, *Familiar Enemy*, ii.

74 E.g., Beidler and Biggs.

75 Ginsberg, *Chaucer's Italian Tradition*, 8.

76 Edwards, *Chaucer and Boccaccio*. On Chaucer's use of Boccaccio's poetry as a window into antiquity, see also Spearing, "Lydgate's Canterbury Tale," 355, who suggests that Chaucer, "guided by his reading of Boccaccio, attempted ... to reimagine a classical pagan culture in its own terms, as possessing its own integrity, its own world-view – a culture imaginable because it had much in common with that of medieval Christianity, but interesting because it was also crucially different." This essay was reprinted in Spearing, *From Medieval to Renaissance*, 86.

77 George Edmondson, *The Neighboring Text*, esp. 3–5.

78 K.P. Clarke, *Chaucer and Italian Textuality*, 5.

79 Other examples include McKinley, *Chaucer's "House of Fame" and Its Boccaccian Intertexts*; Winthrop Wetherbee, *Chaucer and the Poets*; John M. Ganim, "Chaucer, Boccaccio, and the Anxiety of Popularity," 63; Thompson, *Chaucer, Boccaccio, and the Debate of Love*; Barbara Nolan, *Chaucer and the Tradition of the* Roman Antique; and Carol Heffernan, *Comedy in Chaucer and Boccaccio*.

80 Kara Gaston, *Reading Chaucer in Time*.

81 There is an interesting discussion of what constitutes a source taking place in Shakespeare studies as well. See Laurie Maguire and Emma Smith, "What Is a Source?" and *Rethinking Shakespeare Source Study*. Thanks to Elizabeth Scala for pointing me in the direction of this debate.

82 I do not mean to homogenize what is, of course, the rather contentious field of classical studies on intertextuality. Especially in the 1990s and early 2000s, classicists hotly debated issues of authorial intention and the role of the reader (an opposition that Derrida challenged in *Of Grammatology* [1967]). To name a few key players in this debate, Giorgio Pasquali ("Arte allusiva," in *Pagine stravaganti di un filologo*, 2:275 [this essay was originally published in 1942 and reprinted in 1951 and 1968]) insisted that "Le allusioni non producono l'effetto voluto se non su un lettore che si ricordi chiaramente del testo cui si riferiscono." That is, allusions are only effective when properly recognized – when contextualized by the reader who fully comprehends them. Richard F. Thomas, "Virgil's *Georgics* and the Art of Reference," 172n8, prefers the term "reference" to "allusion" to indicate the importance of the author: "Virgil is not so much 'playing' with his models but constantly intends that his reader be 'sent back' to them, consulting them through memory or physically, and that he then return and apply his observation to the Virgilian text; the word *allusion* has implications far too frivolous to suit this process." Don Fowler ("Modern Literary Theory and Latin Poetry") attributes the power of interpretation fully to the reader, suggesting that "the reader is figured as operating on the text to produce meaning, rather than attempting to recover authorial intention" (see also

Fowler, "Intertextuality and Classical Studies"). Conte, *The Rhetoric of Imitation*, 26, who was deeply influenced by Pasquali, nevertheless notes the limitations of his approach, and "its reduction of the poetic function to the moment of willed creation." Conte's own methodology is extreme, removing the author almost entirely as a factor in determining meaning: "one text may resemble another not because it derives directly from it nor because the poet deliberately seeks to emulate but because both poets have recourse to a common literary codification. Even when the resemblances do not appear gratuitous – that is, even where some form of intentionality seems undeniable – my concern is with describing how such resemblances *function* within the literary text." Still, Conte's ambition to move beyond what he calls "'comparisonitis' – collecting [parallels] for the sake of collecting," offers a useful model for us with regard to thinking about influence in less positivistic ways. Carving out a role for the reader that does not preclude the importance of the author, Joseph Pucci (*The Full-Knowing Reader*, 26) claims that the "allusion demands a special sort of reader (the full-knowing reader) – who is just as busy as the author of the literary work and ... just as powerful."

83 Hinds, *Allusion and Intertext*, 23.
84 Hinds, *Allusion and Intertext*, 23.
85 Hinds, *Allusion and Intertext*, 23.
86 Hinds, *Allusion and Intertext*, 25.
87 The field of Virgil's intertextual poetics is vast. Apart from Hinds, major studies include, but are hardly limited to, Georg Nikolaus Knauer's monumental *Homer in the "Aeneid"*; Conte, *The Rhetoric of Imitation* (which is a collection of Conte's essays from 1974 onward, translated from Italian into English); Barchiesi, *La traccia del modello*; R.O.A.M. Lyne, *Further Voices in Vergil's "Aeneid"*; and Joseph Farrell, *Vergil's "Georgics"* and the *Traditions of Ancient Epic*. See also Part 1 of *A Companion to Vergil's "Aeneid" and Its Tradition*, ed. Farrell and Michael C.J. Putnam, as well Farrell's more recent "Intention and Intertext."
88 Hexter, "On First Looking into Vergil's Homer," 32.
89 Hexter, "On First Looking into Vergil's Homer," 35.
90 Pucci, *The Full-Knowing Reader*, 66.
91 Pucci, *The Full-Knowing Reader*, 66.
92 Pucci, *The Full-Knowing Reader*, 66.
93 Pucci, *The Full-Knowing Reader*, 67–8.
94 For the poetics of intertextuality of Ovid and Statius, see Barchiesi, *Speaking Volumes*; Philip Hardie, *The Epic Successors of Virgil*, as well as Hardie's more recent study, *Ovid's Poetics of Illusion*; Charles Martindale, *Redeeming the Text*; Hinds, *The Metamorphosis of Persephone*; and R.A. Smith, *Poetic Allusion and Poetic Embrace in Ovid and Virgil*.

95 "Hoc autem dicebat Gallio Nasoni suo valde placuisse; itaque fecisse illum quod in multis aliis versibus Vergilii fecerat, non subripiendi causa, sed palam mutuandi, hoc animo ut vellet agnosci; esse autem in tragoedia eius: feror huc illuc, vae, plena deo" ("Gallio said that his friend Ovid had very much liked the phrase: and that as a result the poet did something he had done with many other lines of Virgil – with no thought of plagiarism, but meaning that his piece of open borrowing should be noticed. And in his tragedy you may read: 'I am carried hither and thither, alas, full of the god'"). The Latin and its translation are taken from Seneca the Elder, *Controversiae, VII–X. Suasoriae. Fragments*, ed. and trans. Michael Winterbottom, 2:544–5 (*Suasoriae* 3.7).

96 Richard Tarrant, "Ovid and Ancient Literary History," 24.

97 Barchiesi, *Speaking Volumes*, 31.

98 Barchiesi, *Speaking Volumes*, 25.

99 Karla F.L. Pollmann, "Statius' *Thebaid* and the Legacy of Vergil's *Aeneid*," and Randall T. Ganiban, *Statius and Virgil*. See also William J. Dominik, "Following in Whose Footsteps?" For the reception of the *Aeneid* in later works, see, for example, D.C. Feeney, *The Gods in Epic*; Hardie, *Epic Successors of Virgil*; and Martindale, *Redeeming the Text*.

100 Pollmann, "Statius' *Thebaid* and the Legacy of Vergil's *Aeneid*," 16.

101 Rita Copeland, *Rhetoric, Hermeneutics, and Translation in the Middle Ages*, 4.

102 Julia Kristeva, *Desire in Language*, 66. Butterfield, *Familiar Enemy*, rightly notes that Kristeva's model of intertextuality is not entirely useful for studying Chaucer's sources, and describes the "plunge into that 'mosaic of quotations'" as "disorienting." "If we are seeking clues to the compositional process, or to how authors seek to understand and control the meaning of their texts, then we will be as interested in the tiny, local movements of (apparent) choice as in the indiscriminate forces of textual determinism that are certainly present in any one textual instance but indescribable in their vast effect," she suggests (242). But while most scholars agree that Kristeva was the first theorist to use the word "intertextuality" in print, in her essay "Word, Dialogue and Novel" (1966), studies on intertextuality and allusion in classical scholarship have developed less "disorienting" modes of analysis, offering a broader and more diverse approach to authors either deliberately or serendipitously citing one another's works. What is more, as Pucci has noted (*The Full-Knowing Reader*, 15), although Kristeva never intended for "intertextuality" to describe or signify authorial intent, "nor did it function as a term for allusion in any of her writing … by the end of the 1970s, 'intertextuality' had become synonymous with 'allusion,' and in some corners even replaced it."

103 Michèle Lowrie, review of Barchiesi's *Speaking Volumes*. Lowrie is quoting Barchiesi (*Speaking Volumes*, 142).

104 Barchiesi, *Speaking Volumes*, 8. Barchiesi looks back as well to Hinds's own reading of speaking volumes, "Booking the Return Trip."
105 Barchiesi, *Speaking Volumes*, 8.
106 Ovid's reference to his "speaking volumes," is, of course, the origin of Barchiesi's title for this project, which comprises a collection of his previous essays, six originally written in Italian, and translated in this volume by Fox and Marchesi, and two in English.
107 Wallace, *Chaucerian Polity*, 81.
108 I am particularly indebted to David Rollo's two books, *Glamorous Sorcery* and *Historical Fabrication, Ethnic Fable and French Romance in Twelfth-Century England*.
109 Marilyn Desmond, *Reading Dido*; Desmond, "Ovid's *Heroides* 3 and the *inventio* of Criseyde in the Medieval Matter of Troy."
110 Sylvia Federico, *New Troy*; Dominique Battles, *The Medieval Tradition of Thebes*.
111 Douglas, "Eneados," *Prol.* 409–17.
112 In *Sen* IV.5, Petrarch writes: "Et sane cur poeta doctissimus omnium atque optimus nam finxisse constat haec finxerit cur cum vel aliam quamlibet heroidum ex numero eligere, vel personam formare novam suo iure licuisset, unam hanc elegerit ... ut quam studio castitatis ac servandae viduitatis extinctam sciret hanc lascivo amore parentem faciat" ("And why indeed did the most learned and excellent poet of all invent this – for it is well known that he invented it – when it had been permitted by his own rule to choose any other out of a number of heroines or to form a new one; why did he choose one ... who he knew died out of zeal for chastity and the preservation of widowhood and make her yield to a wanton love?"). For the historical Dido and Petrarch's response to Virgil's "invention," see Desmond, *Reading Dido*, 23, from whom I am quoting. For the English translation of Petrarch's *Seniles*, see Petrarch, *Letters of Old Age*. Delaney, *The Naked Text*, 194, likewise observes that "before Virgil, Dido was an emblem of faith and love." In contrast to Petrarch, Boccaccio defended Virgil's adaptation in an important passage from the *Genealogie deorum gentilium*. For an important reading of this defence, see McKinley, *Chaucer's "House of Fame" and Its Boccaccian Intertexts*, 92–5.
113 Citations of Dante's work are taken from *La Commedia*, ed. Giorgio Petrocchi, and are cited by canto and line number; translations are from *The Divine Comedy*, ed. and trans. Robert M. Durling and Ronald L. Martinez. "Salvific misreading" is Simone Marchesi's delightful turn of phrase (*Dante and Augustine*, 176). Of course, by insinuating that Virgil's poetry may contain Christian truths, Dante is also following a tradition of readers who interpreted the Fourth *Eclogue* as a work predicting the birth of Christ. See Karla Taylor, "A Text and Its Afterlives," 3, and the later *Chaucer Reads*

the "Divine Comedy," 56–8. But Dante exploits this tradition to undermine Virgil's poetic authority. While on the surface a statement of unadulterated praise, Statius's claim that he was converted by Virgil's poetry figures him as "a better reader of Virgil's text than its author" (Marchesi, *Dante and Augustine*, 130). Dante uses this episode to wrench Virgil's text out of its own author's control while assuming the posture of the scribe of God. "Quoting Aeneas in Latin, Statius rewrites his Latin into the poetry Vergil would have written had he converted. The author of this translation, which effaces the Roman poet and his poem in the act of citing them, is Dante, but its redemptive authority stems from its congruence with God's Word" (Ginsberg, *Tellers, Tales, and Translation in Chaucer's "Canterbury Tales,"* 44).

114 The Latin text of Statius's *Thebaid*, as well as the English translation, is taken from *Statius*, ed. and trans. D.R. Shackleton Bailey, 2:308–9 (XII.816–17).

115 Edwards, "Medieval Literary Careers," 108. According to Andrew Hui, *The Poetics of Ruins in Renaissance Literature*, 103, "footsteps follow footsteps, epic follows epic."

116 Edwards, "Medieval Literary Careers," 108.

117 McKinley, *Chaucer's "House of Fame" and Its Boccaccian Intertexts*, 94–5, sees in Chaucer's treatment of the Dido narrative in the *House of Fame* an allusion to Boccaccio's earlier analysis of this figure vis-à-vis poets' capacity to convey truth. In her words, "Chaucer would not only borrow from Boccaccio's ekphrastic scenes in his *House of Fame* but also, and perhaps especially, feature Dido as an even more central heroine in a related analysis of poetry's truth claims ... It is clear that as an eager pupil of Boccaccio, Chaucer gleaned this central use of Dido and understood well Boccaccio's varying uses of the myth of Dido and Aeneas."

1 Literary Patricide in the Legend of Thebes

1 An earlier version of this chapter appears in *Studies in the Age of Chaucer* 36 (2014).

2 See especially Robert R. Edwards, *Chaucer and Boccaccio*, 17; Donald R. Howard, *Chaucer*, 189–91; and C. David Benson, "The 'Knight's Tale' as History." William E. Coleman, "The Knight's Tale," 109, speculates that perhaps Chaucer's copy of the *Teseida* lacked Boccaccio's name. Critics have similarly attributed Chaucer's erasure of Boccaccio in *Troilus and Criseyde* to Boccaccio's insufficient authority. See especially George L. Kittredge, "Chaucer's Lollius," 49; Alastair Minnis, *Chaucer and Pagan Antiquity*, 24–5; and David Wallace, *Chaucer and the Early Writings of Boccaccio*, esp. 152.

3 To provide a few examples of this practice, John of Salisbury invents a pseudo-classical and fictional source text, Plutarch's *Institutes of Trajan*, in

the *Polycraticus* (V.2). Guido delle Colonne relies almost singularly on Benoît de Sainte-Maure's *Roman de Troie* for the *Historia Destructionis Troiae*, yet he makes no mention of Benoît's text, purporting instead to translate Dares's *De Excidio Troiae Historia* and Dictys's *Ephemeris Belli Troiani* directly (*Prologus*). (Benoît further minimizes his role in the creation of the *Roman de Troie* by presenting himself as a mere translator of his ancient sources, Dares and Dictys, despite his handsome elaboration of both texts [*Résumé du Poème*]). Finally, Geoffrey of Monmouth credits his knowledge of Trojan history to the discovery of an invented *liber vetustissimus* (*Historia Regum Britanniae* I.1).

4 "Una hystoria antica ... che latino autor non par ne dica." The Italian text of the *Teseida* is taken from Boccaccio, *Teseida delle Nozze d'Emilia*, ed. Edvige Agostinelli and William Coleman (2015), I.2. Passages will be cited in the text by book and stanza, with glosses noted as such. I have chosen this edition over that of Alberto Limentani (who edited the poem in Branca's monumental Mondadori series [1964]) because, while both texts are based on the autograph of the *Teseida* in the Biblioteca Medicea Laurenziana, Florence, Agostinelli and Coleman have used both palaeography and ultraviolet/infrared technology to reveal important information about the manuscript's production. As the editors observe in their introduction to this edition, their research shows that the *Teseida* autograph was "copied in two stages: (I) c. 1350: the poem plus c. 1075 glosses; (2) mid-to-late 1350s: several revisions in the text of the poem plus c. 225 added glosses in Boccaccio's later gothic and cursive hands ... These revisions, which occur in three stages, indicate that amendment was a continuing process for Boccaccio" (xii). After the manuscript endured water damage and a rebinding that resulted in the loss of an entire folio, a sixteenth- or seventeenth-century scribe, C^3, traced over faded text "with an inelegant hand and an often innacurate eye" (xx), unsurprisingly "often producing mistaken readings" (393). While the three twentieth-century editors of the *Teseida* (Salvatore Battaglia [1938], Aurelio Roncaglia [1941], and Limentani [1964]) for the most part accepted the readings of C^3, Agostinelli and Coleman reject these erroneous retracings, which occur predominantly in the glosses. They also uncover new glosses in Boccaccio's hand.

All English translations will be my own, although guided, where suitable, by Bernadette Marie McCoy's translation of *The Book of Theseus* and N.R. Havely's "Teseida and the Marriage of Emilia," in *Chaucer's Boccaccio*, 103–52.

5 Paul Strohm, "Chaucer's Audience(s)," 138.

6 Walter Ong, *Interfaces of the Word*, esp. 53–81. Or, in the words of Gian Biagio Conte, *The Rhetoric of Imitation*, 10, the poet "presupposes" and "establishes the competence of [his] Model Reader."

7 Edwards, "Medieval Literary Careers," 106.

8 J.J.L. Smolenaars, *Statius Thebaid VII: A Commentary*, xvi. For a summary of this critical divide, see Randall T. Ganiban's study, *Statius and Virgil*, 2–6.

9 The Latin text of Statius's *Thebaid*, as well as the English translation, is taken from *Statius*, ed. and trans. D.R. Shackleton Bailey, 2:308–9 (XII.816–17). I have slightly modernized the translation where suitable.

10 Francesco Petrarch, *Le Familiari*, ed. Vittorio Rossi and Umberto Bosco, 4 vols (1933–42), 4:258 (XXIV.12). The fourth volume of these letters is edited by Bosco. The translation of this letter is taken from *Letters on Familiar Matters, Rerum familiarium libri XVII–XXIV*, trans. Aldo Bernardo, 345.

11 The Latin text of the *Aeneid*, as well as the translation, is taken from Virgil, *Eclogues; Georgics; Aeneid I–VI*, ed. H. Rushton Fairclough, revised by G.P. Goold, 342–3 (II.711). According to Michael C.J. Putnam, this passage indicates the "'inferiority' topos of poets' pronouncing their inability to compete with Virgil as Paragon" (*The Virgilian Tradition*, 59).

12 For a reading of Statius's use of allusion in the *Thebaid* to critique the *Aeneid*, see especially Ganiban, *Statius and Virgil*. See also Karla F.L. Pollmann, "Statius' *Thebaid* and the Legacy of Vergil's *Aeneid*."

13 Edwards, "Medieval Literary Careers," 108.

14 *Thebaid*, ed. Bailey, 2:308–9 (XII.818–19).

15 The Hopleus and Dymas episode in *Thebaid* X, which Statius bases on the Nissus and Euryalus episode in *Aeneid* IX, provides another good example of Statius's open erasure of his debt to Virgil. Statius aligns these two Greek warriors with Virgil's soldiers, yet he does not credit the *Aeneid* as his source, writing "vos quoque sacrati, quamvis mea carmina surgant / inferiore lyra, memores superabitis annos. / forsitan et comites non aspernabitur umbras / Euryalus Phrygiique admittet gloria Nisi" ("You too will outlive the mindful years, consecrate, though my songs rise from a lesser lyre, and perhaps Euryalus shall not scorn your attendant shades and Phrygian Nisus's glory shall grant you entry" [*Thebaid*, ed. Bailey, 2:158–9 (X.445–8]). Statius appears to adopt a posture of self-deprecation here, similar to the one he will assume in the epilogue to the *Thebaid*: his characters would be honoured to join Nisus and Euryalus, should they admit them to their ranks. But (again, similar to the epilogue) this passage is not the straightforward expression of reverence that it would seem. Despite his apparent humility, Statius "plays with the possibility that the Hopleus and Dymas episode will rival that of Virgil's Nisus and Euryalus," as Ganiban, *Statius and Virgil*, 3, notes; "by setting his poem alongside the *Aeneid*, the poet invites us to read and interpret these two episodes – and poems – against one another."

16 The Latin text of Statius's *Silvae*, as well as the English translation (slightly adjusted), is taken from vol. 1 of *Statius*, ed. and trans. D.R. Shackleton

Bailey, revised by Christopher A. Parrott, 1:276–7 (IV.7.25–8). Mantua is Virgil's birthplace; "the joys of Mantuan fame" is the *Aeneid*.

17 Stephen Hinds, *Allusion and Intertext*, 93. See also K.M. Coleman's edition of *Silvae* IV. In her commentary on the phrase "audaci fide" (IV.7.27), Coleman notes that whereas in the epilogue of the *Thebaid* Statius was "displaying conventional modesty in presenting his new work before the public, here the circumstances are different" and he can take "legitimate pride in its success" (*Statius: Silvae IV*, 204).

18 *Silvae*, ed. Bailey, 1:334–5 (V.62–3). I have slightly modernized Bailey's translation.

19 The chronology of Boccaccio's Neapolitan works has been a question of debate among scholars, with the long-accepted order being the *Filocolo* (1336–8), the *Filostrato* (1338), and then the *Teseida* (1339–40). Branca ("Filostrato," *Tutte le opere*, 2:3–5) and Pier Giorgio Ricci (*Studi sulla vita e le opere del Boccaccio*, 38–49) amend this chronology to the sequence of *Filostrato*, *Filocolo*, and finally *Teseida*, with the *Filostrato* being written as early as 1335. Luigi Surdich, however (*Boccaccio*, 36), questions such an early placement of the *Filostrato*.

20 Ganiban, *Statius and Virgil*, 1.

21 Tobias Foster Gittes, *Eros, Culture, and the Mythopoetic Imagination*, 6–7, suggests that Boccaccio's "professio[n] of intellectual inadequacy and poetic mediocrity" in the *Filocolo* brackets "a life-long habit of presenting himself as an intellectual subaltern, a mere follower in the path carved out by greater minds."

22 The Italian text of the *Filocolo* is taken from Antonio Enzo Quaglio's edition in *Tutte le opere*, 1:674 (V.97). The English translation is by Donald Cheney, with Thomas Bergin, 470.

23 Citations of Dante's work are taken from *La Commedia*, ed. Giorgio Petrocchi, and are cited by canto and line number; translations are from *The Divine Comedy*, ed. and trans. Robert M. Durling and Ronald L. Martinez.

24 David Anderson, *Before the "Knight's Tale,"* 50. K.P. Clarke, *Chaucer and Italian Textuality*, 59, writes: "Boccaccio's *Teseida* directly interacts with its principal source, the *Thebaid*, not just at a narrative, textual level; it also engages with the source's *auctoritas* by providing his poem with a commentary, elaborating a paratext for his book."

25 Dominique Battles, *The Medieval Tradition of Thebes*, 23.

26 Lee Patterson, *Chaucer and the Subject of History*, 80n88, suggests that Boccaccio is claiming a particular kind of innovativeness, rather than total novelty here: "Boccaccio makes it clear that he is claiming not originality for the *Teseida* but a more profound kind of authenticity than would be the case if his source were Latin ... By returning to an original Greek account, Boccaccio is claiming an authenticity comparable to Dares's or Dictys's accounts

of the Trojan War (both of which were originally written in Greek although known to the Middle Ages in Latin translations)."

27 "By emphasizing Dante's vernacularity and Petrarch's Latinity, Boccaccio was highlighting … his unique authorial identity. He thereby suggested that he was experimenting with more genres in the vernacular *and* in Latin than his two (near) contemporaries" (James C. Kriesel, *Boccaccio's Corpus*, 4).

28 The gloss to the beginning of the following stanza reads, "Cioè, che mai in rima non è stata messa, prima che questa, alcuna hystoria di guerre" ("That is, that no history of wars been put into rhyme before this," XII, 85).

29 Here I am following Havely's translation ("Teseida," *Chaucer's Boccaccio*, 151).

30 The Latin text of *De vulgari eloquentia* is from Pio Rajna's edition (1896), 122 (II.2). The English translation is by Steven Botterill, from Dante, *De vulgari eloquentia*, 53.

31 The Latin text of Virgil's *Georgics*, as well as the translation, is taken from *Eclogues; Georgics; Aeneid I–VI*, ed. Fairclough, revised by Goold, 176–7 (III.10–12).

32 Text and translation are taken from Lucretius, *De rerum natura*, trans. W.H.D. Rouse, revised by Martin F. Smith, 12–13 (I.117–19). For an excellent reading of these lines, see Hinds, *Allusion and Intertext*, 52–5.

33 *De rerum natura*, trans. Rouse, 404–5 (V.336–7).

34 *The Odes of Horace*, ed. and trans. David Ferry, 254. Horace makes a similar claim to primacy in his *Epistles* (I.19.23). See also Propertius, *Elegies* III.1. For a modern analogue, consider Milton's invocation to Book 1 of *Paradise Lost*. Milton claims that his song will pursue "things unattempted yet in Prose or Rhime" (I.13–16), a literal translation of Ludovico Ariosto's promise in *Orlando Furioso*, "Cosa non detta mai in prosa nè in rima" (I.2). Ariosto himself is, moreover, alluding to Matteo Maria Boiardo's *Orlando Innamorato*, in which the narrator declares at the conclusion of Book II that his reader will hear things never before recounted in verse or prose (XXX.1). For a discussion of the textual history of this line, see especially Daniel Shore, "Things Unattempted … Yet Once More." Many thanks to William Robins for bringing this example to my attention. A second modern analogue can be seen in the repeated claims by T.S. Eliot, Picasso, Stravinsky, and Banksy that "good poets borrow" and "great poets steal," which I discuss in this book's Introduction. Like the poets repeatedly designating themselves "first," these artists call attention to their theft of a phrase in the very refrain that conceals that theft.

35 Boccaccio wrote the first thirteen books of the *Genealogie* between 1350 and 1359. He added Books XIV and XV sometime before 1367. He would return to his work, correcting and revising it, until his death.

36 The Latin text of the *Genealogie deorum gentilium* is taken from Vittorio Zaccaria's edition in *Tutte le opere*, 8:1540 (XV.7.5–6); all translated text is

taken from *Boccaccio on Poetry*, trans. Charles G. Osgood, 120, with consideration of David Lummus's modifications of Osgood's translation in his dicussion of this passage ("Boccaccio's Hellenism and the Foundations of Modernity," 129). As Lummus explains, although relying on a primacy topos to explain his role in bringing an interest in the study of Hellenic poetry to Florence, Boccaccio's knowledge of the Greek language was somewhat limited. His engagement with Greek culture was primarily through scholars, especially Leonzo Pilato, under whose tutelage Boccaccio revises, expands, and shapes the final two books of the *Genealogie*.

37 Hinds, *Allusion and Intertext*, 54. On the motif of "firstness" in Roman poetry see also Tony Woodman, "Exegi Monumentum," esp. 211–12, as well as David Meban, "Temple Building, Primus Language, and the Proem to Virgil's Third *Georgic*," 160–7.

38 Hinds, *Allusion and Intertext*, 55.

39 I have followed Havely's translation closely here ("Teseida," *Chaucer's Boccaccio*, 152).

40 For a useful analysis of Boccaccio's glosses in the *Teseida*, see Clarke, *Chaucer and Italian Textuality*, 47–93. Clarke urges readers to move beyond the critical commonplace of interpreting the commentary to the *Teseida* as merely an authenticating device on the part of its author: "It has been a cliché in Boccaccio criticism to describe Boccaccio's desire to provide a commentary on his poem simply as a desire to create, in the (now classic) words of Robert Hollander, 'an instant classic.' Such a characterization of the commentary does an injustice to Boccaccio and to the complexity of his motives. As can be seen in Boccaccio's other impulses to gloss texts … glosses help the reader, they impinge upon the praxis of reading and provide it with a hermeneutics. Being a 'classic' is not quite the point, or rather it is not the *only* point" (56).

41 In the *Thebaid*, it is Athena, not Mars, to whom Tydeus dedicates the spoils of his conquest (II.704–6), and Tydeus fastens his victims' armour, not his own shield, to the tree (II.710–12). These changes seem minor, yet because Boccaccio does not acknowledge the *Thebaid*, they take on the aspect of an alternative account, and one that stands in contrast to the original and even discredits it. It is also worth noting that the Statian passage makes a direct comparison between Athena and Mars – with Mars held as the inferior god (II.715–25). By substituting Athena for Mars, aligning himself with Tydeus, meanwhile reversing the priorities of the Statian scene, Boccaccio inscribes his own superior power as the patron poet of arms. The shield that Tydeus consecrates to Mars – a symbol of victory in the *Teseida* – here signifies Boccaccio's erasure of Statius, with the "hystoria antica" taking Statius's place as the authority on Thebes.

42 For the ways in which the layout of the *Teseida* mimics that of the *Thebaid*, see the appendix of Francesca Malagnini's "Il libro d'autore dal progetto alla realizzazione."

43 Alastair Minnis, *Medieval Theory of Authorship*, xxxii.

44 In Minnis's words, *Medieval Theory of Authorship*, 11, "works of unknown or uncertain authorship were regarded as 'apocryphal' and believed to possess an *auctoritas* far inferior to that of works which circulated under the names of *auctores*."

45 Cf. Barbara Nolan, *Chaucer and the Tradition of the* Roman Antique, 165, who claims that Boccaccio aligns himself here with his classical forbears, and with the French authors of the *romans antiques*, so as to cloak himself in the "authority of the philosophers educated in the liberal arts."

46 *Fingendo* is the gerund of the vernacular verb *fingere*, which derives etymologically from the Latin verb *fingere*, which means "form out of original matter, create," "compose (poems and other literary works)," and "invent." But it could also mean pretend, "make up, feign," and "produce insincerity" (*Vb. fingere*, senses 2; 6a and 6b; 9a and 9b; and 10b: *Oxford Latin Dictionary*). Boccaccio uses the verb "finxere" (to create/to create fictions about) to describe the process of poetic invention. In Lummus's words ("Boccaccio's Poetic Anthropology," 734), the poet's use of *finxere* is "central to how Boccaccio understands the origins of human myth. It means both 'to create' and 'to create fictions about' and thus links myth as poetry (language) and myth as human creation (history)."

47 *Genealogie*, ed. Zaccaria, *Tutte le opere*, 8:1360, 1362 (XIV.2.1, XIV.2.2); trans. Osgood, 17–18. For the history of the *Genealogie*, see vol. 1 of Jon Solomon's edition of *Genealogy of the Pagan Gods: Books V–X*, viii–ix. The second volume of this edition, which includes a translation of Books VI–X, was published in 2017. I am grateful to Michael Papio for his help on this section.

48 Boccaccio lists these as his opponents in the opening of his defence (*Genealogie*, ed. Zaccaria, *Tutte le opere*, 8:1360–1 [XIV.2]; trans. Osgood, 19): "Concurrent, ut fit, ad spectaculum novi operis non solum vulgus ineptum, sed et eruditi convenient homines ... Sunt hi, ut reliquum sinamus vulgus, homines quidam insani, quibus tanta loquacitas est et detestabilis arrogantia, ut adversus omnia quorumcunque probatissimorum hominum presummant clamoribus ferre sententiam" ("Around my book, as usual at the sight of a new work, will gather a crowd of the incompetent. The learned will also attend ... There are, among others in this crowd, certain madmen so garrulous and detestably arrogant that they presume to shout abroad their condemnation of everything that even the best man can do").

49 Petrarch justifies poetry in similar terms in *Fam* X.4.

50 *Genealogie*, ed. Zaccaria, *Tutte le opere*, 8:1416 (XIV.9.13).

51 Lummus, "Boccaccio's Poetic Anthropology."

52 *Genealogie*, ed. Zaccaria, *Tutte le opere*, 7:84 (I.3.8). The translation is taken from Solomon, *Genealogy of the Pagan Gods*, 1:51. As Lummus

notes, "Boccaccio's Poetic Anthropology," 746, "This is clearly a remaking of Dante's example of the allegory of the theologians in his *Epistle to Cangrande.*"

53 Lummus, "Boccaccio's Poetic Anthropology," 747.

54 Lummus, "Boccaccio's Poetic Anthropology," 747.

55 Lummus, "Boccaccio's Poetic Anthropology," 747.

56 Lummus, "Boccaccio's Poetic Anthropology," 747.

57 *Genealogie*, ed. Zaccaria, *Tutte le opere*, 8:1412 (XIV.9.3); trans. Osgood, 47.

58 *Genealogie*, ed. Zaccaria, *Tutte le opere*, 8:1412 (XIV.9.4); trans. Osgood, 47.

59 This definition elevates poetry to the status of philosophy, as Andrew Laird observed ("Fiction, Philosophy, and Logical Closure," 301). Boccaccio believed, "like Aristotle, that poetry tells of the kinds of things that might happen … because it speaks of *universals* – the kinds of thing a certain type of person will say and do in a given situation." Far from requiring exegesis to make them edifying or worthwhile, then, for the author, "all forms of fiction can teach us something."

60 *Genealogie*, ed. Zaccaria, *Tutte le opere*, 8:1414 (XIV. 9.7); trans. Osgood, 48–9.

61 The editor notes that the phrase ("Nec fastidiant obiectores […] usus est") follows in the margins of cod. Plut. LII 9 (an autograph manuscript), but is suppressed in the *Vulgata*. *Genealogia*, ed. Zaccaria, *Tutte le opere*, 8:1707n99. Osgood includes these words in the body of the text of his translation, 49.

62 Patterson, *Negotiating the Past*, 162. Patterson is speaking specifically of medieval adaptations of the *Aeneid*, but his comment characterizes Boccaccio's adaptation of the *Thebaid* as well.

63 As Agostinelli and Coleman note in their edition ("Introduction," xivn4), "While the muses of poetry prefer a formal title, (il) *Theseyda di nozze d'Emilia* (2 concl. Son. 12), the final rubric to [book] 12 entitles it *Theseyda delle nozze d'Emilia.* Elsewhere, the rubrics to the poem most often call it *Theseyda*, but also use *Teseida*, *Teseyda*, and *Theseida*."

64 *Thebaid*, ed. Bailey, 2:306–7 (XII.812–13).

65 Chaucer, *Riverside Chaucer*, I.859; Chaucer also claims to rely on "olde bookes" ("bookes olde") twice in the "Knight's Tale," at I.463 and at I.2294. All quotations from Chaucer's works will be from this edition and cited in the text.

66 To provide a few examples of Chaucer's resurrection of Statius as a Theban authority in his other works, in the *House of Fame* Chaucer records Statius as the sole author holding up the "fame of Thebes" (III.1460–2). In the *Anelida and Arcite*, a shorter work beginning as a translation of the *Teseida*, Chaucer corrects Boccaccio's earlier suggestion that no Latin author had told his story before by claiming to translate an "olde storie, in Latyn which

I finde" (10). He then names "Stace," after "Corynne," as one of the two *auctores* whom he will follow (21), suggesting, as Nolan points out (*Chaucer and the Tradition of the* Roman Antique, 247), that Chaucer recognized Boccaccio's debt to Statius in the *Teseida* and attempted a "similar exercise in creative imitation." Finally, Chaucer names "Stace" as one of the poetic models of whom he will "kis the steppes" in the epilogue to the *Troilus* (V.1792), a passage modelled on the envoy to the *Filocolo*. In recuperating Statius to this assembly of literary exemplars, Chaucer expunges Boccaccio from his own line-up of authors. His adulation of Statius thus involves – even hinges on – the implicit suppression of his Boccaccian source.

67 Chaucer takes his gloss from *Thebaid* XII.519–22. The Latin passage is also included in the *Anelida and Arcite*, between lines 21 and 22.

68 Anderson, *Before the "Knight's Tale,"* 201, argues that Chaucer's alterations to the *Teseida* "generally reflect a concern with preserving and accentuating the *Thebaid* like structure and themes of Boccaccio's narrative." With regard to Chaucer's use of *abbreviato*, Anderson notes that Chaucer "shortens [the *Teseida*] in ways that maintain, or even increase, the underlying patterns from the *Thebaid*" (202).

69 For Boccaccio's expansion of his Statian source, see Edwards, "Medieval Literary Careers," 112, who observes that the *Teseida* is more of an "amplification" than a "vernacular sequel" or translation of the *Thebaid* because it "seeks to resolve" rather than reproduce "the themes and action of Statius's poem." See also Leah Schwebel, "What's in Criseyde's Book?"

70 Cf. Stephen H. Rigby, *Wisdom and Chivalry*, 135, who sees Chaucer's editorial adjustment as a way of ennobling Duke Theseus's achievement: "in massively compressing his source, Chaucer does not have to confront the problems involved in having the chivalrous Theseus overcome a kingdom of women, something which might be considered … an achievement of 'litel worschepe.'"

71 For Chaucer's aesthetic of omission in the "Knight's Tale," see Mark A. Sherman, "The Politics of Discourse in Chaucer's *Knight's Tale*." Sherman explains that the "Knight's Tale" "must be read … with an eye for what is *not* articulated and is in fact blatantly suppressed" (91). By cataloguing the things he *will not* tell us, moreover, the Knight "heighten[s] the reader's awareness of excluded narratives to such a degree that the unsaid exerts greater narrative force than the said, that the utterance stands in the shadow of what it obfuscates" (94). See also Elizabeth Scala, *Absent Narratives, Manuscript Textuality, and Literary Structure in Late Medieval England*, 99, who notes that recent criticism on the tale is grounded "in the Knight's omissions. Revealing the absent narratives of the Knight's story has … emerged as *the* critical drive behind modern readings of his tale, even if such projects have not always articulated their goals in these precise terms." Scala

herself looks at these omissions "as part of the politicized and politicizing content of his tale" (100).

72 *Teseida* VII.72–4. In the original Italian, in addition to perfuming the temple, crowning her hair with cereal oak, and lighting two pyres, Emilia sacrifices turtle doves and lambs, draining the blood from their bodies and tossing the entrails and viscera of the dead animals into the fire. Her proceedings closely echo the process of Tiresias's sacrifice in the *Thebaid.* Chaucer removes these more gruesome details from her rites.

73 For a concise description of some of the parallels between these two episodes, see Anderson, *Before the "Knight's Tale,"* 80.

74 *Thebaid*, ed. Bailey, 3:544–5 (IV.512–17).

75 Here I follow Havely's translation ("Teseida," *Chaucer's Boccaccio*, 134).

76 Coleman, "The Knight's Tale," 2:93, claims that by citing Statius, "the remote source for the passage," Chaucer is "making the point that Statius is available in two forms in the *Knight's Tale*: directly and at second-hand via the *Teseida.*"

77 Coleman, "The Knight's Tale," 2:113–14, suggests Chaucer's version of the *Teseida* likely lacked Boccaccio's original commentary (an argument he first put forth, although not quite so assertively, in "Chaucer's MS and Boccaccio's Commentaries on '*Il Teseida*'"): "The most prudent conclusion regarding the question of Boccaccio's glosses is that the case is not proved. The evidence suggests, however, that Chaucer's *Teseida* was a product of the first redaction of the work and that it was related, not to one of the nine MSS with Boccaccio's glosses, but rather to one of the 38 MSS without them." Coleman's suggestion is based primarily on negative evidence – i.e., what Chaucer would have "responded to … in some way if they were to be found in his MS" (113). Following Robert A. Pratt, "Conjectures Regarding Chaucer's Manuscript of the *Teseida,*" 755, he thus comes to his conclusion on the basis of a "paucity" of "parallels," taking absence as evidence of ignorance. Coleman's demand for positive proof of Chaucer's knowledge of Boccaccio's glosses in a tale that develops according to an aesthetic of omission and erasure (Sherman ["The Politics of Discourse"], Scala [*Absent Narratives*], Schwebel ["Literary Patricide"]) is, I think, delimiting. I am inclined to agree with Clarke (*Chaucer and Italian Textuality*, 59), who suggests that a discussion of Chaucer's use of the *Teseida* that takes the glosses into account can only deepen our understanding of the relationship between these two texts. To Coleman's argument, Clarke responds, "such a cautious position must not preclude a consideration of a broader context of the manuscript textuality in which these texts were produced and read."

78 While the name of Idas is common in epic poetry, the figure of Idas the Pisan, an Olympian who competes in a footrace, is particular to the *Thebaid*. (In his commentary on *Thebaid* VII.266, Smolenaars lists these examples of other figures with this name: *Iliad* IX.558, *Aeneid* IX.575 [Trojan], X.351 [Thracian], *Metamorphoses* V.90, *Fasti* V.701 [Argonaut]).

79 Piero Boitani, *Chaucer and Boccaccio*, 27, has, however, noted that Boccaccio's citation of Virgil here is "curious" for the very reason that he "never acknowledges his much more substantial debt to Statius." Anderson, *Before the "Knight's Tale,"* 115–16, mentions Statius's Idas in his discussion of Boccaccio's games, yet he claims that Boccaccio relies only on Virgil. Commenting on Boccaccio's mention of Virgil here, Clarke, *Chaucer and Italian Textuality*, 57–8, suggests that "there is certainly an appropriation of *auctoritas* via Virgil to Boccaccio in this gloss; he is an *autore* just like Virgil, and the gloss is strongly textual in that it refers to the *autore* who 'scrive,' who writes, rather than 'dice,' who says."

80 *Lactantii Placidi qui dicitur Commentarios in Statii Thebaida et Commentarium in Achilleida*, ed. Richard Jahnke, 313 (VI.296). For Boccaccio's use of Lactantius, and the existence of a copy of the *Thebaid* containing Lactantius's commentary in Boccaccio's possession, see Anderson, *Before the "Knight's Tale,"* 38n1.

81 There is some debate on the chronology of the "Knight's Tale" and the *Troilus*. Yet, the fact that the two poems share many lines speaks to the proximity, perhaps even overlap, of their composition. See Vincent DiMarco's explanatory notes for the "Knight's Tale" in the *Riverside Chaucer*, 826.

82 See Wallace, *Chaucer and the Early Writings of Boccaccio*, 50–3, for a discussion of poets naming themselves sixth of six authors. See also Wallace, *Chaucerian Polity*, 80–1.

83 "If I hadde ytaken for to written / The armes of this ilke worthi man, / Than wolde ich of his batailles endite; / But for that I to writen first bigan / Of his love, I have seyd as I kan – " (V.1765–9).

84 Although we can only speculate on Chaucer's knowledge of *De vulgari eloquentia*, his plea for the *Troilus* to be understood echoes Dante's insistence on the superiority of Italian based on its universal capacity to be understood (*Ve* I.1). It also anticipates his engagement with a debate on the accessibility of Latin versus the vernacular in the "Clerk's Tale," a subject I discuss in chapter 2.

85 Compare *Genealogie* XV, Conclusion, 2–3, in which Boccaccio invites future readers, and especially Petrarch, to correct his work.

86 For a reading of the significance of the dedication, see R.F. Yaeger, "'O Moral Gower.'"

87 *Le Familiari*, ed. Rossi and Bosco, 4:94–100 (XXI.15).

88 Petrarch names Dante only twice in all his poetry, and both times in conjunction with other vernacular love poets writing for the vulgar masses. On these instances, see especially Kevin Brownlee, "Power Plays."

89 Giuseppe Mazzotta, "Petrarch's Dialogue with Dante," 181.

90 Mazzotta, "Petrarch's Dialogue with Dante," 181. This letter was to an unknown correspondent, in response to a letter written in Homer's name, yet

Petrarch addresses the recipient as Homer throughout. Aldo S. Bernardo explains that Petrarch shared his letters, and especially those addressed to the ancients, with his literary friends. We know, for example, that Boccaccio was allowed to copy certain letters from Petrarch's series of letters to the ancient poets in the *Familiares*. See Bernardo, "Introduction," xxiii.

91 *Le Familiari*, ed. Rossi and Bosco, 4:258 (XXIV.12); trans. Bernardo, 345. Homer is named in the *Juvenilia*, but these poems are suspected to be apocryphal.

92 *Le Familiari*, ed. Rossi and Bosco, 4:259 (XXIV.12); trans. Bernardo, 346.

93 *Le Familiari*, ed. Rossi and Bosco, 4:259 (XXIV.12); trans. Bernardo, 346 (I have slightly amended Bernardo's translation).

94 Nor is Dante the only poet that Petrarch erases. Laird, "Re-inventing Virgil's Wheel," 150, points us toward Petrarch's "strategic occlusion" of Virgil, his "clear model" for the *Africa*. Wherever in the *Africa* "one might expect references to the story of the *Aeneid* to prompt an overt or positive acknowledgement of its poet," he notes, "that expectation is confounded" (147).

95 Mazzotta, "Petrarch's Dialogue with Dante," 181–2.

96 Lydgate, *John Lydgate: The Siege of Thebes*, ed. Edwards. James Simpson, "'Dysemol daies and fatal houres," 29, notes that this manoeuvre forces us to reinterpret the "Knight's Tale" through the lens of the *Siege* (which Simpson suggests we call the "Destruction of Thebes"), reinserting Chaucer's text into an "unequivocally historical, political narrative; it equally places the most severe constraints on whatever glimpses of prudential wisdom the *Knight's Tale* might have seemed to offer."

97 For example, Lydgate refers to the "floure of poetes thorghout al Breteyne" in the preface to the *Siege of Thebes* (40).

98 A.C. Spearing, "Renaissance Chaucer and Father Chaucer," 26. See also Daniel T. Kline, "Father Chaucer and the Siege of Thebes."

99 These instances are as follows: 199; 213; 1541; 3171; 3201; 3510; 3541.

100 John Lydgate, *The Fall of Princes*, ed. Henry Bergen, 9.3401–7.

101 Christopher Cannon, *The Making of Chaucer's English*, 185.

102 John Lydgate, *The Life of Saint Alban and Saint Amphibal*, ed. J.E. Van der Westhuizen, 8–14.

103 *The Life of Saint Alban and Saint Amphibal*, ed. Van der Westhuizen, 15–17.

104 Of course, Chaucer also names himself in the *House of Fame* (I.729), through the eagle's address to his narrator. We thus have good reason to question the sincerity of his narrator's fear of recognition. Chaucer's auto-citation in the *House of Fame* recalls *Purgatorio* XXX.55, in which Beatrice names Dante for the first and only time in the entire *Commedia*. After Beatrice names him, Dante insists that he only writes his name out of necessity.

105 Maura Nolan, *John Lydgate and the Making of Public Culture*, 103. David Lawton, "Dullness in the Fifteenth Century," similarly suggests that

Boccaccio's name *became* authoritative in the fifteenth century, even if it was not at the time Chaucer was writing. He suggests that Boccaccio was "useful to Lydgate in the role of authority in ways that he was not to Chaucer" (785). See also Richard Firth Green, *Poets and Princepleasers*, 160.

106 Beyond Maura Nolan's excellent study, see Robert Meyer-Lee, *Poets and Power from Chaucer to Wyatt*, and Mary C. Flannery, *John Lydgate and the Poetics of Fame*.

2 Restoration through Translation in the "Clerk's Tale"

1 An earlier version of this chapter appeared in *Chaucer Review* 47 (2013): 274–99 (https://doi.org/10.5325/chaucerrev.47.3.0274). Used with permission from Penn State University Press.

2 Borges, "Pierre Menard, Author of the *Quixote*," trans. Andrew Hurley, 91.

3 Borges, "Pierre Menard," trans. Hurley, 94.

4 Borges, "Pierre Menard," trans. Hurley, 94.

5 Borges, "Pierre Menard," trans. Hurley, 94.

6 Borges, "Pierre Menard," trans. Hurley, 94.

7 Sergio Gabriel Waisman, *Borges and Translation*, 104.

8 Borges, "Pierre Menard," trans. Hurley, 93.

9 According to Mirko Tavoni ("Linguistic Italy," 253–4), the "terminological opposition" between *gramatica* and *volgare* arose in the last decades of the *Duecento*. In Dante's time, "Latin and the vernacular coexisted, but with clearly defined roles and in a clearly defined hierarchical relationship. To Latin was granted the superior role of language of culture, of written language par excellence, even though it was used orally. To the vernacular was given the lesser role of practical, day-to-day communication, of a language that was primarily spoken, even if it was used in writing" (246).

10 *Vn* XXV.6: "E lo primo che cominciò a dire sì come poeta volgare, si mosse però che volle fare intendere le sue parole a donna, a la quale era malagevole d'intendere li versi latini. E questo è contra coloro che rimano sopra altra matera che amorosa, con ciò sia cosa che cotale modo di parlare fosse dal principio trovato per dire d'amore" ("The first poet to begin writing in the vernacular was moved to do so by a desire to make his words understandable to ladies who found Latin verses difficult to comprehend. And this is an argument against those who compose in the vernacular on a subject other than love, since composition in the vernacular was from the beginning intended for treating of love." The text of the *Vita nuova* is taken from Michele Barbi's edition. The translation is Mark Musa's.

11 The text of the *Decameron* is taken from Vittore Branca's edition in *Tutte le opere*, 4:953 (X.10). The English translation is from *The Decameron*, trans. G.H. McWilliam, 794.

12 Kara Gaston, *Reading Chaucer in Time*, 90.
13 Gaston, *Reading Chaucer*, 90.
14 All quotations of Chaucer are from the *Riverside Chaucer*, here IV.13. Subsequent citations will be noted in the text. K.P. Clarke, *Chaucer and Italian Textuality*, 122, discusses MS Pluteo 42, 1, a manuscript of the *Decameron* copied by Francesco d'Amaretto Mannelli in 1384. Mannelli responds to Griselda's reclothing by her father by noting, "'Nolle dovevan capere essendo ella cresciuta e ingrossata' [*ad Dec.* X.10. 48, fo. 170], 'they [her old clothes] must not have fitted her, having grown and filled out.'" As Clarke observes, "instead of reading the scene as powerfully displaying Griselda's passive acceptance of her husband's will and her father's expectations, Mannelli sees practical life getting in the way" (122). What is more, his response "anticipat[es] an almost exactly similar concern of the French translator," who makes a point of noting the changes to Griselda's body brought on by the passing years.
15 Gaston, *Reading Chaucer*, 92. See also Teodolinda Barolini, "The Marquis of Saluzzo, or the Griselda Story Before It Was Hijacked," 24, who describes Griselda as "unchangeable in her stoicism, and life's contingencies – new events as they unfold – have no purchase over her: 'di niente la novità delle cose la cambiava' [no event, however singular, produced the slightest change in her demeanor]" (*Dec.* X.10, 58).
16 For Chaucer's variety of genres in the *Canterbury Tales*, see especially C. David Benson, *Chaucer's Drama of Style*.
17 Chaucer also changes the very function of Boccaccio's poem. As Robert Hollander, *Boccaccio's Dante and the Shaping Force of Satire*, 69, notes, Boccaccio's narrator invokes Horace ("omne tulit punctum qui miscuit utile dulci, / lectorem delectando pariterque monendo") to promise "diletto" and "utile consiglio" to ladies in love, a "statement of purpose" anticipating Walter's insistence that his trials of Griselda have a didactic incentive. Chaucer's host, however, requests tales of moral profit *first* – "sentence" then "solace" – and for *all.* Chaucer thus reverses and universalizes Boccaccio's Horatian objective.
18 Alison Cornish, "A Lady Asks," 167.
19 Janet Coleman, "English Culture in the Fourteenth Century," 38.
20 Alison Cornish, *Vernacular Translation in Dante's Italy*, 160. The line is worth quoting in full: not only does Petrarch "reverse the tide by flipping one of the very major accomplishments of the vernacular back into the grammatical language, he chooses to do it with a tale of re-clothing that he was perhaps the first to see is itself a parable of translation. In this way, his dressing up of the humble vernacular novella has the opposite effect of vernacularization. While volgarizzamento put high culture into the hands of the *volgo* and, explicitly, of women, Petrarch's elevation of Griselda to the

Latin idiom takes her, explicitly, out of the hands of the female audience to whom the *Decameron* was addressed."

21 As Dolores Warwick Frese, "The 'Buried Bodies' of Dante, Boccaccio, and Petrarch," 251, writes, Dante's treatise is the "never-named but clearly discernible source of inspiration for the narrative plot and governing tropes of *Decameron* X.x."

22 The Latin text of *De vulgari eloquentia* is from Pio Rajna's edition (1896), 6–7 (I.1); The English translation is by Steven Botterill, from Dante, *De vulgari eloquentia*, 3.

23 *Decameron*, ed. Branca, *Tutte le opere*, 4:954 (X.10); trans. McWilliam, 794–5.

24 Chaucer's concept of *gentilezza* likewise derives from Dante's *Convivio*. The crone in the "Wife of Bath's Tale" advises her husband to read Dante, who speaks well on this subject (III.1125–30).

25 Dante, *Convivio*, ed. Franca Brambilla Ageno, Book IV, *Canzone* III.6, 1–2. The English translation is by Richard H. Lansing, *The Convivio*, 145.

26 Alastair Minnis, *Translations of Authority in Medieval English Literature*, 3.

27 Minnis, *Translations of Authority*, 3. Although Dante does not articulate the association between social and linguistic *gentilezza* outright, this connection is, as Minnis rightly observes, "quite implicit in what he actually does say" (3).

28 *Ve*, ed. Rajna (I.1); trans. Botterill, 3.

29 *Ve*, ed. Rajna (I.9); trans. Botterill, 23.

30 Dante reiterates his argument on the universality of the vernacular in the *Convivio* (ed. Ageno [I.9, 4–5]; trans. Lansing, 22), where he contrasts what he calls the *litterati* with those readers who can understand only the vernacular, and praises the vernacular for its ability to include women. "Dico che manifestamente si può vedere come lo latino averebbe a pochi dato lo suo beneficio, ma lo volgare servirà veramente a molti. / Chè la bontà dell'animo, la quale questo servigio attende, è in coloro che per malvagia disusanza del mondo hanno lasciata la litteratura a coloro che l'hanno fatta di donna meretrice; e questi nobili sono principi, baroni, cavalieri e molt'altra nobile gente, non solamente maschi ma femmine, che sono molti e molte in questa lingua, volgari e non litterati" ("I say that it may clearly be seen that Latin would have conferred its benefits on few while the vernacular will be of service to many. / For goodness of mind, which this service attends to, is found in those who because of the world's wicked neglect of good have left literature to those who have changed it from a lady into a whore; and these noble persons comprise princes, barons, knights, and many other noble people, not only men but women, of which there are many in this language who know only the vernacular and are not learned").

31 *Decameron*, ed. Branca, *Tutte le opere*, 4:345 (IV); trans. McWilliam, 284.

32 In the proem, for example, he claims that he will provide "soccorso e rifugio" ("succor and diversion") for ladies in love (*Decameron*, ed. Branca, *Tutte le opere*, 4:5; trans. McWilliam, 3).

33 *Decameron*, ed. Branca, *Tutte le opere*, 4:345–6 (IV); trans. McWilliam, 284.
34 *Decameron*, ed. Branca, *Tutte le opere*, 4:350 (IV); trans. McWilliam, 288.
35 *Decameron*, ed. Branca, *Tutte le opere*, 4:352 (IV); trans. McWilliam, 290.
36 Kristina Olson, "The Language of Women As Written by Men," 52.
37 Lucia Battaglia Ricci, *Boccaccio*, 61–2, attributes Boccaccio's theme of love in his vernacular works, as well as his repeated address to an audience of women, among other things, to Dante: "per tale 'quasi esclusiva insistenza sul tema amoroso' nelle opera volgari ... è verisimile che Boccaccio dipenda da Dante: tematica amorosa, lingua volgare, stile non alto, pubblico femminile sono infatti gli elementi che costituiscono il Sistema di comunicazione letteraria autorizzato da Dante, fattosi storico della letteratura nella *Vita nova* (xxv 6): 'E lo primo che cominciò a dire sí come poeta volgare, si mosse però che volle fare intendere le sue parole a donna, a la quale era malagevole d'intendere li versi latini.'" Likewise invoking this passage from the *Vita nuova*, James C. Kriesel, *Boccaccio's Corpus*, 11–12, observes that "In the late Middle Ages, vernacular texts were associated with women because a male poet had supposedly invented vernacular poetry to communicate with a woman who did not know Latin."
38 Cornish, "A Lady Asks," 173.
39 The legitimacy of the *Stilnovistic* poets' female audience has long been a matter of debate among scholars. As Elena Lombardi notes, *Imagining the Woman Reader in the Age of Dante*, 12, while it is impossible to know whether he had "'real' women in mind" when he defends the vernacular for its capacity to reach them, Dante makes a point of not only including women in his arguments but also *emphasizing* them. "This emphasis on women" is, moreover, "the clue to a female accented lay literacy, and to a subtle and innovative discourse on reading on the part of Dante." Cornish, *Vernacular Translation*, 5, suggests that while women may well have been "a genuine motive" for these poets' choice of Italian over Latin, they were also a "convenient excuse." Speaking in particular of Boccaccio's female audience in the *Decameron*, Olson, "The Language of Women," 54, argues that the poet's claim to write for women is "part of a rhetorical strategy to build vernacular authority." Rhiannon Daniels, "Boccaccio's Narrators and Audiences," 46, considers the "collective audience" that "comes to the fore when the Narrator defends his work against criticisms." This audience "might include female readers," she considers, "but the objection that he is spending too much time writing about women suggests that these are male." Considering the size and format of the autograph manuscript, MS Hamilton 90, Renzo Bragantini, "L'amicizia, la fama, il libro," 112, suggests that the *Decameron* was always intended for an intellectual (male) audience. "L'impaginazione voluta da Boccaccio ... indica senza alcun dubbio che Boccaccio presuppone un pubblico di intellettuali, in grado di affrontare

il testo in profondità, e di coglierne la complessa e ingegnosa macchina, in particolare per quanto riguarda la continua e sottile tramatura intertestuale." Bragantini directs our attention to Boccaccio's later letter to Mainardo Cavalcanti, in which the author expresses concern for the *Decameron*'s reception and advises his friend to keep the women in his house from reading the work. Having designed the poem with a distinct and ideal audience in mind, Bragantini concludes, the author must have felt "un'ansia reale" with regard to the work's reception and dissemination (115).

Examining MS Hamilton 90, Ricci, *Scrivere un libro di novelle*, 27, notes that the volume, "costituito in origine da circa 136 carte di grande formato (mm 371x266), è il più grande dei manoscritti usciti dallo scrittoio di Boccaccio." It is heavy, large, voluminous, and contains only the poem itself. Giancarlo Alfano, *Introduzione alla lettura del "Decameron" di Boccaccio*, 37–8, argues that such a codex was intended primarily for an audience of scholarly men. Indeed, examining the material aspect of a text is important for precisely this reason, "perché dimostra che Boccaccio aveva un preciso progetto culturale: egli aveva, del resto, una grande esperienza di copista ... ed era ben consapevole dei processi editoriali della sua epoca. Un libro di intrattenimento avrebbe dovuto avere caratteri del tutto diversi: avrebbe dovuto essere piccolo e maneggevole, semmai impreziosito da qualque imagine, da potersi portare appresso e legere con comodo anche in compagnia. Realizzare un libro 'da banco,' cioè da studiare sul leggio significava, di conseguenza, selezionare il tipo di lettore: non la dama cortese, non il mercante che si distrae per qualche ora dagli affari, ma l'intellettutuale che legge e ragiona, che s'impegna in un processo di interpretazione e dialogo con il testo." (The term "libro di banco" comes from Armando Petrucci, "Il libro manoscritto." Ricci, *Scrivere un libro di novelle*, 21, finds in the "libri di autori" of Boccaccio and Petrarch "preziosa testimonianza della consapevolezza con cui ... gli autori gestiscono l'allestimento dei loro libri, scegliendo il materiale scrittorio, il formato e il tipo di scrittura," and "costruendo l'assetto grafico-visivo delle pagine," all of which is accomplished for the sake of their reader, "reale o ideale." More recently, Clarke, "Text and (Inter)Face," 28, examined the catchwords of this codex and argued that even these word or words, placed in the margin of the last page of a quire to ensure proper ordering, demonstrate Boccaccio's intense consideration of both his reader and the material text of his works: "Boccaccio emerges as an author in supreme control of the paratext, with an acute awareness of the material complexity of the reader's interpretative encounter with the page."

40 Lombardi, *Imagining the Woman Reader*, 34. For the gender of rhetoric, see Marilyn Migiel, *A Rhetoric of the "Decameron."* In her analysis of the *Decameron*'s male and female narrators, Migiel uses her study to "reflect on the

way that gender is far more controversial in the *Decameron*'s views of sexuality and moral choice than has previously been thought" (63). In her words, the gender of the individual members of the brigata is highly significant, in that Boccaccio uses it to depict "how social and discursive power is divided between sexes. The fictional storytellers of the *Decameron* are marked by their gender and by their express views on sexuality and sexual difference" (82).

41 Dino del Garbo, "La glossa latina di Dino del Garbo," 360, quoted in Alison Cornish, "A Lady Asks," 172. I am quoting directly from Cornish's translations here. Antonio Enzo Quaglio, "Prima Fortuna della Glossa Garbiana a 'Donna me prega' del Cavalcanti," demonstrates that the sole surviving manuscript of Dino's commentary on "Donna me prega" is a Boccaccian autograph; Boccaccio was thus not only familiar with Dino's exposition on the term "la donna," but also largely responsible for its dissemination. In fact, Boccaccio would include Dino's gloss alongside Cavalcanti's poem in his manuscript, the *Chigiano* (now two separate manuscripts), which also contained, among other works, Boccaccio's own *Trattatello in laude di Dante*, Dante's *Vita nuova*, and an earlier version of Petrarch's *Canzoniere*, and which, as Jason M. Houston rightly notes (*Building a Monument to Dante*, 21), "evinces [Boccaccio's] material formulation of a canon of trecento vernacular literature … that persists to this day."

42 Cornish, "A Lady Asks," 177–8.

43 Lombardi, *Imagining the Woman Reader*, 36.

44 Boccaccio responds more overtly to Dante's appeal to poets to compose in the vernacular in the Envoy to the *Teseida* (XII.84), a passage I discuss at length in this book's first chapter.

45 Olson, "The Language of Women," 57, writes, "As the *Decameron*'s Author implies in the Introduction to Day Four, composing in the *volgare* allows Boccaccio to join the ranks of those who also wrote love poetry, such as Dante, Cavalcanti and Cino da Pistoia – and to compete with their lyric production by writing both in the Florentine vernacular *and*, for the first time for the emerging canon of Italian literature, in prose." As Daniels points out, "Boccaccio's Narrators and Audiences," 42, Boccaccio's vision of a vernacular canon is "echoed materially in [his] promotion of Dante as a modern classic, framed by Cavalcanti and Petrarch in his manuscript compilations." Critics have also noted that the story of Filippo Balducci itself contains an allusion to *Purgatorio* XXVI.67–70, an episode in which Dante aligns himself with his *Stilnovist* predecessors by calling Guido Guinizelli his first father. See Robert Hollander, *Boccaccio's Dante and the Shaping Force of Satire*, 75. See also Martin Eisner, "Dante and the Author of the *Decameron*," 293.

46 *Decameron*, ed. Branca, *Tutte le opere*, 4:350 (IV); trans. McWilliam, 288. For Boccaccio's cultivation of the concept of the *tre corone* through his

work as a scribe, see Houston, *Building a Monument*, especially pages 11, 48, and 126. On Boccaccio's formation of his authorial self in relation to a *Stilnovistic* community, see especially Martin Eisner, *Boccaccio and the Invention of Italian Literature*, as well as his recent chapter, "Dante and the Author of the *Decameron*," esp. 290–4. As Eisner observes (*Boccaccio and the Invention of Italian Literature*, 6–7), the poets in this passage from *Decameron* IV are "carefully chosen to show that the Narrator is part of a recent, but nevertheless established, tradition of writing about love. It is a risky strategy precisely because of his fellow poets' relative novelty." Modelling this approach on "strategies of literary affiliation" he found in Ovid's *Tristia* and Dante's *Inferno*, he "invokes these models while departing from them" in that he "does not seek to outdo or surpass the vernacular community of Cavalcanti, Dante, and Cino, but to join it." Francesco Marzano, "Boccaccio storico della letteratura trecentesca l'epistola a Iacopo Pizzinga," explores how, in his letter to Iacopo Pizzinga (1371), Boccaccio presents Dante and Petrarch as the two poets responsible for bringing about the "ritorno delle muse" to Italy, even if they did so in very different ways, and through their use of different languages. Indeed, Dante and Petrarch shared a common love: poetry. Marzano further notes how Boccaccio positions himself as a critical figure: standing in between his two literary fathers, he canonizes their works and perpetuates their glory.

47 Olson, "The Language of Women," 53.

48 In both *Ve* I.1 and *Cv* I.9, Dante specifies his wish to be of service to, and educate, the masses, in particular those who did not know Latin.

49 Boccaccio gives his story collection the surname of "Galeotto," alluding to the role the story of Lancelot and Guinevere played in the downfall of Paolo and Francesca (*Inferno* V.137). As Lombardi points out, *Imagining the Woman Reader*, 187, the poet "devises his own 'libro galeotto' as a form of exchange, amends, and restitution between an author formerly captive to the obsession and pains of love … and a female audience still preoccupied by love. Rescued from hell, the book called Gallehault is now offered as a form of consolation specifically to women in love. In this statement, Boccaccio puts in plain view the courtly heritage of his female readership, and its founding role for vernacular literature."

50 Clarke, "On Copying and Not Copying *Griselda*," 61.

51 Clarke, "On Copying and Not Copying *Griselda*," 62.

52 Clarke, "On Copying and Not Copying *Griselda*," 62. On the timeline and order of these letters, as well as Petrarch's double drafting of the *Historia Griselda*, see also Luca Carlo Rossi, "In margine alla 'Griselda' latina di Petrarca," as well as Monica Berté and Silvia Rizzo, "'Valete amici, valete epistole.'"

53 Petrarch, *Res Seniles*, ed. Silvia Rizzo with Monica Berté, 446–8 (XVII.3); for the translation, see Petrarch, *Letters of Old Age*, trans. Aldo S. Bernardo,

Saul Levin, and Reta A. Bernardo, 656. All citations and translations of the *Seniles* will be taken from these editions.

54 Barolini, "The Marquis of Saluzzo, or the Griselda Story Before It was Hijacked," 26, notes the Dantean allusion in Boccaccio's phrasing. His words, "matta bestialità" echo *Inferno* XI.81–3, where Dante "explicitly cites [Aristotle's] *Ethics* in order to designate nonallegorical categories of sinners in his hell." Barolini further takes issue with McWilliam's translation of this phrase as "senseless brutality," which "is appropriate as a first pass; however, the expression needs ultimately to achieve its full Aristotelian and Dantean patina, rendered in the translation 'mad bestiality,' as per the *Ethics* and the *Inferno*."

55 *Seniles*, ed. Rizzo and Berté, 474 (XVII.3); trans. Bernardo, 668.

56 Petrarch's work has often been read in light of its allegorical transmutation of *Decameron* X.10 – that is, as a "moral reshaping" (Leonard Michael Koff, "Imagining Absence," 289) or "humanist interpretation" of Boccaccio's novella (Emma Campbell, "Sexual Poetics and the Politics of Translation in the Tale of Griselda," 211). See also Wallace, "Whan She Translated Was," esp. 180, a version of which is reprinted in his *Chaucerian Polity*, 261–98; Charlotte C. Morse, "The Exemplary Griselda," esp. 54; and Charles Muscatine, *Chaucer and the French Tradition*, 190–8. William T. Rossiter, *Chaucer and Petrarch*, 135, sees the *Historia Griseldis* as "an allegorical concretization … of Boccaccio's Italian. That is, Boccaccio's deliberately sparse tale and its narrative framework provide … the opportunity for Petrarch to give his translation and, retroactively, Boccaccio's original a definite moral meaning." For two notable exceptions to this approach to the *Historia Griseldis*, see Amy W. Goodwin, "The Griselda Game," and Anne Middleton, "The Clerk and His Tale."

57 Jane Tylus, "Petrarch's Griselda and the Sense of an Ending," 422, notes that Boccaccio "looms large in the *Seniles*," with 18 of the collection's 128 letters intended for him.

58 *Seniles*, ed. Rizzo and Berté, 442–4 (XVII.3); trans. Bernardo, 655.

59 *Seniles*, ed. Rizzo and Berté, 442 (XVII.3).

60 *Seniles*, ed. Rizzo and Berté, 444 (XVII.3); trans. Bernardo, 655. In his letter to Mainardo Cavalcanti, written a few years before his death, Boccaccio urges his friend to avoid skimming his "libellos" (little books), unless he has nothing better to do. He then asks Cavalcanti to keep these works away from the women in his house, noting that if they read them, they will consider the poet a filthy animal and perverted old man. Finally, in words that look back to Petrarch's ironic defence of the work's low style on account of the poet's youth, he laments that not everyone will exonerate him on the basis of his age, saying "Iuvenis scripsit et maioris coactus imperio" ("he wrote this when he was a young man, under the influence of a greater force").

These remarks are probably, although not certainly, in reference to the *Decameron*, and have added to speculation regarding Boccaccio's age at the time of composition, as well as the legitimacy of his female reader. The letter can be found in Ginetta Auzzas and Augusto Campana's edition in *Tutte le opere*, 1:704–7 ("Epistole" XXII.17–24). The translation is my own.

61 Referring to Petrarch's account of his encounter with the *Decameron*, Clarke, "On Copying and Not Copying *Griselda*," 65, points to its "seeming casualness" that "barely hides its studied deliberateness."

62 Olson, "the Language of Women," 53, writes that with the language of the *Decameron*, Boccaccio transforms Dante's "materna locutio" in *Ve* I.6, 2 to a "new literary vernacular in prose, one that is – and is not – different from the 'volgare delle femine' (*Esposizioni Accessus*, 19). He speaks not in an original maternal vernacular, and not in the language of women."

63 Alfredo Stussi, "Lingua," 195–6. I am quoting from Michael Papio's translation of this chapter and volume: "Language," in *The Decameron: A Critical Lexicon*, 180.

64 Tavoni, "Linguistic Italy," ed. Barański and Pertile, *Dante in Context*, 244.

65 Stussi, "Language," trans. Papio, *The Decameron: A Critical Lexicon*, 180.

66 McWilliam, "Translator's Introduction," *The Decameron*, lxi–lxv. For Boccaccio's cultivation in his writings (and especially the *Decameron*) of a middle space between elevated poetry and lower forms like fabliaux, see Francesco Bruni, *Boccaccio*.

67 Giulia Cardillo, "The Tale of Cisti the Baker," 52.

68 Cardillo, "The Tale of Cisti the Baker," 52.

69 Petrarch is not necessarily incorrect in his reference to Boccaccio as a young (as opposed to old) man. Thomas J. Farrell, for one (Farrell and Goodwin, "The Clerk's Tale," 1:109n18), surmises that Boccaccio is about forty when he pens his work, based on Petrarch's own testimony about Boccaccio's birth year. Most scholars agree on this number (see Branca, *Tradizione delle opere di Giovanni Boccaccio*, 2:147n1). Daniels, "Rethinking the Critical History of the *Decameron*," 425n5, notes that Charlton Thomas Lewis and Charles Short (*A Latin Dictionary*) gloss "Juventus" as "the age of youth (from twentieth to the fortieth year)." It is possible, then, that Petrarch's reference to Boccaccio as a "iuvenis" is accurate, if odd.

70 *Le Familiari*, ed. Rossi and Bosco, 4:94–100 (XXI.15).

71 *Le Familiari*, ed. Rossi and Bosco, 4:96 (XXI.15); trans. Bernardo, 204.

72 *Le Familiari*, ed. Rossi and Bosco, 4:97 (XXI.15); trans. Bernardo, 205.

73 *Le Familiari*, ed. Rossi and Bosco, 4:97 (XXI.15); trans. Bernardo, 205.

74 *Le Familiari*, ed. Rossi and Bosco, 4:98 (XXI.15); trans. Bernardo, 205.

75 *Seniles*, ed. Rizzo and Berté (V.2); trans. Bernardo, 162–3.

76 Christopher S. Celenza, "Petrarch, Latin, and Italian Renaissance Latinity," 511.

77 *Seniles*, ed. Rizzo and Berté (IX.1); trans. Bernardo, 312.

78 Theodore J. Cachey, Jr., "Between Petrarch and Dante," 21, notes that "far from having given up on the vernacular, as he claims to have done in *Sen* V.2, Petrarch was working on both the *Canzoniere* and the *Triumphi* when he wrote that letter, and would continue to do so until his death. During the last year of his life, while still working on the *Triumphus eternitatis*, and perhaps even during his last days, he continued to seek the perfect ordering of the poems, and in the right upper-hand corner of Vat. Lat.3195 he renumbered the last thirty-one compositions of the *Canzoniere*."

79 In his commentary on the *Commedia* (1568), Bernardino Daniello points to the resonances of Dante's poem in Petrarch's work. See *L'espositione di Bernardino Daniello da Lucca sopra la Comedia di Dante*. See Paolo Trovato, *Dante in Petrarca*, for a linguistic analysis of "dantismi" in Petrarch's vernacular works. For a survey of more recent studies on the influence of the *Commedia* on Petrarch's vernacular poetry, see Sara Sturm-Maddox, "Dante, Petrarch, and the Laurel Crown," 318n68.

80 As Cornish points out, *Vernacular Translation*, 161, in his claim that he had heard it before ("cum et michi semper ante multos annos audita placuisset"), Petrarch further transforms *Decameron* X.10 "from literary work, contrived by an author (librum tuum) to an artefact of oral storytelling ... The next step is for Petrarch to pluck the story from this oral context he has given it, and to write it down." On *Decameron* X.10 as a spoken work, and on the novella as a genre "situata alla confluenza tra scritto e orale," see Alfano, *Introduzione alla lettura del "Decameron" di Boccaccio*, I.4.

81 Barański, "Petrarch, Dante, Cavalcanti," 79, argues that "it is less Dante and the *Commedia* that aggravate [Petrarch] than their reception."

82 Goodwin, "The Griselda Game," 20.

83 *Seniles*, ed. Rizzo and Berté, 446 (XVII.3); trans. Bernardo, 656. Cornish, *Vernacular Translation*, 161, writes, "Petrarch would seem to be effecting a volgarizzamento, in the sense that he is appropriating [*Decameron* X.10] into his own idiom. Like any translation, its purpose is to make it available to people who do not understand our language ('nostri etiam sermonis ignaros'). Yet Petrarch's 'own' words are not the modern dialect he shares with his fellow-Florentine, but rather Latin, of which Petrarch makes himself out to be a kind of native speaker."

84 *Ve*, ed. Rajna, 3 (I.1); trans. Botterill, 3.

85 Petrarch recounts in *Sen* XVII.4 how one of his two friends must stop reading aloud because he is overcome by emotion. The other, by contrast, does not shed a tear.

86 *Seniles*, ed. Rizzo and Berté, 480 (XVII.4); trans. Bernardo, 670.

87 *Ve* I.7. Ruth Evans, Andrew Taylor, Nicholas Watson, and Jocelyn Wogan-Browne, "The Notion of Vernacular Theory," 318, point out that in describing the "din of the ... vernacular," Dante "equates the vernacular

with the spoken, rather than the written, language and also – by evoking the disorder of Babel – emphasizes the fallen state of all vernaculars, whose very existence is a reminder of the loss of the unitary language spoken by Adam." As Celenza notes, "Petrarch, Latin," 510, Dante also saw Latin as something requiring "reflection and craft." In the *Convivio*, he suggests that "Latin is perpetual and incorruptible" ("lo latino è perpetuo e non corruttibile"), and in the *De vulgari eloquentia*, he notes that vulgar tongues constantly change, because "man is a most unstable, variable animal" ("homo sit instabilissimum atque variabilissimum animal"). Dante was, in this regard, "no nineteenth-century nationalist trying to find the *Volksgeist* of a people in their true, native language. He was more concerned with defending Tuscan against other competing vernaculars; and what he wanted to do in any case was to standardize it, to create in effect a secondary language (a *locutio secundaria*) that would have its own set of more or less permanent rules" (510).

88 *Ve* I.13. Describing the characteristics "di una cosa che non esistenza," Dante, according to Tavoni, *Qualche idea su Dante*, 51, "*inventa* l'Italia linguistica." He does more than defend Italian in the *VE*, in this regard – he also "annuncia l'esistenza di una una lingua italiana"; what this means is that, in the *Cv* and *VE*, he justifies the superiority of this language that he is largely responsible for bringing into being (51).

89 Cf. Clarke, "On Copying and Not Copying *Griselda*," 66, who writes, "This is not a picture of a Petrarch attempting to render the Griselda story more noble in Latin but rather as attempting to work around the deficiencies of those unacquainted with the Tuscan vernacular; it is an attempt to widen access rather than restrict it."

90 Wallace, "Chaucer's Italian Inheritance," 50.

91 Wallace, *Chaucerian Polity*, 264, characterizes Petrarch's followers as "a small, consciously exclusive, masculine group of initiates dedicated to the pursuit of Latin culture: just such a group, in fact, as Petrarch describes in framing his Griselde story."

92 Cornish, *Vernacular Translation*, 162.

93 *Decameron*, ed. Branca, *Tutte le opere*, 4:954 (X.10); trans. McWilliam, 795.

94 For Griselda as an allegorical *figura*, who represents man's relationship with God, see, for example, Branca, *Boccaccio medievale*, 17–18. Guido Martellotti, "Momenti Narrativi Del Petrarca" (reprinted in *Scritti Petrarcheschi*), thinks about Petrarch's Griselda in relation to Roman historiography. He compares the *Historia Griseldis* to the author's own depiction of Joseph in his earlier work, *De viris illustribus*. Robin Kirkpatrick, "The Griselda Story in Boccaccio, Petrarch, and Chaucer," 235, argues that Petrarch "suggests an interpretation that allows Griselda to represent the soul of man – tested but constant – while the Marquis becomes a figure for God himself." For Petrarch's allusions to the biblical stories of Abraham and

Job, see Rossella Bessi, "La Griselda del Petrarca." Berté and Rizzo, "'Valete amici, valete epistolae,'" 87–8, link Griselda's biblically divine patience with Petrarch's own approach to suffering: "La sua versione della novella è un'allegoria della totale, umile e lieta sottomissione che il credente deve tributare con costanza alla volontà divina, come appunto negli esempi biblici di Giobbe e di Abramo, pronto quest'ultimo, come Griselda, a sacrificare il suo stesso figlio … Appare quindi voluta una conclusione altrettanto religiosa dell'ultima raccolta epistolare; e va considerato che Petrarca stesso, come Giobbe, si sentiva nei suoi ultimi anni messo alla prova da Dio con le malattie che lo assediavano e che egli dichiara di accettare umilmente e lietamente." Rossi, "In margine alla 'Griselda' latina di Petrarca," 152–60, locates a possible allusion to Apuleius's story of Cupid and Psyche in Petrarch's translation.

95 *Seniles*, ed. Rizzo and Berté, 474 (XVII.4); trans. Bernardo, 668.

96 *Seniles*, ed. Rizzo and Berté, 448 (XVII.3); trans. Bernardo, 656.

97 Tylus, "Petrarch's Griselda," 435, discusses Petrarch's words in the context of the *stilnovistic tornata*, or final address to one's poem. Drawing on Joan H. Levin's "Sweet, New Endings," she notes that "what is striking about the force of these additions is that they are sometimes articulated in terms of clothing; and that on occasion, a poem is deemed 'nude' and unfinished until it can be dressed by another, an act of dressing explicitly requested in its final lines."

98 Carolyn Dinshaw, *Chaucer's Sexual Poetics*, 133. See also Wallace, *Chaucerian Polity*, 262.

99 Jerome, *Preface to Interpretatio Chronicae Eusebii Pamphili*, in *Patrologia latina* 27:36; trans. W.H. Fremantle, in *The Principal Works of Jerome, Select Library of Nicene and Post-Nicene Fathers of the Christian Church*, 895 (6:483), quoted in Dinshaw, *Chaucer's Sexual Poetics*, 137–8.

100 For Jerome, a text's words (*verba*) were of secondary importance to its sense (*sensus*). See Minnis, *Medieval Theory of Authorship*, 33, 232n149 for this distinction.

101 See Rita Copeland, *Rhetoric, Hermeneutics, and Translation in the Middle Ages*, 94. In *Sen* XVII.3, Petrarch manipulates the tropes that Copeland describes as associated with "primary translations," which "announce themselves as translations by calling attention to their dependence on – and service to – the original text. Yet these translations, Copeland elaborates, "exhibit the rhetorical tendencies of medieval exegetical practice: even as they proclaim themselves to be serving and supplementing the text, they work in effect to contest and supplant that text."

102 *Seniles*, ed. Rizzo and Berté, 448 (XVII.3); trans. Bernardo, 656.

103 John Finlayson, Koff, Dolores Frese, and Jessica Harkins are among the small group of scholars who discuss Boccaccio's influence on the tale;

however, as they rely primarily on tenuous narrative or textual parallels, their arguments, though suggestive, are not wholly convincing. See Finlayson, "Petrarch, Boccaccio, and Chaucer's *Clerk's Tale*"; Koff, "Imagining Absence"; and Frese, "The 'Buried Bodies.'" In her brief study, Frese anchors her reading of the "Clerk's Tale" in an analysis of *De vulgari eloquentia*. Suggesting that there are "radical cultural ideas" passed down from Dante to Chaucer (vis-à-vis Boccaccio and Petrarch), Frese argues that *VE* is the source for not only Petrarch's proem, in which he maps out the various regions of Italy, but also Chaucer's Wife of Bath (250). Harkins, "Chaucer's *Clerk's Tale* and Boccaccio's *Decameron* X.10," searches for what Finlayson has called the "smoking gun" of Chaucer's reliance on Boccaccio in the "Clerk's Tale." She argues that four specific words used by Chaucer – Fortune, dishonest, arraye, and yvele – "provid[e] proof ... that Chaucer must have known and used Boccaccio's *Decameron* X.10" (248), and that "this sentence-by-sentence correspondence ... cannot be accidental" (251).

104 See Farrell and Goodwin, "The Clerk's Tale," ed. Correale and Hamel, at 103.

105 See J. Burke Severs, *The Literary Relationships of Chaucer's "Clerkes Tale,"* 135–211.

106 The idea that Boccaccio's *Decameron* can shed light on our reading of Chaucer's poetry has gained critical traction in the last several decades. See especially Helen Cooper, "The Frame"; Peter Beidler, "Just Say Yes, Chaucer Knew the *Decameron*"; Robert W. Hanning, "The *Decameron* and the *Canterbury Tales*"; N.S. Thompson, *Chaucer, Boccaccio, and the Debate of Love*, esp. 279–312; and Robert R. Edwards, *Chaucer and Boccaccio*, 128–52. Cooper, 1:8, suggests that "the widespread past resistance to recognizing the *Decameron* as a source for, or even an influence on, the *Canterbury Tales*" may stem from an ideological cause: "the *Tales* were seen as representing Chaucer's quintessential Englishness."

107 Most of the surviving manuscripts of the *Historia Griseldis* contain Petrarch's prefatory remarks to Boccaccio, and so the chances are quite good that Chaucer had access to them as well. For a discussion of Chaucer's Latin Source manuscript, see Severs, *The Literary Relationships*, 102–22. Finlayson, "Petrarch," 258, maintains that Chaucer certainly read Petrarch's preface to Boccaccio, the 'Librum tuum' in *Sen* XVII.3, along with the translation when he wrote the "Clerk's Tale." He bases this claim on his assumption that all the manuscripts of the *Historia Griseldis* contain these prefatory words. Thomas Farrell, "Source or Hard Analogue?" 347–8, suggests that Finlayson's assertion of certainty is perhaps overstated, since five of the manuscripts Severs examines do not contain this material, while two manuscripts include it but in an abbreviated form, yet he concedes that Finlayson is "probably right that Chaucer knew the 'Librum tuum' section of Petrarch's letter ... because the vast majority of manuscripts do include

it." With regard to the seven manuscripts that Farrell refers to, which either do not have the "Librum tuum" or contain it in an abbreviated form, there are no apparent similarities among them that would suggest a pattern of exclusion. Rather, these seven manuscripts seem to be isolated variants. The likelihood that Chaucer read the "Librum tuum" is, therefore, very high. Moreover, the ways in which Chaucer appears to draw on and respond to these remarks are extensive, the effects of which are largely evident in the "Clerk's Tale."

108 Middleton, "The Clerk and His Tale," 131.

109 For the polemical aspect of translation in the Griselda story, see especially Dinshaw, *Chaucer's Sexual Poetics*, 132–55; Wallace, *Chaucerian Polity*, 261–98; and Campbell, "Sexual Poetics."

110 For a detailed discussion of Horace's advice against faithful translation, see Copeland, *Rhetoric, Hermeneutics, and Translation*, esp. 168–78. See also Rossiter, *Chaucer and Petrarch*, 1–33, for a comprehensive review of translation in its various forms.

111 In his analysis of Mannelli's 1384 codex of the *Decameron*, Clarke, *Chaucer and Italian Textuality*, 95–128, esp. 113 and following, notes that the scribe exhibits increasing discomfort with Gualtieri's repeated trials of his wife. Hardly a passive conveyer of what he reads, Mannelli goes so far as to write an alternative ending to the tale in the margins. He glosses Griselda's silent and tearful response to Gualtieri's admission of intent with the words: "Pisciarti in mano Gualtieri! Chi mi ristora di dodici anni! le forche?" ("Go piss on your hand, Gualtieri! Who'll give me back twelve years? The gallows?"), 122, quoted in Clarke. Richard Firth Green, "Why Marquis Walter Treats His Wife So Badly," draws our attention to another fourteenth-century response to the Griselda story, that of Thomas III, Marquis of Saluzzo (ca. 1355–1416), who was apparently flummoxed by Walter's cruelty, and goes to some lengths to justify his actions, even providing a back-story detailing Walter's father's marital trouble. I am grateful to Green for having allowed me to read a copy of this article in advance of its publication, and for our many conversations about Griselda since.

112 James R. Andreas, "Chaucer's Defense of the Vulgar Tongue," 25.

113 The Eagle's realization that he can "lewedly to a lewed man / Speke" (*HF* 866–7) echoes the fourth tractate of the *Convivio*, in which Dante reverts to "rima aspra e sottile" ("harsh and subtle rhymes") so that his unlearned reader will better understand his weighty subject matter, the nature of true nobility (ed. Ageno, IV.2, 12; trans. Lansing, 152).

114 Cornish, "A Lady Asks," 178.

115 Evans et al., "The Notion of Vernacular Theory," 325. The full quotation reads, as a "language with immediate access to people's feelings and easily comprehensible – as Latin is not, even to those who can understand it,"

English can "do rather more than provide a practical vernacular means of access to knowledge; it can *signify* clarity and open access and do so even in texts whose projected audience is relatively narrow."

116 Muscatine, *Chaucer and the French Tradition*, 191. See also Michael Raby, "The *Clerk's Tale* and the Forces of Habit," 233, who suggests that the Clerk's "ascetic bent makes him a fitting translator" of Petrarch, "since he is well attuned to the 'ethics of sufficiency' embedded in his source."

117 *Seniles*, ed. Rizzo and Berté, 448–50 (XVII.3); trans. Bernardo, 656–7.

118 *Cv*, ed. Ageno, I.X, 12; trans. Lansing, 25.

119 *Cv*, ed. Ageno, I.X, 12–13; trans. Lansing, 25; italics added.

120 *VE*, ed. Rajna, 112–13 (II.1); trans. Botterill, 49; italics added.

121 *VE*, ed. Rajna, 113 (II.1); trans. Botterill, 49.

122 *Cv*, ed. Ageno, IV.2, 12; trans. Lansing, 152.

123 Glenn D. Burger, *Conduct Becoming*, 143, suggests that a "major reason" for the wide appeal of the Griselda narrative among both authors and readers came from its "ability to function (or not) as a kind of lesson in conduct for married men and women."

124 *Decameron*, ed. Branca, *Tutte le opere*, 4:942 (X.10); the translation is my own.

125 There is some speculation as to whether Chaucer intended his Envoy to be read in conjunction with the "Clerk's Tale" – that is, in the Clerk's narrative voice. Such a question is fuelled by the observation that so many manuscripts of the *Canterbury Tales* attribute the Envoy to Chaucer. For a brief summary of this debate, see Thomas J. Farrell, "The 'Envoy de Chaucer' and the 'Clerk's Tale,'" 329–30. For the sake of narrative smoothness, and because my argument concerns the nature of these remarks and not their speaker, I will continue to refer to the Clerk as the spokesman of the Envoy.

126 *Decameron*, ed. Branca, *Tutte le opere*, 4:954 (X.10); trans. McWilliam, 795; italics added. Boccaccio uses the phrase "scuotere il pilliccione" repeatedly (see also *Decameron* IV.10 and *Decameron* VIII.7) to allude to a sexual act. The idea that this moment can be read as Dioneo's fantasy of a new ending comes from Campbell, "Sexual Poetics," 204: "in fantasizing another woman in Griselda's place, Dioneo offers his audience a possible counter-narrative to the one he has just told, opening up the space that Griselda occupies in the tale to other bodies, writings and readings."

127 On Chaucer's entombment of Petrarch, Wallace, *Chaucerian Polity*, 267, writes, "here we have Petrarch discovered as a living source of poetic inspiration; Petrarch as a corpse; Petrarch as a poet laureate whose rhetoric illuminates a nation; and Petrarch laid low by death, a fate that unites him with us all. The cultural achievement of Petrarch is here accorded great respect, but is insistently brought up hard against the brute facts of mortality."

128 *Le Familiari*, ed. Rossi and Bosco, 4:98 (XXI.15); trans. Bernardo, 205.

129 *Le Familiari*, ed. Rossi and Bosco, 4:98 (XXI.15); trans. Bernardo, 205.

130 For this request in the *Ytalie iam certus honos*, see Eisner, *Boccaccio and the Invention of Italian Literature*, 83–6.
131 See above, note 45.
132 The text of this poem is taken from Giuseppe Velli's edition in *Tutte le opere*, 5/1:97 (CXXVI.9–10). The translation is my own.
133 Many of the excellent essays in Barański and Cachey's *Petrarch and Dante* treat Boccaccio's intermediary role between Dante and Petrarch. See especially Cachey, "Between Petrarch and Dante," esp. 16–35, and Barański, "Petrarch, Dante, Cavalcanti," 50–113. Barański explains that the idea of Dante and Petrarch "represent[ing] two distinct yet complimentary [sic] intellectual and artistic alternatives ... had its roots" in fourteenth-century Italy (52). Wallace, *Chaucerian Polity*, 271, suggests that Boccaccio's divided allegiance between Petrarch and Dante was in part political: his "meetings with Petrarch certainly exerted a powerful influence on Boccaccio's artistic development: he gave up composing vernacular verse and dedicated most of his mature energies to Petrarchan-inspired Latin encyclopaedism. And yet Boccaccio always retained an impressive independence of political judgment. He turned down Petrarch's offers of patronage (even though he was often indigent) and maintained a long and active interest in the civic and diplomatic affairs of Florence. Whereas Petrarch maintained an uneasy, ambiguous attitude towards Dante, Boccaccio envisioned his Dantean discipleship as an integral part of his civic politics."
134 See Copeland, *Rhetoric, Hermeneutics, and Translation*, 3–4, who suggests that "all translation is a vehicle for appropriation ... Like commentary, translation tends to represent itself as a 'service' to an authoritative source; but also like commentary, translation actually displaces the originary force of its models."

3 Power in Flux: Chaucer's Triumphal "Monk's Tale"

1 *The Odes of Horace*, ed. and trans. David Ferry, III.30 (254–5).
2 Ovid, *Metamorphoses*, trans. Frank Justus Miller, revised by G.P. Goold, 2:426–7.
3 For the idea that "medieval culture was fundamentally memorial," see Mary J. Carruthers's foundational work, *The Book of Memory*, 8.
4 In the third book of the *House of Fame*, the narrator sees a mountain of ice on which Fame's castle is built. Carved through this mountain are the names of famous individuals. Some of these names have faded, "so unfamous was woxe hir fame" (III.1146), representing metaphorically the poet's anxiety that his name and works will be lost. All citations from Chaucer's poetry are taken from the *Riverside Chaucer*. Further citations will be noted in the text according to fragment and line number for works from the *Canterbury Tales*, and according to book and line number for Chaucer's other poems.

5 Echoing Boethius's Lady Philosophy, the Monk asserts that we cannot trust the "blynd prosperitee" of Lady Fortune (VII.1997), since all mighty men must eventually fall. For the Boethian elements of Chaucer's "Monk's Tale," see, for example, Bernard L. Jefferson, *Chaucer and the Consolation of Philosophy of Boethius*, 84–7, and 144–5, as well as Douglas Lepley, "The Monk's Boethian Tale." On Chaucer's use of Boethius for his definition of tragedy, see D.W. Robertson, Jr., "Chaucerian Tragedy." For Chaucer's reading of Nicholas Trevet's commentary on the *Consolation* and its influence on his conception of Boethian tragedy, see Henry Ansgar Kelly, *Chaucerian Tragedy*, 51–5. It should be noted that prior to the "Monk's Tale," the idea of tragedy was not intimately connected to the theme of Fortune's transience. Rather, as Helen Cooper observes in the *Oxford Guide* to the *Canterbury Tales*, 327–8, it is "because of the Monk's definition of tragedy, and Lydgate's adoption of it" that "tragedy became synonymous with the *de casibus* tradition, the falls of great men through the instability of Fortune."

6 To name a few examples, Robert K. Root, *The Poetry of Chaucer*, 207–8, protests against the "unspeakable monotony" of the portraits. Howard Rollin Patch, "Chaucer and Lady Fortune," 387, follows the Host's lead and denigrates the Monk for narrating his tragedies "as monotonously as the tolling of his chapel bell." Willard Farnham, *The Medieval Heritage of Elizabethan Tragedy*, 44, dismisses the "Monk's Tale" as a "dreary assembly of tragical stories," and R.M. Lumiansky, *Of Sondry Folk*, 103, describes the work as a series of "tedious and repetitive tragedies." Certain critics, such as M.C. Seymour, "Chaucer's Early Poem *De Casibus Virorum Illustrium*," 164, go so far as to argue that the poem's inferior quality suggests an early date of composition. Seymour claims that the "uneven structure and comparatively flat narrative line ... support an early date, and it is very possible that this is the first poem Chaucer wrote after his return from Italy." Indeed, so ubiquitous is critical condemnation of this work that Terry Jones, "The Monk's Tale," 387, opens his relatively recent essay in defence of the work by characterizing himself as "one of that growing band of awkward customers who don't think that *The Monk's Tale* is a complete and utter disaster."

7 In the introduction to his and Pier Giorgio Ricci's edition of the *De casibus* (*Tutte le opere*, 9:xlviii), Vittorio Zaccaria marks the structural similarities between the *De casibus* and the earlier *Amorosa visione*, attributing our attention to the treatise's innovative form, which contains "una serie di visioni storiche come nell'*Amorosa Visione*," to Attilio Hortis. Guyda Armstrong, *The English Boccaccio*, 33, is one of the few other readers to note the similarities in form linking the *Amorosa visione* to the *De casibus*. In the *Amorosa visione*, she observes, "great figures of the past are presented in a series of *tableaux vivants* as the protagonist moves through the various rooms of the castle," a "mimetic illusion" that is both evoked and "reversed" in the *De*

casibus, "as the narrator-protagonist remains static while the souls come to him." See also Jonathan Usher, "Mural Morality in *Tableaux Vivants*," 119–20, who observes that the *Amorosa visione* has, "in its attempt at sequenced information, a lot in common with the later Latin works, *De casibus virorum illustrium*, *De mulieribus claris*, and even the *Genealogia deorum gentilium*, in that the underlying driver is encyclopedic and categorizing, while any framing narration merely provides the barest presentational excuse for taxonomic organization." He adds that Boccaccio's triumphal poem "clearly herald[s]" the *De casibus*, "as can be seen in Boccaccio's exceptional concentration, in the *Amorosa visione*, on Fame, brought to nought by Fortuna" (122).

For years, scholars upheld a divide between Boccaccio's vernacular and Latin works, which may explain the scarcity of scholarship comparing the *Amorosa visione* to the *De casibus*. (As Rhiannon Daniels notes, *Boccaccio and the Book*, 149, the *De casibus* also had a far more obvious relationship with the Latin *De mulieribus claris*. Both works treated similar subject matter – the lives of great individuals – and were regularly found together in the same manuscript.) David Wallace, for example ("Chaucer and Boccaccio's Early Writings," 143), claims that Boccaccio "came to realize that his passion for Latin learning could not be fully accommodated within the confines of vernacular fiction," a realization "perhaps first formed in writing the *Visione*"; therefore, "Latin learning was saved for the Latin works." Kelly, *Chaucerian Tragedy*, 24, suggests that the *De casibus* "marks the transition between [Boccaccio's] works of fiction and his works of scholarship." See also Warren Ginsberg, *Chaucer's Italian Tradition*, 195–6, who, although noting the stylistic connections between the *Decameron* and *De casibus*, insists on a rupture between Boccaccio's vernacular fictions and his more serious Latin works. "Whenever he wrote in the vernacular," Ginsberg suggests, Boccaccio "hesitated to translate his sense of literary worthiness into social terms," taking care to "insulate his stories from history by establishing an area of play." Once Boccaccio "undertook to write in Latin," by contrast, his "goal was to make the poet's engagement with history part of public discourse."

But if it was once standard practice to separate Boccaccio's Italian poems from his later Latin works (or his Dantean from his Petrarchan writings, as many saw it), several scholars have resisted this trend in recent decades. Zaccaria, for example, *Boccaccio Narratore, Storico, Moralista e Mitografo*, vii, advocates for a more unified reading of Boccaccio's oeuvre, rather than one that distinguishes the storyteller from the scholar ("Non sarebbe comunque giusta una divisione fra il narratore e l'erudito: come se le opere anteriori al capolavoro fossero momenti preparatori della più grande opera narrativa dell'Europa del secolo XIV; e le opere storico-erudite rappresentassero una fase d'involuzione e di ripiegamento dalla creazione letteraria allo studio e alla riflessione moralistica e storico-filosofica, fino alla mitografia"; rather,

"Sono due momenti di un'unica personalità letteraria, che nasce dall'autunno del Medioevo").

8 Although Boccaccio never refers to his treatise as a tragedy, many readers have retroactively characterized the *De casibus* as such, and located it as an origin point for later European examples of this genre. While admitting that Boccaccio himself does not use the word "tragedy," for example, Farnham, *Medieval Heritage*, 78, suggests that Boccaccio's "presupposition or working hypothesis" in the *De casibus* "amounts in its simplest terms only to this: All the notable tragedies which a diligent man can collect from literature, tradition, and observation show without exception that the mortal world ... is ruled by Fortune." Donald Stump, *The Spenser Encyclopedia*, 697, similarly locates a "tradition (broadly termed *de casibus* tragedy)" that was "established by Boccaccio's *De casibus virorum illustrium* and continued in England by Chaucer's *Monk's Tale*, Lydgate's *Fall of Princes*, the *Mirror for Magistrates*, and various Elizabethan plays." Although he does not discuss the *De casibus* itself, Alan S. Downer, *The British Drama*, 125, devotes an entire section of his handbook to what he calls "*De casibus* tragedy," a genre that he suggests deals with "the 'Falls of Princes'": "Man rises only to fall. At the moment of triumph, at the height of earthly glory, Death beckons." More recently, Tom Kräplin, "The Rise of Princes?," 4, characterized *De casibus* tragedy according to its genealogy, "which assumes the original source of these tragedies in Boccaccio's *De casibus*," and further defined it using Chaucer's own words from the "Monk's Tale" (VII.1991–6). Kelly and Paul Budra resist this critical trend of characterizing Boccaccio's treatise as a tragedy. Kelly, *Chaucerian Tragedy*, 11, notes that "throughout the hundreds of 'case histories' which Boccaccio recounts he refrains from calling the stories tragedies, and he shows little inclination to think of the accounts as conforming to the idea of tragedy." Building on Kelly, Budra, *The Mirror for Magistrates and the De casibus Tradition*, xii, observes that our retrospective reading of the *De casibus* through the lens of its fifteenth-century adaptations has skewed our impression of the original work: this "enforced hindsight" has imposed "formal expectations on the *de casibus* literary tradition that have nothing to do with that tradition's own history." Although the *De casibus* was never really a tragedy, Budra notes, "recognizing a transcendent literary form in Shakespeare's tragedies," scholars "have worked backward to earlier sad stories, classified them as tragedies, and dismissed them as simplistically dependent upon a mechanistic pattern of fortune's retributions, not adequately sophisticated to be considered real tragedy" (39). The work functions instead as a moral history, Budra argues. But if Kelly and Budra recuperate the *De casibus* from a tragic tradition, they do so on largely a semantic level. If not tragedies by definition, Boccaccio's biographies are still for both critics stories of inevitable ruin, which demonstrate *ad nauseum* the

vanity of worldly power. Kelly suggests that what Chaucer found in the *De casibus* and identified as tragedies were "simply sad or disastrous stories, for which more or less appropriate morals were drawn, with no generic rationale or consistency beyond that of the moral exemplum, biographical sketch ... and personal complaint" (260). Budra observes that Boccaccio wished to demonstrate "by the weight of the accumulated examples that a falling pattern is typical of the lives of great persons" (16).

9 Simone Marchesi, "Boccaccio on Fortune," 246.

10 Todd Boli, "Review of the *Amorosa Visione*, ed. Hollander," 625.

11 Important studies on the Roman Triumph include Robert Payne, *The Roman Triumph*; H.S. Versnel, *Triumphus*; Michael McCormick, *Eternal Victory*; Mary Beard, *The Roman Triumph*; and Ida Östenberg, *Staging the World*.

12 Zygmunt G. Barański, "The Constraints of Form," 67.

13 Payne, *Roman Triumph*, 12.

14 Beard, *Roman Triumph*, 4.

15 Anthony Miller, *Roman Triumphs and Early Modern English Culture*, 1.

16 Beard, *Roman Triumph*, 3. Italics are Beard's.

17 Beard, *Roman Triumph*, 2.

18 Fifteen manuscripts of the *Canterbury Tales*, including Ellesmere but not Hengwrt, contain as part of the title of the "Monk's Tale" the name of Boccaccio's poem, *De casibus de virorum illustrium*. Nevertheless, some critics are reluctant to suggest Chaucer's reliance on the *De casibus*. Cooper, for example, speculates that it is "unclear just how much Chaucer knew of it" (*Oxford Guide*, 326–7). Boitani, "The *Monk's Tale*," 54, wonders whether Chaucer's manuscript of the *De casibus* was fragmented and unnamed, although he admits that "it is clear that Chaucer knew at last part of the *De Casibus*, that he read it attentively and used it as an authority and as a source on specific subjects." Richard Neuse, "The Monk's *De casibus*," 251, suggests that the "Monk's Tale" "represents a remarkably faithful mirror in miniature" of Boccaccio's poem.

19 Boccaccio completed the first version of the *De casibus* (the A-redaction) between the mid-1350s and 1360. The second, expanded version (the B-redaction) is dedicated to Mainardo Cavalcanti and dated to 1373. For the differences between these two versions, see Zaccaria, "Le due redazioni del *De casibus*," as well as the introduction to Zaccaria and Ricci's edition of the *De casibus* (xv–xx). For Boccaccio's friendship with Cavalcanti, see Todd Boli, "Among Boccaccio's Friends." For the dedicatory epistle to Cavalcanti in the second version of the *De casibus*, see Daniels, "Reading Boccaccio's Paratexts." Daniels observes that "it is clear from both the contents of the letter ... and its material presentation that it was intended by Boccaccio to function as a paratext, in other words, as separate from the text of the *De casibus*, and possibly for the eyes of Mainardo alone, as copies of the first

redaction of the text of *De casibus* had circulated for several years before the dedication was composed. Although it is fairly long, the letter does not stray into the realms of a proem or preface, because it does not introduce the contents of the text in any detail, but limits itself to explaining the process by which Mainardo was selected as the appropriate dedicatee. In material terms, it is clearly set apart from the proem, which is marked with its own rubric and includes the word 'Prohemium' within a rubric addressing Mainardo."

20 The Latin text of the *De casibus* is taken from Ricci and Zaccaria's edition in *Tutte le opere*, 9:27–8 (I.5). All English translations are adapted from *Giovanni Boccaccio: The Downfall of the Famous*, trans. Louis Brewer Hall, 6, with the help of Mark Pearsall. (Hall translates the Paris edition of Jean Gourmont and Jean Petit [1520].) Subsequent citations and translations will be noted in the text, according to book and section of the *De casibus*.

21 Marchesi, "Boccaccio on Fortune," 250.

22 See, for example, Jason M. Houston, *Building a Monument to Dante*, 67, who suggests that Petrarch's "lengthy oration on the virtue of fame seems oddly placed in a text with a fundamental thesis arguing that fame and infamy are subject to the vicissitudes of divine providence (fortune). Furthermore, Petrarca's intervention, coming when it does and including figures from the post-classical period, suggests an important dissonance between Petrarca's opinions on fame and those of his classical sources."

23 *Genealogie deorum gentilium*, ed. Zaccaria, *Tutte le opere*, 7:52 (I, proem 1.21).

24 *Genealogie*, ed. Zaccaria, *Tutte le opere*, 7:52 (I, proem 1.24).

25 Giuseppe Mazzotta, "Boccaccio's Critique of Petrarch," 276.

26 Karl A.E. Enenkel, "Modeling the Humanist," 20.

27 Enenkel, "Modeling the Humanist," 20–1.

28 In *De vita solitaria*, moreover, Petrarch speaks of the pleasure he takes in not only writing, so as to be remembered by posterity, but also celebrating, cherishing, and propagating the glory of his literary ancestors: "Inter hec, ut notiora non sileam, et lectioni dare operam et scripture, et alterum laborem alterno solatio lenire, legere quod scripserunt primi, scribere quod legant ultimi, et beneficii literarum a maioribus accepti, qua in illos non possumus, in posteros saltem gratum ac memorem animum habere, in eos quoque qua possumus non ingratum, sed nomina illorum vel ignota vulgare, vel obsolefacta renovare, vel senio obruta eruere et ad pronepotum populos veneranda transmittere; illos sub pectore, illos ut dulce aliquid in ore gestare, denique modis omnibus amando, memorando, celebrando, si non parem, certe debitam meritis referre gratiam" ("While I am speaking of these, however, let me not pass over in silence the more obvious pleasures: to devote oneself to reading and writing, alternately finding employment and relief in each, to read, what our forerunners have written and to write what later generations may wish to read, to pay to posterity the debt which we cannot pay to the dead for the gift of their writings, and

yet not remain altogether ungrateful to the dead but to make their names more popular if they are little known, to restore them if they have been forgotten, to dig them out if they have been buried in the ruins of time and to hand them down to our grandchildren as objects of veneration, to carry them in the heart and as something sweet in the mouth, and finally, by cherishing, remembering, and celebrating their fame in every way, to pay them the homage that is due to their genius even though it is not commensurate with their greatness"). Petrarch's Latin is taken from Guido Martellotti's edition, *Prose*, 356–8. The English is from Petrarch, *The Life of Solitude*, trans. Jacob Zeitlin, 150–1.

29 The two friends' correspondence began when Boccaccio, tasked with the charge of convincing Petrarch to take up a chair at the University of Florence, wrote Petrarch a letter. The two poets continued to exchange letters with one another for the next quarter of a decade. Their final correspondence took place a month before Petrarch's death, in 1374. For a wide-ranging analysis of this lengthy correspondence, see Gabriella Albanese, "La Corrispondenza fra Petrarca e Boccaccio." See also Rocco Rubini, *Posterity*, 57–65.

30 Petrarch, *Res seniles*, ed. Silvia Rizzo with Monica Berté, I.5. For the English translation, see Petrarch, *Letters of Old Age*, trans. Aldo S. Bernardo, Saul Levin, and Reta A. Bernardo, 2:21–2. The Latin text of the *Aeneid*, as well as the translation, is taken from *Eclogues; Georgics; Aeneid I–VI*, ed. H. Rushton Fairclough, revised by G.P. Goold, X.467–9 (II:204–5).

31 Francesco Petrarch, *Le Familiari*, ed. Rossi and Bosco, 3:314–15 (XIX.3). In this letter, Petrarch describes his meeting with Emperor Charles IV, who asks about the state of the unfinished *De viris illustribus*, with the intention of securing his spot in the work. Petrarch responds frankly that if the emperor lives virtuously, he will be worthy of this title: "id tibi promissum credito, si tibi virtus affuerit, vita michi" (3:314).

32 Wallace, *Chaucerian Polity*, 304. To be sure, Wallace suggests that Boccaccio *refutes* his friend's celebration of worldly glory: "the writings of Boccaccio and Petrarch advance very different political agendas. Petrarch in his *De viris illustribus*, allures great men with the promise of textual immortality. Boccaccio, in his *De casibus virorum illustrium*, repudiates this promise (and the cult of great men) by using his *exempla* to pressurize, hence destabilize, the political present that such men would dominate" (6). Wallace adds that the "Monk's Tale" "articulates a powerful and conscious affirmation of the Boccaccio paradigm." Although Chaucer's work "first recognizes the alluring promise of a 'mighty man,'" it ultimately reveals "the inability of such men to sustain fantasies, especially in the face of death."

33 For the trope of dream-vision initiations in Callimachus, Propertius, and Virgil, see Benjamin Acosta-Hughes and Susan A. Stephens, *Callimachus in Context*, 251–5. For this trope in the Italian tradition, see Sherry Roush, *Speaking Spirits*.

34 Ennius wrote about the Second Punic War in the *Annales* (Books VII–IX), a work covering Roman history from the fall of Troy to the author's present, and again in a panegyric poem on Scipio.

35 Petrarch, *Africa*, ed. Nicola Festa, IX.233–6; the English is from *Petrarch's Africa*, trans. Thomas G. Bergin and Alice S. Wilson, 223. All citations and translations will be taken from this edition and noted in the text.

36 Marchesi, "Petrarch's Philological Epic (Africa)," 127.

37 In *Fam* XXII.2, Petrarch contrasts his singular, hasty reading of Ennius with his more involved perusal of poets like Horace, Virgil, and Boethius. His dedication to revising Ennius's subject in the *Africa* would, however, suggest a more sustained involvement with the Roman poet and his writings.

38 For Petrarch as Ennius's usurper, see Stuart Gillespie, "Literary Afterlives," esp. 214.

39 In the *Annales*, Homer suggests to Ennius that his soul has migrated to Ennius's body. For Ennius's dream of Homer, as reconstructed by fragments, see *The Annals of Quintus Ennius*, ed. Otto Skutsch, 147–66, fragments ii–x, xi. For Ennius as "Homerus Alter," see Mario Citroni, "The Concept of the Classical and the Canons of Model Authors in Roman Literature," 213. For Petrarch's recycling of Ennius's dream, see Kevin Brownlee, "Power Plays," 480–2.

40 Marchesi, "Petrarch's Philological Epic," 127. Ennius himself would seem to anticipate this revival. According to Cicero, *Tusculan Disputations*, ed. and trans. J.E. King, 1.15.34; 40–1, he has written on his tombstone that there is no reason to mourn his death, since he flies living from mouth to mouth of men: "Nemo me lacrumis decoret nec funera fletu / Faxit. Cur? volito vivus per ora virum."

41 Roush, *Speaking Spirits*, 27, insists that the narrator is "pointedly not asleep and not dreaming the encounter [with Petrarch]," nor is Petrarch, in fact, dead at the time of his visit, details that separate this scene from its Petrarchan and Ennian precedents. Even with these minor differences, however, it is clear that Boccaccio is positioning this episode within a tradition of dream initiations.

42 David Lummus, "Boccaccio's Hellenism and the Foundations of Modernity," 103, contrasts Petrarch's vision of antiquity with Boccaccio's: "For Petrarch … I understand modernity as a question of memory and style – as a monumentalization of the past. For Boccaccio, who was just as self-conscious of his age's historical isolation from antiquity, modernity can be understood in terms of the fluid, generative relationship that he establishes between past and present through a process of critical historicization."

43 For Fortune's relationship to *Virtus* in this work, see Marchesi, "Boccaccio on Fortune," 47–9.

44 We cannot say for certain whether Boccaccio was, in fact, born in Certaldo. Luigi Surdich, for example, *Boccaccio*, 4, notes that "tre località sono in

concorrenza nel rivendicare il privilegio di aver dato i natali al padre della narrative europea: Certaldo, Firenza, Parigi." We can expel Paris from this list, according to Surdich, because it appears to be an idealized fantasy of the writer's, but between Certaldo and Florence, the true birthplace of Boccaccio is considered by most (following Branca in his bibliographic profile of the author, in *Tutte le opere*, 1:3–203, at 9) to be Florence. Nevertheless, Boccaccio seems to wish to be remembered as having been born in Certaldo. He composes an epitaph for himself in which he describes his tombstone as marked with the city of Certaldo: "Carmina" in Giuseppe Velli's edition, *Tutte le opere*, 5:404–55, at 454 (X): "Haec sub mole iacent cineres ac ossa Iohannis, / mens sedet ante Deum meritis ornata laborum / mortalis vite; genitor Boccaccius illi, / patria Certaldum, studium fuit alma poesis" ("Under this stone lie the ashes and bones of Giovanni: his spirit, comforted by the merits achieved in the labours of mortal life, sits before God; Father: Boccaccio; homeland: Certaldo; his soul's love: poetry"). Translation is my own.

45 Mary C. Flannery, *John Lydgate and the Poetics of Fame*, 107.

46 For the history and use of *tropaea* in Roman Triumphs, see Gilbert Charles Picard, *Les trophées romains*. Stephen Harrison, editor of *Horace: Odes, Book II*, 127n20, locates a passage in *Odes* 3.32 ("duo … diuerso ex hoste tropaea") in which *tropaeum* is used metaphorically, "to mean simply 'victory' rather than 'victory trophy,'" and suggests that this sense of *tropaeum* has been used since Cicero.

47 For Rome's triumphal monuments, see especially Maggie L. Popkin, *The Architecture of the Roman Triumph*.

48 Beard, *Roman Triumph*, 19. See also Miller, *Roman Triumphs*, 6, who notes that the "ancients had always attempted to perpetuate the memory of triumphal victories, through arches and columns and their sculptured friezes, and through writings. The Roman ceremony itself displayed pictorial and written representations of cities and forts, regions and rivers: it was in a sense a book, unrolling in processional form like the scroll on which a Roman book was written. The award of a triumph was also inscribed on tablets in the Capitol, in historical annals and in poetic odes and epics. These were the records that Renaissance scholars reverently scrutinized as they codified knowledge of the ancient triumph: the ceremony was always in part a literary property."

49 Ovid insists at the conclusion to the *Amores* (I.15.42), for example, that he will endure as long as he continues to be read: "vivam, parsque mei multa superstes erit" ("I'll live, and the better part of me will survive"). *Ovid, Heroides and Amores*, trans. Grant Showerman, 378–9. Ovid ends the *Metamorphoses* with a similar sentiment, which I included as the second gloss to this chapter.

50 Beard, *Roman Triumph*, 37.

51 Beard, *Roman Triumph*, 19.

52 The *Fasti triumphales* registered the names of triumphant generals in marble and once stood in the Roman Forum. The monument does not survive intact, yet fragments were excavated in the sixteenth century near the Temple of Antonius and Faustina. See Beard, *Roman Triumph*, 61–7, as well as Miller, *Roman Triumphs*, 47–51.

53 Beard, *Roman Triumph*, 65.

54 Aldo S. Bernardo, "Triumphal Poetry," 33. Of course, even when they were used by the author to praise himself, poetic triumphs were still political texts. Barański, "The Constraints of Form," 67, describes triumphs as, for example, the "most convenient way to represent concisely and in a poetically telling manner the enduring fame of all that was best and most typically Roman."

55 The text and translation of the *Georgics* is taken from the second volume of Loeb's two-volume Virgil, *Eclogues; Georgics; Aeneid I–VI*, ed. H. Rushton Fairclough, revised by G.P. Goold, III.10–22 (I:176–9).

56 Hardie, "After Rome," 299. For the web of intertextual allusions to Greek and Roman texts in this proem, see David Meban, "Temple Building, Primus Language, and the Proem to Virgil's Third *Georgic.*"

57 A third example of a poet connecting a Roman triumph to his own poetic victory can be found in the *Paradiso*, where Dante moves rapidly from the glory of his subject to his own authorial excellence. After concluding *Purgatorio* with the multi-canto Triumph of the Church, he begins the final canticle by staking a claim to the laurel. He then compares his self-laureation, which he suggests will take place at the close of his work, to the triumph of a Roman victor: poets and warriors are seldom granted the laurel, he laments, and so he will go to Apollo's tree and claim this honour for himself (*Pr* I.25–33).

58 In the final book of the *Africa*, Petrarch looks forward from Scipio's and Ennius's processions, which he relates in the final book of his poem, to his own coronation: "Ipse ego ter centum labentibus ordine lustris / Dumosam tentare viam et vestigia rara / Viribus imparibus fidens utcumque peregi, / Frondibus atque loco simul et cognomine claro / Heroum veterum tantos imitatus honores" ("I too, when fifteen centuries had passed through their appointed cycles, greatly strove with all the means my meager strength allowed to follow o'er the rough and thorny path those precious traces and to imitate with similar crown, like site, and glorious name, the ancient heroes and their dignities sublime" [*Africa*, ed. Festa, IX.404–8; trans. Bergin and Wilson, 237]).

59 James Simpson, "Subjects of Triumph and Literary History," 499.

60 Sextus Propertius, *Elegies*, ed. and trans. G.P. Goold, III.1.9–12; 220–1.

61 The apparent rivalry between authors of poetic triumphs and their predecessors was a feature of the original procession as well. Beard, *Roman Triumph*,

3, notes that it was "part of the history of the triumph to be judged against, to upstage or be upstaged by, the triumphs of predecessors and rivals." For Petrarch's poetics of rivalry in the *Trionfi*, see Leah Schwebel, "Triumphing over Dante in Petrarch's *Trionfi*."

62 Like Propertius, Ovid invokes the Roman triumph to distinguish himself from his epic predecessors, and to root his elegies in an illustrious tradition. Whereas Propertius presents himself as a victor, however, Ovid adopts a posture of powerlessness. He explains that although he wished at first to sing of arms, a vengeful Cupid stole the last foot of his metre, rendering his verse too short for epic: "Arma gravi numero violentaque bella parabam / edere, materia conveniente modis. / par erat inferior versus – risisse Cupido / dicitur atque unum surripuisse pedem. / 'Quis tibi, saeve puer, dedit hoc in carmina iuris?'" (Ovid, *Amores* I.1.1–5 in *Ovid: Heroides and Amores*, ed. and trans. Grant Showerman, 318–19). On Propertius's and Ovid's triumphal poetry, see Kathleen Morgan, *Ovid's Art of Imitation*.

63 Propertius, *Elegies*, ed. and trans. Goold, III.1.25–8; 222–3.

64 "Nec non ille tui casus memorator Homerus / posteritate suum crescere sensit opus; / meque inter seros laudabit Roma nepotes" ("Homer also, the chronicler of your fate, has found his reputation grow with the passage of time. I, too, will be praised by late generations of Rome"). Propertius, *Elegies*, ed. and trans. Goold, III.1.33–5 (222–3).

65 Gianni Guastella, *Word of Mouth*, 252.

66 "Illum post cineres auguror ipse diem. / ne mea contempto lapis indicet ossa sepulcro" ("Not neglected shall be the grave where the tombstone marks my bones"), *Elegies*, ed. and trans. Goold, III.1.36–7 (222–3).

67 The Latin text is taken from John of Salisbury, *Policraticus*, ed. Clement C.J. Webb, Prologue, 385b (12–13). The translation is by Cary J. Nederman, *John of Salisbury: Polycraticus*, 3. In his 1341 laureation speech, Petrarch likewise makes the symbiotic relationship between poets and their patrons in their quest for fame explicit. He laments the many mighty men who merited fame, yet faded from memory because they did not have poets to record their deeds.

68 Branca, "Introduction," *Amorosa visione*, xviii. Branca's introduction was translated into English by Margherita Frankel with the help of Hollander.

69 As Juan Pablo Gil-Osle points out, "Chatty Paintings, Twisted Memories and Other Oddities in Boccaccio's *Amorosa Visione*," 98–9, "in addition to rhetorical weakness in the guide's speeches, she lacks authority. As a result, she wins back the narrator momentarily, but very soon he disobeys her, since his memory does not long retain the *exemplum* she provides."

70 Boccaccio wrote a version of the *Amorosa visione*, called the "A" text, in 1342–3. All of the surviving manuscripts of this poem descend from a now lost archetype of this version. See McKinley, *Chaucer's "House of Fame"*

and Its Boccaccian Intertexts, 22–5, drawing on Branca (*Tutte le opere*, vol. 3), for the manuscript tradition. As McKinley explains, when Branca published his 1944 edition of the poem, he believed the "B" text represented Boccaccio's later version of the *Amorosa visione*, and so he included both "A" and "B" texts. More recently, however, scholars have come to see the "B" version of the *Amorosa visione* as contaminated, with only "A" representing Boccaccio's intended text.

71 Hollander, *Boccaccio's Two Venuses*, 202. Houston, *Building a Monument*, 164, goes so far as to say that he "doubt[s] many readers will argue with [his] characterization that it represents Boccaccio's greatest artistic failure." Usher, "Mural Morality," 122, calls Boccaccio's organization of the poem "untidy and ultimately incoherent." In the notes to his edition (*Tutte le opere*, 3:374), Branca suggests that there is a marked incongruity between the guide's moral lesson and the narrator's obvious refutation of it: "la giustapposizione di motivi diversi e contrastanti, e la contradizione fra la sensualità sempre presente nel suo amore e il tentativo di sublimarla attraverso modi stilnovistici e schemi allegorici, non solo impediscono ogni unità e vita poetica, ma compromettono anche gravemente la coerenza e la chiarezza logica dell'azione rappresentata." For a summary of early criticism on the *Amorosa visione*, see Smarr, "Boccaccio and the Choice of Hercules."

72 Surdich, *Boccaccio*, 68; Giovanni Pozzi, *Poesia per gioco*, 65, by contrast, hails this sequence as the "acrostico più spettacoloso della nostra letteratura."

73 Cf. Houston, *Building a Monument*, 164, who argues that "while not philosophical in nature this rather poetic compendium of tropes of Venus nevertheless closely imitate Dante's poetics."

74 Citations of Boccaccio's *Amorosa visione* are taken from vol. 3 of Branca's *Tutte le opere*, IV.45. Subsequent passages will be taken from this edition and noted in the text according to canto and line number. All translations of this work are my own, with help from Robert Hollander's facing-page edition.

75 For the figure of Dido in the *Amorosa visione*, and its likely influence on Christine de Pizan, see McKinley, "Constructing a Mythic City in the *Book of the City of Ladies*."

76 Margaret Ann Zaho, *Imago Triumphalis*, 30. Despite Boccaccio's extensive borrowings from Dante, Zaho writes, the *Amorosa visione* is, in contrast to the *Commedia*, "dedicated entirely to secular love." Hollander, *Boccaccio's Dante and the Shaping Force of Satire*, 11, calls the *Amorosa visione* "perhaps Boccaccio's most elaborate imitation of Dante," with "fifty canti that seem to put forward Dantean answers to the questions raised by the loves that this world enjoins upon us. The text is shot through with verses and scenes reflecting the verses of the *Commedia.*" Cf. Usher, "Mural Morality," 129, who argues that the poem shows us "a very serious and unsung side

to Boccaccio." The poet does in fact follow Dante's plan and formula of "conversion by exemplum" – that it is a "consciously humble demi-*Divine Comedy* in Dantean *terza rima*, which narrate[s] a vision in which a young man is encouraged to reform, morally and spiritually, after being shown, by a guide, a thematically organized exhibition of portraits of personages representing virtues and vices" (120). For the influence of Andrea Cappellano on the *Amorosa visione*, see Bruno Porcelli, *Nuovi studi su Dante e Boccaccio con analisi della Nencia*, 111–23. Porcelli shows how Boccaccio draws on Cappellano in order to demonstrate the power of love in the poem.

77 Smarr, *Boccaccio and Fiammetta*, 149, draws our attention to the correlation between Augustine's plea for delayed salvation in the *Confessions* and Boccaccio's similar request in the *Amorosa visione*.

78 As Branca notes ("Introduction," *Amorosa visione*, ed. Hollander, xiii), this is the first time Dante is "consecrated as a 'classic.'"

79 McKinley, *Chaucer's "House of Fame" and Its Boccaccian Intertexts*, 160–1.

80 Sylvia Huot, "Poetic Ambiguity and Reader Response in Boccaccio's 'Amorosa Visione,'" 114–15.

81 In *Pg* XI.106–8, Oderisi da Gubbio tells Dante that glory is fleeting, comparing even a thousand years of fame to an eyeblink of heaven's movement.

82 Citations of Dante's work are taken from *La Commedia*, ed. Giorgio Petrocchi, and are cited by canto and line number; translations are from Robert M. Durling and Ronald L. Martinez's *The Divine Comedy*.

83 In Teodolinda Barolini's words, *Dante's Poets*, 202, "[Vergil] does not lose his authority all at once ... but in a more subtle fashion ... When Vergil arrives an hourglass is set, and the grains of sand fall one by one until, in *Purgatorio* XXX, the glass is empty."

84 Huot, "Poetic Ambiguity," 121–2.

85 See Alastair Minnis, "Other Worlds," 430, for the argument that medieval writers (here Chaucer) could, "while recogniz[ing] the force of major cultural differences," at the same time tolerate, even affirm, other value systems and religions. "On this argument, salvation can be attained by a virtuous pagan – someone born in the wrong place and/or at the wrong time and hence unaware of the supreme religion" (419).

86 "Notes," *Amorosa visione*, ed. Hollander, 237–8. Hollander adds, "This deferral of conversion – and hence of closure to the poem – will find its most powerful manifestation in the problematic breaking of the dream itself" (238). McKinley, *Chaucer's "House of Fame" and Its Boccaccian Intertexts*, 25–6, reads Boccaccio's portrayal of his guide in the *Amorosa visione* more ambivalently. In her words, "Throughout the poem, the narrator persists in making the wrong choice, and often the guide reluctantly follows him. In this we see Boccaccio dismantling the didactic and moral force of the guide, and asserting over it the flawed yet autonomous judgement of the narrator.

Yet what must be recognized here is that the very entrances [representing the narrator's desire for earthly glory] that the guide disapproves of, and that the narrator insists on entering in his 'earthly' fashion, lead to Boccaccio's painted narratives on antiquity, Troy, and love, or what make up the heart of the poem. Even as his dreamer does not always manifest good judgement in the poem, it is not entirely clear that Boccaccio endorses the narrow judgements of the guide throughout the poem."

87 McKinley, *Chaucer's "House of Fame" and Its Boccaccian Intertexts*, has argued convincingly for Chaucer's knowledge and use of the *Amorosa visione* in the *House of Fame*, the poem in which Chaucer explores the poet's role in the creation of fame most extensively.

88 L.O. Aranye Fradenburg, *Sacrifice Your Love*, 131, sees the Monk's process as a kind of literary mourning: the tale "memorializes knowledge of and writing about tragedy just as much as it memorializes the falls of unfortunate men": it is "an instance of the 'processes of representation in the work of mourning which have an extended living to the dead'" (Fradenburg is quoting Laurence A. Rickels, *Case of California*, 14). But for Fradenburg, 131, the Monk's moral is not of the revivifying power of poetry – it is ultimately catastrophic, his tale a "traumatic figuration." The Monk "emphasizes that it is the business of tragedy to 'bewail.' He raises the stakes of tragedy, catastrophizes it further; tragedy is not just about an 'overturning' or an unhappy end, but about falling to an end utterly without resources … It is about fallenness as complete dispossession and helplessness, the absolute absence of 'remedie' for unfortunate men of high estate who end 'wrecchedly,' like the 'wrecched ympes' (1956) born to Harry Bailey's shrimp-men" (138).

89 Both the Knight and the Host find fault with the Monk's tale on the basis of its monotony and depressing content. But scholars have also found the tale problematic, and for reasons that go beyond its repetitiveness. Indeed, many have balked at the idea that the materially driven Monk of the "General Prologue" could tell such a listless tale. P.E. Beichner, "Daun Piers, Monk – Business Administrator," suggests that the tale teaches us the truth about the Monk's morality. B.W. Lindeboom, "Chaucer's Monk Illuminated," 339, notes that the "Monk's Tale" is "badly suited to its narrator." For his part, Lindeboom suspects that Chaucer was "ultimately striving for a self-reflecting or self-condemnatory situation, in which the Monk is implicitly or explicitly made to repudiate his fixation on this earthly life through the medium of his own Tale" (340).

90 Neuse, "They Had Their World as in Their Time," 419, suggests that "it would be a mistake to regard the Monk's introductory formula as definitive for each of the stories, since they range in tone and manner from elegiac or tragic to ironic and satiric, the satire frequently being aimed at the chief metanarrative of the Monk's time."

91 For Chaucer's variable representation of Fortune, see Edward Socola, "Chaucer's Development of Fortune in the 'Monk's Tale.'"

92 The idea of the Monk's "accumulation" of the labours of Hercules is Kara Gaston's ("Literary Catalogues and Verse Units"). See also Jahan Ramazani, "Chaucer's Monk," 261, who describes the Monk as a "collector," for whom "stories ... are objects to be gathered."

93 As Boitani notes, "Dante and Boccaccio," 52, the "'moralizing purpose' of the *De Casibus* is lessened in the *Monk's Tale*. The Monk does in fact moralize ... but his are all warnings against man's overweening confidence in Fortune. Boccaccio, on the other hand, recommends a philosophical attitude towards Fortune: he praises specific virtues and condemns specific vices ... All of this is, of course, absent in Chaucer."

94 Neuse, "The Monk's *De casibus*," 252.

95 Winthrop Wetherbee, "The Context of the Monk's Tale," 169, describes this narrative as an "exercise in courtly hyperbole: its hero is the flower of chivalry, and the Monk is so little concerned with the reason for his death by poison that he concludes, in a Chauntecleerian flourish, by 'despising' poison, together with 'Fals Fortune,' as though no human agent had been involved in Alexander's downfall."

96 Lucan, *The Civil War*, trans. J.D. Duff, 2–3 (I. 12). The passage is worth quoting in full: "Quis furor, o cives, quae tanta licentia ferri? / Gentibus invisis Latium praebere cruorem, / Cumque superba foret Babylon spolianda tropaeis / Ausoniis umbraque erraret Crassus inulta, / Bella geri placuit nullos habitura triumphos?" ("What madness was this, my countrymen, what fierce orgy of slaughter? While the ghost of Crassus still wandered unavenged, and it was your duty to rob proud Babylon of her trophies over Italy, did you choose to give to hated nations the spectacle of Roman bloodshed, and to wage wars that could win no triumphs?" [I.8–12]). Of course, by stressing the necessary *absence* of triumphs in civil war, Lucan reconfigures Caesar's "ostensible (and historical very real) victory" into a "resounding defeat" (Mark Thorne, "Lucan's Cato, the Defeat of Victory, the Triumph of Memory," 46). We find Lucan similarly miscited for Caesar's triumph in the "Man of Law's Tale." The Man of Law describes a congregation of Romans and Syrians, measuring this event against the triumph of Caesar. The latter, he suggests, is not nearly as magnificent as the scene he depicts in this tale: "Noght trowe I the triumphe of Julius, / Of which that Lucan maketh swich a boost, / Was roialler ne moore curius / Than was th'assemblee of this blissful hoost" (II.400–3).

97 Chaucer implies his recognition of this intertextual gambit in the "Man of Law's Tale," where he uses a Roman triumph to insinuate the superiority of his poetic theme over Lucan's "boost" of the Triumph of Caesar (a description that, as noted above, does not occur in the *Pharsalia*). Such a gesture

encourages us to seek similar overtones of self-promotion in Chaucer's false recognition of Lucan as his source in the "Monk's Tale."

98 Beard, *Roman Triumph*, 135. See also Pat Southern, *Empress Zenobia*, 156–61, for a useful account of Zenobia's capture and Aurelian's triumph. For the triumph and Zenobia's role in it, see Zosimus, *Historia Nova*, ed. James J. Buchanan and Harold T. Davis, Book I.

99 Beard, *Roman Triumph*, 135.

100 Beard, *Roman Triumph*, 135.

101 For the connection between the mighty Monk and his powerful subjects, see, for example, Wallace, *Chaucerian Polity*, 299–336, Jane Dick Zatta, "Chaucer's Monk," and Stephen Knight, "My Lord, the Monk."

102 *Thebaid* XII.519–22. As I discussed in chapter 1, most manuscripts of the "Knight's Tale" contain this gloss. For the relationship between the Knight and the Monk, see especially R.E. Kaske, "The Knight's Interruption of the *Monk's Tale*," and Jones, "The Monk's Tale," 388, who observed that we "can't understand what *The Monk's Tale* is getting at unless we understand what *The Knight's Tale* is about."

103 As Ramazani notes, "Chaucer's Monk," 65, "the Monk seeks to play a game of presence and absence or *fort/da* with death, representing and reducing it often enough that he masters it, traps it, turns it into something within the control of his will."

104 According to George L. Kittredge, "The Pillars of Hercules and Chaucer's 'Trophee,'" 557, "as a mere word, 'Trophee' is clear enough. It is of course the French *trophée*, Latin *tropaeum* (*tropheum*)" – it is Chaucer's use of Trophee as a name that "causes all the difficulty." Vincent DiMarco, "Another Look at Chaucer's 'Trophee,'" 276, likewise provides the definition of "*tropaeum* (postclassical *trophaeum*, medieval *tropheum*; cf. OF *trophee*)" as "a memorial of victory," yet assumes that Chaucer mistranslates this word, using "Trophee" as a name (the term "proved, perhaps because of its various meanings, notoriously difficult for translators"). Scholars including Walter William Skeat, *Complete Works of Geoffrey Chaucer*, 2nd edn, 2:liv–lvi, George Livingstone Hamilton, *The Indebtedness of Chaucer's "Troilus and Criseyde" to Guido delle Colonne's Historia Trojana*, esp. 55–7 and 150–4, Frederick Tupper, "Chaucer and Trophee," Robert A. Pratt, "Chaucer and the Pillars of Hercules," 122–3, and Oliver Farrar Emerson, "Seith Trophee," 143–4, suggest that the name "Trophee" refers to Guido delle Colonne, who, in the *Historia destructionis Troiae*, describes Hercules establishing pillars at the edges of the world. Emerson, for example, posits that Chaucer uses Trophee for the sake of his rhyme scheme: "in his Hercules story Chaucer was completing an eight-line stanza, and wished a fourth rime with long close *e*. *Guido*, *column*, *pillar* were equally impossible, even if he had not the latter (*piler*) already in mind for his next line. Rather than

recast his stanza, or perhaps by a happy thought rendered unhappy only by our obtuseness, he hit upon *Trophee* for Guido and his stanza was complete" (144–5). Lydgate, *The Fall of Princes*, ed. Henry Bergen, 1.83–7, identifies "a book which callid is Trophe" as the "Lumbard" authority behind *Troilus and Criseyde.* All subsequent citations from the *Fall of Princes* will be taken from this edition and noted in the text.

105 See the *Oxford English Dictionary* entry for both *tropaeum* and (our modern English derivative) trophy. See also the definition of *tropaeum* in Charlton T. Lewis and Charles Short's *Latin Dictionary*, and in the *Dictionary of Medieval Latin from British Sources*. In his 1539 translation of Erasmus's *Proverbes*, Richard Taverner writes that "In olde tyme," victors "were wonte to erecte and set vp some great stone, pyller or other thyng for a sygne of victorie, which marke they called Trophæum."

106 The reading of Trophee in this section reiterates my argument in "'Trophee' and Triumph in the *Monk's Tale*."

107 For Hercules's significant role in the Roman triumph, see, for example, Annalisa Marzano, "Hercules and the Triumphal Feast for the Roman People," 83–97, and Matthew P. Loar, "Hercules, Mummius, and the Roman Triumph in *Aeneid* 8."

108 Loar, "Hercules, Mummius, and the Roman Triumph in *Aeneid* 8," 47.

109 Marzano, "Hercules and the Triumphal Feast," 95.

110 Pliny, *Natural History, Volume IX: Books 33–35*, trans. Harris Rackham, 34.16: "Fuisse autem statuariam artem familiarem Italiae quoque et vetustam, indicant Hercules ab Evandro sacratus, ut produnt, in foro boario, qui triumphalis vocatur atque per triumphos vestitur habitu triumphali" ("That the art of statuary was familiar to Italy also and of long standing there is indicated by the statue of Hercules in the Cattle Market said to have been dedicated by Evander, which is called 'Hercules Triumphant,' and on the occasion of triumphal processions is arrayed in triumphal vestments").

111 See Marzano, "Hercules and the Triumphal Feast," 83–4 and 89.

112 Loar, "Hercules, Mummius, and the Roman Triumph in *Aeneid* 8," 47.

113 Loar, "Hercules, Mummius, and the Roman Triumph in *Aeneid* 8," 47. For the temples dedicated to Hercules, see Popkin, *The Architecture of the Roman Triumph*. For the feasts given in Hercules's honour, see Marzano, "Hercules and the Triumphal Feast," 89.

114 Marzano, "Hercules and the Triumphal Feast," 89. She adds that it seems "very likely that there were various stages in the development of the triumphal celebrations at the Ara Maxima. Hercules at the Ara, in earlier times the recipient of one-tenth of one's profit in thanksgiving, started also to receive the offerings of victorious generals, once the connection of the god to the sphere of war became stronger."

115 Marzano, "Hercules and the Triumphal Feast," 86.
116 Marzano, "Hercules and the Triumphal Feast," 88.
117 According to Lindeboom, "Chaucer's Monk Illuminated," 46, there is "not a jot of doubt that Chaucer follows Boccaccio" for this account.
118 *The Works of Geoffrey Chaucer*, ed. F.N. Robinson, 855. Boitani, "Dante and Boccaccio," 69n35, suggests that the manuscript of the *De casibus* that Chaucer consulted was likely "anonymous and mutilated," and that Chaucer probably assumed that Petrarch wrote it. Neuse, "The Monk's *De casibus*," 249–50, convincingly refutes this argument: not only is Petrarch mentioned in the *De casibus* as a visiting apparition, but also Boccaccio writes *himself* into the poem as a narrative persona.
119 For Petrarch's intertextual methodology in the *Trionfi*, see, for example, Martin Eisner, "Petrarch Reading Boccaccio," Amilcare A. Iannucci, "Petrarch's Intertextual Strategies in the *Triumphs*," and Bernardo, "Triumphal Poetry," 33–45.
120 Citations from Petrarch's *Trionfi* are taken from *Francesco Petrarca: Trionfi, Rime Estravaganti, Codice Degli Abbozzi*, ed. Vinicio Pacca and Laura Paolino, 417–18. Translations are taken from *The Triumphs of Petrarch*, trans. Ernest Hatch Wilkins. All subsequent passages from the *Trionfi* will be noted in the text, and cited according to triumph, part, and line range.
121 Fabio Finotti, "The Poem of Memory (Triumphi)," 66.
122 Miller, *Roman Triumphs*, 53. Miller rightly notes that Petrarch's celebration of fame in the *Trionfi* flouts a Christian charge of piety and humility. "Challenging *Triumphus Mortis* and its empire of death, this poem adduces not the efficacy of faith but the power of triumph and its poetry to reward and perpetuate human attainment. Where the Roman triumphator receives at the height of his fame a reminder of his mortality, Petrarch inverts the practice, reminding the Christian reader of the rewards of fame in spite of mortality" (52).
123 In the *Trionfi*, as Bernardo, *Petrarch, Laura, and the Triumphs*, 95–6, suggests, "no longer is God the only good that does not pass away. Whatever does not pass away is good."
124 As Wallace, *Chaucerian Polity*, 307–8, notes, Petrarch is "more than a source to Chaucer's Monk; his name ... performs the office of the 'author-function.' Such a name, Foucault argues, 'is more than a gesture, a finger pointed at someone; it is, to a certain extent, the equivalent of a description.'" For Wallace, Petrarch's name "may be read as describing Italian humanism as an emergent cultural tradition" (308). I, however, see its function as more poetic, with Chaucer using it to direct his reader to a tradition of triumphal poetry. Like Wallace, Neuse, "The Monk's *De casibus*," 247, sees a special significance in Chaucer's mention of Petrarch. He argues that Chaucer fashions the Monk as an "ironic double" of Boccaccio, and so

mentions Petrarch to restage Boccaccio's own earlier encounters with this figure in the *De casibus.*

125 Although Chaucer does, perhaps, acknowledge his debt to Boccaccio in the surtitle of the poem (see above, note 18). Chaucer credits both Dante and Petrarch among his many sources. As Neuse points out, "The Monk's *De casibus*," 252, by recognizing these poets but not the progenitor of his work, Chaucer makes Boccaccio's absence all the more prominent: "the Monk's 'frankness' in acknowledging his debt to these two seems calculated to make all the more conspicuous his begetter's failure to acknowledge *his* real debt to the third, unnamed one." For Neuse, this is because the Monk "stands *in loco Boccaccii.*" He doesn't name Boccaccio, because he is written to *be* Boccaccio.

126 For Chaucer's exploration of fame, see especially Boitani, *Chaucer and the Imaginary World of Fame*. See also N.R. Havely's more recent "'I Wolde ... han Hadde a Fame."

127 Cf. McKinley, *Chaucer's "House of Fame" and Its Boccaccian Intertexts*, 159, who writes of Chaucer's description of Goddess Fame in *HF* 1341–1418 that "words like satire do not do justice to the complexity of significations we see in these lines. Chaucer is not simply satirizing the 'glory' surrounding fame itself; he is presenting fame as both an object of intellectual-spiritual-erotic desire and an object of horror, for the poet-narrator. For all that Fame is arbitrary and unreliable, the inexperienced poet-narrator finds her power mesmerizing." McKinley demonstrates compellingly that Chaucer's "author gallery" from the third book of *HF* (1460–1509) borrows extensively from Boccaccio's ekphrastic description of the classical poets in Wisdom's Triumph (159–72).

128 Compare C.S. Lewis, *Poetry and Prose in the Sixteenth Century*, 27, who suggests that "poets are, for Chaucer, not the people who receive fame but the people who give it."

129 Indeed, we saw a narrower range of this activity in the *De casibus*. Recording the lives of meritorious individuals as well as those he finds contemptible, Boccaccio cultivates both glory and infamy. This binary is showcased especially in the narrator's encounter with Dante in *De casibus* 9. On Dante's recommendation, Boccaccio foregoes narrating a biography of the author of the *Commedia*, "poetam insignem" and "virum et amplissimis laudibus extollendum" (IX.23). Instead, he tells the story of Walter, Duke of Athens, a man who brought shame to himself and his city. Although Dante, his life, and his works are far worthier of being remembered, Walter's story must take precedence before his own, Dante suggests, since it will act as an exemplum for citizens of Florence. Fame and notoriety serve a similar function here. Distributed by poets, they extend the lives and reputations of those to whom they are granted. The difference, Boccaccio implies, is that

prolonging the memories of individuals who live badly is a punishment, not a reward, since this activity carries with it unending shame as opposed to lasting glory. For the varying forms of fame, both virtuous and vain, and on fame as encompassing infamy, see Boitani, *Chaucer and the Imaginary World of Fame*, 159–88.

130 For Lydgate's pursuit of fame in the *Fall of Princes*, see especially Flannery's fifth chapter in *John Lydgate and the Poetics of Fame*, "Promotion and Self-Promotion," 105–28.

131 For Flannery, *John Lydgate and the Poetics of Fame*, 106, "that Lydgate fully intends to be numbered among these crowned poets through his labors is confirmed by the *Fall*'s closing stanzas, in which Lydgate rewrites Chaucer's farewell to *Troilus and Criseyde* in an explicitly laureate tenor: 'Go kis the steppis of them that wer forthring, / Laureat poetes, which hadde soereynte / Of eloquence to supporte thy makyng' (IX.3605–7)."

132 Laurent de Premierfait's *Des Cas des nobles hommes et femmes* (1400; 1409) likewise celebrates Boccaccio as the author of the text. The 1409 retranslation of the *De casibus*, which was executed in two manuscripts (one for the Duke of Berry and the other for the Duke of Burgundy), included, respectively, cycles of 147 and 153 miniatures. While most images feature the tragic subjects of the *Des cas*, multiple illustrations, which we know Laurent supervised, depict the author, whom we find at his desk, orating, conversing with Petrarch, and asking Fortune for fame. (Anne D. Hedeman, *Translating the Past*, 78, suggests that only the images containing Petrarch and Fortune are of Boccaccio. The other two images are of a generic author figure. According to Hedeman, Laurent "pared down visual references to Boccaccio as author, which effectively enhanced the immediacy of his readers' experience of the translation" (77–8).

133 Flannery, *John Lygdate and the Poetics of Fame*, 90, reminds us that the *Fall* is "as much a collection of stories about fame as it is an encyclopaedia of Fortune's triumphs over great men and women. As part of their rise to prosperity and power, Lydgate's characters obtain glory and good fame, and as part of their sudden fall at the hands of Fortune, they lose them just as quickly. But no matter how they meet their ends, and whether they are perceived as unfortunate but virtuous characters or as cruel or immoral individuals who deserved to get what was coming to them, every one of the Fall's subjects is famous."

134 For Lydgate's engagement with the Roman triumph, and with the commentary tradition on the Roman triumph, in the *Serpent of Division* and "Henry VI's Triumphal Entry into London," see Maura Nolan's "Spectacular Culture: The Roman Triumph," in *John Lydgate and the Making of Public Culture*, 184–255.

135 Flannery, *John Lydgate and the Poetics of Fame*, 107, compares Lydgate's approach to acquiring fame with Chaucer's. Whereas "Chaucer views whatever

ability poets may have to generate and preserve immortal fame (whether for themselves or for others) as extremely limited" (115), Lydgate hails writing as the "preserver of human memory and the tool by which things otherwise absent or past are borne in the mind" (105). For Flannery, this means that Lydgate "proves himself to be an anti-Chaucerian poet, subjecting fame to his will" (157). Certainly, Flannery is correct in her assessment of Lydgate as a poet deeply invested in the immortalizing function of writing, and her work on the ways he exploits this function is groundbreaking and important. To my mind, however, while he is not as explicit as Lydgate in his pursuit of glory, Chaucer is likewise preoccupied with his role as a generator of fame, and he shows a consistent interest in establishing himself within an illustrious authorial genealogy.

4 Myn Auctor Lollius: Chaucer and the Invention of Troy

1 Robert Henryson, "The Testament of Cresseid," 352.

2 Thomas Warton, *The History of English Poetry, from the Eleventh to the Seventeenth Century* (1778), 254n3.

3 Walter Jackson Bate, *John Keats*, 510–11n8, suggests we look to Keats for how to respond to literal-minded critics on a search for his Grecian urn: "Attempts continue to be made to determine a particular vase or urn that Keats may have had in mind when he wrote the ode. Especially with a poem so distinguished by its universality, one thinks of Keats's own remark … that 'They are very shallow people who take everything literal.'"

4 Bella Millett, "Chaucer, Lollius, and the Medieval Theory of Authorship," 102, suggests that Chaucer's feigned reliance on Lollius, particularly before the *Canticus Troili*, should be read as a playful, literary joke: "his emphasis on the authenticity of Troilus' song is more explicable if we take it as a half-private joke, directed to those members of his audience who would have recognized its actual source." For Millett, however, Lollius is also an authorizing device. Comparing Lollius to the fictional authors invented by medieval historiographers, Millett argues that Lollius functions in the *Troilus* as a "warrant of respectability, a cloak under which the writer can decently disguise his fictions" (99). Noting that Chaucer is most outspoken about his fidelity to his "auctour" when he is actually deviating from Boccaccio, Barry Windeatt, *Troilus and Criseyde*, 39, speculates that perhaps Lollius was "a piece of deliberately transparent artifice … designed to foreground the question of sources, and with that the role of interpretation," or a "private joke" between Chaucer and his literary friends. But to the question of why Chaucer fabricates a source, Windeatt, like Millett, rehearses an old critical adage. Insisting that Lollius is an authenticating device, he suggests that Chaucer offers the *Troilus* as a translation of a Latin source

because "the claim to an 'authority' was a claim to authority for *Troilus*" (40). For both Millett and Windeatt, then, Lollius is at once a "joke" or "piece of … transparent artifice" and an authorizing presence, two seemingly conflicting ends. (See also John V. Fleming, *Classical Imitation and Interpretation in Chaucer's "Troilus,"* 191, who argues first that Chaucer's use of Lollius "suggests an act of the poetical imagination rather than a blunder, happy or otherwise," but then qualifies this statement to suggest that Lollius bolsters the historical authority of Chaucer's poem. "For a variety of reasons Chaucer wanted a pseudoantique authority on which to rest the enterprise of the *Troilus* … A pseudoantique 'original' authorized the exercise of his historical imagination, the poetic adaptation of his considerable historical researches, in the vividly augmented 'classicization' of the medieval Troy story" (192). A more convincing reading of Lollius as a recognizable literary device is provided by Richard J. Utz, "'As Writ Myn Auctour Lollius.'" Likening the poet's fictionalizing to the act of divine creation, Utz suggests that Chaucer "create[s] this fictional 'auctour' to draw attention to his own role as a late-medieval vernacular poet who arbitrarily combines and willfully juggles a large variety of available classical and postclassical materials" (140). Building on Windeatt, George Edmondson, *The Neighboring Text*, 189–90, also sees Lollius as a kind of metacritical commentary on pagan and historical authority. He suggests that Lollius serves "as a sly comment on the imbrication of fantasy and history, underscoring the fact that our relation to the past is always, at some level, fake, as fraudulent as Lollius himself. In the case of *Troilus and Criseyde*, in particular, that fraudulency is redoubled; for here, of course, that relation [is] to a pagan past from which the narrator and his contemporaries are utterly estranged."

5 To provide a few examples, Charles M. Hathaway, "Chaucer's Lollius," 161–4, suggests that Chaucer's Lollius was perhaps a thirteenth-century philosopher named Raymond Lull, while Lillian H. Hornstein, "Petrarch's Laelius, Chaucer's Lollius?", argues that Lollius was a pseudonym for Petrarch's friend, a classicist by the name of Lellus Pietri Stephani de Tosettis, who went by the Latinized "Lelius." Hans J. Epstein, "The Identity of Chaucer's Lollius," suggests a third candidate: Bassus Lollius, whose epigrams are dated to 19 CE. For an excellent survey of critical readings of Lollius, see Utz, "As Writ Myn Auctour Called Lollius," 123–7.

6 The theory that "Lollius" owes his existence to Chaucer's misunderstanding of a vocative in Horace's epistles, in which we find an address to "Lollius Maximus" – "Troiani belli scriptorem, maxime Lolli, / Dum tu declamas Romae, Praeneste relegi" – owes its existence to R.G. Lantham, "Chaucer Note" (1868), and Bernhard Ten Brink, *Chaucer* (1870). But it was George L. Kittredge, "Chaucer's Lollius" (1917), who really cemented this theory as the most plausible explanation for Chaucer's invented source. Kittredge's

article was further corroborated by Robert A. Pratt, "A Note on Chaucer's Lollius" (1950), who provided specific manuscript evidence of scribes mistranslating Horace's "Lollius Maximus." See Utz, "'As Writ Myn Auctour Lollius,'" 126–7. Cf. Fleming, *Classical Imitation and Interpretation*, 191, who rejects this line of argument for the reason that it assumes Chaucer to be a bad reader of Latin and also a "dimwit."

7 Kittredge, "Chaucer's Lollius," 49; David Wallace, *Chaucer and the Early Writings of Boccaccio*, 50. Kittredge adds that Chaucer's actual source, Boccaccio's *Filostrato*, "would not answer, for the conditions of the problem required an ancient (or at least antique) personage, and preferably one who had written in a learned language" (49). As I discussed in my introduction, Wallace argues similarly that by naming Lollius, Chaucer affirms that his work "incorporates the historical witness of an *auctour*" and "suggests that his modern vernacular narrative is supported by a backbone of ancient authority." (It is important to note that Wallace, 50, also submits Boccaccio's Ilario as a model for Chaucer's Lollius.) Alastair Minnis, *Chaucer and Pagan Antiquity*, 23–4, maintains that Chaucer did not mention Boccaccio "for the same reason that Guido [delle Colonne] did not mention Benoît's *Roman de Troie*: these writers were casting themselves in the role of historian ... and therefore 'modern' works in whatever vernacular would not serve their purpose. Instead, *auctores* had to be cited, 'ancient' writers who had written in Latin." Richard Firth Green, *Poets and Princepleasers*, 160, suggests that Chaucer names Lollius because "Boccaccio was too recently dead, and too little known in Northern Europe, for Chaucer to be able to cite him as a respected *auctor.* It was not until Premierfait's translations early in the fifteenth century that Boccaccio became popular at the French court."

8 See Anthony Grafton, *Forgers and Critics*, 9, who notes that, by the sixth century BCE, "as authors ceased to claim divine authority for their words, they invented human authoritative sources for facts and texts."

9 The fraudulence of Dares and Dictys was discovered in the early eighteenth century, when Jacob Perizonius proved by means of palaeographic and philological evidence that these diaries were forgeries.

10 Guido considers "Tamen defectum magnorum auctorum, Virgilii, Ouidii, et Homeri, qui in exprimenda ueritate Troyani casus nimium defecerunt ... et specialiter ille summus poetarum Virgilius, quem nichil latuit." This citation is taken from Nathaniel E. Griffin's edition of the *Historia*, 276 (35).

11 Grafton, *Forgers and Critics*; David Rollo, *Historical Fabrication, Ethnic Fable and French Romance in Twelfth-Century England*; and Monika Otter, *Inventiones*. See also Nancy Partner, *Serious Entertainments*. Rollo and Otter demonstrate the ways in which twelfth-century historiographers indicate that they are writing fiction, or, in Rollo's words, "alert their readers or listeners to the inauthenticity of the past they are constructing" (40). William

of Malmsbury's *Gesta Regum Anglorum* is, for example, a work that is "openly dismantled" by its author as it is written, designed "not to deceive, but to invite analysis of the very circumstances that influenced its writing" (20). For Rollo, William of Newburgh's remarks on Geoffrey's *Historia* are "glosses on internal signals of inauthenticity that are already present" in the text: "Geoffrey's innovation was not only to disguise fable as history: it was to do so with a degree of self-dismantling candor" (41). Examining scenes of what she calls "archeological discovery" in the historical writing of twelfth-century England – "episodes of travels and conquests, of searching and finding, of digging" – Otter argues similarly that "these episodes help define the historians' self-image and show their awareness of the complexity of their enterprise" while showing a "latent sense of fictionality" (1). Discussing episodes involving a descent underground or attempts at digging, for example, she notes that these scenes "cause problems ... not only for a referential conception of truth but for most conceptions of historical truth one might think of." In this regard, they "suggest a degree of self-conscious textuality that is usually associated with a high degree of *litterarité*; they encourage us, even force us, to look at the texts as sophisticated literary narratives, not mere utilitarian collections of facts" (5). This practice of thematizing fraudulence as a way of revealing one's own artifice has its roots in antiquity. If the sixth century BCE saw authors inventing human authorities, then the fifth century brought efforts to unmask this invention. As Grafton, *Forgers and Critics*, 10, points out, "already, then, some writers possessed an aptitude for detecting anachronisms – an aptitude essential to anyone trying to either create a plausible document or to expose one. In fact, some evidence from the classical period suggests that the sensitivity to forgery was almost as widespread as its practice."

12 William of Newburgh, *The History of English Affairs, Book 1*, ed. and trans. P.G. Walsh and M.J. Kennedy, 1.28–9 ("Prologue" 2).

13 William of Newburgh, *The History of English Affairs*, 1.30–1 ("Prologue" 5–6).

14 William of Newburgh, *The History of English Affairs*, 1.32–3 ("Prologue" 9).

15 Important figures in this debate include (though are by no means limited to) Isidore of Seville, who contrasts *historia* and *fabula* on the basis of truth and falsehood, defining *historia* as the representation of things that have happened (it is "narratio rei gestae") and *fabula* as the representation of things that have not (*Etymologiae* I.41.1, I.44.5); Alain of Lille, who in his *De planctu Naturae* distinguishes between useful fictions and those that are absolutely unforgiveable, calling authors who use the latter form of fiction pimps; Macrobius, who defends the *narratio fabulosa* in his commentary on Cicero's *Dream of Scipio*; Petrarch, who defends poetry to his brother in *Fam* X.4; and Boccaccio, who includes a lengthy and impassioned defence of poetry in the fourteenth book of the *Genealogie deorum gentilium*.

16 For the semiotics of fraud, see, for example, Teodolinda Barolini, *The Undivine Comedy*, esp. 74–98.

17 *Genealogie deorum gentilium*, ed. Vittorio Zaccaria, *Tutte le opere*, 8:1412 (XIV.9.3). All Latin citations are taken from this edition. The English translations are taken from *Boccaccio on Poetry*, trans. Charles G. Osgood, 47.

18 Chaucer names "Lollius" in the *Troilus* on two occasions: I.3995 and V.1653. Citations from *Troilus* are taken from the *Riverside Chaucer*. Further citations will be noted in the text.

19 For Boccaccio's multilingual sources, see especially Maria Gozzi, "Sulle fonti del *Filostrato*." In another article, "'Filostrato' e 'Roman de Troyle,'" Gozzi examines a fifteenth-century translation of Boccaccio's *Filostrato*, *The Roman de Troyle*, by Louis de Beauvau. Comparing the Italian original and the French translation, she suggests that differences arise predominantly because the latter was rendered into prose.

20 Although, like the other authors this chapter treats, Guido dissimulates his sources in the *Historia destructionis Troiae*, he seems to have little interest in staking out a claim to poetic authority for his work using genealogical strategies. For this reason, I have chosen not to focus on his work. On Guido and the question of authorial genealogy, see, for example, James Simpson, "The Other Troy Book," 404, who argues that the *Historia* "makes no serious play with the genealogical potential of the Troy narrative." Rather, "genealogy guarantees very little indeed in the Guido tradition, either within the Greco-Trojan society represented or between the texts of that pan-European tradition and their readers" (419).

21 This is an argument put forth by Rollo alone, and strictly with regard to Benoît de Sainte-Maure. The first section of my chapter builds on Rollo's valuable work on the *Troie*, especially the sixth chapter of his *Historical Fabrication* (169–89). Rollo, *Historical Fabrication*, 21, asserts that the "widespread inventions" Benoît weaves into *Troie* spring from "an awareness of the fabricated – and therefore already invented – nature of the past he treats." But Rollo is the exception. For the most part, it is taken as a given in scholarship today that writers of the Middle Ages believed wholeheartedly in the historical authority of Dares and Dictys, and that it was not until the early eighteenth century, with Perizonius's discovery, that this authority was dismantled. Writing over a century ago, for example, Griffin, "Un-Homeric Elements in the Story of Troy" (1908), 41–2, remarked that the authors of the pseudepigraphic memoirs of Dares and Dictys "found no difficulty in convincing a credulous public that their spurious productions were genuine relics of antiquity. Both documents, though clearly derived from late and impure sources, were accepted at their face value by subsequent generations, who readily acquiesced in a deception which they lacked the critical acumen to detect." More recently, C. David Benson, *The History of Troy in Middle*

English Literature (1980), 5, argued that readers and writers of the Middle Ages accepted the diaries of Dares and Dictys, as well as their medieval redactions, as "absolutely genuine." Still more recently, Christopher Baswell, *Virgil in Medieval England* (2006), 18, suggests that this counter-tradition of the Troy story "claimed and received greater historical authority than that accorded to the *Aeneid.*"

22 All citations of Benoît are taken from *Le Roman de Troie*, ed. Léopold Constans, here 1:9 ("Prologue" 139–44). All translations are taken from *The Roman de Troie*, trans. Glyn S. Burgess and Douglas Kelly, here 44. Further citations will be noted according to book and line number; translations will be noted according to page number.

23 R.M. Frazer, "Introduction," *The Trojan War*, 13.

24 The Latin is taken from Ferdinand Meister's edition of *De excidio Troiae historia*, 1. The English translation is by Frazer, *The Trojan War*, 133.

25 *De excidio Troiae historia*, 1; trans. Frazer, 133.

26 Frazer, "Introduction," 12–13.

27 David Ganz, "Historia," 10. Ganz provides a few examples of this correlation between history and presence: "Evangelists spoke *veritatis historie* because of eyewitness information. Isidore rejected oral sources in favour of what was seen, a feature which Einhard later grasped and employed. Einhard claims that no one could write more truthfully than he had done, since he was present at the events which he described and as an eyewitness he is reliable: 'oculata ut dicunt fide', with his reference 'as they say' indicating that he is quoting. The expression goes back to Cyprian, referring to Paul's ascent to heaven, when he saw Christ, 'qui occulata fide Ihesum Dominum vidisse se gloriatur' ['who boasts that he saw the Lord Jesus as an eyewitness']."

28 Rollo, *Historical Fabrication*, 180.

29 Rollo, *Historical Fabrication*, 180.

30 Edmondson, *The Neighboring Text*, 91. Edmondson adds that Benoît's identification with Dares here goes beyond a desire for legitimacy. It "can also be viewed as essentially symbolic (as opposed to imaginary), with Dares occupying the structural position of the Father and providing Benoît with a text-based ego ideal: that 'guide beyond the imaginary' from whose vantage point the subject stands in judgement of itself, measuring itself, usually negatively, against the Other's ideals" (91).

31 *Troie*, ed. Constans, 1:3 ("Prologue" 45–6); trans. Burgess and Kelly, 43.

32 *Troie*, ed. Constans, 1:4 ("Prologue" 51–6); trans. Burgess and Kelly, 43–4.

33 *Troie*, ed. Constans, 1:7 ("Prologue" 105–12); trans. Burgess and Kelly, 44.

34 Lee Patterson, *Chaucer and the Subject of History*, 119, sees a metaphorical correspondence between Briseida's fraudulence and the chaos of secular history: "as unreliable as the whirligig world she manipulates, her feminine

treachery is the ethical equivalent to the instability that afflicts the historical world, and her betrayal of Troilus expresses in amorous terms not only the individual betrayals of the Trojan story but the topsy-turvy reversals that characterize all historical action."

35 Edmondson, *The Neighboring Text*, 91.

36 In her article, "Ovid's *Heroides* 3 and the *inventio* of Criseyde in the Medieval Matter of Troy," 149, Desmond considers Benôit's *inventio* with regard to the Briseis storyline: "Since her appearance in Dares's catalogue of Greek heroes and heroines would preclude identifying this figure as the captive Briseis of *Heroides* 3, the lack of agreement between Dares and Ovid allowed Benoît to 'invent' – in the heuristic, rhetorical sense of discovery – the story of a character whose name he translates into French as 'Briseida,' a Trojan woman who is traded to the Greeks." I am very grateful to Desmond for allowing me to read this piece in advance of its publication.

37 Douglas Kelly, "The Invention of Briseida's Story in Benoit de Sainte-Maure's 'Troie,'" 222.

38 See also Desmond, "Ovid's *Heroides* 3 and the *inventio* of Criseyde," for Briseida's transformation.

39 Peter Godman, *The Silent Masters*, 163. Godman's discussion concerns Book 1, Chapter 24 of John of Salisbury's *Metalogiçon*.

40 Kelly, "The Invention of Briseida's Story," 231.

41 Kelly, "The Invention of Briseida's Story," 231.

42 The poem showcases what Lucia Battaglia Ricci, *Boccaccio*, 60, describes as Boccaccio's "incessante sperimentalismo" with literary genres and traditions.

43 For recent contributions on Boccaccio's Angevin Naples, see especially Giancarlo Alfano, Teresa D'Urso, and Alessandra Perriccioli Saggese, eds., *Boccaccio angioino*; Roberta Morosini, "Napoli"; Alfano et al., eds., *Boccaccio e Napoli.* Although her focus is Johanna I, who began her reign as queen of Naples after Boccaccio had departed the city, see also Elizabeth Casteen, "On She-Wolves and Famous Women."

44 The Italian text of *Filostrato* is taken from Vittore Branca's edition in *Tutte le opere*, 2:21 ("Proemio," 28). English translations will be taken for the most part from N.R. Havely, "Il Filostrato," *Chaucer's Boccaccio*, although I have used my own translations in a few places. Further citations will be noted in the text according to section and line number.

45 Desmond, "*Translatio imperii* and the Matter of Troy in Angevin Naples," 189. Desmond observes how in the face of military disappointments, Robert presented himself as a sagacious and effective ruler. "If the Angevins failed to incorporate peripheral territories into their imperial kingdom," she notes, "Angevin bibliophile cultures nonetheless demonstrate how collecting, copying, translating, and illustrating texts could substitute for the peripheral territories that the Angevin monarchy could claim but not conquer" (191).

At the same time, visual programs accompanying Troy narratives were used to influence Robert. Royal 6 E IX, for example, whose illustrations have been attributed to Pacino di Buonaguida, directly "deploys the matter of Troy to appeal directly to Robert as the prudent king who should unify Italy" (182).

46 Jane Gilbert, Catherine Keen, and Ella Williams, "The Italian Angevins," 123.

47 Victoria Kirkham, *Fabulous Vernacular*, 68.

48 As Luigi Surdich, *Boccaccio*, 43–4, points out, Filostrato's opening quest for "truth" in the proem itself functions as "un rifiuto" of his earlier Neapolitan poem, the *Filocolo*, a detail that adds a further, nearly palinodic, reason for our mistrust of his narrator: "A premessa del *Filostrato* ... si assiste alla ritrattazione di una definizione fomulata dall'autore attraverso la sua mediatrice (Fiammetta) nel *Filocolo.* L'undicesima questione d'amore, che proponeva l'interrogativo su 'qual sia maggior diletto all'amante, o vedere presenzialmente la sua donna, o, non vendendola, di lei amorosamente pensare' (*Filocolo* IV 59, 2) e che era stata risolta a favore del pensare, a inizio del *Filostrato* viene ripresa in formulazione più articolata" (Proem, 2). The author's answer in this dedication is thus "preventivamente destuita di fondamento, dal momento che chi la esprime dice di averla espresso 'vinto dal falso parere.'"

49 Kara Gaston, *Reading Chaucer in Time*, 33–4.

50 The text of the *Decameron* is taken from Branca's edition in *Tutte le opere*, 4:Proem, 13. The English translation is from *The Decameron*, trans. G.H. McWilliam, 2nd edn, 3.

51 *Decameron*, ed. Branca, *Tutte le opere*, 4:Proem, 13; trans. McWilliam, 3. The narrator's early claim to tell only "novelle, o favole o parabole o istorie" is not borne out in the body of the *Decameron*, in which members of the brigata regularly invoke recognizable persons and events, and often present their stories as having really happened.

52 *Troie*, 1:3 ("Prologue" 33–4).

53 "Nè altro più atto nella mente mi venne a tale bisogno, che il valoroso giovane Troiolo, figliuolo di Priamo nobilissimo re di Troia" ("And I could think of no-one more suitable for the purpose than the valiant young Troiolo son of Priam, the most illustrious king of Troy" [Proem, 27]).

54 Giulia Natali, *Boccaccio e le controfigure dell'autore*, discusses how in the proems of his early works – the *Filostrato*, the *Filocolo*, and the *Teseida* – Boccaccio presents himself as a storyteller, a vulgarizer of ancient texts, and an intermediary figure critical to the process of transmitting the stories from antiquity to his contemporaries. At the same time, he uses the genre of the lyric and an amorous subject to elevate his vulgar works, "oscillating" in the paratexts between epic and erotic poles (28–9).

55 See also *Filostrato* III.90, where the narrator qualifies a statement with the words, "se non erra la storia."

56 Gozzi, "Sulle fonti del *Filostrato*," 123–209.

57 Surdich, *Boccaccio*, 38. Drawing on Gozzi (1968) for his argument, Wallace, *Chaucer and the Early Writings of Boccaccio*, 74, notes that the *Filostrato* has no one source and reveals Boccaccio's "highly individual purposes."

58 Critics have long recognized Filostrato's lack of trustworthiness. See, for example, Robert Hollander, *Boccaccio's Two Venuses*, 52, who notes that Boccaccio's narrators, including Filostrato, are "not to be trusted as spokesmen for the poet." See also Fabian Alfie, "Reading Boccaccio's Filostrato as a Medieval Parody," 353, who writes that "no matter what the narrator, Filostrato, might say, the astute reader knows him to be a fool, and therefore considers all his utterances to be suspect." Wallace, "Love-Struck in Naples," 78, observes that critics have "long discounted the romantic biographical schemes favored, especially, by nineteenth-century scholars. No evidence suggests that Boccaccio had an early mistress named Giovanna or Filomena, the dedicatee of this romance, or actually had a beloved called Maria d'Aquino or Fiammetta." See also Laura Banella, "'In persona d'alcuno passionato,'" 130, who discusses Boccaccio's movement between the voice of his author and that of his narrator in the *Filostrato* and across his poetry, a movement that Banella identifies as deliberately confusing to the reader.

59 Even though by his own account Criseida takes many measures to hide these exchanges, the narrator knows every detail of Troiolo and Criseida's early correspondence, including the contents of Troiolo's initial letter and where Criseida reads it. On the other hand, the narrator displays a surprising ignorance of things that he perhaps *should* know, given his detailed knowledge of far more private information. When Troiolo falls in love with Criseida, for example, the narrator is unaware of what Criseida perceived: "E qual si fosse non è assai certo: / o che Criseida non se n'accorgesse / per l'operar di lui ch'era coverto, / o che di ciò conoscer s'infignesse" ("And the true state of things is not very clear: whether Criseida because of his discretion perceived nothing of this, or whether she was pretending not to understand" [I.48]).

60 As his story takes a turn for the tragic, Filostrato comments that he no longer cares if he is aided by his lady, because he can narrate Troiolo's sadness using his own narrative skills, unless his feeble memory leads them astray (IV.23).

61 As Frazer, *The Trojan War*, 6, explains in his introduction, a major criticism levelled at Homer from very early on (and a point that pseudo Dares and Dictys sought to correct) was that he frequently described the gods' interference in mortal affairs. Dares and Dictys, on the other hand, "use[d] none of the divine machinery typical of epic poetry, and they tend[ed] to describe supernatural occurrences in rationalistic terms."

62 As Matthew Giancarlo notes about the corresponding scene in the *Troilus* ("The Structure of Fate and the Devising of History in Chaucer's *Troilus*

and Criseyde," 250), even Troilus's repudiation of his sister is historically determined: "By necessity, this correct Cassandran account leads Troilus immediately to disbelieve it and to disbelieve even his own conviction that Criseyde has been 'reft' from him (5.1260)." Indeed, Chaucer amplifies the element of determinism in this scene (already poignant in the *Filostrato* with the incorporation of Cassandra) by having Cassandra look to Thebes for an explanation of Troy's and Troilus's fall. In Patterson's words (*Chaucer and the Subject of History*, 130), she interprets Troilus's dream "not in ethical or even chivalric terms but historiographically." What is more, Troilus must disbelieve her explanation, and history must repeat itself. "History and the understanding of history run on parallel lines of descent, but precisely because they never meet they remain always the same. The relationship between interpretation and event is not causal but specular: just as warriors and lovers perform the same acts, so do poets and historians tell the same stories, parallel events that share an analogous incomprehensibility. And by rejecting Cassandra as a prophetess, Troilus legitimizes her as a historian: denied an understanding of history, he will inevitably repeat it" (131–2).

63 Banella, "'In persona d'alcuno passionate,'" 133, observes that the epistolary frame of the *Filostrato*, as well as the internal letters sent between his characters, has a disorienting effect on the reader (akin to finding oneself in a hall of mirrors), as though Boccaccio wanted to justify the fiction of his narrative with the supposed reality of the narrator. This "struttura epistolare propria del macrotesto e di porzioni interne al testo" induces us to confront "un artificio che rinforza il gioco di specchi" in the poem (133). She further argues that such an experience is reinforced in the manuscript illuminations.

64 For the ways in which Boccaccio and, to a greater degree, Chaucer shape Calkas's speech in Book IV according to medieval understandings of Ciceronian oration, see Rebecca S. Beal, "What Chaucer Did to an Orazion in the *Filostrato*."

65 Drawing on Seneca (*Moral Epistles* 40.1), Phillip Hardie, *Ovid's Poetics of Illusion*, 108–9, observes that "an autograph letter carries 'real traces' of the absent friend in a way that portraits do not, in that the marks on the tablet or papyrus are indexes of the physical motions of the writer's body. The letter may embody its writer in an even more physical way, if its ink is mingled and smudged with body secretions. These blots, *liturae*, threaten the verbal communicative power of *litterae*, but convey an even more powerful non-verbal message. Tears convey directly the lacrimosity of elegy."

66 Elisabetta Menetti, "Appunti di poetica boccacciana," 49.

67 *Genealogie deorum gentilium*, ed. Zaccaria, in *Tutte le opere*, 8:1398 (XIV.7.1); trans. Osgood, 39.

68 *Genealogie*, ed. Zaccaria, *Tutte le opere*, 8:1402 (XIV.7.8); trans. Osgood, 42.

69 *Genealogie*, ed. Zaccaria, *Tutte le opere*, 8:1416 (XIV.9.13); trans. Osgood, 50.

70 Ricci, *Boccaccio*, 47.

71 Ricci, *Boccaccio*, 47.
72 Glending Olson, *Literature as Recreation in the Middle Ages*, 132.
73 Hollander, "Dante Theologus-Poeta," 264–5.
74 David Lummus, "Boccaccio's Poetic Anthropology," reminds us that Boccaccio uses the *Genealogie* to suggest the veracity of the literal/historical sense of poetry as well, something I discuss in chapter 1. It is not only as allegories that fables can be mined for truth.
75 *Genealogie*, ed. Zaccaria, *Tutte le opere*, 8:1412 (XIV.9.3); trans. Osgood, 47.
76 *Genealogie*, ed. Zaccaria, *Tutte le opere*, 8:1414 (XIV.9.7) and 1707n99 (XIV.9). The editor notes that the phrase ("Nec fastidiant obiectores [...] usus est") follows in the margins of cod. Plut. LII 9 (an autograph manuscript). It is suppressed in the *Vulgata.* Osgood (49) includes this passage in the body of the text: "My opponents need not be so squeamish – Christ, who is God, used this sort of fiction again and again in his parables."
77 *Genealogie*, ed. Zaccaria, *Tutte le opere*, 8:1414 (XIV.9.7); trans. Osgood, 48–9.
78 Patterson discusses Troy's root in Theban determinism in his chapter, "*Troilus and Criseyde* and the Subject of History," in *Chaucer and the Subject of History*, 84–164. But see also Giancarlo, "The Structure of Fate and the Devising of History," 30, who observes, "In the poem as a whole, the language of Boethian conjecture on determinism and fate opens our eyes to a wider array of determinisms: one can valuably discuss the importance for the *Troilus* of astral determinism, divine intervention, 'event' causality and 'agent' causality, doctrines of Fortune, the fatedness of the past, the free will of constrained individuals, the limits of human foresight and the problems of providence, and so on."
79 On the ways in which even Homer and his successors dissimulated their sources, see Ralph Hexter, "On First Looking into Vergil's Homer."
80 Here, I dispute the idea, adopted most stridently by Benson in *The History of Troy*, that Chaucer is presenting himself as a historian in the *Troilus.* Benson suggests that, although not to the extent of the medieval historians of Troy, Chaucer "works hard ... to *seem* like a historian, and he succeeds in giving the story a historical plausibility and depth not found in the *Filostrato*" (135–6).
81 For Chaucer's development of the narrator in *Troilus and Criseyde*, see especially E. Talbot Donaldson's *Speaking of Chaucer*. Donaldson sees the narrator as a sentimental lover of Criseyde. In his attempts to defend his subject, however, the narrator shines a lantern on the poet standing behind him, who "jogs his elbow" and causes him to falter (69). In the sense that I think Chaucer constructs a narrator who gradually loses faith in (and in the process, betrays the unreliability of) his sources, I likewise distinguish Chaucer the poet from the narrator of the *Troilus*. Since this question is not central to my argument, however, for the sake of clarity and concision, I refer to both the poet and his narrator as Chaucer in this study.

82 Gaston, "'Save oure tonges difference,'" 260.

83 For a reading of the *Troilus* as "not history," see Sylvia Federico, *New Troy*. Federico argues that, "in Chaucer's poem, the suppression of history is a prerequisite for its inscription" (72). She adds, "to write 'not history' ... is to write history anyway, under the conceit that one is not doing so" (74).

84 In the words of Patricia Thompson, "The 'Canticus Troili,'" 317, "Petrarch is asking whether this incomprehensible feeling of his is love or not. Chaucer has put into the back of Troilus' mind a more general question ... Does love exist or not?" For a general discussion of Chaucer as translator and the *Canticus Troili*, see Fleming, *Classical Imitation and Interpretation*, 179–200. For a close examination of Chaucer's changes to his source, see Gaston, "'Save oure tonges difference,'" 275–83.

85 Gaston, "'Save oure tonges difference,'" 271. Gaston's larger point is that Chaucer is emulating the posture of translation from Latin into the *volgare* here: "Chaucer uses the narrator's professions of incompetence to explore the implications of a certain kind of translation practice, one that shares key details with the importation of Latin syntax and terminology among the later volgarizzatori."

86 Gaston, "'Save oure tonges difference,'" 271.

87 On the concordance of these two losses of faith, see, for example, Carolyn Dinshaw, *Chaucer's Sexual Poetics*, 44–5, who notes, "instability and uncertainty in the fable are centered in Criseyde; the necessary qualifications of the worth of the fable stem from dissatisfactions with the female character. The feminine, again, is the letter's uncontrollability – both its ambiguous and uncertain details and its final, unalterable outcome – especially as it is concentrated in Criseyde."

88 According to Dares and the Greek tradition, Briseis was twenty-one when Helen was abducted. See Stephen Barney's note to *Troilus and Criseyde* V.826 in the *Riverside Chaucer*, 1052. Barney cites Nathaniel E. Griffin, "Un-Homeric Elements in the Medieval Story of Troy."

89 Federico, *New Troy*, 78.

90 Utz, "'As Writ Myn Auctour Lollius,'" 137.

91 Chaucer's refusal to "tell all" has led some critics to question whether his lovers' union was, in fact, consensual. See especially L.O. Aranye Fradenburg, "'Oure owen wo to drynke,'" and Christopher Cannon, "Chaucer and Rape."

92 Chaucer repeats this offer at the end of his poem with the invitation to Gower and Strode to "correct" his work (V.1856–7).

93 Donaldson, "Criseide and Her Narrator," 81–2. Cf. David Lawton, *Chaucer's Narrators*, 87, who sees "no evidence for distinguishing between Chaucer and a wholly fictionalised and unreliable narrator who has fallen in love with Criseyde, strives to extenuate her, and only succeeds in making matters worse for her owing to the poet's cunning acts of sabotage."

94 Wallace, "Chaucer's Italian Inheritance," 48.
95 Wallace, "Chaucer's Italian Inheritance," 48.
96 Guido delle Colonne, *Historia*, ed. Griffin, 276 (35); the translation is from *Historia Destructiones Troiae*, trans. Mary Elizabeth Meek, 265.
97 Benson, *The History of Troy*, 135–6.
98 Citations of Dante's work are taken from *La Commedia*, ed. Giorgio Petrocchi, and are cited by canto and line number; translations are from Robert M. Durling and Ronald L. Martinez's *The Divine Comedy*, 261.
99 *Commedia*, ed. Petrocchi, *Inf* XVI.124–32; trans. Durling and Martinez, 253.
100 Barolini, *The Undivine Comedy*, 59.
101 Barolini, *The Undivine Comedy*, 58.
102 Hollander, "Dante *Theologus-Poeta*," 279–80.
103 I am not claiming that Dante constructs the *Commedia* as a fiction. He does, however, let us know through figures like Geryon that the literal story he tells is embellished, if not wholly invented, even if the pilgrim suggests the opposite. In Charles S. Singleton's famous words, *Dante Studies 1:"Commedia,"* 62, "the fiction of the *Divine Comedy* is that it is not a fiction."
104 Henryson, *Testament*, 352. According to Elizabeth Scala, *Absent Narratives, Manuscript Textuality, and Literary Structure in Late Medieval England*, 200, the "'vther quair' beside Chaucer's is no other than Henryson's *Testament*." If Chaucer directs his *Troilus* to kiss the steps of his epic predecessors, then Henryson does away with any pretence of adulation for previous authors by placing his book immediately adjacent to – and, by implication, as the equivalent of – his precursor, Chaucer's.
105 Monika Otter, "Functions of Fiction in Historical Writing," 111.
106 McKinley, *Chaucer's "House of Fame" and Its Boccaccian Intertexts*, 193, reads the *House of Fame* as just such a Boccaccian manifesto: "In some ways the *House of Fame* is ... almost a theoretical exploration of poetry of the kind seen in *Genealogia deorum*, Book 14, but woven into a dream vision narrative instead."

5 Chaucer through the Looking Glass: Lydgate's Chaucerian Poetics

1 See, for example, *Fall of Princes*, ed. Henry Bergen, *Prol.* 246 and 2.979. Henceforth, all citations from the *Fall* will be taken from this edition and noted in the text according to book and line number.
2 Nicholas Watson, "Outdoing Chaucer," Derek Pearsall, "Chaucer and Lydgate," esp. 47–52, and James Simpson, "Chaucer's Presence and Absence." According to Simpson, "by virtue of building onto his achievement, without underrating or monumentalizing it," fifteenth-century poets "reveal a confident readiness to enter into often competitive and productive conversation with Chaucer, freely adding to his works" (257).

3 Watson, "Outdoing Chaucer," 91. The full quotation reads, "at least two poets, Lydgate and Henryson, had an awareness of Chaucer's significance that went beyond mere imitation to express itself in an ambitious competitiveness worthy of Chaucer himself. Like Dante with Ovid and Lucan, or Boccaccio with Dante, Lydgate and Henryson treat Chaucer not only as a source, but as a challenge, a powerful and even threatening figure, some of whose authority they must annex as a vital part of their self-invention as poets."

4 Pearsall, "Chaucer and Lydgate," 47. Pearsall discusses Lydgate's mirroring and expansion of Chaucer's works on pages 47–52.

5 A.C. Spearing, *From Medieval to Renaissance in English Poetry*, 88–110, and Seth Lerer, *Chaucer and His Readers*. See also Maura Nolan, "Lydgate's Literary History," 61, 72, and Daniel T. Kline, "Father Chaucer and the Siege of Thebes." For a somewhat intermediate perspective, see David Lawton, "Dullness in the Fifteenth Century," 770, who discusses Lydgate's cultivation of dullness in relation to Chaucer, a dullness that is "almost always disingenuous" and developed in imitation of Chaucer's poetry. For Lawton, "dullness" is "the favorite guise in which its poets present themselves," a "humility topos of an intensely specific kind. It owes much to Chaucer, but it is used to a very different end" (762).

6 Lerer, *Chaucer and His Readers*, 3.

7 In chapter 1, I briefly discussed Lydgate's emulation of Chaucer's erasure of Boccaccio in his Oedipal *Siege of Thebes*. In this chapter, I will focus on the *Troy Book* and *Fall of Princes*, exploring how Lydgate emulates yet inverts a Chaucerian poetics by naming his predecessor while eliding the influence of his poetry. Indeed, Lydgate rarely shies away from naming Chaucer. Rather, as Robert Meyer-Lee points out, *Poets and Power from Chaucer to Wyatt*, 57, he was "among those most responsible for giving Chaucer's name [a] sort of currency." R.D. Perry, "Lydgate's Virtual Coteries," 672, suggests that the "frequency with which Chaucer is named in Lydgate's poems has no small part to play in our own understanding of Lydgate as an emphatically *Chaucerian* writer." We should also recall Watson's claim, "Politics of Middle English Writing," 347, that Lydgate "cultivated a relationship of dependence on Chaucer by depicting him as a poet worth citing and imitating, as Chaucer cited and imitated the classical *auctores*, Virgil and Ovid."

8 By "Chaucerian poems" I mean those Lydgate writes that have a clear thematic antecedent in Chaucer's poetry. A survey of these works demonstrates quite clearly that Lydgate positions himself after Chaucer in many literary traditions. As Robert R. Edwards notes, "Medieval Literary Careers," 106, "Writers have careers to the extent and in the way that they position themselves with respect to literary tradition. Patrons may initiate a work and the work may secure memory for its author or (more likely) its topic, but a writer becomes fully part of a literary culture when he creates a place …

within a textual genealogy. This is particularly crucial in the case of vernacular writers, who must locate themselves and their work in relation to classical *auctores* and classical literary models."

9 All citations of the *Troy Book* will be taken from *Troy Book*, ed. Bergen, and noted in the text according to book and line number. I normalize Bergen's *thorn* as th and *yogh* as gh or y.

10 Piero Boitani, "Boccaccio in Western Europe," 12.

11 Guyda Armstrong, *The English Boccaccio*, 20. David Rundle, *Renaissance Reform of the Book and Britain*, discusses the rise of Italian humanism in early fifteenth-century England, a development that no doubt explains why Boccaccio's writings would have gained in prestige and popularity from Chaucer's to Lydgate's time. Hoping to dispel "any shadows of doubt where assumptions lurk that the Renaissance only ventured across the channel during Henry VIII's reign" (273), Rundle argues that "humanism itself was not a static commodity," and "it was with its changing cinquecento identity – expanding and ultimately imploding – that the generations from Wyatt and Surrey to Spenser and Sidney interacted, just as their fifteenth-century predecessors had engaged with humanism's 'classic age' on its own terms." What is more, as Rundle shows with palaeographic evidence, by examining scribes, manuscripts, and books from this period, "The English were not idle spectators of the Renaissance's Quattrocento, but partners in its creation" (17).

12 Speaking of Chaucer's disappearance and then reappearance in the *Troy Book*, Sylvia Federico, *New Troy*, 131, observes that "authorial presence is granted, temporarily and incompletely, only by the dangerous strategy of absencing its others and thus exposing itself to the consequences of being made absent in turn."

13 In the words of Alan S. Ambrisco and Paul Strohm, "Succession and Sovereignty in Lydgate's Prologue to *The Troy Book*," 40, Lydgate's poem has a "recurring concern with matters of succession. Formally, this concern expresses itself within the problematics of the interrupted series, investigating whether, or rather demonstrating how, such an interruption in an ostensibly unbroken line of succession could be overcome and the series continued without affecting its received authority."

14 Edwards, ed., *Troy Book: Selections*, *Prol.* line 22, observes in his notes that Lydgate's praise of Henry "echoes Chaucer's supplication to King Henry IV, where the poet addresses the king as 'conquerour of Brutes Albyon.'"

15 Ambrisco and Strohm, "Succession and Sovereignty," 40.

16 For a discussion of "trouthe" and its significance in the later Middle Ages, see Richard Firth Green, *A Crisis of Truth*.

17 For the role of the Lancastrians in the production of "English" writing, see John Fisher, "A Language Policy for Lancastrian England."

18 Meyer-Lee, *Poets and Power*, 68.

19 Christopher Baswell, "*Troy Book*," 221.
20 Baswell, "*Troy Book*," 221.
21 Baswell, "*Troy Book*," 221. Earlier in this essay, Baswell suggests that Lydgate portrays himself and Henry as "intriguing mirror figures, using words and acts respectively to translate Troy and revive its empire for its British heirs" (218). For Lydgate as a parallel of Henry, see also Lee Patterson, *Negotiating the Past*.
22 In the words of Federico, *New Troy*, 122, from the perspective of the *Troy Book*, Chaucer "was doomed to become a Ricardian poet, despite his repeated refusal to engage overtly with his own political moment."
23 Federico, *New Troy*, 123, suggests that Lydgate's decision to connect the Lancastrians to Troy by forging an illustrious ancestry necessitated the excision of not only Richard but also Chaucer "from the line of literary authorities on the matter of Troy." She attributes Chaucer's absence from Lydgate's lineage to the poet's initial efforts to unseat his predecessor: "Repeating verbatim the list to which Chaucer implicitly joined himself at the end of *Troilus*," she observes, "Lydgate nevertheless fails to include Chaucer himself. It is a telling omission, or rather, replacement: instead of Chaucer, Lydgate claims his literary authority from Guido delle Colonne, one major author noticeably not invoked at the end of *Troilus and Criseyde*."
24 Although not naming Chaucer until the second book of *Troy Book*, Lydgate draws our attention to his imitation of Chaucer's poetry – and Chaucer's poetics – much earlier in the work. At the beginning of the prologue, for example, he praises Guido volubly, but in language borrowed from Chaucer: "Laude and honour & excellence of fame, / O Guydo maister, be vn-to thi name / That excellest by souereinte of stile /… / Whom I schal folwe as nyghe as euer I may" (*Prol.* 371–3, 375). Despite his lack of mention of Chaucer here, this passage contains a clear allusion to the *Legend of Dido* (1–4): "Glory and honour, Virgil Mantuan, / Be to thy name! and I shal, as I can, / Folow thy lantern, as thou gost biforn, / How Eneas to Dido was forsworn." Of course, as I discussed in my Introduction, Chaucer's claim that he will try to emulate Virgil is misleading, because Chaucer does not "follow" Virgil's example at all, instead writing a thoroughly Ovidian version of Dido's story. Lydgate's use of Chaucer's poetry to suggest his fidelity to Guido – a fidelity that is likewise overstated, with Lydgate increasingly turning away from Guido toward Chaucer as a model (see Baswell, "*Troy Book*," 226) – is thus oddly fitting, since this passage shows him dissimulating and effacing his sources (in this case, Chaucer) in a very Chaucerian way. I am grateful to Meyer-Lee for suggesting that I include this passage in my discussion of the *Troy Book*.
25 For Lydgate's reading public, see especially Maura Nolan, *John Lydgate and the Making of Public Culture*, C. David Benson, "Civic Lydgate," Claire

Sponsler, "Lydgate and London's Public Culture," and Sponsler, *The Queen's Dumbshows*, 36–8.

26 Ambrisco and Strohm, "Succession and Sovereignty," 48.

27 Ambrisco and Strohm, "Succession and Sovereignty," 50. See also Strohm, *England's Empty Throne*. Lee Patterson, "Making Identities in Fifteenth-Century England," 77, notes that the "constitutionality of Henry's position" when he became king of England "was far from certain"; heir to a usurper, and active participant from 1410 to 1412 in rebellion against his father, Henry did little to alleviate the public's "grave concern about the capacity of the Lancastrian regime to govern."

28 Ambrisco and Strohm, "Succession and Sovereignty," 50.

29 Strohm, "Hoccleve, Lydgate, and the Lancastrian Court," 653. Italics added.

30 Federico, *New Troy*, 122, argues that excising the former king from Henry's "noble line of descent" was necessary to the process of linking the "new Lancastrian dynasty with the Trojan history previously attached to Richard II."

31 On fifteenth-century poets' use of Chaucer to legitimize their writings, see especially Christopher Cannon, *The Making of Chaucer's English*, 185, who suggests that poets "define[d] their poetic purpose" by using Chaucer's poetry to "claim privileged status for their own efforts," and Lerer, *Chaucer and His Readers*, 18–19, who claims that the poet's successors sought to "establish their relationship to Chaucer by appealing to some kind of personal relationship to [him]." Federico, *New Troy*, 103, addresses "the curious absence of Chaucer in the fifteenth century." Drawing on Stephen Partridge ("Questions of Evidence," 6), she notes the "frequent failure" in surviving manuscripts of his poetry "to attribute Chaucer's works to him," and suggests that this absence was not antithetical to Chaucer's status as an authority. Although it is "well known that it was in the early fifteenth century, rather than in his own day, that Chaucer's imitators flourished and that he was identified as a major figure in English poetry … [T]he silencing, or even murder, of one type of reputation is the prerequisite for the emergence of another" (103).

32 As Patterson observes, "Making Identities in Fifteenth Century England," 74, "at least since the time of Henry II," the Troy narrative "served to support the legitimacy of insecure English kings." See also *Negotiating the Past*, 201–4.

33 In Patterson's words, *Negotiating the Past*, 203, he commissioned for himself "a deluxe manuscript of the finest Trojan poem written in the Middle Ages." Jeanne E. Krochalis, "The Books and Reading of Henry V and His Circle," 63, speculates whether it was reading Chaucer's poem that prompted Henry to patronize Lydgate's *Troy Book*. It should be noted, however, that this manuscript, Morgan MS 817, does not identify Chaucer as the author of the *Troilus*. On the absence of Chaucer's name in fifteenth-century manuscripts of his works, see Partridge, "Questions of Evidence."

34 As Ambrisco and Strohm observe, *Succession and Sovereignty*, 55n7, although "Lydgate does not specifically fault Lollius's version of the Troy story as he does Homer's and Virgil's (a good move, as he could not have said anything specific about the nonexistent text)," in "grouping him with these two authors, it seems reasonable that Lydgate considered Lollius part of the false tradition and distinct from the tradition of which he himself is a part." Robert R. Edwards, alternatively, "John Lydgate and the Remaking of Classical Epic," 472, suggests that Lydgate positions Lollius "ambiguously ... between the supposedly mendacious classical poets imitating Homer and the genealogy of reliable forgers of chronicles." Of course, Lydgate's anti-Homeric rhetoric is in lockstep with the narrative philosophy of Lydgate's anti-Homeric sources. Dares and Dictys, Benoît de Sainte-Maure, and Guido delle Colonne all condemn the fallibility of Homer and his epic successors. The major difference is that Lydgate includes Lollius, Chaucer's fabricated source for *Troilus and Criseyde*, among these fabricators, and so implicates himself and Chaucer in this tradition of fraud.

35 Citations from *Troilus* are taken from the *Riverside Chaucer*. All further citations will be noted in the text.

36 For Lydgate's laureate ambitions, see especially Pearsall, *John Lydgate*, 160–91. For Lydgate's use of Chaucer to establish his laureate pretensions, see Meyer-Lee, *Poets and Power*, esp. 72–3.

37 Lydgate's language of praise hints at this possibility: Chaucer is the "chefe poete thst ever was *yit* in oure langage," the *yet* leaving space for Lydgate's apotheosis.

38 Harold Bloom, *The Anxiety of Influence*, xxiii, argues that "the anxiety of influence *comes out of* a complex act of strong misreading, a creative interpretation that I call 'poetic misprision.'"

39 Watson, "Outdoing Chaucer," 91. Watson further notes that Chaucer is "scarcely mentioned in the *Troy Book* except in association with the [false] Criseyde" (97). The *Troy Book* should thus be viewed as a "complex ac[t] of literary theft," and one in which Lydgate "sets the stage for an extended critique of ... *Troilus and Criseyde*, and through it of Chaucer" (91, 92–3).

40 Pearsall, "Chaucer and Lydgate," 43. While Pearsall is referring here to the *Siege*, he discusses the *Troy Book* in this chapter as well. See also Simpson, "Chaucer's Presence and Absence," 260, who locates a "confidently competitive response to Chaucer in Lydgate's poetry." An example of "fraternal" if not "Oedipal rivalry" (159), the *Troy Book* builds "accretively and conversationally" onto the *Troilus* (260). Edwards, ed. *Troy Book: Selections*, 12, likewise suggests that at the same time that the poem "proclaims discipleship," the *Troy Book* "competes with Chaucer's poem in the scope of its ambition." "Following perhaps the narrator's suggestion in *Troilus and Criseyde* (1.144–5) that 'the Troian gestes' can be found '[i]n Omer, or in Dares, or in Dite' for whoever can read them, Lydgate seeks to go beyond his master" (12).

41 Patterson, "Making Identities in Fifteenth Century England," 131. Henry also unites the crowns of France and England, which Lydgate presents as a moment of unification (e.g., *Troy Book* 5.3375–91, "Henry VI's Triumphal Entry into London," 411). It is possible that, in combining Chaucer and Guido, Lydgate is likewise presenting himself as a figure responsible for unifying disparate factions.

42 See also 3.4197, 3.4215, and 5.3521.

43 Federico, *New Troy*, 125. Strohm, "Hoccleve, Lydgate, and the Lancastrian Court," 645, similarly suggests that Chaucer is for Lydgate a figure of "unquestioned legitimacy." Baswell, "*Troy Book*," 219, 231, qualifies Chaucer as Lydgate's "legitimating beloved," who paves the way for his own poem by enabling its author to "implicitly cas[t] himself as the new if inadequate Chaucer." Meyer-Lee, *Poets and Power*, 72–3, sees Lydgate's praise of Chaucer as, at least in part, self-serving: "By singling out Chaucer's 'rethorik' for praise, Lydgate … cannily creates a verbal basis the inheritability of the retroactively bestowed role of 'poete of Breteyne.'" Since "Chaucer is dead and the seat vacated, he has opened up a space for himself in the present for precisely this role" (72).

44 Watson, "Outdoing Chaucer," 95, suggests that Lydgate is a "confessedly derivative poet, tamely structuring his poem in the same five-book form as Chaucer, taking over the decasyllabic couplets of most of the *Canterbury Tales* and recycling most of Chaucer's imagery, syntax and vocabulary." In the words of Lois Ebin, *John Lydgate*, 47, Lydgate "seizes every opportunity to amplify Guido's matter, routinely expanding the characters' speeches, the descriptive passages about the places the Greeks land, and the appearance and traits of characters."

45 Baswell, "*Troy Book*," 226. For Baswell, Lydgate's open reliance on Chaucer evolves as his poem proceeds: Lydgate "will increasingly replace a Latin model of rhetorical linguistic accomplishment … with a native model of accomplished eloquence in the person of 'My maister Chaucer'" (216).

46 Watson, "Outdoing Chaucer," 93. Edwards, ed., *Troy Book: Selections*, 12, suggests that the "pentameter couplets of the *Troy Book* are modeled on Chaucer's later work in the *Canterbury Tales*, while the rhyme royal stanzas of the Envoy recall the *Parliament of Fowls*, *Troilus*, and works probably composed earlier and then added to the *Canterbury Tales*."

47 Watson, "Outdoing Chaucer," 97, notes that this behaviour is a pattern for Lydgate: "rather than translating Guido's Latin" for the episodes concerning Troilus and Criseyde, Lydgate "ostentatiously turns to his 'maister', basing most of the first of Criseyde's appearances on parts of *Troilus and Criseyde*, and pretending to diffidence in describing her when Chaucer (whose death is lamented at length) has incomparably done so first."

48 See, for example *LGW* 925 and *HF* 143. In both of these instances, Chaucer, too, is "sette … amyddes tweyne," caught between the two conflicting accounts of Dido by Virgil and Ovid.

49 Pearsall, "Chaucer and Lydgate," 40–1. See also Baswell, "*Troy Book*," 229.

50 See Baswell, "*Troy Book*," 232, who suggests that Lydgate "finds himself at an impossible choice between service to the authority of Guido or of Chaucer."

51 "Behind the mask of the seeming 'point to point'-correspondence of original and translation," as Wolfram Keller suggests, *Shakespearean Medievalism*, 134, "one discovers Lydgate's own changeability."

52 For the "sixth of six *topos*," see Wallace, *Chaucer and the Early Writings of Boccaccio*, 50–3, and *Chaucerian Polity*, 80–1.

53 The *Fall* is, as Larry Scanlon has observed (*Narrative, Authority, and Power*, 322), "governed by the trope of translation."

54 Meyer-Lee, *Poets and Power*, 78.

55 Armstrong, *The English Boccaccio*, 74.

56 In form if not in content, Lydgate's literary output is modelled rather precisely on Chaucer's. To provide a few salient examples, the *Complaint of the Black Knight* adapts the *Book of the Duchess*. The *Temple of Glass* mirrors the *House of Fame*. To *Troilus and Criseyde*, Lydgate responds as we have seen with the *Troy Book*. He writes the *Siege of Thebes* as the return journey of the *Canterbury Tales*. As for the "Monk's Tale," it receives its own Lydgatian expansion in the *Fall of Princes*. In these poems, as Pearsall notes ("Chaucer and Lydgate," 52), adding to this list *Reason and Sensuality*, the Marian poems, the saints' legends, and the *Fabula Duorum Mercalorum*, Lydgate "fortif[ies] and improve[s] upon successive Chaucerian models," even if the "improvement ... is generally of the kind that assumes two lines are better than one, and three lines better still." In Simpson's words, "John Lydgate," 207, Lydgate "addresses the Chaucerian oeuvre more consistently and energetically than any other writer except perhaps Henryson." See also Spearing, *From Medieval to Renaissance*, 66–8.

57 Cf. Scanlon, *Narrative, Authority, and Power*, 332, who sees the prologue as not only deferential but also part of a tradition of writings, including Chaucer's, that acknowledges their debts copiously: Lydgate "makes it quite clear that all his authorities owe their authoritative status precisely to their own respect for previous authority," presenting "Bochas as a compiler ... and Chaucer largely as a translator." Similarly, A.S.G. Edwards, "Lydgate's *Fall of Princes*, 24–5, sees Lydgate's pose as an English translator of classical and continental material as self-consciously Chaucerian: "Lydgate saw himself as operating within a tradition of translation established by Chaucer. He invokes his 'maistir' Chaucer as a translator from classical and other sources and as an implicit model."

58 This is not to say Lydgate's motivations for writing the *Fall* were primarily literary, only that he situates his treatment of Chaucer within literary, as opposed to political, history. Indeed, as Armstrong points out (*The English*

Boccaccio, 67), Lydgate's translation of the *De casibus* should be seen "first and foremost as emerging from [a] charged linguistic and political context, in which the creation of an English literary language, canon, and mythos is linked directly to the political fortunes and intentions of the ruling princes; seen in this light, it is nigh-on inevitable that this is the first named work of Boccaccio's to be transmitted into England and turned to the ends of this specific receiving context."

59 Armstrong, *The English Boccaccio*, 11.

60 For Humphrey's role in Lydgate's poetry, see, for example, E.P. Hammond, "Poet and Patron in the *Fall of Princes*," and Alessandra Petrina, *Cultural Politics in Fifteenth-Century England*, 294–312.

61 Armstrong, *The English Boccaccio*, 67–70.

62 For the distinction between these roles, see Alastair Minnis, *Medieval Theory of Authorship*, esp. 73–117, and Rita Copeland, *Rhetoric, Hermeneutics, and Translation in the Middle Ages*.

63 Boccaccio's disingenuous method of attribution has been commented on by critics. Meyer-Lee, for example ("John Lydgate's Major Poems," 66), suggests that Lydgate is practising a strategy of presenting himself as in dialogue with Boccaccio, a strategy "all the more visible to us because we know that Lydgate's actual source is not Boccaccio's mid-fourteenth-century Latin *De casibus virorum illustrium*, but rather Laurent de Premierfait's early fifteenth-century French prose translation of Boccaccio." Indeed, Lydgate's reliance on Laurent de Premierfait is so widely recognized that the only critics to consider his consultation of Boccaccio's original poem are, so far as I know, Petrina, *Cultural Politics*, 295, and Armstrong, *The English Boccaccio*, 71–94, something Armstrong herself notes (71).

64 Perry, "Lydgate's Virtual Coteries," 678, notes that by the time Lydgate wrote the *Fall*, he had already acquired numerous political connections, which suggests that "when Lydgate adds effusive praise to Chaucer throughout the poem that Gloucester commissioned … it likely testifies less to his need to invoke the Chaucer family for pecuniary ends and more to his desire to have Chaucer's skill and success be a part of that poem's creation."

65 Although titles in medieval poetry are not always authorial, Bergen ("Introduction," *The Fall of Princes*, 1:ix) suggests that in this case we may be certain that Lydgate named his poem himself: "there is no doubt that Lydgate himself called his book 'The Fall of Princes.' He refers directly to it in lines VL 304 and IX.3622, and in the same terms to Boccaccio's original, L 51, 77, 270, 471, HL 133, VL 231, and to Chaucer's 'Monk's Tale' of the same title, L 249 and IX.3422. He also used 'fall' as a subject of general interest (in reference to the opinions of Andalus di Nigri), III.174. 'Fallys' he uses once as a subject of general interest, IX.3450, and … four times in reference to the 'fallis' of specific princes." Lydgate refers to the "Monk's Tale" as the "Fall of Princes" again at 9.3422, yet mentions the "Monkys Tale" at 9.3427.

66 It is possible that even Lydgate's description of Chaucer's literary process as an act of complaint, which has a primarily oral, as opposed to textual, connotation, is also intended as deflationary, separating Chaucer from the *Fall*'s textual progenitors. Although by this point the complaint is a literary genre, among the word's possible meanings, the *OED* defines "compleyne" as "to bewail," "to give expression to sorrow," and "to give expression to feelings of illusage," all of which convey this oral usage. This description also suggests that the "Monk's Tale" is *itself* a complaint, a lyric form popular in the Middle Ages, and the provenance of *makers* and court poets. The complaint is a poem in which there is, in the words of Pearsall, *John Lydgate*, 92–3, "no movement, no action, only the lover and his mistress for ever frozen into ritual gestures of beseeching and disdain." For Patterson, *Chaucer and the Subject of History*, 53–4, "like the other kinds of fetishized objects with which the aristocratic world adorned itself (tapestries, jewelry, books): the complaint beautifully stages, over and over again, a reified extravagance, a petrified excess."

67 For Lydgate's Lucretia, see Petrina, *Cultural Politics*, 302–5, as well as her chapter, "A Stranger in the Margins," in *Boccaccio and the European Literary Tradition*. Petrina, "A Stranger in the Margins," 80, suggests that with his portrait of Lucretia, Lydgate means to "stage a philological discussion on the comparative merits of Chaucer's and Coluccio Salutati's versions, a discussion that involves Lydgate's patron and (possibly) advisor, Humphrey ... While Chaucer's version is already available to the English reader, Lydgate undertakes to translate Salutati's." There is also a politics to Lydgate's choice of Salutati, as Jennifer Summit, *Memory's Library*, has discussed. Boccaccio's version "reads Tarquin's exile as a story of tyranny justly punished, a warning against the evils of tyranny, and a reminder of the power of the people to overthrow unjust rulers" (46). As "reread and glossed by Lydgate," however, "the story of Lucrece is made to uphold a very different lesson. Following his faithful translation of Salutati's text, Lydgate reinterprets the story as an example of the tragic aftereffects of bad governance." He "offers Lucrece's story as an extension of his lesson, from *Polycraticus*, that the hierarchical ordering of the kingdom will produce harmonious coexistence, while disorder and riot will ensue when that order is violated" (46–7).

68 For Lydgate's Zenobia, see Nigel Mortimer, *John Lydgate*'s "*Fall of Princes,*" 174–8. Mortimer notes that Lydgate draws primarily on Boccaccio and Laurent for this episode, in this instance alone following Chaucer's previous source. Chaucer's influence is, by constrast, not prominent. Perhaps because Chaucer himself never acknowledges his debt to his Italian source, Lydgate is not concerned, as he is in other instances, with retreading Chaucerian territory here.

69 A particularly striking example of Lydgate evading acknowledging Chaucer's influence occurs in his retelling of the Troy story in the *Fall*. As he has done in nearly every instance involving a textual precedent for his work, Lydgate

prefaces this episode by questioning the need to retell this story. In this case, however, the textual precedent he must contend with is not Chaucer's *Troilus* but rather his own *Troy Book*. The story of Troilus and Criseyde, "and how Cressaide loued Diomeede" (1.6016), is "hool in Troie Book is said, / Reudli endited off my translacioun, / Folwyng vpon the destruccioun." (1.5946–8). For this reason, "as me semeth, the labour were in veyn. / Treuli also I not to what entent, / That I shold[e] write it newe ageyn" (1.5951–2). But if there is ever a place to mention Chaucer's influence on his work, it is here, in Lydgate's discussion of Troilus and Criseyde, especially because Chaucer's *Troilus* is Lydgate's source for much of this material in the *Troy Book*. Lydgate, however, absorbs the *Troilus* into the *Troy Book*, here positioning his earlier poem as his own Trojan authority. If Chaucer's role as the authority on these lovers was recognized in the *Troy Book*, it is all but forgotten here.

70 Elizabeth Scala, *Absent Narratives*, 4.

71 Jacques Derrida, *Of Grammatology*, 23.

72 Gian Biagio Conte, *The Rhetoric of Imitation*, 27, advises readers to look beyond potential psychological motivations for authors imitating one another. The scholar "who seeks at all costs to read intention into imitation will inevitably fall into a psychological reconstruction of motive, whether it is homage, admiring compliment, parody, or the attempt to improve upon the original. If poetic memory is reduced to the impulse to emulate, the production of the text will be devoted to the relationship between two subjectivities, and the literary process will center more on the personal will of two opposing authors than on the structuring reality of the text." Conte takes an extreme view – one in which authorial intention is hardly the most significant factor in reconstructing meaning. And I am by no means suggesting that we take authors out of our study of texts entirely; indeed, Scala's brilliant reading of the *Canterbury Tales* as generated by a series of "misreadings" is incentive enough to consider authorial motivation as a factor in constructing meaning (*Desire in the "Canterbury Tales,"* 41). I do, however, think our focus on the particular desires/aggressions of individual authors sometimes comes at the expense of recognizing larger patterns of emulation – tropes and traditions – skewing our perception toward the subjective in our analysis of literary history.

73 Maura Nolan has commented repeatedly on the ways that Lydgate's intertextual complexity complicates a moral or unilateral reading of his poetry. In her reading of the *Fall* ("'Now Wo, Now Gladnesse,'" 537–8), for example, she rightly notes that the "very mixed bag of authorities and sources that Lydgate employs and attempts to synthesize makes simple moralization impossible." Elsewhere, looking at the "Disguising of London" (*John Lydgate and the Making of Public Culture*, 3), she observes that Lydgate stymies a purely political interpretation of his words: he "presents his audience with a moralized allegory of Fortune and the four cardinal virtues. The lesson seems obvious:

resist the vagaries of Fortune by embracing virtue. On closer examination, however, it becomes clear that the text is both a very complex meditation of the philosophical problem of contingency, and a multilayered response to both Latin and vernacular source texts. Were Lydgate a pure propagandist, he would eschew this kind of intertextuality in favor of didacticism. But he does not."

74 As Simpson writes, "Chaucer's Presence and Absence," 256–7, this is the "fullest fifteenth-century list of Chaucer's works," and serves potentially as a "way of reminding Lydgate's own patron ... of the value of patronage."

75 I discuss the figure of Chaucer's Trophee in chapter 3.

76 Cf. George L. Kittredge, "Chaucer's Lollius," 60, who suggests that while "Chaucer's 'Trophee' may be a mystery ... Lydgate's is not. It has no foundation or genesis save in this passage in *The Monk's Tale*, misapplied by a constitutional blunderer, and it need trouble us no more."

77 Armstrong, *The English Boccaccio*, 32, likens the frame narrative of the *De casibus* to that of the *Decameron*: "As he did in the *Decameron*, Boccaccio organizes his material within a framing superstructure based on the illusion of interaction and conversation. But whereas the third-person narrators of the *Decameron cornice* take it in turns to tell each other stories on each of the ten days of storytelling, here Boccaccio (or better, 'the author-persona') relates the histories as a first-person account as the ghostly shades of the protagonists appear to him in a series of visions while he sits composing the work in his room."

78 See Armstrong, *The English Boccaccio*, 48.

79 Mortimer, *John Lydgate's "Fall of Princes,"* 37.

80 Boccaccio, *De casibus virorum illustrium*, ed. Ricci and Zaccaria, *Tutte le opere*, 9:866 (IX.27), "Pauci flentes et libri conclusio." For Laurent, this is altogether too generous. In his own rendition of this narrative, he supplements Boccaccio's material with personal diatribes against the English and snide remarks in reference to the suspicious circumstances surrounding John's death, all the while upholding the fiction that he is translating Boccaccio precisely. For the King John narrative in all three versions, see Mortimer, *John Lydgate's "Fall of Princes,"* 38–9.

81 Lawton, "Dullness in the Fifteenth Century," 785, suggests that Lydgate focuses on Boccaccio because the Italian poet is "useful to Lydgate in the role of authority in ways that he was not to Chaucer." If Lydgate's repeated emphasis on Boccaccio was motivated by a desire to harness his authoritative prowess, however, why would he be so keen to highlight Boccaccio's prejudices and shortcomings – his "parcial writing" and "ful narwe" thinking?

82 Summit, *Memory's Library*, 37, observes that throughout the *Fall*, Lydgate pictures Bochas "not only in the act of writing but in a place in which he is surrounded by books." Lydgate's studies are, moreover, monuments: the

poem's library setting "supports the book's larger aims and methods. As Lydgate's prologue insists, Bochas intends his book 'for a memoriall,' and he draws on the multiple sources that he 'hath gadred out ... in dyuers bookes which that he hath rad' ... an action of reading across multiple sources that is enabled by the book's library setting" (39). For the importance of memory in the Middle Ages, see Mary J. Carruthers, *The Book of Memory*.

83 Summit, *Memory's Library*, 40.

84 According to Perry, "Lydgate's Virtual Coteries," 671, virtual coteries "place poets, their sources or inspiration, and patrons together as necessary elements in the construction of a poem." They are a "record of distributed agency that details what a poet, a patron, or a source does to make a poem."

85 Mary C. Flannery, *John Lydgate and the Poetics of Fame*, 106. Perhaps the most extensive of these scenes is the lengthy prologue to Book 4, which is devoted to cataloguing the names of authors and their works, and which Flannery discusses at length in her fifth chapter ("Promotion and Self-Promotion," 105–28).

86 Flannery, *John Lydgate and the Poetics of Fame*, 92.

87 Cf. Petrina, "A Stranger in the Margins," 81–2, who, while likewise aligning Lydgate's intertextual poetics with Chaucer's, sees Lydgate's turn away from Chaucer to other authors as motivated by his desire to shape a line of textual continuity: there is a "level at which the Chaucerian influence intersects Lydgate's exploration of Giovanni Boccaccio. In choosing to translate Petrarch's Latin version of Boccaccio's tale of Griselda and propose it as the Clerk's contribution in the Canterbury Tales, Chaucer not only shows once more his interest for Boccaccio's vast literary production, which he explored repeatedly in his works; he also asks his readers to reflect on a line of continuity in the nascent Italian literature, between Petrarch and Boccaccio, which he then openly imitates in the prologue of the *Clerk's Tale* ... The triangulation between Petrarch, Chaucer, and Boccaccio is fruitfully explored by Lydgate in his *Fall.*"

88 Wallace, *Chaucerian Polity*, 80–1. See also Martin Eisner, *Boccaccio and the Invention of Italian Literature*, 6–7.

89 In Meyer-Lee's words, *Poets and Power*, 81, "By the end of the prologue, Lydgate, vis a vis his eulogistic relationships with Gloucester, Chaucer, and other poetic predecessors, has figured himself as ... heir of a long tradition of high-culture poetry."

90 Not only does this moment of "self-canonization" conclude with the inscription of his own name, as Scanlon notes (*Narrative, Authority, and Power*, 334), but by identifying his village Lydgate further replicates Boccaccio's mention of Certaldo in the *De casibus*.

91 Cannon, *The Making of Chaucer's English*, 186.

92 Lewis Carroll, *Alice in Wonderland*, 18.

Bibliography

Primary Sources

Alain of Lille. *De fide catholica contra haereticos. Patrologia latina* 210: cols. 431–82. Ed. J.P. Migne. Turnholt: Brepols Editores Pontificii, 1855, 1976.

Benoît de Sainte-Maure. *Le Roman de Troie*. Ed. Léopold Constans. 6 vols. Paris: Librairie de Firmin Didot, 1904–12.

– *The Roman de Troie*. Trans. Glyn S. Burgess and Douglas Kelly. Cambridge: D.S. Brewer, 2017.

Daniello, Bernardino. *L'espositione di Bernardino Daniello da Lucca sopra la Comedia di Dante*. Ed. Robert Hollander and Jeffrey Schnapp, with Kevin Brownlee and Nancy Vickers. Hanover, NH: University Press of New England, 1989.

Boccaccio, Giovanni. *Amorosa visione*. Bilingual Edition. Trans. Robert Hollander, Timothy Hampton, and Margherita Frankel. Hanover, NH: University Press of New England, 1986.

– *Boccaccio on Poetry, Being the Preface and Fourteenth and Fifteenth Book of Boccaccio's* "Genealogia Deorum." Trans. Charles G. Osgood. Princeton: Princeton University Press, 1930.

– *The Book of Theseus: Teseida delle Nozze d'Emilia*. Trans. Bernadette Marie McCoy. New York: Medieval Text Association, 1974.

– *La caccia di Diana e le rime*. Ed. Aldo Franscesco Massèra. Turin: Unione Tipografica-Editrice Torinese, 1914.

– *Chaucer's Boccaccio: Sources for "Troilus" and the "Knight's" and "Franklin's Tales."* Trans. N.R. Havely. Woodbridge, Suffolk: D.S. Brewer, 1980.

– *The Decameron*. Trans. G.H. McWilliam. 2nd edn. Harmondsworth: Penguin, 1995.

– *Il Filocolo*. Trans. Donald Cheney, with Thomas Bergin. New York: Garland Library of Medieval Literature, 1985.

– *The Filostrato of Giovanni Boccaccio*. Trans. Nathaniel E. Griffin. New York: Biblo and Tannen, 1967.

– *Genealogy of the Pagan Gods.* Trans. John Solomon. Vol. 1. *I Tatti* Renaissance series. Cambridge, MA: Harvard University Press, 2011.
– *Giovanni Boccaccio: The Downfall of the Famous* (originally titled *The Fates of Illustrious Men*). Trans. Louis Brewer Hall. New York: Italica Press, 2018.
– *Teseida delle Nozze d'Emilia.* Ed. Edvige Agostinelli and William Coleman. Florence: SISMEL, 2015.
– *Tutte le opere di Giovanni Boccaccio.* Gen. ed. Vittore Branca. 10 vols. Milan: Mondadori, 1964–98.
Borges, Jorge Luis. "Pierre Menard, Author of the *Quixote.*" *Jorge Luis Borges: Collected Fictions.* Trans. Andrew Hurley, 88–95. New York: Viking Press, 1998.
Carroll, Lewis. *Alice in Wonderland.* Ed. Donald J. Gray. 3rd edn. New York: Norton, 2013.
Cavalcanti, Guido. *Rime.* Ed. Guido Favati. Milan: Ricciardi, 1957.
Chaucer, Geoffrey. *The Complete Works of Geoffrey Chaucer.* Ed. Walter William Skeat. 7 vols. 2nd edn. Oxford: Clarendon Press, 1899.
– *The Riverside Chaucer.* Gen. ed. Larry D. Benson. 3rd edn. Boston: Houghton Mifflin, 1987.
– *The Works of Geoffrey Chaucer.* Ed. F.N. Robinson. 2nd edn. Boston: Houghton Mifflin, 1957.
Cicero. *Tusculan Disputations.* Ed. and trans. J.E. King. Loeb Classical Library. Cambridge, MA: Harvard University Press, 1927.
Dante Alighieri. *La Commedia secondo l'antica vulgata.* Ed. Giorgio Petrocchi. 4 vols. Milan: Mondadori, 1966–7; corr. repr. edn. Florence: Le Lettere, 1994.
– *Convivio.* Ed. Franca Brambilla Ageno. Florence: Le Lettere, 1995.
– *The Convivio.* Trans. Richard H. Lansing. New York: Garland Library of Medieval Literature, 1990.
– *Dante's "Vita Nuova."* Trans. Mark Musa. Bloomington: Indiana University Press, 1973.
– *De vulgari eloquentia.* Ed. Pio Rajna. Florence: Successori Le Monnier, 1896.
– *De vulgari eloquentia.* Trans. Steven Botterill. Cambridge: Cambridge University Press, 1996.
– *The Divine Comedy of Dante Alighieri.* Ed. and trans. Robert M. Durling and Ronald L. Martinez. Oxford: Oxford University Press, 1996–2011.
– *La vita nuova.* Ed. Michele Barbi. Florence: Le Lettere, Edizione nazionale della Società Dantesca Italiana, 1960.
Dares the Phrygian. *De excidio Troiae historia.* Ed. Ferdinand Meister. Leipzig: Teubner, 1873.
"The Fall of Troy: A History." *The Trojan War: The Chronicles of Dictys of Crete and Dares the Phrygian.* Trans. R.M. Frazer, 133–68. Bloomington: Indiana University Press, 1966.
Dictys of Crete. "A Journal of the Trojan War." *The Trojan War: The Chronicles of Dictys of Crete and Dares the Phrygian.* Trans. R.M. Frazer, 19–130. Bloomington: Indiana University Press, 1966.

Dino del Garbo. "La glossa Latina di Dino di Garbo." *Rime, by Guido Cavalcanti.* Ed. Guido Favati, 359–78. Milan: Ricciardi, 1957.

Douglas, Gavin. "Eneados." *Virgil's "Aeneid" Translated into Scottish Verse by Gavin Douglas.* Ed. David F.C. Coldwell. Edinburgh and London: Scottish Text Society, 1957–64.

Ennius. *The Annals of Quintus Ennius.* Ed. Otto Skutsch. Oxford: Oxford University Press, 1985.

Guido delle Colonne. *Historia Destructiones Troiae.* Ed. Nathaniel E. Griffin. Cambridge, MA: Medieval Academy of America, 1936.

– *Historia Destructiones Troiae.* Trans. Mary Elizabeth Meek. Bloomington: Indiana University Press, 1974.

Henryson, Robert. "The Testament of Cresseid." *The Story of Troilus.* Ed. R.K. Gordon, 351–67. Toronto: University of Toronto Press, 1978.

Horace. *Horace: Odes, Book II.* Ed. Stephen Harrison. Cambridge: Cambridge University Press, 2017.

– *The Odes of Horace.* Trans. David Ferry. New York: Farrar, Straus and Giroux, 1997.

Jerome. *Preface to Interpretatio Chronicas Eusebii Pamphili. Patrologia Latina* 27:36. Trans. W.H. Fremantle. *The Principal Works of Jerome, Select Library of Nicene and Post-Nicene Fathers of the Christian Church.* Grand Rapids: William B. Eerdmans, 1959.

John of Salisbury. *John of Salisbury: Polycraticus.* Trans. Cary J. Nederman. Cambridge: Cambridge University Press, 1990.

– *Policraticus: Ioannis Saresberiensis episcopi Carnotensis Policratici sive de nugis curialium et vestigiis philosophorum libri VIII.* 1156–9. Ed. Clement C.J. Webb. 2 vols. Oxford: Clarendon Press, 1909.

Lucan. *The Civil War.* Trans. J.D. Duff. Loeb Classical Library. Cambridge, MA: Harvard University Press, 1928.

Lucretius. *On the Nature of Things.* Trans. W.H.D. Rouse. Rev. Martin F. Smith. Loeb Classical Library. Cambridge, MA: Harvard University Press, 1992.

Lydgate, John. *Fall of Princes.* Ed. Henry Bergen. EETS es 121–4. London: Oxford University Press, 1924.

– *John Lydgate: The Siege of Thebes.* Ed. Robert R. Edwards. Rochester: TEAMS, 2001.

– *The Life of Saint Alban and Saint Amphibal.* Ed. J.E. Van der Westhuizen. Leiden: Brill, 1978.

– *Troy Book.* Ed. Henry Bergen. 4 vols. London: EETS es 97, 103, 106, 126. London: Kegan Paul, Trench, and Trübner, 1906–35.

Lactantius Placidus. *Lactantii Placidi qui dicitur Commentarios in Statii Thebaida et Commentarium in Achilleida.* Ed. Richard Jahnke. Leipzig: Teubner, 1898.

Ovid. *Heroides and Amores.* Trans. Grant Showerman. Loeb Classical Library 41. Cambridge, MA: Harvard University Press, 1914.

– *Metamorphoses*. Trans. Frank Justus Miller, rev. G.P. Goold. Loeb Classical Library. 2 vols. Cambridge, MA: Harvard University Press, 1916.

Oxford Latin Dictionary. Ed. P.G.W. Glare. 2 vols. 2nd edn. Oxford: Oxford University Press, 2012.

Petrarch, Francesco. *Africa*. Ed. Nicola Festa. *Edizione Nazionale*. Florence: G.C. Sansoni, 1926.

– *Le Familiari*. Ed. Vittorio Rossi and Umberto Bosco. 4 vols. (vol. 4 ed. Bosco). Florence: G.C. Sansoni, 1933–42.

– *Letters of Old Age: Rerum senilium libri I–XVII*. Trans. Aldo S. Bernardo, Saul Levin, and Reta A. Bernardo. 2 vols. Baltimore: Johns Hopkins University Press, 1992.

– *Letters on Familiar Matters, Rerum familiarium libri XVII–XXIV*. Trans. Aldo S. Bernardo. Baltimore: Johns Hopkins University Press, 1985.

– *The Life of Solitude*. Trans. Jacob Zeitlin. Urbana: University of Illinois Press, 1924.

– *Petrarch's Africa*. Trans. Thomas G. Bergin and Alice S. Wilson. New Haven: Yale University Press, 1977.

– *Prose*. Ed. Guido Martellotti. Milan: Ricciardi, 1995.

– *Res Seniles*. Ed. Silvia Rizzo and Monica Berté. 5 vols. Florence: Le Lettere, 2006–19.

– *Trionfi*. Ed. Vinicio Pacca and Laura Paolino. *Francesco Petrarca: Trionfi, Rime estravaganti, Codice degli abbozzi*. 2nd edn. Milan: Mondadori, 2000.

– *The Triumphs of Petrarch*. Trans. Ernest Hatch Wilkins. Chicago: University of Chicago Press, 1962.

Pliny. *Natural History, Volume IX: Books 33–35*. Trans. Harris Rackham. Cambridge, MA: Harvard University Press, 1952.

Propertius, Sextus. *Elegies*. Ed. and trans. G.P. Goold. Loeb Classical Library. Cambridge, MA: Harvard University Press, 1990.

Seneca the Elder. *Controversiae, VII–X. Suasoriae. Fragments*. Trans. Michael Winterbottom. Declamations II. 2 vols. Loeb Classical Library. Cambridge, MA: Harvard University Press, 1974.

Statius. *Silvae IV*. Ed. K.M. Coleman. Oxford: Clarendon Press, 1988.

Statius. *Statius*. Ed. and trans. D.R. Shackleton Bailey. Rev. by Christopher A. Parrott. 3 vols. Loeb Classical Library. Cambridge, MA: Harvard University Press, 2004–15 [first issued in 2003].

Virgil. *Eclogues; Georgics; Aeneid I–VI*. [1916; 1918] Ed. and trans. H. Rushton Fairclough. Rev. by G.P. Goold. 2 vols. Loeb Classical Library. Cambridge, MA: Harvard University Press, 1999; 2001.

William of Newburgh. *The History of English Affairs, Book 1*. Ed. and trans. P.G. Walsh and M.J. Kennedy. Warminster: Aris & Philips, 1988.

Zosimus. *Historia Nova*. Ed. James J. Buchanan and Harold T. Davis. San Antonio: Trinity University Press, 1967.

Secondary Sources

Acosta-Hughes, Benjamin, and Susan A. Stephens. *Callimachus in Context: From Plato to the Augustan Poets.* Cambridge: Cambridge University Press, 2012.

"The Afterlife of Origins." Colloquium. *Studies in the Age of Chaucer* 28 (2006): 217–70.

Albanese, Gabriella. "La corrispondenza fra Petrarca e Boccaccio." *Motivi e forme delle "Familiari" di Francesco Petrarca: Gargnano del Garda, 2–5 ottobre 2002.* Ed. Claudia Berrà, 39–98. Milan: Cisalpino, 2003.

Alfano, Giancarlo. *Introduzione alla lettura del "Decameron" di Boccaccio.* Rome: Laterza, 2014.

Alfano, Giancarlo, Teresa D'Urso, and Alessandra Perriccioli Saggese, eds. *Boccaccio angioino: Materiali per la storia culturale di Napoli nel Trecento.* Brussels: Peter Lang, 2012.

Alfano, Giancarlo, E. Grimaldi, S. Martelli, A. Mazzucchi, M. Palumbo, A. Perriccioli Saggese, and C. Vecce, eds. *Boccaccio e Napoli. Nuovi materiali per la storia culturale di Napoli nel Trecento. Atti del Convegno "Boccaccio angioino. Per il VII centenario della nascita di Giovanni Boccaccio." (Napoli–Salerno, 23–25 ottobre 2013).* Florence: Franco Cesati Editore, 2015.

Alfie, Fabian. "Reading Boccaccio's *Filostrato* as a Medieval Parody." *Forum Italicum* 32 (1998): 347–74.

Ambrisco, Alan S., and Paul Strohm. "Succession and Sovereignty in Lydgate's Prologue to *The Troy Book.*" *Chaucer Review* 30 (1995): 40–57.

Anderson, David. *Before the "Knight's Tale": Imitation of Classical Epic in Boccaccio's "Teseida."* Philadelphia: University of Pennsylvania Press, 1988.

Andreas, James R. "Chaucer's Defense of the Vulgar Tongue." *Postscript: The Journal of the Philological Association of the Carolinas* 9 (1992): 19–30.

Armstrong, Guyda. *The English Boccaccio: A History in Books.* Toronto: University of Toronto Press, 2013.

Banella, Laura. "'In persona d'alcuno passionate': Il 'ritratto d'autore' nei manoscritti del *Filostrato.*" *Studi sul Boccaccio* 41 (2013): 129–54.

Barański, Zygmunt G. "The Constraints of Form: Towards a Provisional Definition of Petrarch's *Triumphi.*" *Petrarch's Triumphs: Allegory and Spectacle.* Ed. Konrad Eisenbichler and Amilcare A. Iannucci, 63–83. Ottawa: Dovehouse Editions, 1990.

– "Petrarch, Dante, Cavalcanti." *Petrarch and Dante: Anti-Dantism, Metaphysics, Tradition.* Ed. Zygmunt G. Barański and Theodore J. Cachey, Jr., 50–113. Notre Dame: University of Notre Dame Press, 2009.

Barchiesi, Alessandro. "Future Reflexive: Two Modes of Allusion in the *Heroides.*" *Harvard Studies in Classical Philology* 95 (1993): 333–65.

– *Speaking Volumes: Narrative and Intertext in Ovid and Other Latin Poets.* Ed. and trans. Matt Fox and Simone Marchesi. London: Duckworth, 2001.

– *La traccia del modello: effetti omerici nella narrazione virgiliana; Homeric Effects in Vergil's Narrative.* Trans. Ilaria Marchesi and Matt Fox. Pisa: Giardini; Princeton and Oxford: Princeton University Press, 2015 (originally published 1984).

Barolini, Teodolinda. *Dante's Poets: Textuality and Truth in the "Comedy."* Princeton: Princeton University Press, 1984.

– "The Marquis of Saluzzo, or the Griselda Story Before It Was Hijacked: Calculating Matrimonial Odds in *Decameron* 10.10." *Mediaevalia* 34 (2013): 23–55.

– *The Undivine Comedy: Detheologizing Dante*. Princeton: Princeton University Press, 1992

Baswell, Christopher. "*Troy Book*: How Lydgate Translates Chaucer into Latin." *Translation Theory and Practice in the Middle Ages.* Ed. Jeanette Beer, 215–37. Kalamazoo: Medieval Institute Publications, 1997.

– *Virgil in Medieval England.* Cambridge: Cambridge University Press, 2006.

Bate, Walter Jackson. *John Keats.* Cambridge, MA: Harvard University Press, 1963.

Battles, Dominique. *The Medieval Tradition of Thebes: History and Narrative in the "Roman de Thebes," Boccaccio, Chaucer, and Lydgate.* New York: Routledge, 2004.

Beal, Rebecca S. "What Chaucer Did to an Orazion in the *Filostrato*: Calkas's Speech as Deliberative Oratory." *Chaucer Review* 44 (2010): 440–60.

Beard, Mary. *The Roman Triumph.* Cambridge, MA: Harvard University Press, 2007.

Beichner, P.E. "Daun Piers, Monk – Business Administrator." *Speculum* 34 (1959): 60–9.

Beidler, Peter. "Just Say Yes, Chaucer Knew the *Decameron*: Or, Bringing the Shipman's Tale Out of Limbo." *The Decameron and the Canterbury Tales: New Essays on an Old Question.* Ed. Leonard Michael Koff and Brenda Deen Schildgen, 25–46. Madison, NJ: Fairleigh Dickinson University Press, 2000.

– "New Terminology for Sources and Analogues: Or, Let's Forget the Lost French Source for the *Miller's Tale.*" *Studies in the Age of Chaucer* 28 (2006): 225–30.

Bennett, J.A.W. "Chaucer, Dante, Boccaccio." *Chaucer and the Italian Trecento.* Ed. Piero Boitani, 89–113. Cambridge: Cambridge University Press, 1983.

Benson, C. David. *Chaucer's Drama of Style: Poetic Variety and Contrast in the "Canterbury Tales."* Chapel Hill: University of North Carolina Press, 1986.

– "Civic Lydgate: The Poet and London." *John Lydgate: Poetry, Culture, and Lancastrian England.* Ed. Larry Scanlon and James Simpson, 147–68. Notre Dame: University of Notre Dame Press, 2006.

– *The History of Troy in Middle English Literature: Guido delle Colonne's Historia Destructionis Troiae in Medieval England.* Cambridge: D.S. Brewer, 1980.

– "The 'Knight's Tale' as History." *Chaucer Review* 3 (1968): 107–23.

Bergen, Henry. "Introduction." *The Fall of Princes.* Ed. Henry Bergen. EETS es 121–4. London: Oxford University Press, 1924.

Bernardo, Aldo S. "Introduction." *Rerum familiarium libri: I–VIII.* Albany: State University of New York Press, 1975.

– *Petrarch, Laura, and the Triumphs.* Albany: State University of New York Press, 1974.

– "Triumphal Poetry: Dante, Petrarch and Boccaccio." *Petrarch's Triumphs: Allegory and Spectacle.* Ed. Konrad Eisenbichler and Amilcare Iannucci, 33–45. Ottawa: Dovehouse Editions, 1990.

Berté, Monica, and Silvia Rizzo. "'Valete amici, valete epistole': l'ultimo libro delle *Senili.*" *Studi medievali e umanistici* 12 (2014): 71–108.

Bertelli, Sandro, and Davide Cappi. Eds. *Dentro l'officina di Giovanni Boccaccio. Studi sugli autografi in volgare e su Boccaccio Dantista.* Vatican City: Biblioteca Apostolica Vaticana, 2014.

Bessi, Rossella. "La Griselda del Petrarca." *Umanesimo volgare: studi di letteratura fra Tre e Quattrocento*, 279–92. Florence: Olschki, 2004.

Biggs, Frederick M. *Chaucer's "Decameron" and the Origin of the "Canterbury Tales."* Cambridge: D.S. Brewer, 2017.

Bloom, Harold. *The Anxiety of Influence: A Theory of Poetry.* [1973]. Oxford: Oxford University Press, 1997.

– *A Map of Misreading.* Oxford: Oxford University Press, 1975.

Boitani, Piero. "Boccaccio in Western Europe." *Boccaccio and the European Literary Tradition.* Ed. Piero Boitani and Emilia Di Rocca, 1–17. Rome: Edizioni di Storia e Letteratura, 2014.

– *Chaucer and Boccaccio.* Oxford: Society for the Study of Mediaeval Languages and Literature, 1977.

– *Chaucer and the Imaginary World of Fame.* Cambridge: D.S. Brewer, 1984.

– *Chaucer and the Italian Trecento.* Ed. Piero Boitani. Cambridge: Cambridge University Press, 1983.

– "The 'Monk's Tale': Dante and Boccaccio." *Medium Aevum* 45 (1976): 50–69.

– "'My Tale Is of a Cock,' or, The Problems of Literal Interpretation." *Literature and Religion in the Later Middle Ages: Philological Studies in Honor of Siegfried Wenzel.* Ed. Richard G. Newhauser and John A. Alford, 25–42. Binghamton, NY: Center for Medieval and Early Renaissance Studies, 1995.

– "What Dante Meant to Chaucer." *Chaucer and the Italian Trecento.* Ed. Piero Boitani, 115–40. Cambridge: Cambridge University Press, 1983.

Boli, Todd. "Among Boccaccio's Friends: A Profile of Mainardo Cavalcanti." Ed. Olivia Holmes and Dana E. Stewart, 98–106. *Reconsidering Boccaccio: Medieval Contexts and Global Intertexts.* Toronto: University of Toronto Press, 2018.

– "Review of the *Amorosa Visione*, ed. Hollander." *Speculum* 63 (1988): 625–7.

Bragantini, Renzo. "L'amicizia, la fama, il libro: sulla seconda epistola a Mainardo Cavalcanti." *Boccaccio 1313–2013.* Ed. Francesco Ciabattoni, Elsa Filosa, and Kristina Olson, 107–15. Ravenna: Longo Editore, 2015.

Branca, Vittore. *Boccaccio medievale*. 5th edn. Florence: Sansoni, 1981.

– "Copisti per passione, tradizione caratterizzante, tradizione di memoria." *Studi e problemi di critica testuale: Convegno di studi di filologia italiana nel centenario della Commisione per i testi di lingua, 7–9 aprile 1960*, 69–83. Bologna: Commissione per i testi di lingua, 1961.

– "Introduction." *Amorosa visione*. Ed. Robert Hollander. Hanover, NH: University Press of New England, 1986.

– *Tradizione delle opere di Giovanni Boccaccio*. Vol 2: *Un secondo elenco di manoscritti e studi sul testo del "Decameron" con due appendici*. Rome: Edizioni di Storia e Letteratura, 1991 [first printed in 1958].

Branca, Vittore, ed. *Boccaccio visualizzato: Narrare per parole e per immagini fra Medioevo e Rinascimento*. 3 vols. Turin: Einaudi, 1999.

Branca, Vittore, and Pier Giorgio Ricci. *Un autografo del "Decameron": Codice Hamiltoniano 90*. Florence: Olschki, 1962.

Bright, J.W. "Chaucer and Lollius" *PMLA* 18 (1903), xxii–xxiii.

Brink, Bernhard Ten. *Chaucer: Studien zur Geschichte seiner Entwicklung und zur Chronologie seiner Schriften*. Munster, Leipzig: Russell, 1870.

Brownlee, Kevin. "Power Plays: Petrarch's Genealogical Strategies." *Journal of Medieval and Early Modern Studies* 35 (2005): 467–88.

Bruni, Anna Bettarini, Giancarlo Breschi, and Giuliano Tanturli. "Giovanni Boccaccio e la tradizone dei testi volgari." *Boccaccio letterato. Atti del convegno internazionale: Firenze-Certaldo, 10–12 ottobre 2013*. Ed. Michaelangiola Marchiaro and Stefano Zamponi, 9–104. Florence: Accademia della Crusca, 2015.

Bruni, Francesco. *Boccaccio: l'invenzione della letteratura mezzana*. Bologna: Il Mulino, 1990.

Budra, Paul. *The Mirror for Magistrates and the De casibus Tradition*. Toronto: University of Toronto Press, 2000.

Burger, Glenn D. *Conduct Becoming: Good Wives and Husbands in the Later Middle Ages*. Philadelphia: University of Pennsylvania Press, 2017.

Burgess, Glyn S., and Douglas Kelly. *The Roman de Troie*. Cambridge: D.S. Brewer, 2017.

Bush, Douglas. "Chaucer's '*Corinne*.'" *Speculum* 4 (1929): 106–8.

Butterfield, Ardis. "The *Book of the Duchess*, Machaut, and the Image of the Archive." *Chaucer's "Book of the Duchess": Contexts and Interpretations*. Ed. Jamie C. Fumo, 199–212. London: D.S. Brewer, 2018.

– *The Familiar Enemy: Chaucer, Language, and Nation in the Hundred Years War*. Oxford: Oxford University Press, 2009.

Cachey, Theodore J., Jr. "Between Petrarch and Dante: Prolegomenon to a Critical Discourse." *Petrarch and Dante: Anti-Dantism, Metaphysics, Tradition*. Ed. Zygmunt G. Barański and Theodore J. Cachey, Jr., 3–49. Notre Dame: University of Notre Dame Press, 2009.

Campbell, Emma. "Sexual Poetics and the Politics of Translation in the Tale of Griselda." *Comparative Literature* 55 (2003): 191–216.

Cannon, Christopher. "Chaucer and Rape: Uncertainty's Certainties." *Representing Rape in Medieval and Early Modern Literature.* Ed. Elizabeth Robertson and Christine M. Rose, 255–79. New York: Palgrave, 2001.

– *From Literacy to Literature: England 1300–1400.* Oxford: Oxford University Press, 2016.

– *The Making of Chaucer's English: A Study of Words.* Cambridge: Cambridge University Press, 1998.

Cardillo, Giulia. "The Tale of Cisti the Baker: VI.2." *Decameron Sixth Day in Perspective*. Ed. David Lummus, 35–55. Toronto: University of Toronto Press, 2021.

Carruthers, Mary J. *The Book of Memory: A Study of Memory in Medieval Culture*. Cambridge. Cambridge University Press, 1990.

Casteen, Elizabeth. "On She-Wolves and Famous Women: Boccaccio, Politics, and the Neapolitan Court." *Reconsidering Boccaccio: Medieval Contexts and Global Intertexts.* Ed. Olivia Holmes and Dana Stewart, 219–45. Toronto: University of Toronto Press, 2018.

Celenza, Christopher S. "Petrarch, Latin, and Italian Renaissance Latinity." *Journal of Medieval and Early Modern Studies* 35 (2005): 509–36.

Chaucer and Fame: Reputation and Reception. Ed. Isabel Davis and Catherine Nall. Cambridge: D.S. Brewer, 2015.

Citroni, Mario. "The Concept of the Classical and the Canons of Model Authors in Roman Literature." *Classical Pasts: The Classical Traditions of Greece and Rome.* Ed. James I. Porter, 204–69. Princeton: Princeton University Press, 2005.

Clarke, K.P. *Chaucer and Italian Textuality.* Oxford: Oxford University Press, 2011.

– "On Copying and Not Copying *Griselda*: Petrarch and Boccaccio." *Boccaccio and the European Literary Tradition.* Ed. Piero Boitani and Emilia Di Rocco, 57–71. Rome: Edizioni di Storia e Letteratura, 2014.

– "Text and (Inter)Face: The Catchwords of Boccaccio's Autograph of the *Decameron*." *Reconsidering Boccaccio: Medieval Contexts and Global Intertexts*. Ed. Olivia Holmes and Dana Stewart, 27–47. Toronto: University of Toronto Press, 2018.

Coleman, Janet. "English Culture in the Fourteenth Century." *Chaucer and the Italian Trecento.* Ed. Piero Boitani, 33–64. Cambridge: Cambridge University Press, 1983.

Coleman, William E. "Chaucer's MS and Boccaccio's Commentaries on *Il Teseida*." *Chaucer Newsletter* 9 (1987): 1, 6.

– "The Knight's Tale." *Sources and Analogues of the Canterbury Tales.* Ed. Robert M. Correale and Mary Hamel. 2 vols. 2:87–247. Cambridge: D.S. Brewer, 2005.

A Companion to Vergil's "Aeneid" and Its Tradition. Ed. Joseph Farrell and Michael C.J. Putnam. Chichester: Wiley-Blackwell, 2010.

Conte, Gian Biagio. *The Rhetoric of Imitation: Genre and Poetic Memory in Virgil and Other Latin Poets.* Ed. Charles Segal. Ithaca: Cornell University Press, 1986.

Cooper, Helen. "The Four Last Things in Dante and Chaucer: Hugolino and the House of Rumour." *New Medieval Literatures* 3 (1999): 39–66.

– "The Frame." *Sources and Analogues of the "Canterbury Tales."* Ed. Robert M. Correale and Mary Hamel. 2 vols. 1:1–22. Cambridge: D.S. Brewer, 2002.

– *Oxford Guides to Chaucer: The Canterbury Tales*. 2nd edn. Oxford: Oxford University Press, 1996.

Copeland, Rita. *Rhetoric, Hermeneutics, and Translation in the Middle Ages: Academic Traditions and Vernacular Texts.* Cambridge: Cambridge University Press, 1991.

Cornish, Alison. "A Lady Asks: The Gender of Vulgarization in Late Medieval Italy." *PMLA* 115 (2000): 166–80.

– *Vernacular Translation in Dante's Italy: Illiterate Literature*. Cambridge: Cambridge University Press, 2010.

Cummings, Hubertis M. "The Indebtedness of Chaucer's Works to the Italian Works of Boccaccio." PhD Dissertation. Cincinnati: University of Cincinnati Studies, 1916.

Cursi, Marco. "Authorial Strategies and Manuscript Tradition." *Mediaevalia* 34 (2013): 87–110.

– "Boccaccio architetto e artefice di libri: i manoscritti danteschi e petrarcheschi." *Critica del testo* 16 (2013): 35–62.

– *La scrittura e i libri di Giovanni Boccaccio*. Rome: Viella, 2013.

Daniels, Rhiannon. *Boccaccio and the Book: Production and Reading in Italy 1340–1520.* London: Legenda, 2009.

– "Boccaccio's Narrators and Audiences." *The Cambridge Companion to Boccaccio*. Ed. Guyda Armstrong, Rhiannon Daniels, and Stephen J. Milner, 36–52. Cambridge: Cambridge University Press, 2015.

– "Reading Boccaccio's Paratexts: Dedications as Thresholds between Worlds." *Reconsidering Boccaccio: Medieval Contexts and Global Intertexts*. Ed. Olivia Holmes and Dana Stewart, 48–76. Toronto: University of Toronto Press, 2018.

– "Rethinking the Critical History of the *Decameron*: Boccaccio's Epistle XXII to Mainardo Cavalcanti." *MLR* 106 (2011): 423–47.

D'Avray, David L. *Medieval Marriage: Symbolism and Society.* Oxford: Oxford University Press, 2005.

Delaney, Sheila. *The Naked Text: Chaucer's "Legend of Good Women."* Berkeley: University of California Press, 1994.

Derrida, Jacques. *Of Grammatology.* [1974]. Trans. Gayatri Chakravorty Spivak. Baltimore: Johns Hopkins University Press, 1997.

DeRobertis, Teresa, Carla Maria Monti, Marco Petoletti, Giuliano Tanturli, and Stefano Zamponi, eds. *Boccaccio autore e copista*. Florence: Mandragora, 2013.

Desmond, Marilyn. "Chaucer and the Textualities of Troy." *The Oxford Handbook of Chaucer*. Ed. Suzanne Conklin Akbari and James Simpson, 238–51. Oxford: Oxford University Press, 2020.

– "Ovid's *Heroides* 3 and the *inventio* of Criseyde in the Medieval Matter of Troy." *Illinois Classical Studies* 46 (2021): 139–61.

– *Reading Dido: Gender, Textuality, and the Medieval "Aeneid."* Minneapolis: University of Minnesota Press, 1994.

– "*Translatio imperii* and the Matter of Troy in Angevin Naples: BL Royal MS 20 D I and Royal MS 6 E IX." *Italian Studies* 72 (2017): 177–91.

DiMarco, Vincent. "Another Look at Chaucer's 'Trophee.'" *Names: A Journal of Onomastics* 34 (1986): 275–83.

Dinshaw, Carolyn. *Chaucer's Sexual Poetics.* Madison: University of Wisconsin Press, 1989.

Dominik, William J. "Following in Whose Footsteps? The Epilogue to Statius' *Thebaid.*" *Literature, Art, History: Studies on Classical Antiquity and Tradition.* Ed. André Basson and William J. Dominik, 91–110. Frankfurt: Peter Lang, 2003.

Donaldson, E. Talbot. "Criseide and Her Narrator." *Speaking of Chaucer*, 65–83. Durham, NC: Labyrinth Press, 1983.

– *Speaking of Chaucer.* Durham, NC: Labyrinth Press, 1983.

Downer, Alan S. *The British Drama: A Handbook and Brief Chronicle.* New York: Appleton-Century-Crofts, 1950.

Ebin, Lois. *John Lydgate.* Boston: Twayne, 1985.

Edmondson, George. *The Neighboring Text: Chaucer, Boccaccio, Henryson.* Notre Dame: University of Notre Dame Press, 2011.

Edwards, A.S.G. "Lydgate's *Fall of Princes*: Translation, Re-Translation and History." *Renaissance Cultural Crossroads: Translation, Print and Culture in Britain, 1473–1640*, ed. Sara K. Barker and Brenda M. Hosington, 21–34. Leiden: Brill, 2013.

Edwards, Robert R. *Chaucer and Boccaccio: Antiquity and Modernity.* Basingstoke, Houndmills, Hampshire, New York: Palgrave, 2002.

– "John Lydgate and the Remaking of Classical Epic." *Oxford History of Classical Reception in English Literature*. Ed. Rita Copeland, 465–86. Oxford: Oxford University Press, 2016.

– "Medieval Literary Careers: The Theban Track." *European Literary Careers: The Author from Antiquity to the Renaissance.* Ed. Patrick Cheney and Frederic A. de Armas, 104–28. Toronto: University of Toronto Press, 2002.

Edwards, Robert R., ed. *Troy Book: Selections*. TEAMS: Middle English Text Series. Kalamazoo: Medieval Institute Publications, 1998.

Eisner, Martin. *Boccaccio and the Invention of Italian Literature: Dante, Petrarch, Cavalcanti, and the Authority of the Vernacular.* Cambridge: Cambridge University Press, 2013.

– "Dante and the Author of the *Decameron*: Love, Literature, and Authority in Boccaccio." *The Oxford Handbook of Chaucer*. Ed. Suzanne Conklin Akbari and James Simpson, 286–302. Oxford: Oxford University Press, 2020.

– "Petrarch Reading Boccaccio: Revisiting the Genesis of the Triumphi." *Petrarch and the Textual Origins of Interpretation*. Ed. Teodolinda Barolini and Wayne H. Storey, 131–46. Leiden: Brill, 2007.

Eliot, T.S. "Philip Massinger." *Selected Essays: 1917–1932.* New York: Harcourt, 1932.

Emerson, Oliver Farrar. "Seith Trophee." *MLN* 31 (1916): 142–6.

Enenkel, Karl A.E. "Modelling the Humanist: Petrarch's Letter to Posterity and Boccaccio's Biography of the Poet Laureate." *Modelling the Individual: Biography and Portrait in the Renaissance*. Ed. Karl A.E. Enenkel, Betsy de Jong-Crane, and Peter Liebregts, 11–49. Leiden: Brill, 1998.

Epstein, Hans J. "The Identity of Chaucer's Lollius." *Modern Language Quarterly* 3 (1942): 391–400.

Evans, Ruth. "Textual Forensics." *Studies in the Age of Chaucer* 28 (2006): 263–70.

Evans, Ruth, Andrew Taylor, Nicholas Watson, and Jocelyn Wogan-Browne. "The Notion of Vernacular Theory." *The Idea of the Vernacular: An Anthology of Middle English Literary Theory, 1280–1520.* Ed. Jocelyn Wogan-Browne, Nicholas Watson, Andrew Taylor, and Ruth Evans, 314–30. University Park: Penn State University Press, 1999.

Farnham, Willard. "England's Discovery of the *Decameron.*" *PMLA* 39 (1924): 123–39.

– *The Medieval Heritage of Elizabethan Tragedy.* Berkeley: University of California Press, 1936.

Farrell, Joseph. "Intention and Intertext." *Phoenix* 59 (2005): 98–111.

– *Vergil's Georgics and the Traditions of Ancient Epic: The Art of Allusion in Literary History*. Oxford: Oxford University Press, 1991.

Farrell, Thomas J. "The 'Envoy de Chaucer' and the 'Clerk's Tale.'" *Chaucer Review* 24 (1990): 329–36.

– "Source or Hard Analogue? 'Decameron X,10' and the 'Clerk's Tale.'" *Chaucer Review* 37 (2003): 346–64.

Farrell, Thomas J., and Amy Goodwin. "The Clerk's Tale." *Sources and Analogues of the "Canterbury Tales."* 2 vols. Ed. Robert M. Correale and Mary Hamel, 1:103–29. Cambridge: D.S. Brewer, 2002.

Federico, Sylvia. *New Troy: Fantasies of Empire in the Late Middle Ages.* Minneapolis: University of Minnesota Press, 2003.

Feeney, D.C. *The Gods in Epic: Poets and Critics of the Classical Tradition.* Oxford: Oxford University Press, 1991.

Flannery, Mary C. *John Lydgate and the Poetics of Fame.* Cambridge: D.S. Brewer, 2012.

Fleming, John V. *Classical Imitation and Interpretation in Chaucer's "Troilus."* Lincoln: University of Nebraska Press, 1990.

Finlayson, John. "Petrarch, Boccaccio and Chaucer's *Clerk's Tale.*" *Studies in Philology* 97 (2000): 255–75.

Finotti, Fabio. "The Poem of Memory (Triumphi)." *Petrarch: A Critical Guide to the Complete Works.* Ed. Victoria Kirkham and Armando Maggi, 63–84. Chicago: University of Chicago Press, 2009.

Fisher, John. "A Language Policy for Lancastrian England." *PMLA* 107 (1992): 1168–80.

Foscolo, Ugo. *Saggi di letteratura italiana. Parte prima: Epoche della lingua italiana.* Ed. Cesare Foligno. Florence: Le Monnier 1958.

Fowler, Don. "Intertextuality and Classical Studies." *MD* 39 (1997): 13–34.

– "Modern Literary Theory and Latin Poetry: Some Anglo-American Perspectives." *Arachnion* 1 (1995): unpaginated.

Fradenburg, L.O. Aranye. "'Oure owen wo to drynke': Loss, Gender, and Chivalry in Troilus and Criseyde." *Chaucer's "Troilus and Criseyde": "Subjit to alle Poesy": Essays in Criticism.* Ed. R.A. Shoaf, 88–106. Binghamton, NY: Pegasus Paperbooks, 1992.

– *Sacrifice Your Love: Psychoanalysis, Historicism, Chaucer.* Minneapolis: University of Minnesota Press, 1992.

Frazer, R.M., Jr., trans. *The Trojan War: The Chronicles of Dictys of Crete and Dares the Phrygian.* Bloomington: Indiana University Press, 1966.

Frese, Dolores Warwick. "The 'Buried Bodies' of Dante, Boccaccio, and Petrarch: Chaucerian 'Sources' for the Critical Fiction of Obedient Wives." *Studies in the Age of Chaucer* 28 (2006): 249–56.

Fumo, Jamie C. *The Legacy of Apollo: Antiquity, Authority, and Chaucerian Poetics.* Toronto: University of Toronto Press, 2010.

Furnivall, Frederick James, Edmund Brock, and W.A. Clouston. *Originals and Analogues of Some of Chaucer's "Canterbury Tales."* London: Trübner, 1872.

Fyler, John M. *Language and the Declining World in Chaucer, Dante, and Jean de Meun.* Cambridge: Cambridge University Press, 2007.

Ganiban, Randall T. *Statius and Virgil: The "Thebaid" and the Reinterpretation of the "Aeneid."* Cambridge: Cambridge University Press, 2007.

Ganim, John M. "Chaucer, Boccaccio, and the Anxiety of Popularity." *Assays* 4 (1987): 51–66.

Ganz, David. "Historia: Some Lexicographical Considerations." *Medieval Cantors and Their Craft: Music, Liturgy, and the Shaping of History, 800–1500.* Ed. Katie Ann-Marie Bugyis, A.B. Kraebel, and Margot E. Fassler, 8–22. Suffolk: York Medical Press, 2017.

Gaston, Kara. "Literary Catalogues and Verse Units." *International Congress of the New Chaucer Society.* Reykjavik, Iceland. July 16–20, 2014.
– *Reading Chaucer in Time: Literary Formation in England and Italy.* Oxford: Oxford University Press, 2020.
– "'Save oure tonges difference': Translation, Literary Histories, and *Troilus and Criseyde.*" *Chaucer Review* 48 (2014): 258–83.
Giancarlo, Matthew. "The Structure of Fate and the Devising of History in Chaucer's *Troilus and Criseyde.*" *Studies in the Age of Chaucer* 26 (2004): 227–66.
Gilbert, Jane, Catherine Keen, and Ella Williams. "The Italian Angevins: Naples and Beyond, 1266–1343." *Italian Studies* 72 (2017): 121–7.
Gillespie, Alexandra. "Reading Chaucer's Words to Adam." *Chaucer Review* 42 (2007): 269–83.
Gillespie, Stuart. "Literary Afterlives: Metempsychosis from Ennius to Jorge Luis Borges." *Classical Literary Careers.* Ed. Philip Hardie and Helen Moore, 209–25. Cambridge: Cambridge University Press, 2010.
Gil-Osle, Juan Pablo. "Chatty Paintings, Twisted Memories and Other Oddities in Boccaccio's *Amorosa visione.*" *Studi Sul Boccaccio* 38 (2010): 89–104.
Ginsberg, Warren. *Chaucer's Italian Tradition.* Ann Arbor: University of Michigan Press, 2002.
– *Tellers, Tales, and Translation in Chaucer's "Canterbury Tales."* Oxford: Oxford University Press, 2015.
Gittes, Tobias Foster. *Eros, Culture, and the Mythopoetic Imagination.* Toronto: University of Toronto Press, 2008.
Godman, Peter. *The Silent Masters: Latin Literature and Its Censors in the High Middle Ages.* Princeton: Princeton University Press, 2000.
Goodwin, Amy W. "The Griselda Game." *Chaucer Review* 39 (2004): 41–69.
Gozzi, Maria. "'Filostrato' e 'Roman de Troyle.'" *Studi sul Boccaccio* 29 (2001): 145–85.
– "Sulle fonti del *Filostrato.* Le narrazioni di argomento troiano." *Studi sul Boccaccio* 5 (1968): 123–209.
Grafton, Anthony. *Forgers and Critics: Creativity and Duplicity in Western Scholarship.* Princeton: Princeton University Press, 1990.
Green, Richard Firth. *A Crisis of Truth: Literature and Law in Ricardian England.* Philadelphia: University of Pennsylvania Press, 2002.
– *Poets and Princepleasers: Literature and the English Court in the Late Middle Ages.* Toronto: University of Toronto Press, 1980.
– "Why Marquis Walter Treats His Wife So Badly." *Chaucer Review* 47 (2012): 48–62.
Griffin, Nathaniel E. "Introduction." *The Filostrato of Giovanni Boccaccio.* Trans. Nathaniel E. Griffin. New York: Biblo and Tannen, 1967.
– "Un-Homeric Elements in the Story of Troy." *Journal of English and Germanic Philology* 7 (1908): 32–52.

Gross, Karen Elizabeth. "Chaucer's Silent Italy." *Studies in Philology* 109 (2012): 19–44.

Guastella, Gianni. *Word of Mouth: Fama and Its Personifications in Art and Literature*. Oxford: Oxford University Press, 2017.

Hagedorn, Suzanne C. *Abandoned Women: Rewriting the Classics in Dante, Boccaccio, and Chaucer.* Ann Arbor: University of Michigan Press, 2004.

Hamilton, George Livingstone. *The Indebtedness of Chaucer's "Troilus and Criseyde" to Guido delle Colonne's Historia Trojana.* New York: Columbia University Press, 1903.

Hammond, E.P. "Poet and Patron in the *Fall of Princes:* Lydgate and Humphrey of Gloucester." *Anglia* 38 (1914): 121–36.

Hanning, Robert W. "The *Decameron* and the *Canterbury Tales.*" *Approaches to Teaching Boccaccio's Decameron.* Ed. James H. McGregor, 103–18. New York: Modern Language Association, 2000.

Hardie, Philip. "After Rome: Renaissance Epic." *Roman Epic.* Ed. Anthony James Boyle, 294–313. New York: Routledge, 1993.

– *The Epic Successors of Virgil: A Study in the Dynamic of a Tradition.* Cambridge: Cambridge University Press, 1993.

– *Ovid's Poetics of Illusion.* Cambridge: Cambridge University Press, 2002.

Harkins, Jessica. "Chaucer's *Clerk's Tale* and Boccaccio's *Decameron* X.10." *Chaucer Review* 47 (2013): 247–73.

Hathaway, Charles M. "Chaucer's Lollius." *Englische Studien* 44 (1911): 159–64.

Havely, N.R. *Chaucer's Boccaccio: Sources for "Troilus" and the "Knight's" and "Franklin's Tales."* Woodbridge, Suffolk: D.S. Brewer, 1980.

– "Il Filostrato." *Chaucer's Boccaccio: Sources for "Troilus" and the "Knight's" and "Franklin's Tales."* Cambridge: D.S. Brewer, 1992.

– "'I Wolde ... han Hadde a Fame': Dante, Fame and Infamy in Chaucer's *House of Fame.*" *Chaucer and Fame: Reputation and Reception.* Ed. Isabel Davis and Catherine Nall, 43–56. Cambridge: D.S. Brewer, 2015.

Hedeman, Anne D. *Translating the Past: Laurent de Premierfait and Boccaccio's "De Casibus."* Los Angeles: J. Paul Getty Museum, 2008.

Heffernan, Carol. *Comedy in Chaucer and Boccaccio.* Cambridge: D.S. Brewer, 2009.

Hexter, Ralph. "On First Looking into Vergil's Homer." *A Companion to Vergil's "Aeneid."* Ed. Joseph Farrell and Michael C.J. Putnam, 26–36. Chichester: Wiley-Blackwell, 2010.

Hinds, Stephen. *Allusion and Intertext: Dynamics of Appropriation in Roman Poetry.* Cambridge: Cambridge University Press, 1998.

– "Booking the Return Trip: Ovid and *Tristia* 1." *Cambridge Classical Journal* 31 (1985): 13–32.

– *The Metamorphosis of Persephone: Ovid and the Self-Conscious Muse.* Cambridge: Cambridge University Press, 1997.

Hollander, Robert. *Boccaccio's Dante and the Shaping Force of Satire.* Ann Arbor: University of Michigan Press, 1997.
– *Boccaccio's Two Venuses.* New York: Columbia University Press, 1977.
– "Dante Theologus-Poeta." *Dante Studies* 94 (1976), reprinted in *Studies in Dante* (Ravenna: Longo, 1980), and in *Dante Studies* 118 (2000): 261–302.
Hornstein, Lillian H. "Petrarch's Laelius, Chaucer's Lollius?" *PMLA* 63 (1948): 64–84.
Horobin, Simon, and Linne R. Mooney. "A Piers Plowman Manuscript by the Hengwrt/Ellesmere Scribe and Its Implications for London Standard English." *Studies in the Age of Chaucer* 26 (2004): 65–112.
Houston, Jason M. *Building a Monument to Dante: Boccaccio as* Dantista. Toronto: University of Toronto Press, 2010.
Howard, Donald R. *Chaucer: His Life, His Works, His World.* New York: Fawcett Columbine, 1987.
Hui, Andrew. *The Poetics of Ruins in Renaissance Literature*. Oxford: Oxford University Press, 2017.
Huot, Sylvia. "Poetic Ambiguity and Reader Response in Boccaccio's 'Amorosa Visione.'" *Modern Philology* 83 (1985): 109–22.
Iannucci, Amilcare A. "Petrarch's Intertextual Strategies in the *Triumphs.*" *Petrarch's Triumphs: Allegory and Spectacle.* Ed. Konrad Eisenbichler and Amilcare A. Iannuci, 3–10. Ottawa: Dovehouse Editions, 1990.
The Idea of the Vernacular: An Anthology of Middle English Literary Theory, 1280–1520. Ed. Jocelyn Wogan-Browne, Nicholas Watson, Andrew Taylor, and Ruth Evans. University Park: Penn State University Press, 1999.
Jefferson, Bernard L. *Chaucer and the Consolation of Philosophy of Boethius.* Princeton: Princeton University Press, 1917.
Jones, Terry. "The Monk's Tale." *Studies in the Age of Chaucer* 22 (2000): 387–97.
Kaske, R.E. "The Knight's Interruption of the *Monk's Tale.*" *ELH* 24 (1957): 249–68.
Keller, Wolfram. "Shakespearean Medievalism: Conceptions of Literary Authorship in *Richard II* and John Lydgate's *Troy Book.*" *European Journal of English Studies* 15 (2011): 129–42.
Kelly, Douglas. "The Invention of Briseida's Story in Benoit de Sainte-Maure's 'Troie.'" *Romance Philology* 48 (1995): 221–41.
Kelly, Henry Ansgar. *Chaucerian Tragedy.* Cambridge: D.S. Brewer, 2000.
Kircher, Timothy. "Boccaccio's Humanist *Brigata*: Reading the *Decameron* in the Quattrocento." *Essays on the Early Modern Impact of Giovanni Boccaccio and His Works.* Ed. Martin Eisner and David Lummus, 36–55. Notre Dame: University of Notre Dame Press, 2019.
Kirkham, Victoria. *Fabulous Vernacular: Boccaccio's "Filocolo" and the Art of Medieval Fiction.* Ann Arbor: University of Michigan Press, 2001.
– "A Visual Legacy (Boccaccio as Artist)." *Boccaccio: A Critical Guide to the Complete Works.* Ed. Victoria Kirkham, Michael Sherberg, and Janet Levarie Smarr, 501–29. Chicago: University of Chicago Press, 2014.

Kirkpatrick, Robin. *English and Italian Literature from Dante to Shakespeare: A Study of Source, Analogue, and Divergence.* London: Longman, 1995.

– "The Griselda Story in Boccaccio, Petrarch, and Chaucer." *Chaucer and the Italian Trecento.* Ed. Piero Boitani, 231–48. Cambridge: Cambridge University Press, 1983.

Kittredge, George L. "Chaucer's Lollius." *Harvard Studies in Classical Philology* 28 (1917): 47–132.

– "The Pillars of Hercules and Chaucer's Trophee." The Putman Anniversary Volume. Ed. F. Boas, 545–66. Cedar Rapids: Torch; New York: Stechert, 1909.

Kline, Daniel T. "Father Chaucer and the Siege of Thebes: Literary Paternity, Aggressive Deference, and the Prologue to Lydgate's Oedipal Canterbury Tale." *Chaucer Review* 34 (1991): 217–35.

Knauer, Georg Nikolaus. *Homer in the "Aeneid." Die Aeneis und Homer. Studien zur poetischen Technik Vergils.* Göttingen: Vandenhoeck and Ruprecht, 1964.

Knight, Stephen. "My Lord, the Monk." *Studies in the Age of Chaucer* 22 (2000): 381–6.

Koff, Leonard Michael. *The "Decameron" and the "Canterbury Tales": New Essays on an Old Question.* Ed. Leonard Michael Koff and Brenda Deen Schildgen. Madison, NJ: Farleigh Dickinson University Press, 2000.

– "Imagining Absence: Chaucer's Griselda and Walter without Petrarch." *The "Decameron" and the "Canterbury Tales": New Essays on an Old Question.* Ed. Leonard Michael Koff and Brenda Dean Schildgen, 278–315. Madison, NJ: Farleigh Dickinson University Press, 2000.

Koonce, B.G. *Chaucer and the Tradition of Fame: Symbolism in "The House of Fame."* Princeton: Princeton University Press, 1966.

Kräplin, Tom. "The Rise of Princes?: A Discussion Concerning a Possible Existence of Unbalance in the Theory of 'de casibus' Tragedy in the Emphasis Given to the Rise and Fall of Its Protagonist." Norderstedt: GRIN Verlag, 2010.

Kriesel, James C. *Boccaccio's Corpus: Allegory, Ethics, and Vernacularity.* Notre Dame: University of Notre Dame Press, 2018.

Kristeva, Julia. *Desire in Language: A Semiotic Approach to Language and Art.* Trans. Thomas Gora, Alice Jardine, and Leon S. Roudiez. Ed. Leon S. Roudiez, 64–91. New York: Columbia University Press, 1977–80.

Krochalis, Jeanne E. "The Books and Reading of Henry V and His Circle." *Chaucer Review* 23 (1988): 50–77.

Lantham, R.G. "Chaucer Note." *Athenaeum* 2 (1869): 433.

Laird, Andrew. "Fiction, Philosophy, and Logical Closure." *Classical Constructions: Papers in Memory of Don Fowler.* Ed. S.J. Heyworth, 281–309. Oxford: Oxford University Press, 2007.

– "Re-inventing Virgil's Wheel." *Classical Literary Careers and Their Reception.* Ed. Philip Hardie and Helen Moore. Cambridge: Cambridge University Press, 2010.

Lawton, David. *Chaucer's Narrators.* Cambridge: D.S. Brewer, 1985.
– "Dullness in the Fifteenth Century." *ELH* 54 (1987): 761–99.
Lennon, Paul. "Ludic Language: The Case of the Punning Echoic Allusion." *Brno Studies in English* 37 (2011): 79–95.
Lepley, Douglas. "The Monk's Boethian Tale." *Chaucer Review* 12 (1977–8): 162–70.
Lerer, Seth. *Chaucer and His Readers: Imagining the Author in Late-Medieval England.* Princeton: Princeton University Press, 1993.
Levin, Joan H. "Sweet, New Endings: A Look at the Tornada in the Stilnovistic and Petrarchan *Canzone*." *Italica* 61 (1984): 297–311.
Lewis, Charlton T., and Charles Short, eds. *A Latin Dictionary.* Oxford: Clarendon Press, 1975.
Lewis, C.S. *Poetry and Prose in the Sixteenth Century*. Oxford: Clarendon Press, 1954.
– "What Chaucer Really Did to *Il Filostrato*." *Chaucer's "Troilus": Essays in Criticism.* Ed. Stephen A. Barney. Hamden, CT: Archon Books: 1980.
Lindeboom, B.W. "Chaucer's Monk Illuminated: Zenobia as Role Model." *Neophilologus* 92 (2009): 339–50.
The Literary Context of Chaucer's Fabliaux. Ed. Larry D. Benson and Theodore M. Andersson. Indianapolis and New York: Bobbs-Merrill, 1971.
Loar, Matthew P. "Hercules, Mummius, and the Roman Triumph in *Aeneid* 8." *Classical Philology* 112 (2017): 45–62.
Lombardi, Elena. *Imagining the Women Readers in the Age of Dante.* Oxford: Oxford University Press, 2018.
Lowrie, Michèle. Review. *Speaking Volumes: Narrative and Intertext in Ovid and Other Latin Poets* by Alessandro Barchiesi. *Bryn Mawr Classical Review*, 2002.
Lumiansky, R.M. *Of Sondry Folk: The Dramatic Principle in the "Canterbury Tales."* Austin: University of Texas Press, 1955.
Lummus, David. "Boccaccio's Hellenism and the Foundations of Modernity." *Mediaevalia* 33 (2012): 101–67.
– "Boccaccio's Poetic Anthropology: Allegories of History in the *Genealogie deorum gentilium libri*." *Speculum* 87 (2012): 724–65.
Lyne, R.O.A.M. *Further Voices in Vergil's "Aeneid."* Oxford: Clarendon, 1987.
Maguire, Laurie, and Emma Smith. *Rethinking Shakespeare Source Study: Audiences, Authors, and Digital Technologies.* Ed. Dennis Austin Britton and Melissa Walter. Abingdon: Routledge, 2018.
– "What Is a Source? Or, How Shakespeare Read His Marlowe." *Shakespeare Survey* 68 (2015): 15–31.
Malagnini, Francesca. "Il libro d'autore dal progetto alla realizzazione: il 'Teseida delle nozze di Emilia,' con un'appendice sugli autografi di Boccaccio." *Studi sul Boccaccio* 34 (2006): 3–102.

Marchesi, Simone. "Boccaccio on Fortune (De casibus virorum illustrium)." *Boccaccio: A Critical Guide to the Complete Works.* Ed. Victoria Kirkham, Michael Sherberg, and Janet Levarie Smarr, 245–54. Chicago: University of Chicago Press, 2014.

– *Dante and Augustine: Linguistics, Poetics, Hermeneutics.* Toronto: University of Toronto Press, 2011.

– "Petrarch's Philological Epic (Africa)." *Petrarch: A Critical Guide to the Complete Works.* Ed. Victoria Kirkham and Armando Maggi, 113–30. Chicago: University of Chicago Press, 2009.

Martellotti, Guido. "Momenti Narrativi Del Petrarca." *Scritti Petrarcheschi* 4 (1951): 7–33; reprinted in *Scritti Petrarcheschi.* Ed. Michele Feo and Silvia Rizzo, 179–206. Padua: Antenore, 1983.

Marzano, Annalisa. "Hercules and the Triumphal Feast for the Roman People." *Transforming Historical Landscapes in the Ancient Empires.* Ed. Borja Antela-Bernárdez and Toni Ñaco del Hoyo, 83–97. Oxford: British Archaeological Reports, 2009.

Marzano, Francesco. "Boccaccio storico della letteratura trecentesca l'epistola a Iacopo Pizzinga." *Intorno a Boccaccio/Boccaccio e dintorni 2015. Atti del seminario internazionale di studi (Certaldo Alta, Casa di Giovanni Boccaccio, 9 settembre 2015).* Ed. Stefano Zamponi, 1–13. Florence: Firenze University Press, 2016.

Martindale, Charles. *Redeeming the Text: Latin Poetry and the Hermeneutics of Reception.* Cambridge: Cambridge University Press, 1993.

Mazzotta, Giuseppe. "Boccaccio's Critique of Petrarch." *Petrarch and Boccaccio: The Unity of Knowledge in the Pre-Modern World.* Ed. Igor Candido, 270–86. Berlin: de Gruyter, 2018.

– "Petrarch's Dialogue with Dante." In *Petrarch & Dante: Anti-Dantism, Metaphysics, Tradition.* Ed. Zygmunt G. Barański and Theodore J. Cachey, Jr., 177–94. Notre Dame: University of Notre Dame Press, 2009.

McCormick, Michael. *Eternal Victory: Triumphal Rulership in Late Antiquity, Byzantium, and the Early Medieval West.* Cambridge: Cambridge University Press, 1986.

McKinley, Kathryn. *Chaucer's "House of Fame" and Its Boccaccian Intertexts: Image, Vision, and the Vernacular.* Toronto: Pontifical Institute of Mediaeval Studies, 2016.

– "Constructing a Mythic City in the *Book of the City of Ladies*: A New Space for Women in Late Medieval Culture." *A Handbook to the Reception of Classical Mythology*. Ed. Vanda Zajko and Helena Hoyle, 353–66. Malden, MA: Wiley Blackwell, 2017.

Meban, David. "Temple Building, Primus Language, and the Proem to Virgil's Third *Georgic.*" *Classical Philology* 103 (2008): 150–74.

Menetti, Elisabetta. "Appunti di poetica boccacciana: l'autore e le sue verità." *Boccaccio angioino.* Ed. Giancarlo Alfano, Teresa D'Urso, and Alessandra Perriccioli Saggese, 47–68. Brussels: Peter Lang, 2012.

Meyer-Lee, Robert. "John Lydgate's Major Poems." *A Companion to Fifteenth-Century English Poetry*. Ed. Julia Boffey and A.S.G. Edwards, 59–72. Cambridge: D.S. Brewer, 2013.

– *Poets and Power from Chaucer to Wyatt.* Cambridge: Cambridge University Press, 2007.

Middleton, Anne. "The Clerk and His Tale: Some Literary Contexts." *Studies in the Age of Chaucer* 2 (1980): 121–50.

Migiel, Marilyn. *A Rhetoric of the "Decameron."* Toronto: University of Toronto Press, 2003.

Miller, Anthony. *Roman Triumphs and Early Modern English Culture.* London: Palgrave Macmillan, 2001.

Millett, Bella. "Chaucer, Lollius, and the Medieval Theory of Authorship." *Studies in the Age of Chaucer* 1 (1985): 93–103.

Minnis, Alastair. *Chaucer and Pagan Antiquity.* Cambridge: D.S. Brewer, 1982.

– *Fallible Authors: Chaucer's Pardoner and Wife of Bath.* Philadelphia: University of Pennsylvania Press, 2008.

– *Magister Amoris: The "Roman de la Rose" and Vernacular Hermeneutics.* Oxford: Oxford University Press, 2001.

– *Medieval Theory of Authorship: Scholastic Literary Attitudes in the Later Middle Ages.* [1984]. 2nd edn. London: Scholar Press; Philadelphia: University of Pennsylvania Press, 1988.

– "Other Worlds: Chaucer's Classicism." *Oxford History of Classical Reception in English Literature.* Ed. Rita Copeland. 5 vols. 1:413–34. Oxford: Oxford University Press, 2016.

– *Translations of Authority in Middle English Literature: Valuing the Vernacular.* Cambridge: Cambridge University Press, 2009.

Minnis, Alastair, and Ian Johnson, eds. *The Cambridge History of Literary Criticism.* Vol. 2, *The Middle Ages.* Cambridge: Cambridge University Press, 2005.

Mooney, Linne R. "Chaucer's Scribe." *Speculum* 81 (2006): 97–138.

Mooney, Linne R., and Estelle Stubbs. *Scribes and the City: London Guildhall Clerks and the Dissemination of Middle English Literature, 1375–1425.* York: York University Press, and Woodbridge: Boydell & Brewer, 2013.

Moore, Edward. *Scripture and Classical Authors in Dante.* Oxford: Clarendon Press, 1896.

Morgan, Kathleen. *Ovid's Art of Imitation: Propertius in the "Amores."* Leiden: Brill, 1977.

Morosini, Roberta. "Napoli: Spazi rappresentativi della memoria." *Boccaccio geografo*. Ed. Roberta Morosini, 179–204. Florence: Mauro Pagliai, 2010.

Morse, Charlotte C. "The Exemplary Griselda." *Studies in the Age of Chaucer* 7 (1985): 51–86.

Mortimer, Nigel. *John Lydgate's "Fall of Princes": Narrative Tragedy in Its Literary and Political Contexts.* Oxford: Oxford University Press, 2005.

Muscatine, Charles. *Chaucer and the French Tradition.* Berkeley and Los Angeles: University of California Press, 1957.

Natali, Giulia. *Boccaccio e le controfigure dell'autore.* L'Aquila: Japadre, 1990.

Neddermeyer, Uwe. *Von der Handschrift zum gedruckten Buch*. 2 vols. 1:72–85. Wiesbaden: Harrassowitz, 1998.

Neuse, Richard. *Chaucer's Dante: Allegory and Epic Theater in "The Canterbury Tales."* Berkeley: University of California Press, 1991.

– "The Monk's *De casibus:* The Boccaccio Case Reopened." *The "Decameron" and the "Canterbury Tales": New Essays on an Old Question.* Ed. Leonard Michael Koff and Brenda Deen Schildgen, 247–77. Madison, NJ: Farleigh Dickinson University Press, 2000.

– "They Had Their World As in Their Time: The Monk's *Little Narratives.*" *Studies in the Age of Chaucer* 22 (2000): 415–23.

– "*Troilus and Criseyde*: Another Dantean Reading." *Chaucer's "Troilus and Criseyde," "Subgit to alle Poesye": Essays in Criticism.* Ed. R.A. Shoaf, 199–210. Binghamton, NY: Pegasus Paperbooks, 1992.

Nolan, Barbara. *Chaucer and the Traditions of the* Roman Antique. Cambridge: Cambridge University Press, 1992.

Nolan, Maura. *John Lydgate and the Making of Public Culture.* Cambridge: Cambridge University Press, 2005.

– "Lydgate's Literary History: Chaucer, Gower, Canace." *Studies in the Age of Chaucer* 27 (2005): 59–92.

– "'Now Wo, Now Gladnesse': Ovidianism in the *Fall of Princes.*" *ELH* 71 (2004): 531–55.

O'Keeffe, Katherine O'Brien. "Source, Method, Theory, Practice: On Reading Two Old English Verse Texts." *Bulletin of the John Rylands Library* 76 (1994): 51–73.

Olson, Glending. *Literature as Recreation in the Middle Ages.* Ithaca: Cornell University Press, 1982.

Olson, Kristina. "The Language of Women As Written by Men: Boccaccio, Dante and Gendered Histories of the Vernacular." *Heliotropia* 8–9 (2011–12): 51–78.

Ong, Walter. *Interfaces of the Word: Studies in the Evolution of Consciousness and Culture.* Ithaca: Cornell University Press, 1977.

Östenberg, Ida. *Staging the World: Spoils, Captives, and Representations in the Roman Triumphal Procession.* Oxford: Oxford University Press, 2009.

Otter, Monika. "Functions of Fiction in Historical Writing." *Writing Medieval History.* Ed. Nancy Partner. London: Hodder Arnold, 2005.

– *Inventiones: Fiction and Referentiality in Twelfth Century English Historical Writing*. Chapel Hill: University of North Carolina Press, 1996.

Papio, Michael. Trans. *The Decameron: A Critical Lexicon.* Tempe: Arizona Center for Medieval & Renaissance Studies, 2019.

Partridge, Stephen. "Questions of Evidence: Manuscripts and the Early History of Chaucer's Works." *Writing after Chaucer: Essential Readings in Chaucer and the Fifteenth Century.* Ed. Daniel Pinti, 1–26. New York: Garland, 1998.

Partner, Nancy. *Serious Entertainments: The Writing of History in Twelfth-Century England.* Chicago: University of Chicago Press, 1977.

Pasquali, Giorgio. "Arte allusiva." *Pagine stravaganti di un filologo.* 2 vols. Florence: Le Lettere, 1994.

Patch, Howard Rollin. "Chaucer and Lady Fortune." *MLT* 22 (1927): 377–88.

Patterson, Lee. *Chaucer and the Subject of History.* Madison: University of Wisconsin Press, 1991.

– "Making Identities in Fifteenth Century England: Henry V and John Lydgate." *New Historical Literary Study.* Ed. Jeffrey N. Cox and Larry J. Reynolds, 69–107. Princeton: Princeton University Press, 1993.

– *Negotiating the Past: The Historical Understanding of Medieval Literature.* Madison: University of Wisconsin Press. 1987.

Payne, Robert. *The Roman Triumph.* London: Hale, 1962.

Pearsall, Derek A. "Chaucer and Lydgate." *Chaucer Traditions: Studies in Honour of Derek Brewer.* Ed. Ruth Morse and Barry Windeatt, 39–53. Cambridge: Cambridge University Press, 2006.

– *John Lydgate.* Charlottesville: University Press of Virginia; London: Routledge and Kegan Paul, 1970.

Perry, R.D. "Lydgate's Virtual Coteries: Chaucer's Family and Gower's Pacifism in the Fifteenth Century." *Speculum* 93 (2018): 669–98.

Petrina, Alessandra. *Cultural Politics in Fifteenth-Century England: The Case of Humphrey, Duke of Gloucester.* Leiden: Brill, 2004.

– "A Stranger in the Margins: Giovanni Boccaccio in John Lydgate's Work." *Boccaccio and the European Literary Tradition.* Ed. Piero Boitani and Emilia Di Rocco, 73–88. Rome: Edizioni di Storia e Letteratura, 2014.

Petrucci, Armando. "Il libro manoscritto." *Letteratura italiana.* 2 vols. Vol. 2: *Produzione e consumo.* Ed. Alberto Asor Rosa, 2: 499–524. Turin: Einaudi, 1983.

– "Minuta, autografo, libro d'autore." *Atti del convegno internazionale il libro e il testo, Urbino, 20–23 settembre 1982.* Ed. Renato Raffaelli and Cesare Questa, 397–414. Urbino: Università di Urbino, 1984.

Picard, Gilbert Charles. *Les trophées romains: contribution à l'histoire de la religion et de l'art triomphal de Rome.* Paris: de Boccard, 1957.

Pollmann, Karla F.L. "Statius' *Thebaid* and the Legacy of Vergil's *Aeneid.*" *Mnemosyne* 54 (2001): 10–24.

Popkin, Maggie L. *The Architecture of the Roman Triumph: Monuments, Memory, and Identity.* Cambridge: Cambridge University Press, 2016.

Porcelli, Bruno. *Nuovi studi su Dante e Boccaccio con analisi della Nencia.* Pisa: Istituti editoriali e poligrafici internazionali, 1997.

Pozzi, Giovanni. *Poesia per gioco: Prontuario di figure artificiose.* Bologna: Il Mulino, 1984.

Pratt, Robert A. "Chaucer and the Pillars of Hercules." *Studies in Honor of Ullman*. Ed. Lillian B. Lawler, Dorothy M. Robathon, and William C. Korfmacher, 118–25. St. Louis: Classical Bulletin, 1960.

– "Conjectures Regarding Chaucer's Manuscript of the *Teseida.*" *Studies in Philology* 42 (1945): 745–63.

– "A Note on Chaucer's Lollius." *Modern Language Notes* 65 (1950): 183–7.

Pucci, Joseph. *The Full-Knowing Reader: Allusion and the Power of the Reader in the Western Tradition.* New Haven: Yale University Press, 1998.

Putnam, Michael C.J. *The Virgilian Tradition.* Ed. Jan M. Ziolkowski and Michael C.J. Putnam. New Haven: Yale University Press, 2008.

Quaglio, Antonio Enzo. "Prima Fortuna della Glossa Garbiana a 'Donna me prega' del Cavalcanti." *GSLI* 141 (1964): 336–68.

Raby, Michael. "The *Clerk's Tale* and the Forces of Habit." *Chaucer Review* 47 (2013): 223–46.

Ramazani, Jahan. "Chaucer's Monk: The Poetics of Abbreviation, Aggression, and Tragedy." *Chaucer Review* 27 (1993): 260–76.

Ricci, Lucia Battaglia. *Boccaccio.* Rome: Salerno, 2000.

– *Scrivere un libro di novelle: Giovanni Boccaccio autore, lettore, editore.* Ravenna: Longo Editore, 2013.

Ricci, Pier Giorgio. *Studi sulla vita e le opere del Boccaccio.* Milan and Naples: Ricciardi, 1985.

Rickels, Laurence A. *Case of California.* Baltimore: Johns Hopkins University Press, 1991.

Rigby, Stephen H. *Wisdom and Chivalry: Chaucer's "Knight's Tale" and Medieval Political Theory.* Leiden: Brill, 2009.

Robertson, D.W., Jr. "Chaucerian Tragedy." *ELH* 19 (1952): 1–37.

Rollo, David. *Glamorous Sorcery: Magic and Literacy in the High Middle Ages.* Minneapolis: University of Minnesota Press, 2000.

– *Historical Fabrication, Ethnic Fable and French Romance in Twelfth-Century England.* Lexington, KY: French Forum, 1998.

Root, Robert K. *The Poetry of Chaucer: A Guide to Its Study and Appreciation.* Boston: Houghton Mifflin, 1906.

Rossi, Luca Carlo. "In margine alla 'Griselda' latina di Petrarca." *Acme* 53 (2000): 139–60.

Rossiter, William. *Chaucer and Petrarch.* Cambridge: D.S. Brewer, 2010.

Roush, Sherry. *Speaking Spirits: Ventriloquizing the Dead in Renaissance Italy.* Toronto: University of Toronto Press, 2015.

Rubini, Rocco. *Posterity: Inventing Tradition from Petrarch to Gramsci.* Chicago: University of Chicago Press, 2022.

Rundle, David. *Renaissance Reform of the Book and Britain: The English Quattrocento.* Cambridge: Cambridge University Press, 2019.

Rundle, David, ed. *Humanism in Fifteenth-Century Europe.* Oxford: Medium Ævum Monographs, 2012.

Scala, Elizabeth. *Absent Narratives, Manuscript Textuality, and Literary Structure in Late Medieval England.* New York: Palgrave, 2002.

– *Desire in the "Canterbury Tales."* Columbus: Ohio State University Press, 2015.

Scanlon, Larry. *Narrative, Authority, and Power: The Medieval Exemplum and the Chaucerian Tradition.* Cambridge: Cambridge University Press, 1994.

Scanlon, Larry, and James Simpson, eds. *John Lydgate: Poetry, Culture, and Lancastrian England.* Notre Dame: University of Notre Dame Press, 2006.

Schless, Howard H. *Chaucer and Dante: A Revaluation.* Norman, OK: Pilgrim Books, 1984.

Schibanoff, Susan. *Chaucer's Queer Poetics: Rereading the Dream Trio.* Toronto: University of Toronto Press, 2006.

Schwebel, Leah. "Literary Patricide in the Legend of Thebes." *Studies in the Age of Chaucer* 36 (2014): 139–68.

– "Redressing Griselda: Restoration through Translation in the Clerk's Tale." *Chaucer Review* 47 (2013): 274–99.

– "Triumphing Over Dante in Petrarch's *Trionfi*." *Mediaevalia* 39 (2018): 87–111.

– '"Trophee' and Triumph in the *Monk's Tale*." *Chaucer and Italian Culture*. Ed. Helen Fulton, 193–216. Cardiff: University of Wales Press, 2021.

– "What's in Criseyde's Book?" *Chaucer Review* 54 (2019): 91–115.

Severs, J. Burke. *The Literary Relationships of Chaucer's "Clerkes Tale."* New Haven: Yale University Press, 1942.

Seymour, M.C. "Chaucer's Early Poem *De Casibus Virorum Illustrium*." *Chaucer Review* 24 (1989): 163–5.

Sherman, Mark A. "The Politics of Discourse in Chaucer's *Knight's Tale*." *Exemplaria* 6 (1994): 87–114.

Shoaf, R.A. *Dante, Chaucer, and the Currency of the Word: Money, Images, and References in Late Medieval Poetry.* Norman, OK: Pilgrim Books, 1983.

Shore, Daniel. "Things Unattempted … Yet Once More." *Milton Quarterly* 43 (2009): 195–200.

Simpson, James. "Chaucer's Presence and Absence: 1400–1550." *Cambridge Companion to Chaucer*. 2nd edn. Ed. Piero Boitani and Jill Mann, 251–69. Cambridge: Cambridge University Press, 2003.

– "Dysemol daies and fatal hours: Lydgate's *Destruction of Thebes* and Chaucer's *Knight's Tale*." In *The Long Fifteenth Century: Essays for Douglas Gray.* Ed. Helen Cooper and Sally Mapstone, 15–33. Oxford: Clarendon Press, 1997.

– "John Lydgate." *Cambridge Companion to Medieval English Literature, 1100–1500*. Ed. Larry Scanlon, 205–16. Cambridge: Cambridge University Press, 2009.

– "The Other Troy Book: Guido delle Colonne's *Historia destructionis Troiae* in Fourteenth- and Fifteenth-Century England." *Speculum* 73 (1998): 397–423.

– "Subjects of Triumph and Literary History: Dido and Petrarch in Petrarch's *Africa* and *Trionfi*." *JMEMS* 35 (2005): 490–508.

Singleton, Charles S. *Dante Studies 1: "Commedia": Elements of Structure Dante and Myth*. Cambridge, MA: Harvard University Press, 1954.

Smarr, Janet Levarie. *Boccaccio and Fiammetta: The Narrator as Lover.* Urbana: University of Illinois Press, 1986.

– "Boccaccio and the Choice of Hercules." *MLN* 92 (1977): 146–52.

Smith, R.A. *Poetic Allusion and Poetic Embrace in Ovid and Virgil.* Ann Arbor: University of Michigan Press, 1997.

Smolenaars, J.J.L. *Statius Thebaid VII: A Commentary*. Leiden: Brill, 1994; repr. 2018.

Socola, Edward. "Chaucer's Development of Fortune in the *Monk's Tale*." *JEGP* 49 (1950): 159–71.

Sources and Analogues of Chaucer's "Canterbury Tales." Ed. W.F. Bryan and Germaine Dempster. Chicago: University of Chicago Press, 1941; repr. Humanities Press, 1958.

Sources and Analogues of the "Canterbury Tales." 2 vols. Ed. Robert M. Correale and Mary Hamel. Cambridge: D.S. Brewer, 2002 (vol. 1) and 2005 (vol. 2).

Southern, Pat. *Empress Zenobia: Palmyra's Rebel Queen*. New York: Continuum US, 2008.

Spearing, A.C. "Classical Antiquity in Chaucer's Chivalric Romances." *Chivalry, Knighthood, and War in the Middle Ages*. Ed. Susan J. Ridyard, 57–73. Sewanee: University of the South Press, 1999.

– *From Medieval to Renaissance in English Poetry.* Cambridge: Cambridge University Press, 1985.

– "Lydgate's Canterbury Tale: *The Siege of Thebes* and Fifteenth Century Chaucerianism." *Fifteenth-Century Studies: Recent Essays.* Ed. Robert F. Yeager. Hamden, CT: Archon, 1984.

– "Renaissance Chaucer and Father Chaucer." *English: The Journal of the English Association* 34 (1985): 1–38.

Spelman, Henry. *Pindar and the Poetics of Permanence.* Oxford: Oxford University Press, 2018.

Spense, Sarah. "Felix Casus: The Dares and Dictys Legends of Aeneas." *A Companion to Vergil's "Aeneid" and Its Tradition.* Ed. Joseph Farrell and Michael C.J. Putnam, 133–46. Chichester: Wiley-Blackwell, 2010.

Sponsler, Claire. "Lydgate and London's Public Culture." *Lydgate Matters: Poetry and Material Culture in the Fifteenth Century.* Ed. Lisa H. Cooper and Andrea Denny Brown, 13–33. New York: Palgrave, 2008.

– *The Queen's Dumbshows: John Lydgate and the Making of Early Theater.* Philadelphia: University of Pennsylvania Press, 2014.

Stocchi, Manlio Pastore. "Su alcuni autografi del Boccaccio." *Studi sul Boccaccio* 10 (1977): 123–43.
Strohm, Paul. "Chaucer's Audience(s): Fictional, Implied, Intended, Actual." *Chaucer Review* 18 (1983): 137–45.
– *England's Empty Throne.* [1998]. Notre Dame: University of Notre Dame Press, 2006.
– "Hoccleve, Lydgate, and the Lancastrian Court." *The Cambridge History of Medieval English Literature.* Ed. David Wallace, 640–61. Cambridge: Cambridge University Press, 1999.
Stump, Donald. *The Spenser Encyclopedia.* Gen. ed. A.C. Hamilton. Toronto: University of Toronto Press, 1990.
Sturm-Maddox, Sara. "Dante, Petrarch, and the Laurel Crown." *Petrarch and Dante: Anti-Dantism, Metaphysics, Tradition.* Ed. Zygmunt G. Barański and Theodore J. Cachey, Jr., 290–319. Notre Dame: University of Notre Dame Press, 2009.
Stussi, Alfredo. "Lingua." *Lessico critico decameroniano.* Ed. Renzo Bragantini and Pier Massimo Forni, 192–221. Turin: Bollati Boringhieri, 1995.
Summit, Jennifer. *Memory's Library: Medieval Books in Early Modern England.* Chicago: University of Chicago Press, 2008.
Surdich, Luigi. *Boccaccio.* Rome: Editori Laterza, 2001.
Tarrant, Richard. "Ovid and Ancient Literary History." *The Cambridge Companion to Ovid.* Ed. Philip Hardie, 13–33. Cambridge: Cambridge University Press, 2002.
Tavoni, Mirko. "Linguistic Italy." *Dante in Context.* Ed. Zygmunt G. Barański and Lino Pertile, 243–59. Cambridge, New York: Cambridge University Press, 2015.
– *Qualche idea su Dante.* Bologna: Il Mulino, 2015.
Taylor, Karla. *Chaucer Reads the "Divine Comedy."* Stanford: Stanford University Press, 1989.
– "A Text and Its Afterlives: Dante and Chaucer." *Comparative Literature* 35 (1983): 1–20.
Thomas, Hugh M. *The Secular Clergy in England, 1066–1216.* Oxford: Oxford University Press, 2014.
Thomas, Richard F. *Virgil and the Augustan Reception.* Cambridge: Cambridge University Press, 2001.
– "Virgil's *Georgics* and the Art of Reference." *Harvard Studies in Classical Philology* 90 (1986): 171–98.
Thompson, N.S. *Chaucer, Boccaccio, and the Debate of Love: A Comparative Study of the "Decameron" and the "Canterbury Tales."* Oxford: Oxford University Press, 1996.
Thompson, Patricia. "The 'Canticus Troili': Chaucer and Petrarch." *Comparative Literature* 11 (1959): 313–28.

Thorne, Mark. "Lucan's Cato, the Defeat of Victory, the Triumph of Memory." PhD Dissertation, University of Iowa, 2010. ProQuest Dissertation Publishing.

Trovato, Paolo. *Dante in Petrarca: per un inventario dei dantismi nei "Rerum vulgarium fragmenta."* Florence: Olschki, 1979.

Tupper, Frederick. "Chaucer and Trophee." *MLN* 31 (1916): 11–14.

Tylus, Jane. "Petrarch's Griselda and the Sense of an Ending." *Nottingham Medieval Studies* 56 (2012): 421–45.

Usher, Jonathan. "Mural Morality in *Tableaux Vivants: Amorosa Visione.*" *Boccaccio: A Critical Guide to the Complete Works.* Ed. Victoria Kirkham, Michael Sherberg, and Janet Levarie Smarr, 119–29. Chicago: University of Chicago Press, 2014.

Utz, Richard J. "'As Writ Myn Auctour Lollius': Divine and Authorial Omnipotence in Chaucer's *Troilus and Criseyde.*" *Nominalism and Literary Discourse: New Perspectives.* Ed. Hugo Keiper, Christoph Bode, and Richard J. Utz, 123–44. Amsterdam: Rodopi, 1997.

Versnel, H.S. *Triumphus: An Inquiry into the Origin, Development and Meaning of the Roman Triumph.* Leiden: Brill, 1970.

Waisman, Sergio Gabriel. *Borges and Translation: The Irreverence of the Periphery.* Lewisburg: Bucknell University Press, 2015.

Wakelin, Daniel. *Scribal Correction and Literary Craft: English Manuscripts 1375–1510.* Cambridge: Cambridge University Press, 2014.

Wallace, David. "Chaucer and Boccaccio's Early Writings." *Chaucer and the Italian Trecento.* Ed. Piero Boitani, 141–62. Cambridge: Cambridge University Press, 1983.

– *Chaucer and the Early Writings of Boccaccio.* Cambridge, Suffolk: D.S. Brewer, 1985.

– *Chaucerian Polity: Absolutist Lineages and Associational Forms in England and Italy.* Stanford: Stanford University Press, 1997.

– "Chaucer's Italian Inheritance." *The Cambridge Companion to Chaucer.* Ed. Piero Boitani and Jill Mann, 36–57. Cambridge: Cambridge University Press, 2004.

– "Letters of Old Age: Love between Men, Griselda, and Farewell to Letters *Rerum senilium libri.*" *Petrarch: A Critical Guide to the Complete Works.* Ed. Victoria Kirkham and Armando Maggi, 321–32. Chicago: University of Chicago Press, 2009.

– "Love-Struck in Naples." *Boccaccio: A Critical Guide to the Complete Works.* Ed. Victoria Kirkham, Michael Sherberg, and Janet Levarie Smarr, 77–86. Chicago: University of Chicago Press, 2014.

– "Whan She Translated Was: A Chaucerian Critique of the Petrarchan Academy." *Literary Practice and Social Change in Britain, 1380–1530.* Ed. Lee Patterson, 156–215. Berkeley: University of California Press, 1990.

Warner, Lawrence. *Chaucer's Scribes: London Textual Production, 1384–1432.* Cambridge: Cambridge University Press, 2018.

Warton, Thomas. *The History of English Poetry, from the Eleventh to the Seventeenth Century.* London: Ward, Lock, and Tyler, Warwick House, 1778.

Watson, Nicholas. "Outdoing Chaucer: Lydgate's Troy Book and Henryson's Testament of Cresseid as Competitive Imitations of Troilus and Criseyde." *Shifts and Transpositions in Medieval Narrative: A Festchrift for Elspeth Kennedy.* Ed. Karen Pratt, 89–108. Cambridge: D.S. Brewer, 1994.

– "The Politics of Middle English Writing." *The Idea of the Vernacular: An Anthology of Middle English Literary Theory 1280–1520.* Ed. Jocelyn Wogan-Browne, Nicholas Watson, Andrew Taylor, and Ruth Evans, 331–52. Exeter: University of Exeter Press; University Park: Penn State University, 1999.

Wetherbee, Winthrop. *Chaucer and the Poets: An Essay on "Troilus and Criseyde."* Ithaca: Cornell University Press, 1984.

– "The Context of the *Monk's Tale.*" *Language and Style in English Literature: Essays in Honour of Michio Masui.* Ed. Michio Kawai, 159–77. Hiroshima: English Research Association of Hiroshima, 1991.

Windeatt, Barry. *Chaucer's Dream Poetry: Sources and Analogues.* Cambridge: D.S. Brewer, 1982.

– *Troilus and Criseyde: Oxford Guides to Chaucer.* Oxford: Clarendon Press, 1992.

Wise, Boyd Ashby. *The Influence of Statius upon Chaucer.* Baltimore: J.H. Furst, 1911.

Woodman, Tony. "Exegi Monumentum: Horace, Odes 3:30." *Why Horace? A Collection of Interpretations.* Ed. William Scovil Anderson, 205–22. Wauconda: Bolchazy-Carducci Publishers, 1991.

Wright, Herbert G. *Boccaccio in England: From Chaucer to Tennyson.* [1957]. London: Bloomsbury, 2013.

Yaeger, R.F. "'O Moral Gower': Chaucer's Dedication of *Troilus and Criseyde.*" *Chaucer Review* 19 (1984): 87–99.

Yates, Peter. *Twentieth Century Music: Its Evolution from the End of the Harmonic Era into the Present Era of Sound.* New York: Pantheon Books, 1967.

Young, Karl. *The Origin and Development of The Story of Troilus and Criseyde.* London: Chaucer Society, 1908.

Zaccarello, Michelangelo. "Boccaccio as a Scribal Editor: Book Concept, Language Innovation, Cultural Intermediation." *Heliotropia* 11 (2014): 65–72.

Zaccaria, Vittorio. *Boccaccio Narratore, Storica, Moralista e Mitografo.* Florence: L.S. Olschki, 2001.

– "Le due redazioni del *De casibus.*" *Studi sul Boccaccio* 10 (1977–8): 1–26.

Zaho, Margaret Ann. *Imago Triumphalis: The Function and Significance of Triumphal Imagery for Italian Renaissance Rulers.* New York: Peter Lang, 2004.

Zatta, Jane Dick. "Chaucer's Monk: A Mighty Hunter before the Lord." *Chaucer Review* 29 (1994): 111–33.

Index